Jan 84
from U. of C. press

EXPERIENCE

AND

ENLIGHTENMENT

EXPERIENCE

AND

ENLIGHTENMENT

*Socialization
for Cultural Change
in Eighteenth-Century
Scotland*

CHARLES CAMIC

The University of Chicago Press

CHARLES CAMIC is assistant professor of sociology
at the University of Wisconsin, Madison.

THE UNIVERSITY OF CHICAGO PRESS, CHICAGO 60637
EDINBURGH UNIVERSITY PRESS
© *1983 by The University of Chicago*
All rights reserved. Published 1983
Printed in the United States of America
5 4 3 2 1   83 84 85 86 87 88 89

Library of Congress Cataloging in Publication Data

Camic, Charles.
  Experience and enlightenment.

  Bibliography: p.
  Includes index.
  1. Scotland—Social conditions. 2. Enlightenment.
3. Socialization. 4. Scotland—History—18th century.
I. Title.
HN398.S3C35 1983   306'.09411   83-4992
ISBN 0-226-09238-0

For Nina

Contents

Acknowledgments

During the time I have been involved in the various activities that resulted in the following study, I have received advice and support in good measure, and would like very much to thank the responsible parties. At the dissertation stage, I benefited enormously from the incisive criticism and tolerant understanding of Donald Levine, who also provided me with matchless lessons (to which I hope someday to do a bit of justice) on the demands of serious scholarship. I am grateful as well to Morris Janowitz and Michael Schudson for reliable help with assorted dissertation-related problems and to Charles Bidwell for this and for sharing with me his vast knowledge of the subtle workings of educational institutions. Since moving on to new surroundings, I have profited from the instructive suggestions that Bert Adams, Kent Geiger, Richard Schoenherr, and Elizabeth Thomson made on an early draft and from the frequent encouragement and careful readings of Warren Hagstrom, who never failed to return chapters that had been many months in the making within days or to return them without astute advice on matters big and small. Apart from these specific debts, I also count it lucky to have found myself in so hospitable an intellectual environment as the Department of Sociology at the University of Wisconsin at Madison.

As things were nearing an end, the bulk of the manuscript was obligingly read by Robert Merton and Robert Dreeben and, as one might expect, its argument now stands markedly improved as a result. I likewise owe special thanks to Vern Bullough for supplying the data presented in the Appendix. These have been of major use to me and I do not care even to think of the time that would have been spent floundering had they not been so generously given over for the cause.

The Graduate School Research Committee of the University of Wisconsin at Madison helped by providing funds for analyzing the Bullough data, and Charles Halaby patiently answered numerous questions that came up when this analysis was underway. My life was made easier too by my persevering secretaries, Cindy Braun, who typed and retyped this document with great speed and accuracy, and Margarette Hanson, who finished up the task in time for final deadlines. I am thankful to both, and also to the editors of *Comparative Studies in Society and History* for allowing me to draw from an article of mine which appeared in that journal.

Of course, for me, no more than for the characters in this study, can educational and professional experiences be acknowledged without those of family. I am grateful to my mother and father for their years of support and to my daughter, Susannah, for bounding in at the start of chapter 6 and filling the period to the Conclusion, and since, with such unexpected joy.

For reasons not entirely clear to me, I managed to make each day that I was at work on this more turbulent by far than there was need to do. That the years went by so well anyway, that the turbulence was so often calmed and even converted—when the resistance from my side was not too much—into a rewarding adventure in learning and in living is due to my wife Nina. All the intellectual, professional, technical, and personal considerations that constituted the enterprise became hers as well as mine, and the author and the outcome are both much the better for it all.

Note on Citations

In this book, source citations are given parenthetically within the text to the extent that this is possible without causing too much distraction. In all other cases, sources of documentation are reported in the accompanying notes.

To understand the makings of early modern cultures we need to understand the makings of early modern minds.

Benjamin Nelson, "Weber's Protestant Ethic," p. 93

Much . . . may be made of a Scotchman, if he be caught young.

Samuel Johnson, *Boswell's Life of Johnson,* vol. 2, p. 194

Introduction

Surveying a variety of anthropological work on cultural evolution, Jack Goody has recently objected to the widespread habit of assuming a Great Divide, a "single breaking point" when human culture moved "from myth to history, from magic to science, from status to contract, cold to hot, concrete to abstract, collective to individual, ritual to rationality" (1977, p. 3). Such an assumption, Goody argues, has had the regrettable result of provoking endless controversy over when and where the Great Divide is really located, while deflecting anthropological attention from the more fundamental problem of investigating the multiple steps in human cultural development.

Although the situation has been little noticed, sociology too has long been plagued by the Great Divide assumption, and with similar consequences. The assumption has particularly governed discussions of the metamorphosis of medieval Europe into the modern Western world. Here, while several competing candidates for the Great Divide have ineluctably appeared, it has been most common to draw rather freely from Max Weber in *The Protestant Ethic and the Spirit of Capitalism* and to regard the Reformation as the decisive turning point. Talcott Parsons has expressed this view in the baldest form: "The Reformation was the culmination . . . of the trend of social and cultural change away from the medieval system and toward modernity" (1968, p. 436).[1] Accompanying this conclusion has been the further claim that the "implications [of the Reformation] took long to unfold" (Parsons 1968, p. 436) and, conjoined

1. The ellipses signify the omission of the phrase "in the strictly religious sphere" since, in the present context, this would suggest a qualification to Parsons's position out of line with the whole trend of his thought. As the remainder of this paragraph indicates, Parsons does not limit the direct consequences of the Reformation to the

with this, a well-rehearsed, streamlined account of the episodes that constituted the unfolding—an account devised to corroborate the notion that the Reformation was indeed the watershed in the emergence of modern society and culture. Beginning in the early sixteenth century with the Lutheran Reformation (or with its antecedents), the familiar plot quickly cuts to the inner-worldly ascetic spirit generated a few decades later by the Calvinist branches of the Reformation; the saga then hastens to mid-seventeenth-century England to trace how that spirit was channelled into economic, political, and cultural activities, promoting modern capitalism, the proto-democratic developments associated with the Puritan Revolution, and modern philosophy and science; next the story proceeds to the late eighteenth century, when the French Revolution erupted and when the several seventeenth-century English developments coalesced to foster the beginnings of the Industrial Revolution, from which it is but a short leap to the present (for renditions of this, see esp. Parsons 1968, p. 439, 1971, pp. 45–84; and Bellah 1965, pp. 194–99).

Whatever merit this tale may have as an overview of the emergence of certain modern social institutions, the assumption that, with the Calvinist Reformation or in its direct shadows, modern culture sprang into the world essentially complete[2] truncates a complex developmental process so severely that it is untenable. Perhaps the most striking gaps that those concerned with the making of modern culture may notice in the sketch are its bypassing the first approximately three-quarters of the eighteenth century and, in the process, its omitting those cultural changes that are known as the

---

strictly religious sphere, but instead insists that they constituted a watershed in "the general development of secular culture" and "the major turning point in the development of modern society" (1968, p. 425, 1971, p. 69).

2. "Essentially complete" does not mean complete in every detail. Bellah, for example, has observed that Calvinism initially retained some "lingering medievalism" and expressed itself "not yet in fully secular form" (1965, pp. 196–97). But the difference between so reluctant a nod to the nonmodern aspects of Reformation culture and the view that is developed in chapter 1 and announced in the quotation by Troeltsch following in the text will readily be seen. Bellah's remarks reduce the medieval features of Calvinism to incidental remnants (reminiscent of those scientific issues that, according to Kuhn [1962, p. 24], entail a little "mop-up work" in the aftermath of paradigm changes), so inconsequential that their eventual disappearance is not even analyzed beyond claiming that this took place "partly in accordance with the logic of Protestantism itself" (Bellah 1965, p. 198). Such addenda reinforce, rather than revise, the image of the Reformation under discussion.

Enlightenment.[3] The argument is not new. Long ago Ernst Troeltsch, while granting to Weber that Calvinism promoted the growth of capitalism, insisted that in the cultural sphere "Protestantism cannot be supposed to have directly paved the way for the modern world, [for it swept] away such beginnings of a free and secular civilization as had already been toilsomely established [and forced Europe] to experience two centuries more of the medieval spirit," which was not dispelled until the Enlightenment, "the beginning and foundation of the really modern period in European culture" (1912, pp. 85–86, 1897, pp. 338–39 [my translation]). Almost a century has elapsed and Troeltsch's resounding conclusion has been confirmed on many counts by subsequent historical research,[4] but never has it penetrated historical sociology. Wedded to the Great Divide as-

3. Works that treat the Reformation as the Great Divide are not the only instances of historical sociology with these characteristics. A number of otherwise divergent sociological perspectives share the tendency first to situate the turning point in the emergence of the modern world in developments that occurred in (or immediately bordering decades of) the sixteenth century and then to proceed straightaway to trace the crystallization of these same developments in mid-seventeenth-century England and in one or more late eighteenth-century revolutions, all the while ignoring the bulk of the eighteenth century and, with it, the Enlightenment. Reinhard Bendix, for example, holds that the key to "the great social and intellectual transformation of European societies" was the process of "intellectual mobilization" that commenced in "the decades around 1500," both with the Reformation and with "economic growth, European expansion overseas, . . . the rise of Humanism, the invention of printing, and the early development of modern science" (1978, pp. 9–10; on Bendix's definition of "intellectual mobilization," see chap. 2, sec. II below). In his view, the next major stages in the process were "the revolutions of seventeenth-century England, the French Revolution, [and] the English industrial revolution" (1978, p. 4). Eisenstadt (1968) and Nelson (1973) offer a similar approach; they begin the story with a plurality of factors, including the Reformation, but then retain the familiar litany of later events. While the traditional Marxist account of centuries past naturally accords the Reformation a very different role (see esp. Hill 1961), it too dates the "opening phase" of its Great Divide, the emergence of the capitalist mode of production, from "the latter half of the sixteenth and early seventeenth century" (Dobb 1963, p. 18). The account continues: "In the career of Capitalism since this date it is evident that there are two decisive moments. One of them resides in the seventeenth century: in the political and social transformations [that reached their] apex in the Cromwellian revolution. . . . The second consists of the industrial revolution of the late eighteenth . . . century" (Dobb 1963, pp. 18–19; see also Marx 1867, pp. 713–60). The series of historical events that Moore (1966) and Wallerstein (1974, 1980a) emphasize in their analyses of the making of the modern world should also be noted here.

4. See, e.g., Cassirer (1932), Hampson (1968), Mosse (1960), Trevor-Roper (1969b), and above all Gay (1966, 1969). The contrary position, put forth in a famous essay by Becker (1932), has been effectively countered by Gay (1957); see also Venturi (1971).

sumption, the field has persistently neglected the role of the Enlightenment in the formation of various attitudes, values, viewpoints, and orientations that are now regarded as integral features of modern culture.

None of this is to say that sociologists have never mentioned the Enlightenment, for in two types of research they have considered it in some detail. In both cases, however, its broad significance in the early development of modern Western culture has been obfuscated. In the first instance, the Enlightenment has been treated as a brief installment in the history of sociological ideas. Comte (1822) and Durkheim (1892–1901), in their writings on the precursors of sociology, inaugurated this practice, and today histories of sociology frequently provide at least a few introductory remarks on the Enlightenment's sociological insights.[5] Unfortunately, ransacking the Enlightenment for its specifically "sociological" passages has generally masked the much more fundamental cultural transformation that it wrought.

The only other place where the Enlightenment has typically received sociological attention is in work that has pondered the great events of modern French history. By an interesting twist, such work has often been produced by the same scholars who see the Reformation as the watershed in the emergence of the modern world and otherwise have so ignored the Enlightenment. Unable to pass over the French Revolution and unable, since it occurred in a Catholic country, to see it simply as an outgrowth of the Reformation, these scholars have adduced the writings of the *philosophes* of the French Enlightenment as one of the main sources of the Revolution,[6] and then suggested that these writings "developed . . . under the influence of English [Protestant] thought and institutions" (Bellah 1968, p. 68). Although such reasoning may suffice perhaps in

5. Thus, to take a recent example, Bottomore and Nisbet begin their collection on the *History of Sociological Analysis* with an essay in which Robert Bierstedt (1978) comprehensively describes the explicitly sociological ideas of the men of the Enlightenment, but quickly skips over the larger implications of their work for cultural change in the eighteenth century. This reservation notwithstanding, Bierstedt's article should be appreciated as a valuable corrective to sociology's long-distorted view of the Enlightenment as the age of abstract rationalism, the age of those obsolete social theories that overstressed the cognitive and overlooked all the irrational and nonrational dimensions of social life (for an example of this view, see Bellah 1970, pp. 237–48).

6. See esp. Bellah (1965, 1968), and Parsons (1968, 1971). See also the classic formulation of Tocqueville (1856, pp. 138–69), and the more recent analysis of Weinstein and Platt (1969, pp. 45–81).

the context of some general speculation on the causes of the French Revolution, the tendency to regard the ideas of the French Enlightenment as functional alternatives to the doctrines of the Reformation has been a serious impediment to a more general appreciation of the Enlightenment. Above all, concentration on the French Enlightenment has deflected historical sociology from recognizing that the Enlightenment was a development that transformed previous cultural patterns throughout much of Western Europe, not only in lands where the Reformation failed, but in lands where it triumphed.

This study examines this transformation as it unfolded in Scotland, a country where the Calvinist Reformation had been an unparalleled success. The first two chapters describe the specific nature of the cultural change that took place in eighteenth-century Scotland—a task that, curiously enough, has been as little pursued by the European intellectual historians who have identified the discontinuities between the beliefs and values of Reformation and those of the Enlightenment as by the sociologists who have persistently neglected such discontinuities. Chapter 1 analyzes Scottish culture during the decades immediately prior to the Enlightenment and finds that the "medieval," Calvinist attitudes of dependency and particularism thoroughly pervaded religious belief and secular thought as late as the early eighteenth century. Chapter 2 considers Scottish culture in the mid-eighteenth century, the Age of the Enlightenment. Here the discussion demonstrates that, although the Calvinist attitudes that were common early in the century persisted throughout much of Scotland, in the writings of the intellectuals who constitute the Scottish Enlightenment—viz. Adam Ferguson, David Hume, John Millar, William Robertson, and Adam Smith—they were again and again displaced by the modern orientations of independence and universalism.

In dwelling at length upon how these elemental conceptions were articulated in Scotland by the Enlightenment rather than the Reformation, my objective is to indicate through a strategic illustration why historical sociology needs to abandon Great Divide approaches to the emergence of modern culture, not to advance any exaggerated claims on behalf of the Scottish Enlightenment. It is certainly not my intention to offer, in place of the notion that the Reformation was the turning point in the development of all things modern, the assertion that it was the Scottish Enlightenment—or, *pace* Troeltsch, the European Enlightenment—that began the "really" modern cultural period. Nor does this study aim to replace the orthodox view by suggesting that the Scottish Enlightenment was "the watershed of modern intellectual thought" (Hamowy 1969, p. iv) and "one of the major sources of contemporary Western culture" (Phillipson 1973, p. 125). To take such positions is to posit anew a Great Divide assumption or, at least, to postulate that there are long, intricate chains of influence that bind us to a handful of eighteenth-century Scots. The existence of chains of this sort has not been convincingly established one way or the other and must be left to other research, since it is nowise relevant to this inquiry.[7] The Scottish Enlightenment commands our attention as a moment when a generation's major intellectuals decisively shed some of the most basic orientations of preceding generations for those that, despite their rather tenuous hold even in our times, we now regard as essential components of the modern *mentalité*. Whether this moment was soon followed by moments when Scottish culture and cultures elsewhere marched further from the past and discarded dependency, particularism, and other age-old attitudes on a broader scale, or whether, during ensuing periods, one and all retained such attitudes partially or completely, the general thesis is that the multiple steps in the shaping of the various dimensions of modern culture must be explored—not forgotten upon the mention of the role of the Reformation *or* the Enlightenment in the process by which contemporary cultures came into being. Initial appearances to the contrary, this position, it is worth noting, is actually very close to Weber's own. For all the times that his work has been used in support of the proposition that the Reformation was the springboard into the modern world, Weber himself not only insisted that there was no one, linear route to the modern era (see esp. 1904–5, pp. 76–78), but provided, almost without exception, that rare kind of historical sociology that dispensed with any form of the Great Divide.

To surmount the Great Divide by acknowledging the multiplicity of phases in the shaping of modern cultures is only a prologue, of course, to the real task: understanding why the various changes

7. This statement does not mean that there currently is no evidence that the Scottish Enlightenment made its mark. Though it sometimes leans too heavily on the troublesome notion of "intellectual influence," research of the impact of certain aspects of the Scottish Enlightenment upon selected areas, particularly upon American culture in the latter part of the eighteenth century and the first half of the nineteenth, has been undertaken on several occasions (see Hook 1975; Lehmann 1978; May 1976*b*; Sloan 1971; Wills 1978*b*, 1981). The conclusions of specialized work of this type do not, however, yet provide a basis for the grander claims quoted above.

took place. In the present case, this task entails moving beyond a description of the development of independence and universalism during the Scottish Enlightenment to an explanation of this cultural transformation. Chapters 3 through 7 attempt to provide that explanation and, in the process, they become a study in both the sociology of knowledge and the sociology of cultural change, though not the kind of study that has traditionally characterized these areas. To some, it may at first glance seem that accounting for the emergence of the orientations of universalism and independence in the work of Scotland's enlightened intellectuals requires little else than tapping the explanatory resources that have accumulated in the sociology of knowledge and using these to analyze the distinctive social and cultural circumstances of eighteenth-century Scotland. And this would all be very well if the appropriate resources were there waiting to be tapped. Such, however, is scarcely the case. The sociology of knowledge (particularly as it has developed in this country) has not lived up to much of its youthful promise, and studies in the field that have tried to supply explanations for specific intellectual developments have too often done no more than point to some of the eye-catching aspects of the general historical scene in which the intellectual changes of concern first occurred.

We need not wonder what such tactics would amount to if extended to the problem posed by the Scottish Enlightenment. For it happens that, although rarely cognizant of research in the sociology of knowledge as such, all previous efforts to explain the Enlightenment have proceeded in exactly the way that the sociology of knowledge would typically counsel: they have treated the Enlightenment primarily as a product of outstanding antecedent historical developments. Thus Weber, departing from his otherwise more judicious reflections on the topic,[8] regarded the Enlightenment as the "laughing heir" of the good old "spirit of religious asceticism" that was born with the Calvinist Reformation (1904–5, pp. 181–82), and thus modern historians, as chapter 3 indicates, have seen the Scottish Enlightenment as the outcome of divers social and intellectual landmarks, ranging all the way from the growth of the capitalist economy to the writings of Isaac Newton.

8. In these other remarks, Weber commented on the differences between the orientations of the Enlightenment and those propagated by Calvinism and observed that the path to the "worldly rational philosophy [of the Enlightenment thinkers] of the eighteenth century" did not parallel the path from Calvinism to capitalism (1904–5, pp. 45, 77, 106).

Were explanations of this type adequate, they would completely vitiate the claim that the Scottish Enlightenment attests of the need to give up Great Divide approaches to the making of modern culture since, in all these explanations, the Scottish Enlightenment itself collapses into some prior watershed. But chapter 3 finds such explanations to be marred by serious shortcomings—generic shortcomings, which will be readily recognized by those familiar with studies in the sociology of knowledge—and consequently insufficient to provide an account of the cultural change that is the Scottish Enlightenment. It then constructs an alternative approach by turning to a little known social-psychological theory which has shown that the experiences that individuals receive in microlevel socialization settings can give rise to entirely new types of cultural orientations.

When applied to the question at hand, this theory suggests the hypothesis that the independence and the universalism of the Scottish Enlightenment first emerged out of the social experiences of the five intellectuals who comprise the Enlightenment. The remaining chapters of the study assess the validity of this hypothesis, interweaving biographical materials and institutional histories to produce a general picture of the experiences that Ferguson, Hume, Millar, Robertson, and Smith encountered in the context of four social settings—the Calvinist households in which they were raised (chapter 4); the simple primary schools where they began their formal educations (chapter 5); the renowned universities where they passed their undergraduate and postgraduate years (chapter 6); and the patronage-dominated job market in which they sought to obtain suitable professional positions for themselves (chapter 7). Most of these chapters contain a fair amount of relatively intricate material on socialization arrangements in eighteenth-century Scotland, but in presenting this my purpose throughout is not merely to sustain a new interpretation of a particular episode in the history of modern culture. It is also to advocate, by the device of a detailed example, a way of looking at basic changes in values and beliefs that is pliable and might as well be brought to bear in the analysis of cultural transformations that differ markedly in form and content from the Scottish Enlightenment. So bringing the approach exemplified here to bear would actually seem to constitute a general means for overcoming long-standing limitations of the explanatory framework that the sociology of knowledge offers, though whether or not this judgment is genuinely warranted will not be known until the results of pertinent further research are in. But while looking ahead to future possibilities, it is equally important to realize that, because of certain currently unbridgeable theoretical and (above all) evidential gaps, the following examination of the Scottish Enlightenment is itself—to borrow a remark from Lawrence Stone (1969, p. 69)—often more of a trial balloon than the final flight. The lessons of the first outing are discussed in the Conclusion.

Apart from brief visits to libraries in Edinburgh and London to examine certain scarce sources that were essential for treating some of the issues broached in the following chapters, this book was researched by consulting materials in various accessible midwestern libraries. For the most part, these were "secondary materials," writings published by historians on questions addressed in this study. I am, of course, aware that there are several reasons why this kind of methodology has fallen into considerable disfavor. Since I generally find myself in agreement with these reasons, it may be appropriate to outline why, in this particular case, I nonetheless have opted to proceed by means of secondary sources.

The most insistent objections to heavy reliance on sources of this kind would naturally be raised by historians. To the historical community, any procedure that so flagrantly violates hallowed canons about the value of primary documents reeks of being dilettantish and unscholarly. And this certainly is not a groundless assessment, for, on the basis of my secondary research, I can hardly be regarded as an expert on any of the many aspects of Scotland's past that are discussed here. Areas like Scottish economic, political, and ecclesiastical history have long been the subjects of highly detailed inquiries, and specialists in these fields—as one should keep in mind throughout—doubtless would often wish to amend my generalizations on their topics. But unless this study is mistaken for an introduction to Scottish social history, this situation is not particularly problematic, since the precision of the analysis of these issues is rarely essential to the main argument. Of far more serious concern are those areas where I am inexpert not because there are so many experts, but because there are so few. Several matters that are of greatest consequence here—the nature of family life in eighteenth-century Scotland, the internal organization of certain Scottish grammar schools, the structure of the professional job market, even the life of William Robertson—have yet to receive adequate historical treatment. It is in this predicament that most historians would advise mining the primary sources in order to make a solid beginning in just one of these areas, rather than attempting to advance at once on all fronts with only the bits and pieces that can be gathered from the existing literature.

This is a sage recommendation, but accepting it unfortunately would mean indefinitely postponing getting on with the task of this study. Determining whether or not the revolutionary attitudes of the Scottish Enlightenment were rooted in the socialization experiences of the men who formed the Enlightenment requires that one first establish what patterns of experience these men actually encountered as they passed through a series of socialization settings. But to follow the historians' suggestion and investigate all the primary materials either on one man or on one social setting would in no way reveal such general patterns, and it is scarcely viable to wait until the numerous specialized studies desired here accumulate one by one. This leaves three alternatives: to adopt the practice of previous students of the Scottish Enlightenment and to explain this cultural transformation without recourse to those topics that the secondary materials treat imperfectly, the experiences of the enlightened intellectuals and the character of the settings where these took place; to abandon the Scottish Enlightenment and explore the relationship between social experience and cultural change under contemporary conditions where fuller data are available; or to proceed with the existing secondary sources, aware of their deficiencies, but alert to how even these documents can be exploited to disclose something important about the experiences that the intellectuals of the Scottish Enlightenment received in their families, schools, and early professional lives. The first alternative would perpetuate inadequate ways of explaining cultural change, while the second would sacrifice the historical-sociological objectives of this study; I have therefore opted for the third. And in this connection it may be worth observing that, as often as I have despaired at the limitations of secondary sources, I have been encouraged by what a search of these materials can reveal: by how often some systematic sifting uncovers a pattern that has been overlooked in writings more fully grounded on primary documents.

Historians have not been the only scholars to express their dissatisfaction with research that is based principally on secondary sources. Sociologists too have become increasingly wary of such a methodology. Their reasons for this reaction have not been stated as formally as the objections of historians, but (if I read these correctly) seem to involve a diffuse suspicion over research that is so quick and easy, so much a simple recycling of the intricate inquiries of historians. In light of all those specimens of historical

sociology whose historical side amounts to little more than a rep-
etition of conclusions gleaned from glancing at the summary chapters of a few general history texts, this feeling is quite understandable.
But a historical sociology that proceeds by utilizing secondary materials is not inherently of this shallow sort; this has been made
abundantly clear through certain recent works that have canvassed
the relevant materials rigorously and comprehensively. In approaching the existing historical literature on eighteenth-century
Scotland, this study has tried generally to conform to these new
standards, and given the many questions that are left unexplored
in the available literature, this strategy has proved even less quick
and easy than it would otherwise have been.

To say this is not in the least to deny that, in matters of fact and
judgment alike, this book is enormously indebted to the sundry
secondary materials and to the generations of scholars that have
produced them. While the text will follow convention and omit
source citations for those basic facts that are common knowledge
to all who study eighteenth-century Scotland (though, of course, I
learned of these from many sources), it will try to make evident
the broad extent of my obligations in all other areas. As I have
already suggested, however, the secondary materials cannot be
blamed for everything said in this study. Not infrequently, the way
existing materials are combined, the configurations inferred from
the information they report, and the resulting interpretations are
my own. This should all be fairly evident in the last five chapters,
for chapter 3 explicitly criticizes previous explanations of the Scottish Enlightenment, while chapters 4 through 7 examine the widely
neglected subject of the social experiences that the intellectuals of
the Scottish Enlightenment underwent in their families, schools,
and early professional careers. But the same general point holds
as well for the first two chapters, which portray both early and mid-
eighteenth-century Scottish culture in a way that is quite different
from that of the majority of historians. This is the reason the initial
chapters are so disproportionately lengthy; as it became clear that
many historians have sociologically misconstrued the evidence upon
which they base their views on Scottish culture before and during
the Age of the Enlightenment, it became necessary for chapters 1
and 2 to undertake a fairly thorough reevaluation and reinterpretation of that evidence. Still, if these chapters have departed from
dominant trends in Scottish historiography, they have nevertheless
been informed by one source that no number of citations could
accurately acknowledge, the writings of Peter Gay (1957, 1966,

1969, 1970, 1973) on the European Enlightenment. Although these treat the Scottish Enlightenment only occasionally, examine the rest of Scottish culture not at all, and account for the Enlightenment in a way that differs substantially from the account of the Scottish Enlightenment proposed here, they have been my constant guide for understanding pre-Enlightenment and Enlightenment culture, for formulating the nature of the change that separated the one from the other, and for acquiring a general sense of intellectual history. That this sense is no better than it is certainly is no fault of the guide.

As this study proceeds, it will become apparent that there is one place where I have reversed the policy of passing over original sources while attempting to be reasonably complete with respect to the appropriate secondary materials. The writings of the intellectuals of the Scottish Enlightenment, particularly Adam Smith and David Hume, are the subjects of massive, highly specialized, and often quite technical literatures that were not systematically consulted for the purposes of this inquiry.[9] I like to believe that I know the main contributions here well enough to hope that, however much the fuller literatures might entail refinement of my remarks on specific features of the works of the Enlightenment, they would not alter my general conclusions. But I will willingly grant that specialists may not share this optimistic assessment. In any event, I have sought to counterbalance this handling of the secondary materials on Hume, Smith, and the others with a direct examination of their original writings. These are the cynosure for all who wish to understand the Scottish Enlightenment and what it reveals about the development of modern culture.

9. The amount of material on Hume alone is astonishing. Jessop's (1938) bibliography on Humian scholarship was compiled before the full flowering of Hume's modern popularity and fills thirty pages; Hall's (1978) more recent catalogue, for the 1900–1976 period, runs on, growing annually, for some ninety-seven dense pages.

1

Scottish Culture in the Early Eighteenth Century

The massive central block of the International Monument to the Reformation in Geneva merges for the ages the granite figures of John Calvin and John Knox. It is a fitting conjunction. In 1560, only five years after Calvin's final Genevan triumph, the preaching of his disciple Knox precipitated in medieval Scotland a reformation which would establish what has been aptly described as "a kind of Calvinist society par excellence" (Burrell 1960, p. 136). Scotland had long been awaiting reform, and success had thus come to Knox and his followers more completely, swiftly, and peacefully than was the lot of reformers elsewhere. Yet, ironically, within years of Knox's death a decade later, the reformed Church of Scotland had been rent internally into Presbyterian and Episcopalian factions, whose arid controversy over the organization of church government—over whether parity should exist among ministers, with religious and ecclesiastical affairs regulated by courts comprised both of ministers and elders, or whether the office of bishop should be established to superintend ministers and the life of the church—became one of the vital questions of Scottish history. The century after the Reformation records the frequently bitter, even bloody, conflicts of Presbyterians and Episcopalians and their partial, transient victories as episcopacy became the form of the Church of Scotland in 1584, presbytery in 1592, episcopacy in 1610, presbytery in 1638, episcopacy in 1661, and—setting the pattern down to the twentieth century—presbytery in 1690.[1] But throughout this protracted and divisive whirl of church polities, the Scots never abandoned the message at the heart of John Knox's Reformation. For the entire period, they remained strongly committed to the

1. For an excellent brief account of these developments and of how and why the Reformation came to Scotland, see Donaldson (1960, pp. 36–94).

tenets of Calvinism. These they carried with them into the eighteenth century.

This chapter analyzes Scottish culture from the beginning of that century until the onset of the Age of the Enlightenment some forty years later.[2] The first section describes two basic cultural orientations, dependency and particularism, that were inherent in the teachings of Scottish Calvinism. In so doing, it attempts to display some of the deeply traditional aspects of the creed propagated through the Scottish Reformation and thus to demonstrate the fallacy of regarding the Calvinist Reformation as the Great Divide in the emergence in Scotland of modern cultural orientations.[3] The second section of the chapter examines the mechanisms that enabled the Church of Scotland to disseminate its message so widely and completely during the early eighteenth century that Calvinist orientations came to dominate the cultural life of the nation. In the third section, the discussion turns to several of the age's more innovative religious, legal, and philosophical developments, in the course of which many particulars of the Calvinist heritage were surrendered, while its ultimate assumptions were nonetheless retained. The final section considers the main secular branch of early eighteenth-century Scottish culture in order to show that, even in cases where the religious foundations of Calvinism were finally eroded, the medieval orientations of dependency and particularism tenaciously persisted. As this preview makes clear, this chapter does not portray Scottish culture during the decades prior to the Enlightenment in all its richness and fullness. The following sections are limited to certain spheres of Scottish culture and to certain specific cultural themes, and these considerations neither exhaust

2. The argument of this book requires that this treatment of Scottish culture precede an examination of the nature of Scottish society during the eighteenth century. But those who would prefer to begin with some information on the latter may wish to consult chap. 3, sec. I before continuing with the current chapter.

3. To the extent that the following inquiry cites authorities who are not writing exclusively about Scotland, it may be taken to suggest that this argument is not limited to *Scottish* Calvinism. But it must be left for later research to determine the other places and times for which this suggestion is actually valid. The fact that the text often abbreviates "Scottish Calvinism" as "Calvinism" is by no means intended either to mask the need for this research or to encourage the common sociological habit of treating Calvinism as if it were always the same. Just as one should be alert to the characteristics that Calvinism retained from situation to situation, one must (for reasons that emerge in notes 11, 12, and 15 below, and in the literature cited in note 6) be wary of overhasty generalizations—as in the popular practice of using seventeenth-century English developments as the model for Calvinism everywhere, or even for "Great Britain (including Scotland)" (Parsons 1968, p. 439).

nor summarize the whole of Scottish culture in the early eighteenth century. The matters selected for attention are those that provide the necessary background for understanding the particular cultural changes that formed the Scottish Enlightenment, but concentration upon such matters is not intended to devalue the significance of elements of Scottish culture that either remained largely stable throughout the eighteenth century, or changed in ways little connected with the Scottish Enlightenment itself.

I

Typically, it is an exceedingly difficult task to uncover the fundamental components of a social group's system of religious beliefs. The essential features of Scottish Calvinism, however, are simply and lucidly announced in a remarkable set of documents which rank among the classics of Calvinist literature everywhere: *The Westminster Confession of Faith, The Larger Catechism,* and *The Shorter Catechism.* Proclaimed at Westminster in 1647 by an assemblage composed chiefly of English divines, these celebrated texts, as G. D. Henderson has observed, actually contained "nothing new or strange in the sphere of doctrine" from a Scottish point of view, but succeeded in formulating the Calvinism of Knox and other Scottish reformers in a manner that was more "carefully complete [and] rigidly systematic" (1957, p. 31). As such, they were quickly adopted by the Church of Scotland, where they retained their official status until presbytery gave way to episcopacy in 1661. When the Presbyterian system returned again in 1690, *The Westminster Confession* was soon "ratified and established by acts of Parliament . . . as the publick and avowed confession of the Church of Scotland" (*CF,* p. 17). Thus installed, this testament and the accompanying catechisms constituted the basic framework within which the clergy and the laity of the eighteenth century learned the principles of their religion (Clark 1964, p. 246), and it is for this reason that these sources provide—along with what is known of Scottish theology and preaching during the early eighteenth century—an ideal point of access to Calvinist culture in Scotland.

The Great Divide thesis discussed in the Introduction prepares one to find in a Calvinist culture the signs of a decisive transition toward beliefs and values of the kind customarily described as modern. But when the cardinal documents of Scottish Calvinism are examined what instead becomes apparent is the prominent place still occupied by two highly traditional cultural orientations, hereafter labelled "dependency" and "particularism." Since they recur frequently in this study, these two terms require formal introduction, though formalization in this instance is not without its dangers. To attach definitions to dependency and particularism is to offer retrospective abstractions which may quietly obscure the fact that the exact meaning of each orientation cannot be appreciated until one explores the various contemporary contexts where it surfaced. Particularism, in fact, is not even an eighteenth-century Scottish word; it is simply a convenient means of describing an important commonality among several, seemingly unrelated attitudes which must also be viewed in their own terms. Only if such safeguards are employed is it sensible to utilize the following general formulations for these cultural orientations:[4] dependency will here designate the orientation, or set of orientations, which renders the action, judgment, or situation of human beings primarily subservient to agents regarded as removed in essence from human control; particularism designates the orientation, or cluster of orientations, which treats individuals, groups, and things, not "in conformity with a general standard, [but] rather in light of their possession of properties [that] have a particular relation" to one's own properties (Parsons and Shils 1951, p. 82).[5]

These two orientations are of special interest because they were among the most elemental components of early eighteenth-century Scottish culture. Not only did both then find expression in numerous cultural contexts, both actually played a major role in structuring a disparate variety of more specific beliefs and values. And this is why dependency and particularism, rather than more tan-

4. Cultural orientations may themselves be formally defined as those explicit or implicit conceptions or criteria that channel the ways in which individuals relate to their world. Such orientations are one among many components of a social group's system of meaningful symbols—its culture, in a word—and correspond closely to what Parsons and others have called value orientations. The expression "cultural orientations" is preferred here to a more common term like "beliefs" in order to emphasize that such ideas have cognitive, appreciative, and moral aspects: they may establish (the standards for evaluating) not only what exists, but what is satisfying, and what ought to be (for more rigorous formulations on these matters, see Kluckhohn 1951, pp. 395–412; Parsons 1951, pp. 12–14; Parsons and Shils 1951, pp. 55–60). For the sake of variety, however, terms like "beliefs," "values," "attitudes," "assumptions," "themes," "principles," "views," and so on will be substituted for cultural orientations in passages where misunderstandings are unlikely to arise.

5. The formulation here attributed to Parsons and Shils has been taken from an analysis of particularism and universalism that is considerably more elaborate, but unfortunately much too technical to insert unedited into the text at this point. The complete analysis is, however, a very instructive one (see also Parsons 1951, pp. 62–63).

gible cultural items such as political, scientific, or aesthetic opinions, have been chosen as the focus of this discussion. Dependency and particularism must not be indiscriminately lumped together, however, and for current analytical purposes the two are best seen as relatively autonomous. Neither orientation, in other words, logically entailed the other, even though in reality both sometimes operated in tandem, and even though dependency seems to have been by far the more fundamental cultural element in the pair; for in eighteenth-century Scotland, attenuation of particularistic conceptions meant less, and less substantial, reorganization of other aspects of culture than similar changes with regard to dependency.

The heavy emphasis placed here on these two themes should not be misunderstood. To stress the centrality of particularism and dependency is in no way to deny the independent presence of other, equally basic orientations and to assert that these various orientations permeated every dimension of Scottish culture. Nor should the distinction between those cultural components that are elemental and those that are not be taken to imply that the former fully shaped and then remained unaffected by the latter, or to suggest an absence of inconsistency, ambiguity, or internal contradiction among the diverse constituents of Scottish culture in the early eighteenth century. It is also useful to recognize that neither dependency nor particularism is an absolute, all-or-nothing term, however often stylistic considerations require speaking as if this were the case. Scottish Calvinism naturally was comprised of many doctrines, and some of these exhibited particularism and dependency to a much lesser degree than others. Moreover, what appears as a clear manifestation of dependency or particularism from the perspective of the eighteenth century may well seem striking evidence of independence or universalism to students of far more distant epochs and of certain non-Western cultures. That concepts of this type are of an intrinsically relative character is a basic premise of this study.

There is one more preliminary matter that needs to be cleared aside. This examination of Scottish Calvinism is not designed to offer a general introduction to the main terms and the overall logic of Calvinist theology and ethics. Not, of course, that these topics are unimportant, but sociological research has already channelled so much attention here that knowledge of such issues can be presupposed in order to proceed directly to other aspects of Scottish Calvinism, aspects that elsewhere have been too little noticed. Focusing on these is intended to complement the view of Calvinism

presented in previous studies for that view, although closely mod-
elled after the analysis of Calvinism in *The Protestant Ethic,* has
typically omitted Weber's careful warning about the "artificial sim-
plicity" of his approach (see 1904–5, p. 98). Weber's famous argument was concerned principally with those elements of Calvinism
that looked forward to the spirit of capitalism and related developments, particularly the elements that fostered inner-worldly asceticism.[6] Given this starting point, his investigation, as well as the
long excerpt from *The Westminster Confession* that accompanied it,
concentrated on Calvinism's "most characteristic dogma," the doctrine of predestination, and passed over "the question of what [the
Calvinist creed] theoretically and officially taught [in other areas],
however much practical significance this may have had" (1904–5,
pp. 98, 97). Subsequently, however, sociological treatments of Calvinism have tended to ignore these additional teachings altogether,
entirely forgetting that Weber had merely abstracted some pertinent items from a great complex of religious ideas and precepts.
Among the casualties of this research have been those features of
Calvinism that looked backward—according to Troeltsch, all the
way back to the Middle Ages (1912, p. 45). In the following discussion, two of these neglected features are selected for consideration. The full picture, the picture that incorporates all the
medieval and modern dimensions of Calvinism, must be drawn
elsewhere.[7]

A constant refrain in the major documents of Scottish Calvinism
is human dependency, the conviction that in their being and in
their believing, in practice and in theory, existentially and intellec-
tually, individuals are not their own. The inescapable message of
the Calvinist teachings was, as Troeltsch frequently reiterated, that
humans and their world are wholly and absolutely dependent upon
the will and the grace of God (see esp. 1911, 2:579–90). Not for a

6. For varying assessments of the applicability of the Protestant ethic–spirit of
capitalism thesis to Scotland, see Burrell (1960), Campbell and Wilson (1975, pp.
21–23), Cunningham (1914, pp. 66–70), Hagen (1962, pp. 294–98), Hechter (1975,
p. 104), Henderson (1951, pp. 44–46, 1957, p. 136), Hill (1961), Mathieson (1902,
1:202–3), Robertson (1933, pp. 88–100), Samuelsson (1957, p. 51), Smout (1969*a*,
pp. 88–93), Trevor-Roper (1969*a*, p. 6), and Weber himself (1904–5, p. 44, 1910,
pp. 1125–26). Additional previous work on this question is cited by Marshall (1980*a*,
1980*b*), whose own research throws a new light on the whole issue.

7. In lieu of the full picture, Marshall's (1980*b*, pp. 39–109) remarkable Weberian
analysis of the forward-looking aspects of Scottish Calvinism provides a valuable
supplement to the view now to be presented.

moment did Scottish Calvinism abandon this position. Rather, it was conveyed and reinforced through three of the most fundamental postulates of Calvinist theology. These reveal the orientation of dependency in its most striking form.

The first of these postulates announced the condition that precluded genuine human autonomy: the complete corruption and impotence of human nature. In place of the Renaissance's elevated view of human virtues and capabilities, the Lutheran Reformation firmly instated the Augustinian dogmas of the fall and of original sin (see, e.g., Skinner 1978, 2:4), and these were then carried over into Calvinism and, from there, into Scotland. *The Larger Catechism* held that, by Adam's sin, man "is utterly indisposed, disabled, and made opposite unto all that is spiritually good, and wholly inclined to all evil, and that continually" (*LC*, p. 140). It averred: "all men are not only utterly unable and unwilling to know and do the will of God, but prone to rebel against his word, to repine and murmur against his providence, . . . wholly inclined to do the will of the flesh and of the devil, [and marred by] blindness, weakness, indisposedness, and perverseness of heart" (*LC*, p. 276). And this uncompromisingly bleak view of human nature was not confined to catechistical passages. Instead, from the Reformation onward "the doctrines of man's fallen and guilty state [were] doctrines which Scotch theology . . . always taught and Scotch preachers . . . always strongly proclaimed" (Walker 1872, p. 159).[8]

Fused with these beliefs was a second aspect of Calvinist theology through which the orientation of dependency was promoted and expressed. This was the assumption that, in Troeltsch's words, "over against the absolute corruption caused by sin and the helplessness of natural man" stood an unflawed being upon whom all depended, a God whose "majestic sovereign will [was] the basis of the world, and the cause of its whole course" (1911, 2:580, 582). *The Westminster Confession* defined God as he "who is infinite in being and perfection, . . . immense, eternal, incomprehensible, almighty, most wise, most holy, most free, most absolute, working all things according to the counsel of his most immutable and righteous will . . . alone in and unto himself all-sufficient . . . alone fountain of all being, [with] sovereign domain over [all things] to do by them, for them, or upon them, whatsoever himself pleaseth" (*CF*, pp. 24–26).

8. On the place of these doctrines in popular sermons, see Graham (1899, pp. 294–95, 394–99), Henderson (1951, pp. 41–42, 1957, p. 148), and Letwin (1965, p. 20).

These were not pat phrases. The idea that "God . . . doth uphold, direct, dispose, and govern all creatures, actions, and things . . . by the most wise and holy providence" (*CF,* p. 33) was integral to Calvinist thought in Scotland for centuries after the Reformation (Henderson 1951, p. 41; Graham 1899, pp. 336–37; Walker 1872, pp. 81–91). The reformers' doctrines may have done their part to spur scientific investigation of the laws of nature in England (see Merton 1938), but the Scots maintained, as James Walker pointed out long ago, that:

> The essence of God . . . is everywhere directly and imme-diately energetic. In regard to the material world all motion and action in it spring from God and are sustained by His immediate influence. . . . In no vague or distant sense the Almighty shines in the sun, breathes in the life, brings gales of spring, refreshes in the summer dew or the summer shower, utters His voice in the rolling thunder. The idea of a mighty mechanism kept going by inherent laws and forces . . . was utterly rejected. . . . In every case God is not merely the cause supreme, but the cause immediate—more immediate . . . than the natural agents along with which he works.
>
> . . . .
>
> God's Living power is the real thing that binds, and moves, and changes. You cannot think or will, motives cannot do their part without His immanent energy. [Walker 1872, pp. 81–82, 90][9]

The idea that in this not yet disenchanted world a sovereign God is the source of everything from predestination for everlasting life to a summer shower was pursued with such relentless logic that when it came to Sin, that vile development for which a perfect God could not be made responsible, Scottish theologians were driven to formulate the paradoxical nonentitive theory of sin—the view that this ever ubiquitous and consequential force was simultaneously "a nonentity, a nothing" (Walker 1872, p. 85). In the simpler terms of the *Confession:* "The most wise, righteous, and gracious God, doth oftentimes leave for a season his own children to manifold temp-tations . . . that they may be humbled and to raise them to a more close and constant dependence for their support upon himself"

9. See also Donovan (1975, pp. 8–9). In the early eighteenth century, there was some recognition of the existence of natural laws, but these "were merely regarded as conventional arrangements of Providence which could be lightly changed, stopped, or reversed" (Graham 1899, p. 339).

(*CF*, p. 36). All paths, even the path of sin, led to "constant dependence" on God.

The centrality of dependency is apparent in a third area of Calvinist theology, its insistence that humans not only must believe, but must believe certain specific teachings. "Whoever believes in him shall be saved": in Calvinism, faith, that absolute miracle wrought by the Holy Spirit, was the bridge between the sovereign God and the corrupt human, the vehicle by which the elect were "made partakers in the redemption purchased by Christ" (*LC*, p. 160, *SC*, p. 245). "Unbelief," "misbelief," "distrust," "bold and curious searching into his secrets," "immoderate setting of our mind . . . upon other things, and taking off from him in whole or in part"—hallmarks of independent judgment—were sins forbidden by the first commandment, for those living in "unbelief do never truly come to Jesus Christ" (*LC*, pp. 162, 188).

What precisely "man ought to believe concerning God," the sum of saving knowledge, was conveyed, Scottish Calvinism taught, by the Old and New Testaments of the Bible, "which are given by the inspiration by God, to be the rule of faith and life" (*LC*, pp. 130–131, *CF*, p. 21). As Troeltsch observed, if in Catholicism the "heart of religion [was the] hierarchical-sacramental system," in Protestantism everywhere it became the spirit of faith effected by the Word of God (1911, 2:469). In Scotland, the *Confession* hailed the Bible as "infallible truth, and divine authority," as the "whole counsel of God, concerning all things necessary for his own glory, man's salvation, faith and life . . . unto which nothing at any time is to be added" (*CF*, p. 22). It further insisted that the "infallible rule of interpretation of scripture is scripture itself" (*CF*, p. 24). These convictions ever suffused Scottish theological writing. So much was this the case that while Europe was alive with biblical criticism, while England was developing historical apologetics (or external evidences) for the Bible, Scottish theologians held the line that the scriptures were their own evidence (Walker 1872, p. 67; see also Henderson 1957, p. 150). Indeed, Henderson has suggested that these can actually be regarded as "the supreme constitutional document in Scottish history and experience. [From the Reformation onward,] the Bible was the test for everything. . . . Sabbath observance was based on the Bible. . . . The political philosophy of Knox . . . was upheld on Bible grounds. The same may be said of the political principles [of other Scottish theologians]. . . . Social customs were regulated by Scripture. The subordination of wife to husband was plain Scripture teaching and therefore unquestioned.

. . . Christmas was not observed because it was not in the Bible. . . . For centuries the verbal inspiration of the Bible and the infallibility of each statement was unquestioned" (1951, pp. 20–23). Such pervasive unquestioning, which forms so basic a dimension of the orientation of dependency that runs throughout the sources of Scottish Calvinism, vividly reveals the chasm between a culture wrought by the Reformation and what is conventionally considered modern Western culture.

The chasm is found elsewhere as well. The manifestos of Scottish Calvinism exhibit a pronounced tendency toward particularism, toward erecting barriers within the human community and then awarding priority to the resulting subcommunities insofar as they resembled the preferred Scottish Calvinist subcommunity. Four prominent examples of this tendency particularly stand out.

First, at the global level, Scottish Calvinism accentuated the differences between Christians and non-Christians and allowed the ultimate desideratum, salvation, only to the former group, its group. Although Calvin could personally preach that "even a Moor or a Barbarian is 'our brother and neighbor' " (McNeill 1954, p. 234), such a notion was generally quite atypical wherever the Reformation took root. By making belief in the absolute truth of both testaments of the Bible the only basis for salvation, the doctrines of the Reformation, as Cassirer has remarked, excluded those beyond this "temporally and geographically limited proclamation of the divine," and thus eroded much of the "religious universalism" of Renaissance humanism (1932, p. 139). In Scotland, theologians and preachers taught that "the Christian is the only really happy person, for he enjoys the presence of God, . . . deliverance from all sin and assurance of eternal felicity" (Henderson 1951, p. 42), and the *Confession* declared that "men not professing the Christian religion [cannot be saved] be they ever so diligent to frame their laws according to the light of nature, and the law of that religion they do profess; and to assert and maintain that they may, is very pernicious and to be detested" (*CF*, p. 56).

This was not the end of the matter, for Scottish Calvinism imposed further barriers among the different churches that composed the exclusive Christian subcommunity. In this one sees the second and third manifestations of the particularistic orientation of Scottish Calvinism: on the one hand, it disparaged that branch of Christianity that, in contrast to itself, was unreformed and, on the other hand, it celebrated the distinct virtues of one particular reformed Christian church, the Church of Scotland. It is true that Scottish theologians insisted that the Church of Christ "is catholic, [made up not of] an indefinite number of Parochial, or Congregational, or National Churches . . . but one great spiritual republic" (Walker 1872, p. 95; see also, *CF,* pp. 107–8). Yet there was an important proviso here: "particular churches, which are members [of the "catholick church"], are more or less pure, according as the doctrine of the gospel is taught and embraced, ordinances administered, and publick worship performed more or less purely in them. . . . Some have so degenerated as to become no churches of Christ, but synagogues of Satan" (*CF,* p. 109). The chief such synagogue was, of course, the Church of Rome. The *Confession* regarded the pope as "that antichrist, that man of sin, and son of perdition, that exalteth himself in the church against Christ, and all that is called God" (*CF,* pp. 109–10), and for centuries fierce anti-Catholic sentiment was a staple of Scottish Calvinist culture.

Equally persistent was its claim that of all the reformed churches of Christianity, its own Church of Scotland was uniquely sanctified. "The idea that the Scots were a specially favored people, and even a Chosen People," Donaldson (1960, p. 84) has demonstrated, goes back centuries before the Scottish Reformation. But, he continues, "belief in the exceptional purity of the Scottish reformed church strengthened this particular form of national conceit; Knox claimed that all other churches retained 'some footsteps of Antichrist and some dregs of papistry,' whereas 'we . . . have nothing within our churches that ever flowed from that Man of Sin'" (1965, p. 315). This extremely particularistic notion did not die with the father of the Scottish Reformation. It recurred in Scottish theological writings in the seventeenth and in the eighteenth centuries.[10]

The fourth illustration of the particularistic orientation that pervaded Scottish Calvinism can be seen in the way in which the subcommunity that was Christian and reformed and Scottish further subdivided into factions which accorded little tolerance to one another's views. The century of acrimony between the most renowned of these factions, the Episcopalian and Presbyterian parties within the Church of Scotland, has been mentioned previously. What is worth observing here is that the ecclesiastical events that began the eighteenth century—the establishment of the Presbyterian system

10. See Donaldson (1965, p. 316) and Walker (1872, pp. 58–60). It is worth noting that among Calvinists elsewhere as well, Weber discovered that "the belief that they were God's chosen people saw . . . a great renaissance" (1904–5, p. 166); see also Troeltsch (1912, p. 69).

in 1690 and the departure of the supporters of episcopacy from the Church of Scotland—only intensified the rancor between these Calvinist subgroups (Ferguson 1968, p. 102). This was generally an era that managed to publish little more than theological and devotional writings, but it issued volumes where Presbyterians and Episcopalians raged against each other. If universalism implies a measure of objectivity by entailing criteria that (to some degree at least) transcend one's own group (see Merton 1942, pp. 270–73; Parsons 1951, pp. 62–63), the extreme particularism permeating these Calvinist volumes is nowhere so evident as in their partisan judgments of all the persons and events that they treated. Henry Grey Graham has described the situation as follows:

> In the incessant war of pamphlets which was maintained for a generation by tracts—"replies," "rejoinders," "letters," "plain dealings," "vindications," "apologies," "exposures" from either side—there is a spirit of intense virulence. "Foul calumnies," "gross imposters," "base lyar," "false witness," are the sort of epithets which besprinkle every page. So charged with venom, so abounding in evident misrepresentation, are the accusations of Presbyterian and Episcopalian alike, that it is well-nigh impossible to clear the way to truth amidst the jungle of reproaches, recriminations, charges, and countercharges. [Graham 1899, p. 277]

However little these developments are anticipated by the claim that the Calvinist Reformation was the watershed in the emergence of modern culture, they too were integral to the Scottish Calvinist heritage.

   Scottish Calvinism was not of one piece. The point, though stated at the outset, needs to be emphasized, since black-and-white perceptions die hard. There were in Scottish Calvinism propensities to level certain of the barriers that previously divided humans: to raze the hierarchical arrangements of the medieval church; to give the laity a real place in church affairs and thus mitigate the division between clergy and laity; to accentuate a dichotomy—the elect-reprobate distinction—that, since no one in this life knew in which of the dichotomy's classes anyone belonged, practically meant that individuals in all stations were "alike sinners and in that sense . . . equals, as at the same time equal in connexion with the hope of life to come" (Henderson 1957, p. 120). Scottish Calvinism also exhibited tendencies to root out human docility and submissiveness:

in its transformation of the role of the church so as to leave individuals more on their own in the all-important matter of salvation; in its encouragement of "industry," "diligence," "prudence," "sobriety," "a sense of vocation," "backbone," "discipline," and "self-control" (Henderson 1951, pp. 44–45, 1957, p. 136); in its emphasis on liberty of conscience (*CF*, pp. 84–89); and in its support of the cause of political liberty that Knox had championed when holding that each individual has "a sacred duty to help resist and remove all idolatrous or tyrannical magistrates" (Henderson 1951, pp. 46–47; Skinner 1978, 2:237). Were this an exhaustive examination of Scottish Calvinism, it would be necessary to add to these descriptions an analysis of the various other features in Scottish Calvinism that measurably inhibited the realization of its levelling propensities and of its tendencies toward "autonomy" (on some of the previous scholarship on this point, see Camic 1979*a*, pp. 25–29). Such an analysis is unnecessary here. These several developments, however fully realized, neither eradicated the distinctive strains of dependency and particularism that have been identified, nor altered their fundamental position in the Calvinist system. Even as it promoted instrumental activism, liberty of conscience, and political liberty, Calvinism, by leaving humans on the path of salvation without the traditional assistance of the church,[11] enhanced (as Troeltsch's observation above suggested) the belief that they were absolutely dependent upon the will and word of God. Further, the clergy and laity could be given an identical voice in church affairs and all those within a congregation could equally be regarded as sinners, while the attitude that treated Presbyterians and Episcopalians, Scots and non-Scots, Protestants and Catholics, and Christians and non-Christians differently was retained, or even reinforced. To be sure, these

11. Like earlier comments, this remark has assumed, for the sake of a more general argument, that one of the most important features of the conventional wisdom about Calvinism is correct. But as sec. II indicates, the Presbyterian Church of Scotland cannot really be said to have left individuals on their own by the elimination of hierarchical control. It is interesting to note, moreover, that while Parsons has asserted that the Reformation "deprived any Protestant church and its clergy of the 'power of the keys,' the capacity to mediate salvation through the sacraments" (1971, pp. 47–48), *The Westminster Confession* explicitly stated that it is to the officers of the church that "the keys of the kingdom of heaven are committed, by virtue whereof they have the power respectively to retain and remit sins [and] to shut that kingdom against the impenitent, both by word and censures" (*CF*, p. 120). The *Confession* also stressed that the sacraments, one of the means by which God relays the benefits of redemption (*SC*, p. 311), could be dispensed only by "a minister of the word, lawfully ordained" (*CF*, p. 113).

are complex states of affairs, poorly represented in the assumption that the elements of Calvinist culture all tended in essentially the same direction. But that assumption, so much a part of the standard view of the consequences of the Reformation, is the very one that an appreciation of the role of the orientations of dependency and particularism in Scottish Calvinism forces us to abandon.

II

In eighteenth-century America, Henry May has remarked, Calvinism was in a position much like "economic laissez-faire in mid-nineteenth-century England or democracy in twentieth-century America": it was the society's "normal doctrine," received "with different degrees of conviction," but widely and firmly upheld nevertheless (1976b, p. 46). Much the same may be said of Calvinism in early eighteenth-century Scotland. In the round of daily affairs, the orientations just examined were not always uppermost, but neither were they relegated to unnoticed doctrinal statements, sermons, and theological writings. In this era, the Church of Scotland was organized[12] to propagate so broadly its creed of dependency, particularism, and the rest and to limit so effectively the spread of discordant beliefs that Scottish culture was a thoroughly Calvinist culture.[13]

To understand the organization of the Church of Scotland in the early decades of the eighteenth century, it is necessary to return to 1690 when the change in ecclesiastical polity brought, in Hender-

12. It is remarkable how many sociological discussions of Calvinism's historical significance have been altogether silent on the way the Calvinist churches were organized. Here they have followed Weber's policy in *The Protestant Ethic* of passing over matters of church government and discipline, without recognizing that Weber put such matters aside only for his immediate purposes (see 1904–5, p, 96). He was, however, very far from denying an important role to organizational factors (see Weber 1906, 1910), and he quickly tempered his overall argument about the Protestant ethic and the spririt of capitalism with the qualification that "the ecclesiastical supervision of the life of the individual, which, as it was practised in the Calvinistic State Churches, almost amounted to an inquisition, might even retard that liberation of individual powers which was conditioned by the rational ascetic pursuit of salvation, and in some cases actually did so" (1904–5, p. 152).

13. The Church of Scotland is the focus of this discussion because its role in fostering Calvinist orientations was the most obvious. The Church did not stand alone, however. As chap. 4–7 should make clear, certain familial, educational, and occupational arrangements in eighteenth-century Scotland likewise did much to promote dependency and particularism. One could also trace here the ways in which the economic and political structures of the age sustained (and were sustained by) Calvinist beliefs and values.

son's words, "the triumph of [an] intransigent and unimaginative Presbyterianism" (1957, p. 110). Concretely this meant that the powerful General Assembly, the high governing court of the Church of Scotland, was overtaken by sixty aged Presbyterian ministers, the only living remnant of a large band of Presbyterian clerics that had been evicted from the Church when episcopacy was instituted in 1661. The sixty resolved to use the leadership positions they had finally reacquired "to lead Scotland back to a narrower path of morality than the one in which the[se] puritans thought she had walked since 1660" (Smout 1969*a*, p. 213). Their task was not an easy one: episcopacy was (and would long be) revered in the north-eastern parts of Scotland and in the Highlands, while Presbyterian ministers to fill the many parish positions that Episcopalians had vacated were in short supply (Ferguson 1968, pp. 103, 105). Within a generation, however, especially throughout the Scottish Low-lands, Presbyterian Calvinism was victorious,[14] its doctrine pure, its mechanisms for socialization and social control firmly entrenched.[15] Whatever challenges the Church's hegemony would face in later generations, during this period its capacity to disseminate Calvinist orientations was awesome.

A vehicle central to this process, in a way that may now be difficult to appreciate, was the minister's Sunday sermon. "The importance of the pulpit in Scotland," Henderson has observed, "can scarcely be over-estimated. By character and education the minister was the leader of his parishioners. The sermon was their chief source of information and instruction on all matters of . . . moral and spiritual concern" (1937, p. 219; see also Henderson 1951, p. 73). In form, the sermon was an hour long lecture on a brief scriptural passage which often went unchanged for weeks; in content, this lecture was undiluted Westminster Confession Calvinism (Graham 1899, p.

14. Its victory even withstood various political developments at the start of the eighteenth century which, by favoring Scottish Episcopalians, gave anxious Pres-byterians grounds to fear that their hold over Scottish religious life would eventually erode (on these developments, see Clive 1970, p. 236; Ferguson 1968, p. 110).

15. See Cameron (1967, p. 1939), Henderson (1957, pp. 410–41), Sloan (1971, p. 10), and Walker (1872, p. 27).

It is important to recognize the sociological distinctiveness of the state of affairs that has just been described, for Calvinist churches were not always as effective as the Church of Scotland in the early eighteenth century in dominating the culture of which they were a part. For a fascinating example of how un-Calvinist elements penetrated a culture where Calvinist religious regulation had broken down, see Schuma (1979); see also Weber (1904–5, pp. 168–69).

344),[16] giving ample room, as section I indicated, to the themes of dependency and particularism. To guarantee such doctrinal uniformity, presbyteries—church courts intermediate between the national level General Assembly and the parish level kirk-sessions—were well known to send visitation committees to monitor the sermons of local ministers (Graham 1899, p. 333). The setting in which these sermons were preached is also significant. They were the centerpiece of the mandatory, austere Scottish Sabbath service, which typically consisted of two periods of two or more hours in church broken with an interval during which parishioners—lest they forget their Calvinism—could listen to local school boys ask and answer questions from *The Shorter* and *Larger Catechisms* (Graham 1899, p. 291).

The church did much to insinuate Calvinism into the remainder of the week as well, and not only during Wednesday services and sermons. Ministers insisted that parishioners conduct daily family exercises in their homes, and praying and scripture reading punctuated the days of many (Graham 1899, pp. 336, 344–46). "The Scots were Bible reading people till well into the nineteenth century [and] the Bible soaked itself into the thinking and vocabulary and habits of all classes" (Henderson 1951, p. 13; see also Henderson 1957, p. 105). To fill the spare hours of younger souls, there was also an extensive network of primary schools, a network designed—the General Assembly reminded the nation in 1705—to "instruct scholars in the principles of the Christian reformed religion, according to the Holy Scriptures, Our Confession of Faith, or such books as are entirely agreeable thereto" (cited by Grant 1876, p. 417). That exhortation did not go unheeded. Schools "worked within a completely religious framework," where orthodox teachings formed a major component of the curriculum, the Bible served as the typical primer for new readers, and *The Shorter Catechism* regularly provided the basis for a "searching and abstruse doctrinal inquisition" of young pupils (Bain 1965, p. 83; Beale 1953, pp. 81–82; Grant 1876, p. 419). Little wonder that eighteenth-century Scots learned a thing or two about Calvinist orientations.

16. Using Macleod's listing of the "specimens of the orthodox pulpit" (1943, p. 112) and some hints from Graham (1899, pp. 393–413) as guides to representative collections of sermons during this period, the works of Gray (1789), Meldrum (1704), Spalding (1703), and Wedderburn (1713) were selected and briefly consulted to check the accuracy of this standard picture of Scottish sermons (the first and last of the sources mentioned were actually composed earlier, but remained popular throughout the early eighteenth century). The picture was found to be satisfactory.

That Scottish churches and schools were amply filled year after year and had their commandments widely obeyed was not accidental. The Church of Scotland backed socialization and social pressure with elaborate disciplinary machinery. The origins of this were in Calvinist theology. Calvin had placed great stress on the Communion service and insisted "that none dare to present himself at it save holily and with singular reverence" (quoted by McNeill 1954, p. 138). To guard against the participation of unworthy persons in the holy sacrament, he had proposed a complex system of discipline for the visible church (McNeill 1954, p. 151). In Scotland from the Reformation until well past the early eighteenth century, this system was organized around parish level church courts, or kirk-sessions, which were composed of the local minister and a variable number of elders chosen from the laity. A principal task for these courts was to examine the beliefs and morals of the potential communicants in their districts prior to the Communion season and to issue admission tickets to the sacrament to those found worthy (Henderson 1935, pp. 49–50). But kirk-sessions did not stop here, and though their activities do not merit Buckle's famous comparison with the Spanish Inquisition (1861, p. 234), it remains the case that there was little in the lives of parishioners that was outside of kirk-sessions jurisdiction. During the early eighteenth century, session members monitored Sunday church attendance in a manner that, if not always wholehearted and universally successful, was nevertheless inevitably strict, and then brought the same spirit to bear in a puritanical regulation of gambling, drinking, wayward sexual activities, and the like.[17] Most important for understanding pre-Enlightenment Scottish culture was the church's insistence upon enforcing orthodoxy in belief from the home to the university, its intolerance of anything suggesting heterodox sentiments, and the perpetual readiness of kirk-sessions "to detect and call to heel a [confessional] deviant before he imperilled his own soul and began to infect those of the rest of the flock" (Smout 1969a, p. 480; see also Cameron 1967, p. 1939).

To ensure the effectiveness of such policies, kirk-sessions were empowered with a variety of sanctions. These ranged from censures and fines, through required weekly appearances on a stool of repentence before the church congregation, to several shades of excommunication (see Henderson 1935, pp. 116–18). Prior to 1690

17. On church attendance, see Brackenridge (1969), and Graham (1899, pp. 314–21); more generally, see Burleigh (1960, p. 268), Henderson (1957, pp. 146–47), Letwin (1965, p. 22), and Reid (1960, pp. 114–15).

those excommunicated from the church faced severe civil penalties as well, and up to 1712 state authorities could legally compel sinners to submit to the sentences of kirk-sessions. Ultimately, the combined force of the legislation of these years reduced some of the Church of Scotland's control over behavior and belief (see Smout 1969*a*, pp. 480–81), but this effect developed slowly. Civil authorities lent assistance to kirk-sessions for some time after 1712, and due to the social stigma that resulted from kirk-session penalties (especially excommunication), such sanctions remained efficacious long into the eighteenth century (see Graham 1899, pp. 315–17, 324; Ferguson 1968, pp. 110–11). Indeed, it has been argued that not until the nineteenth century "did minister and kirk-session lose their position of parochial authority" (Henderson 1951, p. 176). Whether or not their position was that long-lived, it was so firm in the early eighteenth century that the fundamental cultural orientations of Calvinism were given a commanding "hold over great masses of the people of all classes" (Graham 1899, p. 336).

III

Scottish Calvinist culture was not monochromatic. No system of socialization and social control functions flawlessly and, however mighty the Church of Scotland's capacity to spread its beliefs, to claim that every breathing soul in Scotland from 1700 until 1740 accepted an identical brand of Westminster Confession Calvinism would be to propose a sociological miracle. Let us anticipate the Enlightenment and banish the miraculous: if most early eighteenth-century Scots adopted the teachings of the Church of Scotland with little hesitation, deviance from the standard creed was also to be found. Previous commentators, using a miraculously monolithic culture as their norm,[18] have taken all signs of such deviance as indications that Calvinist cultural preeminence was in jeopardy. But that interpretation is not sustained by a more realistic reading of the evidence. Scholarship on the period prior to the Scottish Enlightenment does well of course to take note of those developments

18. Here scholars have too often accepted uncritically the testimony of eighteenth-century Scottish Calvinists, who *did* expect a uniform culture and panicked over the most trivial departures from the orthodox creed. The reaction of at least one contemporary, however, was more temperate. In a 1756 pamphlet, Robert Wallace (see note 28) observed that "religion has been said to be declining as long as he can remember and that he is not a young man [Wallace was born in 1698]. . . . He adds 'if men would believe you in this they . . . would allmost wonder there is any Religion left at all' " (Sefton 1966, pp. 19–20).

that are harbingers of the Enlightenment itself, and in this regard certain breaches that were made in the code of particularism especially stand out. At the same time, however, it is important not to mistake wisps of smoke for a conflagration. Departures here and there from the Calvinist gospel were not the end, or even the beginning of the end, of the Calvinist *mentalité*. In early eighteenth-century Scotland, divergence from the received doctrines, even in the area of particularism, occurred well within a framework of otherwise orthodox assumptions and was everywhere restrained by the overriding supposition that humans and their world are dependent in all things upon the will of God. The fact that this conviction still persisted in the most extreme instances of doctrinal deviance is striking testimony to the utter tenacity of Calvinist culture at this time. Before taking up the extreme cases, however, three more routine exceptions to the general pattern of Calvinist belief should be mentioned.

The first of these was composed of those outside of the Presbyterian establishment. However much it may have wished to, the Church of Scotland did not eliminate Episcopalians, Catholics, and other, generally small, sects with their own traditions, patterns of education, and social institutions (on the eighteenth-century fate of the principals here, see Donaldson 1960, pp. 104–8). But in the present context, these groups are of little concern; during this period, they had a very limited effect on the Church and its system of belief, although—at the price of various kinds of harassment from the Church and state—they may have provided Scotland with something of "a leven in the presbyterian lump" (Trevor-Roper 1967, p. 1644).[19]

A second kind of departure from orthodoxy was exhibited in the periodic doctrinal prevarications of certain minor Presbyterian heretics. Peter Gay has observed that even the medieval world had its share of "heretics questioning aspects of Catholic doctrine. But

19. Trevor-Roper views the intellectual activities of some of these groups as a stimulus to the Enlightenment (see 1967, pp. 1642–46; see also Clive 1970, pp. 232–37; Meilke 1947), and it certainly is the case that they sometimes operated as channels through which novel foreign ideas reached Scotland. The text will make clear, however, that there were numerous other channels of this sort and that the infiltration of foreign ideas—themselves not of the Enlightenment—did not the Enlightenment make. It is also worth noting that research on many of those whom Trevor-Roper mentions has found that they shared, for all their differences from those in the Church of Scotland, a majority of the traditional cultural orientations that the Church propagated (see Duncan 1965, pp. 15–23; Henderson 1957, pp. 105–19; Kenrick 1956, pp. 40–49; and sec. IV below).

no one, not even the heretic, doubted the religious foundation of the world" (1966, p. 254). Much the same was true in early eighteenth-century Scotland, as the case of the egregious James Allan reveals. Allan was a Presbyterian minister who in 1706 was deposed of his clerical charge for refusing to endorse those passages of *The Westminster Confession* that concerned "the fate of the heathen. He said he failed to see how it could contribute to one's salvation to believe that 'the greatest part of mankind' is fore-ordained to everlasting death [and] declared that men might share a Christian spirit who had never heard of Christ" (Mathieson 1905, p. 223). Naturally, the Church found such hints of universalism quite shocking,[20] but we need not succumb to its fear that they undermined the Calvinist heritage. Not only did the kirk swiftly detect and punish Allan's errors, but of themselves these entailed little rupture in the Calvinist universe. The source of Allan's novel sentiments was nothing more subversive than the work of the devout Richard Baxter— the English divine whom Weber (1904–5, p. 155) and almost everyone else except for the membership of the Church of Scotland has taken as a model Calvinist thinker—and, after all, even the provocative Allan did not scruple to affirm the vast bulk of the Westminster Confession.

The third type of divergence from standard Calvinist beliefs was more innocuous still: those Scottish Presbyterians who took their Calvinism so very seriously that they were driven—momentarily— to doubt it. Not a few of the age's most renowned ministers, craving strong religious sentiments and not content without them, worried themselves into grave "struggles with unbelief," but, to the relief of all, the Bible ultimately guided these skeptics back to the straight and narrow (Walker 1872, pp. 70–71).

Calvinism in early eighteenth-century Scotland experienced what appear to be more serious attacks. It was already fairly clear, as early as 1690, that the members of the Church of Scotland were not exactly of one theological voice (Donaldson 1960, p. 96). Yet

20. That the Church reacted this way each time the slightest suggestion of universalism surfaced is a powerful commentary on the entrenchment of particularistic orientations. It is not surprising, therefore, that when a group of Episcopalian theologians adopted the loosely universalistic ideas of the French mystic Antoinette Bourignon (on these, see Mathieson 1910, p. 187) and asserted that "those who are govern'd by the spirit of divine love are the children of God . . . wherever they are" (James Garden's remark, quoted by Henderson 1957, p. 111), Bourignonism was repeatedly condemned by the General Assembly (Henderson 1957, pp. 110, 118).

for some years they all managed to coexist, their slightly different emphases, "the traditional, the new evangelical, the evangelical-moderate, the semi-rationalistic, all . . . shading off into one another" (Walker 1872, p. 27; see also Mechie 1967, pp. 267–70). Between 1714 and 1730, however, the concern of men of these varying persuasions with strict orthodoxy generated throughout the Church certain theological disputes that have often been taken to indicate the weakening of Calvinism.[21] The kind of challenge to Calvinist orientations actually implied here is best seen in the two most famous theological controversies of the period.

In 1717 John Simson, professor of divinity at the University of Glasgow, was tried before the General Assembly for holding such reckless opinions as "that there was no natural inability in man to seek saving grace; that the heathen had a glimmering of gospel truth and would be lost only if they rejected this 'obscure discovery and offer'; that the soul was created pure and became corrupt only when united to the body inherited from Adam; [and] that the elect might be expected to outnumber the damned" (Mathieson 1905, p. 225). The General Assembly did not hesitate to declare the fallacy of these views, but eventually decided—since Simson avowed his adherence to the Confession and since the evidence against him was shaky—to let their alleged author resume his teaching. In 1726 Simson was less fortunate. While still endorsing the Confession, he lost his Glasgow position for following the pious English divine, Samuel Clarke, and maintaining that the three persons of the trinity are not numerically one.

If Simson was called to task for steering a little "left" of the Confession, in 1720 the General Assembly condemned *The Marrow of Modern Divinity*, a favorite work of several Evangelical ministers who veered in the opposite direction. Among its five heretical departures from the Confession, the *Marrow* was especially attacked for implying, through its claim "that it is part of the direct act of faith to believe that Christ died for me," the doctrine of universal redemption. Although supporters of the work insisted that they "rejected the 'sheer universalism' that Christ died for every man," the work was nonetheless banned (Walker 1872, pp. 53–54).[22]

21. That it was a desire for orthodoxy that actually provoked these various disputes is the position suggested by Burleigh (1960, p. 291).

22. This did not repress the Evangelical ministers and in 1733, in the midst of controversy over the proper way of appointing parish ministers, several of them broke from the Church of Scotland to form the Associate Presbytery, the first major Secession church.

Historians have overinterpreted these theological controversies. They have found in the General Assembly's initial acquittal of Simson and in its condemnation of the Evangelical *Marrow* tract a "liberalizing of Calvinism" (Cameron 1967, p. 1944), and they have seen in Simson himself an "anticipa[tion of] the attitudes of the Enlightenment" (Ferguson 1968, p. 116). There is something in such judgments, but not much. In point of fact, the *Marrow* did go beyond the Calvinism of the Confession, so that to condemn it was actually to provide a faithful defense of the old orthodoxy (see Drummond and Bulloch 1973, p. 37; Mechie 1967, pp. 267–68; Walker 1872, pp. 57–58). Simson was let off, but only for a time and with a warning; and in any event, he was—in his worries over how many beings comprise the trinity, over the proportion of elect and reprobate, over the moment the soul becomes corrupt—a character far better equipped for a role in hairsplitting, medieval debates over the characteristics of a God-saturated universe than for the Enlightenment's secular stage. More important, Simson's "errors," such as they were, were probably "the most serious that had been broached in Scotland since the Reformation" (Mathieson 1905, p. 233; see also Mechie 1967, p. 272). Can a cultural system which produced no more outrageous a deviant in belief than a Professor Simson—and which had courts that caught and eventually punished and silenced him—seriously be regarded as weakened? Theological "wrangling about minute points of doctrine and forms of words" there was as a matter of course in early eighteenth-century Scotland (Mechie 1967, p. 266). Educated men reflecting daily on such issues were bound to clash occasionally. Never, however, did these men stray too far from Calvinist orthodoxies and, wherever they wandered, they were closely watched by church courts.[23]

George Davie has criticized Scottish historical research for neglecting fields like law and philosophy and, in so doing, exaggerating "the religious monopoly on Scottish culture"(1961*a*, pp. xii–xiv). At one level, this is a sound observation. For no more than the Reformation extinguished poetry and the accumulation of medical and agricultural lore did it bring legal and philosophical speculation to a halt. It is true that, for many generations, such speculation was all quite sterile and sterilized (see Meilke 1947, p. 11; Morgan 1933, p. 63; Veitch 1877, pp. 86–87). But there is also

23. This conclusion is further supported by the history of the other main theological controversy that has been adduced to demonstrate the decay of orthodoxy, the case of Archibald Campbell (see Camic 1979*a*, pp. 41–42).

considerable evidence that, at least by the early decades of the eighteenth century, things were at last very dramatically coming to life. In the later seventeenth century, many of the seminal intellectual developments then underway in Europe were already making their way to Scotland through diverse channels, and the influx thereafter proceeded apace, with the result that there were few major philosophical, legal, or scientific currents that had left Scotland untouched by the 1730s. Hobbes, Descartes, Leibniz, Malebranche, the writings on natural law by Grotius, Pufendorf, and Cumberland, historical skepticism, deism, Shaftesbury, Mandeville, Clarke, Butler, Berkeley, and, not least, John Locke and Isaac Newton had at this point all made their appearance; and in the literary circles of Edinburgh, Glasgow, and Aberdeen, in classrooms of the universities, and even on the shelves of devout Presbyterian ministers, the stimulating new materials were everywhere to be found.[24]

In this massive penetration of foreign work into Scotland by the early eighteenth century, previous students of Scottish culture have predictably seen signs foreboding that Calvinism was decaying and that the Enlightenment itself was nearly at hand.[25] Such scholars would be at home with those who are so bothered about Professor Simson's heresies. It is undeniable that the ideas imported into Scotland during this era were not those found in *The Westminster Confession;* that, furthermore, they provoked some quite heterodox discussion of metaphysical, ethical, psychological, and sundry other issues; and that they were a great boon to the "improving movement," which sought so thoroughly to modernize nearly all aspects of Scottish life (see Clive 1970, p. 234; Phillipson 1974, p. 441; on the improving movement, see chap. 2, sec. II below). To ignore these facts is to render the cultural background of the Enlightenment incomprehensible. But, once again, it is essential not to conflate departures from certain specific doctrines of Calvinism with a transformation of its basic postulates.

However novel, none of the work filtering into Scotland at this time—not that of the natural law theorists, nor that of Locke, nor

24. On this series of developments, see Clark (1964, pp. 212–14), Clive (1970, pp. 230–33), Davie (1961*b*, pp. 11–12), Drummond and Bulloch (1973, pp. 86–91), Emerson (1977, pp. 464–70), Henderson (1951, p. 51), McCosh (1875, pp. 36–49), Mechie (1967, p. 258), Mossner (1954, p. 49), Murray (1927, pp. 507, 511), Phillipson (1974, pp. 438, 440), Rae (1973, pp. 204–6), Rendall (1978, p. 22), Ross (1972, p. 28), Trevor-Roper (1967, pp. 1642–49), and Walker (1872, pp. 71–73).

25. See Clive (1970, esp. p. 235), Ferguson (1968, p. 113), Mechie (1967, p. 258), Phillipson (1974, p. 440), and Ross (1972, p. 14).

surely that of the saintly Newton—was of the Enlightenment (see, e.g., Forbes 1975a, pp. 3–90; and Gay 1966, 1969). Like the Scottish Enlightenment, the European Enlightenment was still gestating and it would have been most extraordinary if the entry into Scotland of a few, or even a few score, pre-Enlightenment documents dissolved the foundations of a religious system so widely accepted and so well institutionalized as Calvinism. Indeed, early eighteenth-century Scotland abounds with instances where encounters with the most subversive foreign ideas available failed to produce this magical dissolution of existing beliefs. The legendary Presbyterian theologian Thomas Halyburton read Locke and the deists, only to subject the former to a spiritual reinterpretation and to reject the latter's religion of nature in favor of revelation (Walker 1872, pp. 71–73). Judging from the General Assembly's constant outrage over the vile deist literature, this kind of response to new suggestions was quite typical (see Cameron 1967, pp. 1940, 1946; Ferguson 1968, pp. 113–14; Mechie 1967, pp. 258–59). Things were not much different in the universities. The same curricula that introduced a certain amount of Descartes, Hobbes, and Locke remained "suffused with a Calvinist religiosity," and in the moral philosophy courses where religious issues were broached, there was little change for decades (Emerson 1977, pp. 465–69). To be sure, Presbyterian theologians, General Assemblies, and college courses were not the age's most forward-looking forces. But even the work of the legal and philosophical figures who were most progressive and most receptive to foreign intellectual currents is meager evidence with which to dispute the "religious monopoly." Rather, this work demonstrates that, in early eighteenth-century Scotland, Calvinism's most fundamental assumptions thoroughly pervaded the most vital spheres of nonreligious culture.

In legal matters, the pioneer was undoubtedly James Dalrymple, first Viscount Stair. Stair was a late seventeenth-century Scottish scholar who, drawing from the Continental natural lawyers (especially Grotius and Pufendorf), insisted that Scottish law conform to the dictates of Reason and then set about transforming Scotland's previously chaotic catalogues of court decisions into a coherent and logical system of legal rules (Stein 1970, p. 148). Although his great work, *The Institutions of the Law of Scotland,* appeared in 1681, a generation prior to the period of direct concern here, it provided the paradigm for Scottish legal thought throughout the first half of the eighteenth century (Stein 1970, p. 151) and has been celebrated for giving "a vigorous push to intellectual activities pointing to the Scottish Enlightenment" (Ross 1972, p. 14). In the end, however, Stair's conception of law was, as Peter Stein has shown, even less "independent of theological assumptions" than the natural law tradition on which it was based. Law, according to Stair, "is founded primarily on the will of God. Reason is rather a subsidiary instrument . . . given to man that . . . he might deduce God's law in more particular cases. As [A. H.] Campbell puts it, 'Stair was prepared to rely on God at an indefinite number of points as the author of an indefinite number of principles of human action, which are directly known without reasoning or experience, [and] which therefore did not require logical proof of their validity' " (1970, pp. 148–49; see also Clive 1970, p. 220; Millar 1903, p. 306; Young 1967, p. 1970). Stair's views, it is scarcely surprising, required no defense before the cautious courts of his beloved Presbyterian church.

The Calvinist orientation of dependency was also preserved in the writings of the most avant-garde early eighteenth-century Scottish philosophers. Gershom Carmichael (1672–1729) was, for example, a very generous proponent of the philosophies of Grotius and Pufendorf, Leibniz and Descartes, Locke and Newton. Through them all, however, he remained "wrapt in . . . Calvinism" (Rae 1895, p. 12), affirming scriptural standards, emphasizing man's duties to God, publishing works designed to establish His perfections, and insisting that things corporeal only "exist so long as they have being from the creative efficacy of God" (McCosh 1875, pp. 36–42). Andrew Baxter (1686–1750) was of a similar ilk. Having immersed himself in Leibniz, Clarke, Locke, and Newton, he then used these up-to-date sources to establish what Calvinist theologians always established: "the necessity of incessant Providence . . . the ceaseless activity of the Divine cause" (Laurie 1902, pp. 36, 39). Only superficially is the case of George Turnbull (1698–1748) any different. At nearly the same time that David Hume was extending Newtonian procedures to the field of moral philosophy in the *Treatise of Human Nature* and inaugurating the Scottish Enlightenment in the process, the widely read Turnbull completed his *Principles of Moral Philosophy,* which likewise attempted to apply Newton's experimental methods to the analysis of moral subjects. But his au courant readings and intentions did not make him a Hume. Occasional innovations notwithstanding, Turnbull was still sufficiently encased within the Calvinist framework that, to his mind, the laws of nature were equivalent with the laws of God, just as a proper philosophical view of human duties ever corresponded to the scriptural view (Forbes 1975a, pp. 42, 45).[26]

A final illustration of the immunity of ingrained Calvinist presuppositions to unorthodox philosophical developments is the most remarkable. Francis Hutcheson (1694–1746) was a hybrid, part early eighteenth-century Scot, part imported philosophical novelty. He was born to a Scottish Presbyterian family in Ireland, lived there until he was seventeen, spent probably the next six years in Glasgow as a student of the notorious Simson, returned to Ireland, joined a circle where radical philosophical ideas (Shaftesbury, Berkeley, and deism) were in the air, published his first philosophical inquiries, and in 1730 sailed again for Glasgow to replace the now-departed Carmichael in the moral philosophy chair until his own death (see Scott 1900). The arrival of this Irishman in Scotland has often been regarded as the real beginning of the Scottish Enlightenment,[27] and there surely is no gainsaying the magnitude of Hutcheson's achievement. His celebrated proclamations on economics, politics, psychology, and ethics challenged a solid phalanx of received wisdoms and anticipated many of the specific arguments that would subsequently be advanced by the likes of Hume and Smith. What is most significant here, moreover, is that, despite Hutcheson's Calvinist training, his lectures and writings not only allowed comparatively little place to original sin and the innate corruption of human nature, and not only proposed to establish a science of morality without the aid of the Bible, they also exhibited a hardy strain of universalism, particularly evident in their advocacy of religious tolerance and in their unprecedented opposition to slavery.[28]

26. On this side of Turnbull's thought, see also Norton (1975, pp. 712–16). On his involvement in modern intellectual trends, see Forbes (1975a, pp. 2–3), Fraser (1898, pp. 21–23), McCosh (1875, pp. 95–106), Norton (1975, pp. 702–4), Ross (1972, p. 70), and Veitch (1877, pp. 212–13); on Carmichael's involvement, see Murray (1927, pp. 507, 511), Taylor (1965, pp. 26–28), and Veitch (1877, p. 209); on Baxter, see McCosh (1875, pp. 42–49). For an interpretation of Baxter differing from the one offered in the text, see Davie (1961b, p. 15).

27. See Bryson (1945), Davie (1967, p. 25), Nybakken (1980, p. 1128), Taylor (1965), and Wills (1978b, p. 149). Note also the formulations of Deanina (1763), Rendall (1978, pp. 74–78), Smout (1969a, p. 452), and Stewart (1821, p. 428).

28. On Hutcheson's economics, see Taylor (1965); on his politics, see Forbes (1975a, pp. 161–62), Robbins (1954, pp. 243–51, 1959, pp. 188–95), and Winch (1978, pp. 46–66); on his psychology and ethics, Blackstone (1965, pp. 11–40), Jensen (1971, pp. 8–65), Raphael (1947, pp. 15–46), and Smith (1941, pp. 23–51). For a stimulating, more general analysis of Hutcheson's work, see Wills (1978b). As to the

For all this, however, Hutcheson accepted the most essential premises of Calvinism. His work, as Duncan Forbes has demonstrated, was not genuinely independent of theological supports and "one cannot make it independent without destroying its whole structure" (1975a, p. 45, and more generally, pp. 41–60). Hutcheson's philosophy everywhere rested on the belief that "an omnipotent and good God governs the world," "that the Deity is the original independent Being, compleat in all possible perfection, of boundless power, wisdom and goodness" (*Works* 6:379–80, 4:72). As for humans: "we are such dependent creatures," full of "manifold weaknesses and disorders of soul," "intangled in many errors and misapprehensions," and molded for "submission, resignation, and trust in God's Providence" (*Works* 4:73–74, 76). And again:

> We ought always to keep this in our thoughts, that we entirely depend on God; that all the goods either of mind or body, all our virtues, have been derived from him, and must be preserved or increased by his gracious Providence. ... There can be no other stable foundation of tranquility and joy than a constant trust in the goodness, wisdom, and power of God, by which we commit to him ourselves, our friends, and the whole universe, persuaded that he will order all things well. [*Works*, 4:59–60]

various "enlightened" elements in his thought: see Graham (1899, p. 352), Laurie (1902, p. 32), and Rendall (1978, p. 75), along with the works on psychology just enumerated, on the reevaluation of original sin; Forbes (1975a, p. 41) on the proposed science of morality; Clark (1964, pp. 224–25), Laurie (1902, pp. 14, 33–34), and Robbins (1954, p. 249) on religious tolerance; and Sypher (1939) on slavery.

Given Hutcheson's tolerance toward differences in religious belief, as well as his general flexibility in the area of dogma, it has become customary to see him also as an intellectual ancestor of the Moderate party that later emerged within the Church of Scotland (see Clark 1964, pp. 223–25; Mathieson 1905, pp. 253–55, 1910, pp. 190–96; on the Moderates, see chap. 2, sec. II). It is important to emphasize, however, that in this respect he did not stand alone, for a handful of other "earnest and devout" clerics of his generation likewise stressed "tolerance [more] than correctness of dogma" (Mechie 1967, pp. 269–71; see also Mathieson 1910, pp. 194–95). The most radical of this band was probably the versatile Robert Wallace (1698–1771), who was probably closer to the Scottish Enlightenment, particularly in the matter of universalism, than any other early eighteenth-century Scot (see Mossner 1943, p. 123; Robbins 1959, pp. 202–8; Sefton 1966, pp. 18, 22). Nevertheless, to follow Mossner and actually make him "a member of the Scottish Enlightenment" (1943, p. 105) is to obscure his essential orthodoxy, especially his views on divine revelation and his abiding interest in vindicating to humans the ways of Providence (see Robbins 1959, pp. 203–5, 209–11; Sefton 1966, pp. 17–18).

Thus does the "most forward-looking thinker [of the Scotland] of his day" (Forbes 1975a, p. 32) return time after time to the verities of *Westminster Confession* Calvinism. No wonder Hume had his reservations about Hutcheson, and Hutcheson about Hume (see Mossner 1954, p. 134; Ross 1966). The Scottish Enlightenment was not yet at hand.

IV

Well into the early eighteenth century, Scottish presses issued a kind of literature that was integral to the cultural life of Presbyterians and Episcopalians alike but finds no place in the preceding remarks. Merging at one end into antiquarianism and, at the other, into contemporary political commentary, this literature is usually described generically as historical writing.[29] By and large, it was historical writing of an unexpected type, however. For while some Scottish historiography followed the Calvinist model and concerned itself chiefly with chronicling God's miraculous ordering of past events (see Henderson 1951, p. 43; Millar 1912, pp. 8–29), a large portion of the historical work of the age was—in comparison not only with *The Westminster Confession,* but also with the most advanced philosophical ideas of the early eighteenth century—markedly secular. Though generally penned by devout believers and rarely silent about divine doings, this work proffered accounts of the events of this world that were not vitally dependent upon the will of God, accounts that can be loosened from what theological foundations they have without losing their structure. Despite this most un-Calvinist of characteristics, historiography in early eighteenth-century Scotland nevertheless retained in various guises the orientations of particularism and dependency which were at the base of Scottish Calvinist culture.[30]

The particularism is blatant. Douglas Duncan has, in fact, aptly termed this entire body of work "controversial history" to indicate that, above all else, it was of "fiercely partisan" nature (1965, p. 125). Rather than attempting to view past persons and events in

29. See, e.g., Beattie (1949), Graham (1899, pp. 112–13, 1901, p. 5), National Library of Scotland (1958, pp. 6–11), and Pryde (1962, p. 110).

30. It is immaterial in this context whether this congruence was due to the influence of Calvinism on the historical writers of this period, or to the impact upon both Scottish Calvinism and Scottish historiography of similar social and cultural factors not yet mentioned, or to the fact that, while each of these two spheres of Scottish culture was affected by different factors, these factors nevertheless shaped the two spheres in similar ways.

terms of general, relatively objective standards designed to appeal beyond any particular human subgroup, Scottish historians emphasized the boundaries that divided the human community and considered historical phenomena in light of criteria peculiar to the subcommunity to which they belonged. Consistently, these historians regarded the past through the filter of their own political commitments and employed historical materials as polemical weapons on behalf of the cause of their social group (Duncan 1965, p. 126, and more generally, pp. 122–44; Ross and Scobie 1974).

One manifestation of this was the spate of patriotic histories that appeared in early eighteenth-century Scotland. To understand this outpouring, it is necessary to realize that for many centuries Scotland had cherished a quaint legend concerning its origin. This legend proclaimed the great antiquity of the Scottish people and their line of monarchs, and was frequently used to justify Scotland's political independence from England (see Rae 1973, pp. 207–8). In the late seventeenth and early eighteenth centuries, English scholars, grinding axes of their own, challenged the historical evidence for the independence of Scotland, denied the legend of its origin and, in the process, deprived Scotland of nine hundred years of its history and forty of its kings (Rae 1973, p. 209). This was much too much for patriotic Scottish historians, who naturally responded by treating the historical record in ways that vindicated the claims of their own nation. Particularly when the question of the union of the English and Scottish parliaments revived the issue of Scottish political independence, historical writers in Scotland furiously produced tracts asserting the historicity of Scotland's mythical kings and tomes (notably James Anderson's bluntly titled *Historical Essay Showing that the Crown and Kingdom of Scotland is Imperial and Independent*) attacking the nationalist English historians and providing Scotland, for better or worse, with its own tendentious renditions of the past (see Duncan 1965, pp. 124–25; Phillipson 1974, p. 429; Ross and Scobie 1974, pp. 103, 116).

A second illustration of the particularism that pervaded Scottish historical literature emerges from the writings of spokesmen for the different political parties—Whig or Whig-Presbyterian, Tory or Tory-Episcopalian.[31] Party histories, which were a much more

31. It is unnecessary to enter at this point into the vagaries of Scottish political alignments in the eighteenth century. The party labels used in the text here and below are illustrative and should not be taken for a description of political life in this age. In fact, for Scotland, as for England, the court-country dichotomy was often more apposite than the Whig-Tory one, and frequently "the Scots did not fit

typical feature of Scottish culture than patriotic histories, actually exhibited such pronounced partisanship that they make patriotic histories seem like objectivity itself. During the course of the seventeenth century, supporters of different parties had produced histories of Scotland which, as Millar has commented, "naturally dwell on circumstances which tell in favour of their own views, and make light of such as tell against them" (1903, p. 276), and the practice persisted. By the first decades of the eighteenth century, according to Duncan, "men of party . . . could scarcely reflect on any character or incident from their country's past without finding it fraught with controversial significance," while as late as the 1740s major scholars were still attempting "to force the facts of [Scottish] history into the mould of modern political ideas" (1965, pp. 129, 137). The historical habits of earlier times continued into the eighteenth century even though Scottish historians had recently become aware of work in which their European counterparts, having decided that partisan commitments thoroughly bias historical research, advocated a thoroughgoing historical skepticism (see Hay 1977; Popkin 1965; Rae 1973). This work did have some effect. In 1708 George Mackenzie, sounding a suitably skeptical note, fairly remarked that in Scotland "all parties misrepresent Facts, . . . each side displaying what is most to their Advantage; or dissembling, or but faintly representing, what is not in their Favours" (cited by Duncan 1965, p. 127), while, a generation later, Charles Mackie, professor of civil history at the University of Edinburgh, taught that historical "writers have often been blinded by passion and strong prejudices . . . to favour a particular sect or *party* in a country" (cited by Horn 1956, p. 159). But, in the early eighteenth century, even the men who recognized the extent to which particularism colored Scottish historiography did not provide a historical literature that treated the events of the past more universalistically. Mackie compiled chronological tables, but wrote no historical work at all and always remained a staunch Whig (see Horn 1967, p. 38;

into English categories" (Riley 1974, p. 12), but rather combined, dissolved, and recombined into factions of their own which intersected, in complex ways, with Scottish ecclesiastical parties (see Ferguson 1968, pp. 53, 63, 137; Riley 1964, pp. 17–23, 1974, pp. 12–17; see also Hume *Essays*, p. 73, note 1; on English political alignments and the relevance of the concept of party to its political situation, see Speck 1977, pp. 1–7; Owen 1974, pp. 94–122, 277–94; Plumb 1967, pp. 129–72). How parties and factions were constituted and denominated does not affect the argument that early eighteenth-century Scottish historians regarded historical phenomena in terms of the political claims of the particular party or faction to which they belonged.

Sharp 1946, pp. 37–51); Mackenzie produced *The Lives and Characters of the Most Eminent Writers of the Scots Nation,* which did not "rise above the party-political approach to history" (Duncan 1965, p. 128). The tendency to award the laurels of history to one's own political subgroup was as entrenched as the practice of alloting more divine rewards to those with the good fortune of belonging to the right subcommunity of reformed Scottish Christians.

A no less fundamental attribute of the historiographic sphere of Scottish culture was dependency. This orientation, in its secularized form, rendered human judgment subservient to the unquestioned requirements and shibboleths of superpersonal political units (nation, party, faction) rather than to the ways and words of God, but its manifestations were much the same.[32] Above all, as Charles Mackie pointedly observed, Scottish historians operated with a "too great credulity in receiving anything yt makes for ye honour of one's country" or party (cited by Horn 1956, p. 159). Thus, Robert Wodrow (1679–1734), a Whiggish Presbyterian historian and "probably the most industrious collector of facts and documents . . . among the historians of Scotland," was a most undiscriminating scholar: "No story to [his opponents'] discredit is too improbable to be received by him with eager welcome, and of anything like a critical method he is absolutely innocent" (Millar 1903, pp. 299–300; see also Ferguson 1968, p. 217; Millar 1912, pp. 149–65). The Tory Episcopalian, Thomas Ruddiman (1674–1757), "the foremost literary scholar in the Scotland of his day and one of the most versatile and industrious that Scotland has ever known" (Duncan 1965, p. 1), was of a similar breed. Perhaps more than any other early eighteenth-century Scottish intellectual, he understood and endorsed the European historiographic injunction that the "historian's duty [is] to tell the truth," not for any particular group, but for the public as a whole (Duncan 1965, p. 130). Ruddiman's own historical judgments, however, were ever governed by received political orthodoxies that were as sacred and indubitable to him as

32. In certain of the other quasi-secular branches of pre-Enlightenment culture, it appears that political convictions—and, with them, attitudes of particularism and dependency—may have run as deep as they did in the historical scholarship of the period. Ross and Scobie (1974, pp. 111–16) have found that partisan (party and patriotic) sentiments suffused major poetic writings in early eighteenth-century Scotland, and Riley (1978, pp. 220–45) has detected, throughout the extensive literature that debated the parliamentary union with England, an orientation whereby the evaluation of situational phenomena depended upon automatically accepted political beliefs (see also Ferguson 1968, pp. 48–49).

the word of God was to other Scottish Calvinists. In his historical writings, Duncan concludes, " 'Truth' . . . was not a distant ideal to be pursued but a long-cherished political . . . philosophy to be defended," "a mystery already . . . vouchsafed to Tories and Episcopalians" (1965, pp. 136, 139).[33]

Ruddiman was a hardy man. He lived well past the early decades of the eighteenth century to see the Scottish Enlightenment come to life in his Edinburgh. But Ruddiman was always removed from this development by a deep "gulf of incomprehension" (Duncan 1965, p. 146), something that had never separated him and other early eighteenth-century historians from the world of Scottish Calvinism. It would take men of rather different experiences to transcend the culture of particularism and dependency.

33. These comments on Wodrow and Ruddiman should not be interpreted to mean that all early eighteenth-century Scottish historians were so unswerving in their political loyalties. Although the matter has yet to be investigated systematically, it is not unlikely that some historical writers resembled the paid political propagandists of the age who were no "more devoted to principle than their masters" (Riley 1978, p. 229) and quickly altered the slant of their tracts when more profitable political connections arose. It would be erroneous, however, to impute an orientation of independence to the work of men of this sort, since in abandoning the ideas of the political group to which they belonged, what they opted for was not some more detached standard, but simply a newly acquired, and again unquestioned, political program (see Riley 1978, p. 233).

2

Scottish Culture in the Age of the Enlightenment

A quiet, perhaps ephemeral, but revolutionary cultural change took place in mid-eighteenth-century Scotland. The Scottish Enlightenment displaced the dependency and particularism that were at the root of Scottish Calvinist culture with the distinctively modern attitudes of independence and universalism. The first section of this chapter describes this fundamental transformation which has found so little place in Great Divide accounts of the making of the contemporary Western world. The second section briefly analyzes the broader cultural milieu of mid-eighteenth-century Scotland, the world that the Enlightenment wrote for and against, the age that, despite the Enlightenment and those who shared something of its values, largely retained the orientations that had been integral to pre-Enlightenment Scottish culture. This wider cultural context of the Scottish Enlightenment is considered only as far as it is pertinent to the task of understanding the development of the Scottish Enlightenment itself. No attempt is made here to unravel innumerable other threads, old and new, that composed the rich tapestry that was Scottish culture in the middle decades of the eighteenth century.

I

In the eighteenth century the French could speak of the *siècle des lumières*, Germans of the *Aufklärung*, but Scots would have found talk of a Scottish "Enlightenment" meaningless. "The British," as Peter Gay has observed, "did not naturalize the name 'Enlightenment' until the nineteenth century" (1966, p. 21), which was long after the fact. Even the fact itself was not, by any name, a clearly identifiable entity to eighteenth-century Scots or to most of their contemporaries. But as generations of schoolbooks have reiterated the word, the Enlightenment has taken on the appearance not only of a concrete historical event, but often of a more or less crystallized social movement, complete with leaders and followers out to spread light in the world. Although such an image may not lead too far astray if one's concern is with mid-eighteenth-century France, more generally it is inappropriate to regard the Enlightenment as a discrete historical event or social movement. Rather it is a historical construct, a label applied to embrace a variety of disparate cultural objects or expressions that retrospectively seem jointly to constitute a basic kind of cultural change, a term employed because and "to the extent that it appears meaningful to isolate certain beliefs and ways of thinking" and to treat these as distinctive developments in the eighteenth century (Hampson 1968, p. 9).

While there has been considerable diversity of opinion concerning the exact nature of the Enlightenment's characteristic beliefs and ways of thinking, following a major tradition of scholarship on the European Enlightenment, which is best represented in the work of Gay (1966, 1969), the "Scottish Enlightenment" is employed in this study as a collective label for all the cultural products in eighteenth-century Scotland that departed from the prevailing creed of dependency and particularism and exhibited instead a sustained commitment to the orientations of independence and universalism.[1] If the previous reservations about formally defining orientations of this sort are recalled, this conception of the Scottish Enlightenment can be clarified by pointing out that "independence" is used here to describe the orientation, or family of orientations, which regards the human condition (human actions, judgments, or situations) as essentially autonomous, rather than as primarily subordinate to agents transcending human control, while "universalism" designates the orientation, or group of orientations, which

1. Gay, to be sure, has not formulated his conception of the Enlightenment in exactly this way. In his view, the basic elements of the program of the Enlightenment were "secularism, humanity, cosmopolitanism, and freedom" (1966, p. 3). But Gay freely substitutes "independence" for "freedom," and seems to regard "secularism" more as a manifestation of this attitude than as a separate characteristic of the Enlightenment (see 1966, p. 256, 1969, pp. 159, 389–90). He treats "humanity" and "cosmopolitanism," moreover, as more or less interchangeable terms, whose meaning is much like that given here to universalism (see 1966, pp. 13, 333, 1969, pp. 29–38). Patterson has explicitly stated that the "Enlightenment thinkers restored the principle of universalism . . . in Western thought" (1977, p. 246; see also Simmel 1908, p. 286). Among earlier students of the Scottish Enlightenment, Phillipson has probably come the closest to officially countenancing Gay's general approach, even though his own remarks on the independence theme tap issues analytically and substantively different from those central to Gay's argument and to the argument of this chapter (see 1974, pp. 407–8, note 2, 1981, pp. 21, 36).

treats individuals, groups, and things "in conformity with a general standard rather than in light of their possession of properties [that] have a particular relation" to one's own properties (Parsons and Shils 1951, p. 82). The Scottish Enlightenment has not previously been defined, or even seen, in terms of this pair of elemental conceptions. Earlier commentators, insofar as they have not simply taken the meaning of the Scottish Enlightenment for granted, have tended to approach it more descriptively, concentrating on its views of human progress and social evolution, its commitment to extend the empirical methods of the natural sciences to the secular analysis and eventual improvement of the condition of humans in society, its assertion of human capabilities and their worldly uses against the customary restraints of received faiths and traditions, and the like. Such accounts have been invaluable, but their descriptive treatment of the Scottish Enlightenment is not duplicated here,[2] since this is a study of the development of certain fundamental and deepset cultural orientations, not an inquiry into the vicissitudes of numerous more specific and more narrowly "intellectual" conceptions— not an essay in the history of ideas.[3] It should subsequently become clear, however, that by analyzing the Scottish Enlightenment in terms of independence and universalism, one actually subsumes to a considerable extent many of the Enlightenment's more concrete and more typically discussed notions, including its proc-

2. Those seeking such a treatment may find the references later in this section a useful guide to the large existing literature here.

3. To prevent several possible misinterpretations, this point should be underscored. The approach to the Scottish Enlightenment used here is in no way intended to negate definitions and treatments of the Scottish Enlightenment that bring out themes other than the underlying orientations of independence and universalism. The current study is organized around these conceptions because of its larger sociological concern with the emergence of modern cultural orientations, but this is scarcely the only concern that might attract one to the Scottish Enlightenment, and those with different historical interests are fully justified in bracketing this rather sweeping perspecitve and focusing upon other aspects of the Enlightenment. Of course, this does not mean that all definitions of the Enlightenment are equally adequate; definitions that are overly idiosyncratic, overly restrictive, overly broad, and the like all have serious scholarly drawbacks (see Ford 1968), and there are appealing conceptualizations of the Scottish Enlightenment that can be faulted on grounds such as these (see sec. II of this chapter). But it is interesting to note that, even though it has characterized the content of the Scottish Enlightenment variously and without reference to universalism and independence, the majority of work in this area has agreed in identifying the Scottish Enlightenment with a set of individuals whose membership tends to approximate the membership of the Enlightenment as it is here defined (for a listing identical to the one proposed in the next paragraph, see Chitnis 1976, p. 92).

lamation of human potentialities, its scientism and secularism, and its approach to human history.[4]

When the cultural terrain of mid-eighteenth-century Scotland is surveyed, it quickly becomes apparent that the sustained commitment to independence and universalism that defines the cultural change represented by the term Enlightenment appeared in the writings or cultural productions of five men: Adam Ferguson (1723–1816), a crusty, moralistic Highlander who occupied the chair of pneumatics and moral philosophy at the University of Edinburgh; David Hume (1711–76), the cheerful and controversial skeptical philosopher who was his age's most versatile, cosmopolitan, and accomplished man-of-letters; John Millar (1735–1801), a wide-ranging historian, outspoken political commentator, and long-time professor of civil law at the University of Glasgow; William Robertson (1721–93), a reserved Presbyterian minister and eloquent modern historian, who was the principal of the University of Edinburgh during its golden age; and Adam Smith (1723–90), a beloved Glasgow professor of moral philosophy, an absentminded commissioner of Scottish Customs and Salt Duties, and a premier student of rhetoric, psychology, jurisprudence, and political economy.[5] For the purposes of this study, the change in cultural orientations that took place in the works of these five *is* the Scottish Enlightenment, while the five themselves are the "intellectuals" of the Scottish Enlightenment, the "enlightened intellectuals," or—to risk a neologism—the "enlighteners." These terms are no more than convenient anachronisms, however, and it is always necessary to recognize that the intellectual organization of eighteenth-century Scotland looked rather different to contemporaries than it does to us (see Gibson 1978), and that although Ferguson, Hume, Millar, Robertson, and Smith knew one another and were for the most part bound together by ties of friendship, they neither formed a cohesive group nor typically regarded themselves as united in a common cultural enterprise (cf. Bryson 1945, p. 2).

4. In greater detail than is appropriate in this chapter, Gay's (1966, 1969) analysis of the European Enlightenment has also argued that these and other typical Enlightenment themes were part and parcel of the more basic change in attitude that the Enlightenment produced.

5. The character and the adult careers of these five figures have been amply discussed many times and need not be sketched more fully in this study. Those wishing more background here, however, may want to consult the literature cited in chap. 3, note 20.

Five is an odd number for a sociological investigation, so odd that it may introduce certain misunderstandings which it is important to eliminate. *Pace* Kreiger (1970, p. 172), Ferguson, Hume, Millar, Robertson, and Smith should not, given the current state of knowledge about eighteenth-century Scottish culture, be seen as the "leaders" of the Scottish Enlightenment, the great men who diffused independence and universalism to their fellows and to later generations. Even if such orientations were widely distributed in eighteenth-century Scotland—which, in fact, they were not—there would be no warrant for asserting that Scotland was led to these by the Scottish enlighteners. Scholarship on the French Enlightenment has indicated that only refined studies of book readership and its effects permit conclusions about how much (or whether) the Enlightenment enlightened (see Darnton 1971*b*, pp. 124–31, 1971*c*), but since pertinent research of this sort has yet to be done for the Scottish Enlightenment,[6] it is misleading to speak of its members as leaders and to look upon them as the towering figures who reshaped the fundamental attitudes of their contemporaries. It is essential to recall this argument whenever the following discussion announces that the Scottish Enlightenment altered basic elements of Scottish culture, wrought a radical transformation in Scottish cultural orientations, and the like. Comments of this type are not meant to gloss over the scarcity of relevant evidence on the impact of the Scottish Enlightenment and to insinuate that the writings of the enlightened intellectuals somehow produced universalism and independence in others; the point rather is that, whatever their role in causing further cultural change, the enlighteners' works were themselves the locus of cultural change—of the emergence, that is, of a set of cultural orientations that had found no place in Scottish Calvinist culture. And to remark that these works altered certain features of, or wrought a major transformation in, Scottish culture is simply to put *this* point, which is really no more than a restatement of the current definition of the Scottish Enlightenment, in other words.

6. The scattered studies that have been conducted on the foreign diffusion of some of the specific works and ideas of the Scottish Enlightenment (see Phillipson 1981, pp. 19–20; and note 7 of the Introduction) do not speak to the matter being raised here: the problem of the extent to which the writings of Ferguson, Hume, Millar, Robertson, and Smith caused, or at least precipitated, a shift to independence and universalism on the part of other Scots who lived at approximately the same time.

As these observations suggest, the five men who are the subjects of this study should not be regarded as a sample from a broader population of eighteenth-century Scots. The second section of this chapter demonstrates the continuity of orthodox Calvinist attitudes and assumptions among the vast majority of Scots during the relevant decades of the eighteenth century, as well as the persistence of dependency in the works of even those subgroups that previous scholarship has seen as having the greatest affinities with the Scottish Enlightenment. It is true that these other works occasionally displayed—as did a few documents in the early part of the eighteenth century—a commitment to universalism not unlike that found in the Enlightenment itself and, in this one sense, the writings of the enlighteners can be taken to represent a somewhat more ubiquitous cultural shift. However, in the decisive matter of independence, and thus in the combination of independence and universalism, the Scottish Enlightenment seems to have stood apart from its age.

For this reason, it is appropriate to treat Ferguson, Hume, Millar, Robertson, and Smith as the known population of enlightened individuals in mid-eighteenth-century Scotland, the universe of those who now appear to have participated fully in the development of independent and universalistic cultural orientations. As the wording of these remarks indicates, future research could well reveal others who belong here along with Ferguson, Hume, and the rest. That is to say, the work of these five has been identified as the Scottish Enlightenment, while the work of others has been excluded, by integrating existing scholarship on mid-eighteenth-century Scottish culture. Yet not only may later research modify the conclusions that this scholarship has reached about the matters it considers, but to date such scholarship has cast its net very narrowly. It has focused too exclusively on the purely technical accomplishments of those renowned in fields like the natural sciences, poetry, and fiction,[7] and it has virtually ignored those who published nothing and are knowable only through letters, journals, and the testimony of contemporaries, as well as those who published works

7. Donovan has asserted that the chemists Joseph Black and William Cullen "should be seen as figures in the Scottish Enlightenment" (1975, p. vi), and Smart (1952) had made a similar claim on behalf of the artist Allan Ramsay, Jr. (see also Ferguson 1968, p. 226). And while these contentions may well turn out to be true, it is at present impossible to know this since these scholars neither specify their definition of the Enlightenment, nor offer evidence sufficient to enable one to determine if the figures discussed were committed to independence and universalism.

little noticed at the time or since forgotten (including here the "literary low life" which work on the French Enlightenment has begun to discover [see Darnton 1971a]). In each of these cases, it is currently impossible to know whether a sustained commitment to independence and universalism was present or absent. Were time infinite, the orientations of all those included here would be uncovered before proceeding with this investigation in order to determine if the list of enlighteners should be extended. As it is, however, that enumeration remains within the bounds of what is now known of mid-eighteenth-century culture in Scotland and subject, along with the conclusions to which it leads, to revision when those bounds are finally outgrown.

It ought also to be noted at this juncture that, even in cases where some information on their opinions was available, individuals born in the second half of the eighteenth century, or, in other words, after the generations to which those who first shed the attitudes of dependency and particularism belonged, were not eligible for inclusion in the analysis here. Because this is a study of cultural change, it is appropriate to concentrate upon the cohort that initially effected the change at issue. Hence, Ferguson, Hume, Millar, Robertson, and Smith, all of whom were born in the quarter century after 1710. This brought them to maturity in the mid-eighteenth century and, indeed, the great majority of their writings appeared between 1740 and 1780,[8] which may thus be regarded as the dates of the Scottish Enlightenment.

What subsequently became of the Enlightenment, its fate in later birth cohorts, is a problem of a different sort and one that remains inadequately resolved. The traditional judgment on this point, which unfortunately is based on little solid documentation, is that by the end of the eighteenth century "the light . . . had . . . gone out," extinguished both by the reactionary spirit evoked by the French Revolution and by the rise of Common-sense philosophy.[9] Although a conception of the Enlightenment different from the one used here underlies this contention (and although its explanation for

8. Ferguson's *Principles of Moral and Political Science* and Millar's *Historical View of the English Government* were the only major works of the Scottish Enlightenment completed after 1780. Smith's *Essays on Philosophical Subjects,* though (posthumously) published in 1795, was among his earliest writings (see Wightman 1975, pp. 44–59).

9. On the former factor, see Mathieson (1910, p. 241), the source of the remark quoted, and Thornton (1968, p. 415). On the latter factor, see Phillipson (1973, p. 45, 1976a, p. 823), and note 87 in this chapter.

the demise of the Enlightenment seems to oversimplify a complex development), a cursory glance at Scottish culture in the last decades of the eighteenth and early decades of the nineteenth centuries suggests that independence, though perhaps not universalism, was also smothered. Poorly documented judgments and cursory glances must obviously be replaced by research on the evolution or devolution of the Scottish Enlightenment, but that is a large task for another study.

Taken together, the preceding considerations allow that future scholarship may determine that the change that occurred in the work of the men of the Scottish Enlightenment was short-lived, that these men influenced none of their contemporaries, and that they expressed orientations that were otherwise quite foreign to the Scotland of their day. To appreciate the rationale for what follows, it is necessary to realize that even this possibility would in no way diminish the significance of investigating the Scottish Enlightenment. For all their limitations, studies in the sociology of knowledge (not to mention intellectual biographies) have done much to enrich understanding of the ways in which cultures develop, and those studies have generally confined themselves to the esoteric ideas of single individuals. This study examines, in the work of five major intellectuals, a more elemental kind of cultural transformation, the emergence of a set of modern cultural orientations from the midst of a Calvinist culture which upheld antithetical beliefs and values. So marked a change constitutes by itself an essential chapter in the history of the development of modern culture. And that chapter becomes retroactively no less important should it prove difficult to write its whiggish sequel: the installment that shows that the achievements of the Scottish Enlightenment were pervasive, deeply influential, and lasting.

This argument should make clear that in this study universalism and, even more so, independence are regarded as among the most fundamental components of the work that comprises the Scottish Enlightenment. Not only were these orientations displayed in the Enlightenment's treatment of a plentitude of concrete issues, frequently they were essential in structuring its whole approach in the realm of particulars. This is a primary reason for concentrating on these two conceptions, rather than upon the Enlightenment's more specific philosophical, ethical, historical, psychological, legal, economic, political, anthropological, and sociological speculations,[10] or upon its more familiar themes like scientism, societal development, and the rest. Yet, while such themes and speculations can up to a point be seen as expressions or manifestations of the universalism and independence of the Enlightenment, the former cannot merely be regarded as reducible to the latter.[11] Since this inquiry is concerned with the development of modern cultural orientations upon the medieval soil of Calvinism, it naturally accords prominence to the independence and universalism of the Scottish Enlightenment, but these attitudes do not represent all of the Enlightenment's innovations, let alone every element that it reproduced from the varied religious and secular traditions that it inherited.[12]

To emphasize the centrality of independence and universalism in the Scottish Enlightenment as a whole is not to claim that these orientations were expressed with the same degree, kind, and consistency of commitment by each of the five enlighteners. In fact, in ways that will become clear, Hume's work exhibited independence more fully than did that of Smith and after him Millar, while their writings went further in this regard than those of Robertson and particularly of Ferguson. For the most part the same ordering repeats itself in the area of universalism, though on one important matter, which is discussed below, Smith, Millar and Robertson were markedly more universalistic than Hume and especially Ferguson.

10. The literature on these speculations is vast. The "sociological" side of the Scottish Enlightenment has particularly received considerable recent attention: see Bierstedt (1978), Burke (1980), Bryson (1945), Burrow (1966, pp. 7–12), Camic (1979b, 1983a), Campbell (1971), Chitnis (1976, pp. 91–123), Forbes (1954), Gay (1969, pp. 332–43), Hawthorn (1976, pp. 28–33), Höpfl (1978), Lehmann (1930, 1960, esp. 91–108), Macfie (1955, 1961), MacRae (1961, pp. 140–42, 1969), Meek (1954, 1971, 1976b), Nisbet (1969, pp. 126–28, 150–57, 1980, pp. 189–93), Pascal (1938), Reisman (1976), Rendall (1978, pp. 148–205), Schneider (1967, 1971–72), Skinner (1965, 1967, 1975), Swingewood (1969, 1970a, 1970b), and Trevor-Roper (1967).

11. This is so not only for the reasons indicated in the next sentence, but also because the several qualifications entered in the earlier discussion of the place of dependency and particularism in early eighteenth-century culture (see p. 17 above) apply as well to the position of independence and universalism in the Scottish Enlightenment. There is no need to restate these stipulations here.

12. On the continuities between Calvinism and the Enlightenment, see Camic (1979a, pp. 82–83), Campbell (1974, pp. 67–68), Ferguson (1968, p. 209), Lehmann (1960, pp. 93–94), and Robbins (1959, p. 178). On the broader debt of the Scottish Enlightenment to its past, see Bryson (1945), Brumfitt (1967), Chitnis (1976), Clive (1970), Gay (1966, 1969), Lehmann (1960, pp. 118–19), Meek (1976b, pp. 37–67), Pocock (1965, p. 582, 1975, pp. 483–505), Rendall (1978), Stein (1970), Trevor-Roper (1967), as well as chap. 1, sec. III, and chap. 3, sec. I.

As these two orientations fused with one another and with other basic features of the Enlightenment and spread out to a host of specifics, those differences with respect to independence and universalism added up to significant variations among the enlightened intellectuals in their attachment to the more general modern outlook that is sometimes called "the philosophy of the Enlightenment" (for descriptions of this, see Cassirer 1932; Gay 1966, 1969; Hampson 1968). While this outlook was fully in evidence in the work of Hume, Smith, and Millar—most assertively in the instance of Hume, least so in Millar's case[13]—the situation was otherwise for Robertson and Ferguson.[14] Even as he articulated and affirmed many of the Enlightenment's fundamental assumptions, Robertson remained far more loyal to received Calvinist beliefs than any of the other enlighteners. As Felix Gilbert has pointed out, while enlightened principles were the ones that governed Robertson's thought, these frequently combined, without much palpable tension or conflict, with a sincere "Christian religiosity," and it is "this combination of a modern and a traditional element [that] constitutes the peculiar and distinctive character of his . . . work" (1972, pp. xx, xiv).

The same elements, but not in an equally harmonious combination, are found in Ferguson's writings. Intellectual historians are usually reluctant to maintain that their subjects formulated views that in their essence were internally discordant; scholars instead typically seek to identify the unity that underlay apparent incompatabilities. But research on Ferguson, even though it has discerned some unifying characteristics, has nevertheless repeatedly concluded that there were tensions and "conflicting commitments" throughout his work (Kettler 1965, p. 293; and, more generally, Bernstein 1978; Hamowy 1969; Kettler 1965, 1978). These distin-

13. On this general point, see Gay (1966, pp. 401–19, 1969, pp. 359–68, 416–20); on Hume, see Mossner (1965); on Smith, Lindgren (1973); on Millar, Lehmann (1960).

14. Obviously, this remark is referring to the way that Hume and the others expressed the philosophy of the Enlightenment in their writings. Since this is a study of *cultural* change, it focuses throughout on what the enlighteners wrote, not upon how they otherwise acted. Had there been a substantial discrepancy between their words and deeds, this procedure could be extremely misleading. But, in fact, there was little discrepancy: Ginsberg has aptly observed how Hume matched "theory and theorist [and] lived his philosophy" (1972, p. 645; see also Gay 1966, pp. 401–19; Price 1967, p. 373; and esp. Mossner 1954), and—insofar as one allows for the fact that their theories and philosophies differ somewhat—the same observation could well be made for each of the other Scottish enlighteners (see the literature cited in chap. 3, note 20).

guished Ferguson's kind of Enlightenment sharply from that which emerged in the hands of Hume, Smith, Millar, and Robertson.[15] Nor is this the only way in which Ferguson stood apart. The enlighteners' intellectual careers extended over several decades and, during these, their ideas on many concrete topics underwent considerable development.[16] Yet despite this, Hume, Smith, Millar, and Robertson all remained basically consistent in the nature and extent of their adherence to the constituent attitudes of the Enlightenment.[17] While Ferguson's later and more renowned writings reveal a somewhat similar stability of enlightened opinion,[18] his earliest

15. This is not to imply that the writings of these figures were without certain more superficial discrepancies or, at a very different level of abstraction, certain ultimate contradictions.

16. For an interesting recent account of Hume's philosophical development, see Noxon (1973). The evolution of Adam Smith's moral-philosophical and economic theories has been very extensively studied (on the former, see Raphael 1969, 1975; Raphael and Macfie 1976; on the latter, Meek 1976a; Meek and Skinner 1973; Skinner 1976). Much effort has also been consumed with "Das Adam Smith Problem": with the development, or shift, in attitude that Smith is said to have undergone between his two major works, *The Theory of Moral Sentiments* and *The Wealth of Nations* (see, e.g., Viner 1927). The claim that there is genuine discontinuity between the two works has, however, been persuasively challenged by several generations of scholarship (see Anspach 1972; Campbell 1971; Cropsey 1957; Macfie 1967, pp. 59–81; Morrow 1923; Teichgraeber 1981; Wills 1978a; Winch 1978, pp. 5–12).

17. The following discussion briefly attempts to document this by citations from works that these intellectuals produced at different points in their careers. Recent research (with the exceptions pointed out in notes 31 and 65 of this chapter) has also emphasized that the enlighteners' fundamental views remained stable throughout their intellectual lifetimes (on Hume, see Forbes 1975a, pp. 136, 139; Noxon 1973, p. 153; Stewart 1963, p. vi; on Millar, Lehmann 1960, pp. 114, 143; on Smith, Viner, 1968, p. 328, and the preceding note). The validity of the claim that Hume, Millar, Robertson, and Smith were consistent in their various writings is not, however, of decisive consequence for this study. Substantively more important, for reasons that will emerge in the next chapter, is the fact that in contrast to Ferguson, the other four enlighteners exhibited independence and universalism in their first works. From these, therefore, the following analysis draws most heavily. It should also be noted that, while Millar, Robertson and Smith were somewhat older than Hume when they completed their earliest work, there is evidence to suggest that they may well have formulated the main ideas contained in their first writings at considerably earlier dates (on Millar, see Lehmann 1960, pp. 57–58, 114, 407–9, 1970, p. 60; on Robertson, Stewart 1796, p. 112; on Smith, Macfie 1961, pp. 12–13; Meek 1971, pp. 16–17, 1976a; Rae 1895, pp. 36, 54, 61–62, 141, 203, 216; Scott 1937, pp. 50–61; Stewart 1793, pp. 11–13, 66–68).

18. The argument here is David Kettler's: although there are still important discrepancies among these later writings—due to certain substantive developments and the fact that the *Essay on the History of Civil Society* and the *Institutes of Moral Philosophy* were designed for very different audiences, while the *Principles of Moral*

work—particularly *A Sermon Preached in the Ersh Language*—contains little hint of his subsequent departures from Calvinist culture. The novel orientations of the Enlightenment appear to have crystallized at a later stage in his intellectual development than in that of his fellow enlighteners. A proper interpretation of the Scottish Enlightenment requires recognizing the variation among these men in their commitment to independence and universalism.

The Scottish Enlightenment held that humans are, or ought to be, their own. While in early eighteenth-century Scotland, even so avant-garde a thinker as Francis Hutcheson believed with Calvinism that "we are such dependent creatures" (*Works*, 4:73), the enlightened intellectuals of the mid-eighteenth century condemned dependency and championed human independence in context after context. David Hume's celebration of "Independency" extends from his first known letter in 1727 through to his final autobiographical note in 1776, and his "Disdain of all Dependence" was no less tirelessly expressed (see *HL* 1:10, 365, *Essays*, p. 608).[19] The ideal character, he emphasized, is "entirely master of his own disposition," and thus "every wise man will endeavour to place his happiness on such objects chiefly as depend upon himself" (*Essays*, pp. 3–4; see also Stewart 1963, p. 187). For Smith too, it is the perfection of human nature "to be more and more master of itself," "to live free, fearless and independent," to acquire "the highest degree of self-command" (*TMS*, pp. 245, 122, 254).[20] "Nothing," he told his Glasgow pupils in the midst of a lecture on the police, "tends so much to corrupt and enervate and debase the mind as dependency, and nothing gives such noble and generous notions of probity as freedom and independency" (*LJA*, p. 333). The same lessons emerged from Millar's writings which asserted "the independence of the inquiring mind" and insisted that "every act, condition, institution or value [be] viewed and judged in its relation . . . to some end-goal of human striving and desire" (Lehmann 1960, p. 35).

and Political Philosophy combined themes from both of these works—taken together they indicate that, during the period they encompass, "Ferguson never changed the general tendency of his opinions" (1965, p. 153; see also p. 283; cf. Kettler 1978, pp. 209, 221).

19. For other relevant remarks from Hume's correspondence, see *HL* 1:86, 161, 170, 193, 355, 392, 451, 504, *NHL*, p. 26; see also Forbes (1975a, p. 125, note 2).

20. On Smith's novel notion of self-command and its importance in his thought, see Campbell (1975, p. 74), Cropsey (1957, pp. 11–12, 37), Mizuta (1975, pp. 123–27), Raphael (1975, p. 89), and Raphael and Macfie (1976, p. 6).

Human autonomy was also proclaimed, though in rather different ways, in the works of Robertson and Ferguson. Robertson combined his belief that humans are finally "only instruments in the divine hand" with sharp indictments of whatever leads the human mind from its natural condition of "independence" into "servitude" (*SW*, pp. liii–liv, *HA* 9:143). In his estimation, "independence [is] one of the noblest privilege[s]" of human nature, and he accordingly praised those primitive people who, "conscious of their own dignity, and capable of the greatest efforts in asserting it, aspire[d] to independence" (*SW*, p. lvi, *HA* 9:136; cf. *HA* 9:223–24). Although Ferguson more often urged man to be "a willing instrument [of divine purposes] in what depends on his own will; and . . . a conscious instrument, at the disposal of providence, in matters which are out of his power" (*PMPS* 1:313; see also *PMPS* 1:166, 333, 2:61, 103), on the whole he too clearly demonstrated, as Kettler has concluded, a "commitment to man's ultimate independence" (1965, p. 176). Whether asserting that every individual is "the master of his own actions," or proposing that a "wonderful character" would be formed were the "mind always master of itself," for Ferguson the essential point was that "man is his own master" (*PMPS* 1:130–31, *EHCS*, p. 39; see also *HPM*, p. 183).

However eloquent, such remarks no more than hint at the full nature of the Scottish Enlightenment's transformation of the Calvinist assumption of human dependency. The real indication of that change is not this variety of brief comments from all sorts of contexts,[21] but the sweeping revision by the Scottish enlighteners of each of the three postulates through which Calvinist theology exhibited and promoted the orientation of dependency.

The first feature of this revision was a full-scale reevaluation of human nature. The Enlightenment supplanted the fall and original sin with the premise that man is born "pure and untainted" (Hume *EHU*, p. 379) and "the talents he may afterward acquire, as well as the virtues he may be rendered capable of exercising, depend, in a great measure, upon the state of society in which he is placed" (Robertson *HA* 9:219; see also *SW*, p. lv). Observations of this sort, so characteristic of the Enlightenment, take for granted that talents and virtues, rather than impotence and corruption, are the prov-

---

21. In fact, without the analysis to follow, this variety of comments would provide little evidence for the shift from dependency to independence. For, as previously suggested, there were certain restricted contexts in which Scottish Calvinism itself condemned "dependency" and employed "independence" as a term of commendation (see chap. 1, sec. I; see also Phillipson 1981, pp. 22–26).

ince of human nature. Each of the enlighteners expressed this conviction in his own way. With Calvinism, Ferguson averred that "perfection is no where to be found short of the infinite mind," and acknowledged both the "depravity" of human nature and the frightful effects of "the evil passions." Simultaneously, however, he suggested that "progression is the gift of God to all his intelligent creatures and is within the competence of the lowest of mankind," recognized—as Calvinism never had—various desirable human passions and mankind's natural "sense of right," and then repeatedly affirmed the integrity and the dignity of human nature.[22] For Robertson too, there was "dignity and lustre" in human nature. To attain "pure and undefiled virtue," humans may require the "assistance of divine revelation," but even without this they have developed something Scottish Calvinism nowhere acknowledged: viz. such "noble . . . human passions [as] temperance, frugality, decency, public spirit, love of their fellow citizens, [and] magnanimity" (*SW*, pp. liii–lvi; see also *India*, pp. 245–47).

The other intellectuals of the Scottish Enlightenment rehabilitated human nature without any heavenly help. In Millar's view, man has a "wonderful capacity for the improvement of his faculties" and, depending on the organization of his society, can acquire "the virtues of courage and fortitude, of sobriety and temperance, of justice and generosity" (*Ranks*, p. 218, *HV* 4:176). Such ideas had been previously developed in rich detail in the first major work of Millar's favorite professor, Adam Smith. Smith's *Theory of Moral Sentiments* can, in fact, be seen as an extended indictment of the stark image of human nature presented in *The Westminster Confession*. As Cropsey has argued, rather than advocating the familiar "conquest of the passions," Smith saw these attributes of human character as the very source of virtue (1957, p. 23). He also held that many of the passions, particularly "generosity, humanity, kindness, compassion, [and] mutual friendship," were primarily of a "social and benevolent" nature (*TMS*, p. 94). Not that this was true of all of them. Instead of replacing Calvinism's view of human nature with another one-dimensional picture, Smith—and the other Scottish enlighteners in their turn—wrote at length of unsocial and selfish passions. According to Smith, however, even passions of this

22. The direct quotations from Ferguson contained in the last two sentences are taken from *PMPS* 1:136, 180, 2:403, and *EHCS*, p. 35. For Ferguson's mixed assessment of the passions, see also *EHCS*, pp. 35–36, *IMP*, pp. 77–78, 90–95, 102–3, and *PMPS*, 1:128–29, 131, 141. On his belief in the dignity of human nature, see Kettler (1965, pp. 115, 118, 134, 273, 295); see also Forbes (1967, p. 42).

sort had their uses and, in all events, they were regulated both by conscience and by internalized normative rules, which were mechanisms that humans acquired naturally through "sympathy," or the interpersonal communication process that occurred in all societies (see *TMS*, pp. 85–89, 97, 203–68).[23] For these and other reasons, Smith consistently maintained with the Enlightenment that beyond the weakness of human nature there is ever dignity and grandeur (*TMS*, pp. 70, 229; see also Lindgren 1973). Hume's reappraisal of humankind was no less thorough. Before Smith had published any of his daring opinions, Hume had systematically examined humanity's moral potentialities, as well as sympathy, normative rules, and the vicissitudes of the passions (*THN*, pp. 275–621; see also Camic 1979*b*, pp. 526–31). He had even refurbished the motives that Calvinism had most condemned, suggesting that pride "is not always vicious," that "vanity is . . . closely allied to virtue," and that the "affection between the sexes . . . begets a friendship and mutual sympathy, which runs through the whole tenor of their lives" (*THN*, p. 297, *Essays*, pp. 87, 131). Rejecting the practice of demeaning man by elusive comparisons between his being and "beings of most perfect wisdom," Hume above all insisted upon the essential dignity of human nature (*Essays*, pp. 81–88; more generally, Mossner 1954, p. 5). One can easily become inured to this recurrent theme, but for the Enlightenment it was a cultural innovation with far-reaching implications. The humans who were deprived in Calvinism of moral and intellectual worth were predestined to everlasting dependency. Those whose dignity was constantly proclaimed were already on their own.

A universe composed of such capable beings no longer demanded perpetual supernatural assistance. In the works of the Scottish Enlightenment, the hallowed belief that, in the most immediate sense, "God . . . doth uphold, direct, dispose, and govern all creatures, actions, and things" was displaced by a deeply secular comprehension of this world and of the life within it (see Bryson 1945, p. 28; Gay 1969, p. 390; Lehmann 1971–72, p. 2102; Swingewood 1970*b*, p. 165). Divine Providence thus finally gave way to perspectives on and explanations of natural phenomena that were not vitally dependent upon the will of God or other theological supports (for the application of a similar conception of secularization to the Scottish Enlightenment, see Lehmann 1960, p. 92,

23. For more extended treatment of Smith's views on internalized regulation and sympathy, see Brissenden (1969), Camic (1979*b*, pp. 531–35), Campbell (1971, esp. pp. 87–165, 1975), and Lindgren (1973, pp. 20–38).

1971, pp. 157–58). By means of this development, the Scottish Enlightenment supplanted the second dependency-sustaining postulate of Calvinism. Secular accounts were, to be sure, not a complete novelty in mid-eighteenth-century Scotland. A degree of secularization had surfaced earlier in Scottish historical literature. But there the orientation of independence remained submerged: dependence on God was simply replaced by dependence on political programs. This, as will subsequently become clear, is not what happened in the case of the Scottish Enlightenment. Its secularism, as Lehmann has justly observed, was part and parcel of its assertion of human autonomy (1960, pp. 91–92).

To speak of the Scottish Enlightenment's secular comprehension of the world is not to claim that the enlightened intellectuals abandoned their personal belief in God. The private religious convictions of the five were actually most various. Hume's were the most unconventional. Today he is typically described as an agnostic for, beyond rejecting all the central tenets of Calvinism, he granted no more to any theology than the "one simple, though somewhat ambiguous, at least undefined proposition: That the cause or causes of order in the universe probably bear some remote analogy to human intelligence" (*DNR*, p. 516).[24] Less consensus has emerged about Adam Smith's, perhaps "deliberately ambiguous," religious sentiments.[25] Like Hume, Smith set himself apart from "Whining Christian[s]" and accepted no established creeds or churches (*Corr*, p. 203; Macfie 1967, p. 111). On the other hand, his writings betray a belief in the existence of God and possibly in an afterlife, freely invoke empirical arguments to corroborate theological presuppositions, and generally leave the impression of an unmistakably pious spirit at work.[26] Millar's writings, in contrast, reveal virtually nothing of his own religious beliefs—no mean accomplishment in a religious age—and these thus remain something of a mystery. It now appears that, in addition to departing from many specific Calvinist teachings, Millar was generally skeptical or indifferent toward religious dogmas and practices (see *Ranks*, pp. 310–11, *HV*

24. On Hume's rejection of Calvinism, see Smith (1948, pp. 9–10, 13, 30). For use of the agnostic label, see Mossner (1965, p. 57), and Stewart (1963, pp. 261, 269).

25. The expression quoted is from Lindgren (1973, p. 133). Scholarly opinion concerning Smith's religious outlook has ranged from Viner's judgment that Smith was an optimistic theist (1927, p. 217) to Reisman's remark that "he may have been an agnostic" (1976, p. 86).

26. Campbell (1971, pp. 60, 213, 229–30), Lindgren (1973, pp. 144–52), Macfie (1967, pp. 107, 111), and Raphael and Macfie (1976, p. 19).

4:267–75; Lehmann 1960, pp. 35, 80, 84–85, 118). But rather than ever denying the truth of Christianity, he directly acknowledged its pure, holy, and enlightened character (Lehmann 1960, pp. 79–80). Robertson is less of a puzzle; if Calvinist orthodoxies were rarely endorsed, or even broached, in his published work, this devout Presbyterian minister was, to his bones, a firm believer in the "true God" of Christianity and His scriptural precepts (for the quotation, see *Progress*, p. 20; see also *India*, pp. 260–67). Predictably, tensions were far more pronounced in Ferguson's case. Unlike Millar and Robertson, Ferguson consciously surrendered the essentials of his Christian heritage (Kettler 1965, pp. 131, 171–78). Despite this loss of faith, however, his works, alone among those of the enlighteners, explicitly attempted to "justify the ways of God to men," insisting that "to those who are qualified with intelligence and a grateful mind, every circumstance or event in the order of nature may serve to manifest, and to extol the supreme wisdom and goodness of God" (*PMPS* 1:172, 187).[27]

For all this diversity, the intellectuals of the Scottish Enlightenment united in grasping the things and events of this world in a manner so thoroughly secular that, even at its most equivocal, it was without parallel in the culture in which they were raised. In his only published sermon, Robertson in all good faith preached that God's providence, "powerful, wise, and good," governs the world, that "there is a skillful hand directing the revolutions of human affairs" (*SW*, p. li). But he then asserted what Scottish thought repeatedly denied: "the Supreme Being conducteth all his operations by general laws [and] seldom effects by supernatural means anything which could have been accomplished by such as are natural" (*SW*, pp. lii–liii; see also *Progress*, p. 43).[28] Under the guise of describing superstitious practices prevailing prior to the Reformation, he ridiculed the Scottish theological premise that natural phenomena like "the thunder, the hurricane, and the earthquake,

27. See also *PMPS* 1:179, 338, *EHCS*, p. 6, and *IMP*, pp. 121–28; as well as Bernstein (1978, p. 105), and Rendall (1978, p. 100).

28. Outside the ranks of the Scottish Enlightenment, the traditional Scottish conception of the laws of nature proved remarkably durable throughout the second half of the eighteenth century. In 1758, the Moderate minister William Leechman held "that this visible world has a superior, who can alter and change its order and laws at his pleasure" (1758, p. 243); some forty years later, the scientist John Robinson was still "keen to involve God in His created universe and to keep Him active there." Robinson insisted upon "the continuing superintendence and dominance by God of His universe from moment to moment" (Morrell 1971a, p. 48).

are the effects of [supernatural] interposition."[29] Robertson's own work so seriously underplayed such interposition that even his sermonic reflections on the reasons underlying the triumph of Christ's mission concentrated upon sociopolitical conditions at the time of the birth of Christ (*SW*, p. liii). Making the success of the Son of God contingent upon social circumstances was in itself quite a transmogrification of Calvinism. Almost everywhere, however, the Scottish Enlightenment repeated Robertson's procedure. Thus Ferguson, after acknowledging that the "world is governed by the wisdom of God," maintained that "wise providence" operates by the "fixed and determinate laws" of nature (*EHCS*, pp. 55, 90–91, *PMPS* 1:180), and then undertook extensive researches to uncover how such laws operated in the social world. The treatment of the origins of religion that resulted may well be more "deistically theological" than "sociological,"[30] but otherwise the analyses Ferguson produced were, as Forbes remarks, "utterly matter of fact, dry and secular" (1966, p. xviii). These were also the characteristics of Millar's writings (see Lehmann 1960, pp. 123–24; Macfie 1961, p. 206). His youthful masterpiece, *The Origin of the Distinction of Ranks,* for example, accounted for the forms assumed in different societies by a diversity of authority relations (men over women, fathers over children, masters over servants, chiefs over tribes, sovereigns over nations) without once invoking a Supreme Authority to account, directly or indirectly, for anything. For Millar, the "wise and good Author of nature" had left nature entirely to itself (for the quotation, see Lehmann 1960, p. 355, note).

The wide-ranging investigations of social life that Adam Smith offered were also independent of supernatural supports, although this is not something that may be evident at first glance. In *The Theory of Moral Sentiments,* he did advert frequently to the "all-wise Author of Nature" and propose that the "administration of the great system of the universe . . . is the business of God" (*TMS*, p. 386). It has been effectively argued by Lindgren that Smith also "postulated a final theological sanction to human morality" and that "key aspects of his overall philosophic position appear to have been suggested to him by his religious experience" (1973, pp. 146, 149). None of this blunts the unmistakably secular thrust of his

29. *HA* 9:192, *ER*, p. 70, *Progress*, p. 43, and *India*, pp. 263–64. The interventionist premise was one that Adam Smith also made light of (see *EPS*, pp. 85–87, *WN*, pp. 723–24).

30. Such is the judgment of Lehmann (1930, p. 136). For Ferguson's discussion of the origins of religion, see *PMPS* 1:163–71.

work, however. For not only was Smith remarkably silent about the Author of Nature in lectures and writings other than the *Moral Sentiments*,[31] but consistently his "principal doctrines—both positive and normative—were . . . altogether independent of his belief in final theological sanctions" (Lindgren 1973, p. 148). Like his beloved friend Hume, Smith allowed Providence no role in the explanation of the causes of human action and granted God no direct entry whatever into the natural sequence of earthly events (Campbell 1971, p. 61).[32]

In Hume's own writings, the secular orientation of the Scottish Enlightenment was most fully expressed. Wherever the first enlightener turned, to epistemology or psychology, economics or politics, law or morals, he turned without anything supernatural, providential, or divine.[33] For Hume, religious beliefs and practices themselves were nothing more than natural phenomena to be accounted for by completely human causes (see *NHR*).[34] He rejected the very idea that the natural order could be violated by supernatural or miraculous means: "A miracle is a violation of the laws of nature; and as a firm and unalterable experience has established

31. Viner (1927, pp. 221–22) long ago noticed that Smith's deity virtually disappeared in *The Wealth of Nations*, which was published seventeen years after *The Theory of Moral Sentiments*. This disappearance, when coupled with Smith's deletion of certain allegedly Christian passages from a subsequent edition of the latter work, has prompted the claim that Smith formed his unorthodox religious views rather late in life (see esp. Raphael 1969; see also Rae 1895, pp. 425–30; Raphael and Macfie 1976, p. 19). But recent research, while not denying that Smith may have grown somewhat more heterodox with age, has convincingly countered the idea that he underwent a basic change in belief, as well as the supposition that his original position in the *Moral Sentiments* was essentially an orthodox one (Campbell 1971, pp. 227–29; cf. Raphael 1969, p. 246). It is also pertinent to record the fact that well before Smith undertook *The Wealth of Nations*, he had substantially removed the hand of God from the scene. Already in the philosophical *Essays* that he chiefly composed prior to publishing the *Moral Sentiments*, the Author of Nature was almost entirely missing (cf. *EPS*, pp. 374, 392).

32. For further support of the views on Smith presented in this paragraph, see Brissenden (1969, p. 962), Campbell (1971, pp. 60–61, 231), and Macfie (1967, p. 102). For a more general treatment of secularization in Smith's work, see Cropsey (1957).

33. For the most recent demonstration, see Forbes (1975*a*, pp. 59, 65). This aspect of Hume's thought is already apparent in his first known essay, a composition which, according to Mossner (1954, p. 47), was produced when Hume was only fourteen years old (see *EC*).

34. For discussion of this point, see Cassirer (1932, pp. 179–81), and Stewart (1963, pp. 260, 270–79). Millar (*Ranks*, pp. 256–57), Robertson (*HA* 9:186–206), and Smith (*EPS*, pp. 84–87, 206–15; see also Lindgren 1973, pp. 135–39) also adopted a "sociological" approach to the origin and development of religion.

these laws, the proof against a miracle, from the very nature of the fact, is as entire as any argument from experience"—the only valid kind of argument in Humian philosophy—"can possibly be imagined" (*Essays,* p. 524). The breach with Calvinism here was total, its implications radical. "Hume makes plain," Gay has written, "that since God is silent, man is his own master: he must live in a disenchanted world . . . and make his own way" (1966, p. 419).

The same conclusion emerged in another context. Calvinism taught that salvation derived from belief and that saving knowledge derived from the Bible. Unbelief, misbelief, and bold speculations about things that were the business of God were thus sins of the highest order. Yet such were the sins that the Scottish Enlightenment committed time and again: in asserting human autonomy it inevitably rejected the third premise that accompanied the Calvinist code of dependency. For faith and the word of God, it substituted a boundless "lust for knowledge," a perpetual "doubting and seeking, tearing down and building up" through philosophy or science—then virtually interchangeable terms that referred not to specialized academic fields, but to a comprehensive, empirically rooted, disciplined and systematic, critical analysis of the human situation.[35] The Scottish Enlightenment repeatedly preferred such organized skepticism to dogmatism of any sort.

That preference is most manifest in Hume's writings. Relentlessly these urged humans to "shake off the yoke of authority [and] to think for themselves"—without religious doctrines which are "but sick men's dreams," and without sacred books which "contain nothing but sophistry and illusion" and thus deserve "the flames." To Hume's mind, it was only philosophy, by contenting itself "with assigning new causes and principles to the phenomena which appear in the visible world," and "nothing but philosophy [that enables humans] entirely to conquer the . . . unaccountable terrors" that otherwise drive them to religious chimeras. Accordingly, when Hume developed his own epistemology, appropriately known as "moderate skepticism," it was with the express intention of establishing rules for the evaluation of all pregiven ideas, exempting none from critical scrutiny.[36] Its purpose, even at its most abstruse, was ever

35. The quoted expressions are drawn from Cassirer (1932, pp. ix, 14). For a more general treatment of "philosophy as criticism" during the Enlightenment, see Cassirer (1932) and Gay (1966, esp. pp. 127–32, 1973, p. 17).

36. For the direct quotations from Hume in the preceding lines, see *Abst,* p. 4, *Essays,* p. 77, *EHU,* p. 430, *NHR,* p. 75, and *THN,* p. 271; see also *Essays,* pp. 543–44, *HEM,* pp. 500–502, and *HL* 1:13, 16. On the rules for the evaluation of estab-

enlightenment: "to free men from unexamined beliefs" (Stewart 1963, p. 323), to render them, in a word, independent.

Each of the other intellectuals of the Enlightenment joined Hume's campaign for the liberation of human judgment. Smith repeatedly celebrated philosophy and science and the moral, intellectual, and practical consequences of their searching inquiries into the principles of nature.[37] Indeed, as Cropsey points out, he proposed "to rely upon philosophy and science for the very defense of society against the power of other worldly influence" (1957, p. 28). In a similar fashion, Millar condemned Christians, Roman and reformed alike, for denying "freedom of opinion" and regarding "any remarkable deviation from their own tenets in the light of a damnable error." Such attitudes, he claimed, were only "mellowed and softened" by philosophy, "the fuller light of science," and "cool and dispassionate inquiry" as these revealed "the circumstances which contribute to the perfection of the social order" (*HV* 3:144, 4:305). Even Ferguson more or less assented to the Enlightenment's devaluation of fixed belief. Not that he endorsed something so rash as Hume's skepticism. This Ferguson forcefully opposed for its apparent tendency to destroy the certain foundations of all knowledge (see Kettler 1965, pp. 107–35). Nevertheless, he too warmly welcomed modern science and philosophy as loyal allies in the long march against all manner of human credulity (Kettler 1965, pp. 4–5; Lehmann 1930, pp. 131–32).

In his own way, pious William Robertson was the most remarkable figure in the process of elevating intense inquiry over bridled believing. He did regard the Bible as the repository of the purest moral code and hold that "the facts which inspired writers relate are no less instructive than the doctrines they teach" (*SW*, p. li). Beyond this, however, his unquestioning acceptance did not extend. Robertson was a pioneer in the critical examination of historical documents and even sought extrascriptural corroboration for empirical statements made by the apostles.[38] His historical works, moreover, always hastened to praise those developments through which humans "recovered the powers of inquiry," of "venturing to

---

lished beliefs, see *THN*, pp. 173–75; and, for discussion, Mossner (1965, p. 52), and Stewart (1963, pp. 44–56).

37. See *EPS*, p. 80, *LJB*, pp. 167–68, and *WN*, pp. 725–26, 748. On Smith's conception of science, see Raphael (1975, p. 83), Skinner (1972, 1974, p. 170), and Wightman (1975, pp. 46–47).

38. See *SW*, p. liii; and, on Robertson's critical historiographic methods, Black (1926, pp. 118–19), and Horn (1956, p. 166).

move . . . in every subject, with great boldness," and of "thinking for themselves" (*HC* 5:154, *HS* 1:150). Like other Calvinists, Robertson strongly believed that the medieval church had stifled human thought; yet when explaining the process of the mind's emancipation, he gave chief emphasis not to the Reformation—not to the teachings of Luther, Calvin, and Knox, or to some return to the infallible truth of the Bible—but instead to the progress of science and philosophy.[39] Again and again, he championed a vigorous "spirit of enquiry," even when it went astray (see *Progress*, pp. 60–63), over any catalogue of prescribed beliefs and, in so doing, reaffirmed the Scottish Enlightenment's abiding commitment to human independence.

The Scottish Enlightenment was also firmly committed to a broader universalism. The writings of the enlighteners cognitively and evaluatively eroded the particularistic boundaries that Scottish Calvinism imposed within the human community. For a world divided into non-Christians and Christians, unreformed and reformed Christians, non-Scottish and Scottish reformed Christians, and Episcopalian and Presbyterian Scottish reformed Christians, the Scottish Enlightenment tended to substitute humanity, the human community as a whole.[40] In the process, it quickly shed Scottish Calvinism's practice of awarding priority to subcommunities whose characteristics were most like its own for more general standards, standards not weighted in favor of its particular social group. This basic change in orientation appears in a great variety of contexts throughout the work of the enlightened intellectuals.

Robertson continually professed his allegiance to "humanity," his "love of the human species," and his regard for "the voice of mankind."[41] With his fellow enlighteners, he insisted that a "human

39. See *ER*, p. 23, *HS* 1:150–51, and *Progress*, pp. 43–44; cf. *HC* 5:134–60.

40. Loubser has observed: "Universalism . . . implies a refusal to draw boundaries, to exclude others because they lack a particularistic relation to the actor. The moral community most consistent with this component is mankind as a whole," or "humanity" (1970, pp. 105, 109; a similar view is implied by Weber 1915, pp. 330–36). However little such a formulation may accommodate the historically variable nature of "universalism," it is extremely appropriate for an analysis of the universalism of the Scottish Enlightenment (on some of the difficulties contained in this notion of universalism, see Barnard 1965, pp. 88–108).

41. The phrase next to the last is cited by Stewart (1796, p. 161); otherwise, see *ER*, p. 6, *HA* 9:93, *HS* 2:32, *India*, pp. 287–89, *Progress*, p. 29, and *SW*, p. lvi.

It should be emphasized that what is pertinent here is the pervasive importance that the attitude designated by "humanity" and related expressions had for the

being, as he comes originally from the hand of nature, is every-where the same" (*HA* 9:218)[42] and that, Calvinism to the contrary, all such beings can attain happiness. This conclusion was an-nounced in both religious and secular terms. In his early sermon, Robertson extolled the Gospel for declaring "all men, of every condition . . . to be offspring of the same God, and the heirs of the same heavenly inheritance" (*SW*, p. lvi). Elsewhere he remarked that "there is a species of happiness which [corresponds to] every situation where a human being can be placed" (*HA* 9:232–33). Robertson's universalism was not confined to these abstract proc-lamations; it extended as well to his practical prescriptions. In spite of his own rather benighted judgments on the Catholic church (see, e.g., *HC* 5:103–4), he chastised the Scottish reformers for lacking a "spirit of toleration" toward those from "the Romish church" and supported, at great personal cost, the unpopular movement to re-peal certain repressive anti-Catholic laws (*HS* 2:32; Clark 1964, p. 405; Stewart 1796, pp. 187–91). In addition, he commended the growth of international commerce for wearing off "those prejudices which maintain distinction and animosity between nations," and went on vigorously to attack slavery for its "ignominious depression of human nature," its destruction of "that original equality in which [humans] were at first placed, and are still viewed by their impartial Creator" (*Progress,* p. 67, *SW*, p. lvi).[43]

This attack appears especially striking when one realizes that it emerged from a nation and an age where slavery was an economic mainstay that passed largely unopposed (see Hill 1967, pp. 227–30), but Robertson was not the only enlightener to speak out. Each of the enlightened intellectuals built a case against slavery,[44] Millar

Scottish Enlightenment, not the mere recurrence of particular terms. By consulting enough works, "humanity" no doubt could be found throughout pre-Enlightenment writings. One does not, however, trace cultural developments by extracting words from their contexts.

42. On the Scottish Enlightenment's postulate of the uniformity of human nature, see Bryson (1945, pp. 114–47), Forbes (1975*a*, pp. 102–21), and Schneider (1967, pp. xxi–xxv).

43. See also *India*, pp. 181–82, *SW*, p. lii; and Clark (1964, pp. 22, 42, note 29, 1970, p. 208), Gilbert (1972, p. xvi), and Hirschman (1977, p. 61).

44. See Ferguson *EHCS*, p. 185; Hume *Essays*, pp. 385–97; and Smith *AN*, pp. 475–76, *LJB*, pp. 99–101, 226–31, *WN*, p. 365; for discussion, see Gay (1969, pp. 416–19). Hume's views here were not as unequivocal as those of the other enlight-eners. When condemning slavery in the American colonies, he held that slaves and their masters were "fellow-creatures," but never retracted an earlier remark that stated: "I am apt to suspect the Negroes to be naturally inferior to the Whites" (*Essays*, pp. 386, 213, note 1).

doing so most systematically and incisively. Ever the advocate of "humanity" and its "privileges," he inveighed against those who "should make no scruple of reducing a great proportion of their fellow-creatures into circumstances by which they are not only deprived of property, but almost of every species of right" (*Ranks,* pp. 302–11, 315–18, 321). Whether in ancient cities, on American plantations, or in the coal mines and salt pits of Scotland,[45] "the institution of slavery . . . appears equally inconvenient and pernicious" (*Ranks,* p. 316). Like Smith on an earlier occasion (*LJB,* p. 104), Millar decried Christianity and its biblical precepts for so long countenancing such an oppressive institution (*Ranks,* pp. 310–11). Returning to favorite Enlightenment themes, he maintained that more humane sentiments about slavery were fostered rather by the "advancement of commerce and the arts, together with the diffusion of knowledge" as these dissolved the prejudices and barriers that divided the human community (*Ranks,* p. 322).

Universalistic elements were also preeminent in the work of Adam Smith. As Smith saw the matter, human morality is itself rooted in "the general fellow-feeling which we have with every man, merely because he is our fellow-creature" (*TMS,* p. 172). Proper moral judgments, he further argued, emerge when humans, on the one hand, view situations through the eyes of an "impartial spectator . . . who has no particular connection" to themselves and, on the other hand, employ "general rules [that] counterbalance the impulse of . . . weak and partial humanity, by the dictates of a humanity that is more generous and comprehensive" (*TMS,* pp. 235, 233, 172, 170).[46] Cropsey has put the point as follows: "The constructive standard of 'universal mankind' is fundamental to the version of [moral philosophy] taught by Smith" (1963, p. 136). It also found expression in his economic inquiries. Behind Smith's renowned case for freer international trade was a cosmopolitan proposal for "an equality of treatment to all nations," a proposal that always railed against provincial, "national prejudices" (*Corr,* p.

45. Excepting Millar, Viner (1965, pp. 111–16) has faulted the Scottish Enlightenment for its silence on those forms of slavery that existed on Scottish soil. But Adam Smith had actually indicted these long before Millar published his own attack (see *AN,* p. 456, *LJB,* p. 99).

46. For further discussion of these features of Smith's analysis, see Campbell (1971, pp. 127–65), Cropsey (1957, p. 19), and Lindgren (1973, pp. 20–38). The specific positions just mentioned in the text were not fully developed in the earliest known draft (c. 1752; this is reproduced in Raphael 1969) or in the first edition of *The Theory of Moral Sentiments.* Even in the draft, however, universalistic elements were much in evidence (see Raphael 1975, pp. 88–89).

271, *LJB*, p. 206; see also *Letter*, pp. 567, 576). His recommendations on intranational religious affairs were equally generous and an impressive indication of the cultural distance between the Enlightenment and the Scottish tradition of interconfessional intolerance. Smith suggested that everyone be allowed "to chuse his own priest and his own religion as he thought proper. There would be in this case . . . a great multitude of religious sects. [Together these would be] productive of the most philosophical good temper and moderation, [for religious] zeal must be altogether innocent where the society is divided into two or three hundred, or perhaps as many thousand small sects" (*WN*, pp. 744–45; see also *LJB*, pp. 57–58, *TMS*, p. 291). For Smith, none of these groups had a place above the others either in heaven or on earth. The only affiliation that mattered was membership in what Hume had aptly called "the party of humankind" (*IPM*, p. 96).

Hume himself consistently demonstrated his loyalty to this party. He scorned the Bible's "arbitrary choice of one people"—"that people the countrymen of the author"—"as the favourites of heaven" and staunchly advocated religious toleration (*Essays*, p. 544; Stewart 1963, pp. 283–86). His social philosophy too, as Stewart has remarked, "implies universalism: if any distinction, for example the distinction made manifest by the existence of a separate dynastic or national state, is introduced between each and all, its introduction can be explained only in terms of some secondary consideration. [Hume held that the] world is the natural economic unit. Any more confined economic system is irrational and perverse" (1963, pp. 191–92). He thus "pray[ed] for the flourishing commerce of Germany, Spain, Italy and even France," not for Britain alone (*Essays*, p. 338), and acclaimed the contribution that international trade would make to the erosion of particularistic divisions between groups.[47] Policy recommendations aside, Hume was also of the more general belief that, whereas an ordinary man of the world sees "the characters of men [more in] relation to his interest than as they stand in themselves, and [thereby] has his judgment warped on every occasion," it is "the chief business of philosophers"—those guardians of enlightenment—"to regard the general course of things" (*Essays*, pp. 562, 260).[48] Valid judgments, he urged, require rising above every "private and particular situation" and considering "not whether the persons [judged] be our acquaintance or

47. See *Essays*, pp. 202–20; Camic (1979*b*, pp. 530–31), and Chamley (1975).

48. There is an uncanny resemblance between Hume's formulations here and Parsons's (1951, p. 62) observations on particularism and universalism.

strangers, countrymen or foreigners": they require "general points of view," "some universal principle in the human frame," "sentiments which arise from humanity [and] are not only the same in all human creatures . . . but . . . also comprehend all human creatures," or, more simply, "the principle of humanity" (*IPM*, pp. 93–94, *THN*, pp. 581–82).[49] With very little ado, the more exclusive criteria that were ingrained in Scottish Calvinist culture have been resolutely abandoned.

Ferguson's writings present a more complicated picture. Abstractly, these valued the passion of "general humanity" and the "principle of candour, which knows no partial distinctions," "is confined to no bounds," and makes "us feel a relation to the universe, and to the whole creation of God" (*EHCS*, pp. 51–52). Sounding thoroughly universalistic, Ferguson caustically observed that too many nations, "having chosen themselves . . . the judges and models of what is excellent, [place themselves] first in their own opinion, and give to others consideration or eminence, so far only as they approach to their own condition" (*EHCS*, p. 204). In the same vein, he taught generations of his moral philosophy students that the "greatest good competent to man's nature is the love of mankind" and that "the highest point to which moral science conducts the mind of man, is that eminence of thought, from which he can view himself as but part in the community of living natures" (*IMP*, p. 171, *PMPS* 1:313).

All this, however, was only one side of Ferguson. When commenting upon his world in less theoretical language, he was wont to maintain that, without the invigorating effects of conflict, a society loses its moral strength and falls into a state of corruption (see Forbes 1966, pp. xxxvi–xli). Upholding the distinctions between human subgroups was Ferguson's antidote to this dreadful possibility, and he generally opposed the tendency of the other enlighteners to level such differences. "Could we at once, in the case of any nation, extinguish the emulation which is excited from abroad, we should probably break or weaken the bonds of society at home, and close the busiest scenes of national occupations and virtues" (*EHCS*, p. 25). Nor was it only international struggles that, according to Ferguson, "bring out the best in man" (Forbes 1966, p. xl). "When we are involved in any of the divisions into which mankind are separated . . . the sentiments of the heart, and the talents of the understanding, find their natural exercise. Wisdom,

49. See also *HEM*, p. 500, *HL* 1:12; and Raphael (1975, p. 87).

vigilance, fidelity, and fortitude are the characters requisite in such a scene, and the qualities which it tends to improve" (*EHCS*, pp. 218–19). None of the intellectuals of the Scottish Enlightenment was the complete universalist: Robertson held the Jews to be naturally perverse and was scarcely more generous when it came to the Jesuits; Hume has, with some justice, been accused of a "westernizing narcissism," which can be detected elsewhere in the Enlightenment as well; all of the enlighteners exuded a certain local pride in Scottish achievements; and so it goes.[50] Only in the case of Ferguson, however, was the lingering provincialism sufficiently consequential to entail a modification of the Enlightenment's program to break down the divisions between different religious, political, and national groups. If Ferguson eventually subdued his early fulminations against the Papists, and the French, and others unlike himself to become far more universalistic than Scottish Calvinism, he continually set himself apart from his fellow enlighteners by defending the principle and practice of patriotism and partisanship.[51] As ever, his Enlightenment was a compromise.

The limits of Ferguson's universalism surface in one other context, which is essential for understanding the whole of the Scottish Enlightenment. As will become clear, the Enlightenment nowhere handled the situation of the masses in a way that would now be regarded as satisfactory. But within the bounds of their common inadequacies, the enlightened intellectuals differed among themselves in the extent to which their universalistic sentiments encompassed those from "the lower orders." Here three enlighteners were, for their age, extraordinarily inclusive. Robertson maintained that,

50. For Robertson's views on the Jesuits and the Jews, see *HC* 6:189–209, and *SW*, p. liv; for Hume's contrary opinions on the latter, see *HE*, pp. 119–26, and *HL*, 1:423. Chamley (1975, p. 304) advances the charge of "westernizing narcissism," which is also discussed, in other words, by Forbes (1978, p. 61). Lehmann (1971, p. xiii) stresses the point about local pride; and notes 44, 45, and 59 in this chapter call attention to other limitations in the universalism of the Enlightenment.

The Scottish Enlightenment's feminism, or lack thereof, should also be mentioned at this juncture, although this fundamental issue has yet to be investigated systematically. The evidence at hand (Ferguson *EHCS* p. 185; Hume *Essays*, pp. 133–34, *THN*, pp. 570–75; Millar *Ranks*, pp. 183–228; Robertson *SW*, p. lv; Smith *LJB*, pp. 78, 115, 122; see also Battersby 1980; Gay 1969, pp. 33–34; Swingewood 1970*b*, pp. 168–69) indicates that here again there were variations among the enlightened intellectuals and that these variations were generally congruent with other differences among the enlighteners in terms of universalism. More research on this topic, however, is clearly necessary.

51. See *SPE*, pp. 16–22, *MSP*, p. 5; Forbes (1966, pp. xxxv), and Kettler (1977, pp. 452–54).

whatever their "exterior distinctions," human beings are fundamentally equal (*SW*, p. lvi). Millar adjudged social arrangements
that serve to make "the common people [virtual] dupes of their
superiors . . . revolting to all feelings of humanity" (*HV* 4:156, 159).
And Smith, despairing that "the great never look upon their in-
feriors as fellow-creatures," generally held the same moral standards to apply to all social classes and embraced "the principle of
the radical equality of human beings" (*TMS*, p. 120; Cropsey 1957,
p. 64, 1963, p. 144).[52] Ferguson was more particularistic. Despite
occasional remarks to the contrary, he generally "accorded differential treatment," Kettler has shown, to "the lower and upper classes,
. . . applied different criteria to men at opposite ends of the social
scale, and treated them as not even equal in principle" (1965, pp.
285–86).[53] David Hume, otherwise the most ardent proponent of
the Enlightenment's novel attitudes, took a similar position. Central
to his work was, as Stewart has demonstrated, a dichotomy between
the "vulgar," the vast, ignorant, and dangerous multitude, and "men
of true principles," an enlightened minority drawn primarily from
the landed gentry into which Hume himself had been born. To the
latter, Hume allowed the nirvana of "moderate skepticism" and,
with it, the capacity to govern, but he did not regard this elite "as
a vanguard leading the vulgar to a new order in which all will be
cautious and suitably sceptical" (1963, p. 319). The masses, rather,
were to be given a dogmatically bland, but ceremonial religion "to
reinforce their morality and to tame their spirits, [for] notions of
a vast general enlightenment are vain and silly" (1963, pp. 287,
320).[54] Like Ferguson, Hume had by no means eradicated all the
fundamental divisions within the human community. Everywhere
in the Scottish Enlightenment, however, that community had be-

52. For additional indications of Robertson's position, see *ER*, p. 6, and *HS* 1:151,
3:189–94. For Millar, see the passage cited by Lehmann (1960, p. 394), and Schneider (1971–72, p. 2094). For Smith, see *Letter*, p. 578; and Campbell (1971, pp. 172–
73); cf. Reisman (1976, pp. 159–60). On Smith's extensive sympathies for the lower
classes, see Macfie (1967, p. 120), Robbins (1959, p. 196), and Viner (1927, p. 245).

53. See esp. *MSP*, pp. 23–25, and *PMPS* 2:61, 93–94, 462–64; cf. *EHCS*, pp. 249–
50; Robbins (1959, pp. 178, 194).

54. For Hume's earliest expression of such views, see *THN*, pp. xiv–xviii, 272–
73, 402.

Adam Smith, it is true, also distinguished "the bulk of mankind" from "philosophers" and described the social utility of religion for the "common people" (*EPS*,
p. 79, *WN*, pp. 746–48). In his writings, however, these were but occasional, descriptive observations and, as such, did not lead him to trade his general class
universalism for the overall Humian position.

come vastly more comprehensive than the particularistically partitioned world of Scottish Calvinism.

The Scottish Enlightenment is usually described as the "age of history."[55] That characterization in certain ways is most curious: the Scots produced a mass of historical literature long before the Enlightenment and the majority of enlighteners wrote on numerous nonhistorical topics.[56] Still, history was a genre in which all of the enlighteners intensively worked and where their achievement has been loudly proclaimed. Ordinarily, however, that achievement has been defined to include only some of the Enlightenment's historical writings. Historians of the social sciences, for example, have seen the accomplishment of the Scottish Enlightenment in the wideranging, protoevolutionary speculations on the stages and laws of societal development that Smith, Millar, and Ferguson put forward.[57] Historians of historiography, on the other hand, have located the Scottish achievement in the way that the more temporally and geographically delimited histories of Hume and Robertson welded the scholarly techniques of the earlier antiquary "to the exposition of the [pre-Enlightenment] historian, so that the discipline of historical research that we are familiar with . . . was established" (Hay 1977, p. 184).[58] What the disparate species of the historical work of the Enlightenment shared, however, were the attitudes of independence and universalism. Whatever else it may have been, history was a wide field where the Enlightenment's novel orientations came alive, converging in an approach fundamentally at odds with the traditional Calvinist historiography.

55. The expression is Skinner's (1967, p. 33). The sentiment is one that infuses virtually all recent scholarship on the Scottish Enlightenment (see notes 10 and 58 in this chapter).

56. Particularly noteworthy here are the essential moral-philosophical works of Ferguson (*Institutes of Moral Philosophy, Principles of Moral and Political Science*), Hume (*A Treatise of Human Nature, An Enquiry Concerning Human Understanding, An Inquiry Concerning the Principles of Morals*), and Smith (*The Theory of Moral Sentiments*), critical sections of which become altogether lost when the Scottish Enlightenment is seen simply as the "age of history."

57. See Burrow (1966, pp. 7–12), Chitnis (1976, pp. 94–106), Höpfl (1978), Lehmann (1960, pp. 98–104, 1971, pp. 117–18), Meek (1954, 1971, 1976b, pp. 99–130), Pascal (1938), Rendall (1978, pp. 123–26), and Skinner (1965, 1967, 1975).

58. See also Black (1926), Birley (1962, pp. 110–35), Gay (1969, pp. 373–75), and Peardon (1933, 19–29).

The two preceding sentences in the text have continued the customary associations of Smith (in his *Lectures on Justice* and in the fifth book of *The Wealth of Nations*),

There are many indications of this. The enlighteners' historical writings robbed the Scottish people of their special status as God's chosen people. Except for Robertson's *History of Scotland,* none of these writings regarded Scotland even as an area of particular historical concern. The enlightened intellectuals either concentrated on the affairs of other regions (America, Continental Europe, England) and by and large left their own country out of the picture, or considered all the societies they knew of in an evolutionary perspective that placed those at comparable developmental stages on the same plane and reduced Scotland to just one more, relatively backward land. In the process, the provincial distinctions that Calvinism had imposed within the human community were inevitably abandoned for a more universal, world history (see Bryson 1945, p. 14; Gay 1969, pp. 391–93).[59] The recurrent plot of that history was also of a piece with the spirit of the Enlightenment. The his-

---

Millar (in *The Origin of the Distinction of Ranks* and parts of *An Historical View of the English Government*), and Ferguson (in the *Essay on the History of Civil Society*) with broad evolutionary notions (on some of the differences between Ferguson and the others here, see Forbes 1966, pp. xxii–xxiii), and of Hume (in *The History of England*) and Robertson (especially in *The History of Scotland* and most of *The History of the Reign of Charles V*) with more concrete historical inquiries. Although it does not change the argument being made above, it is worth observing that such associations are imperfect. The former three intellectuals often offered somewhat more restricted historical analyses (Smith in the third book of *The Wealth of Nations,* Millar in much of his *Historical View,* Ferguson in *The History of the Progress and Termination of the Roman Republic*), while Robertson provided his own reflections on the laws and stages of societal development (particularly in the Appendix of his *Disquisition on India* and in sections of *The History of America;* on the latter, see Meek 1976*b*, pp. 136–45). Stewart (1963, pp. 167–71, 292–93) has made a similar claim about Hume (cf. Meek 1976*b*, pp. 30–31; the best discussion of Hume's views on "the progress of society" and of its uniqueness is provided by Forbes 1975*a*, pp. 279–323). It is also important to note here that the suggestion that follows in the text does not claim that independence and universalism are the only themes sufficiently general to encompass the Enlightenment's various historical writings.

59. This is not to deny the considerable justice of the common observation that there are serious limits to the historical relativism of the intellectuals of the Enlightenment (see, e.g., Burrow 1966, pp. 14, 48–49, 58; Forbes 1951, pp. 20–23, 31; Gilbert 1972, p. xiv; Peardon 1933, pp. 19–29). But in acknowledging this, it is equally important not only to recognize the Scottish enlighteners' belief that "in passing judgment upon the characters of men, we ought to try them by principles and maxims of their own age, not by those of another" (the remark is Robertson's [*HC* 6:313]; see also Hume *Dialogue,* pp. 146–47; Millar *Ranks,* pp. 197–98; Robertson *India,* p. 201), but also to realize that, considering the period, their own historical writings actually brought this injunction to bear with surprising frequency (this has been most fully documented for Hume, see Forbes 1975*a*, pp. 102–21, 286–92; see also Gay 1969, pp. 381–83).

torical works of the Scottish Enlightenment treated a varied multitude of tangible past events, yet in so doing they time and again
traced the history of human independence, recording the forward
and backward march of various forms of human autonomy, and
analyzing the sources of and impediments to their further development.[60] But not only was independence a principal protagonist
in the Enlightenment's histories, the episodes in those histories
unfolded independently of Providence. The secularism that so
thoroughly permeated other aspects of the Scottish Enlightenment
suffused its historical productions as well. This was even the case
in the work of William Robertson, the most orthodox of the enlighteners. Robertson did begin his account of the Reformation by
remarking how that development emerged "by a singular disposition of Providence," "which, with infinite ease, can bring about
events which to human sagacity appear impossible" (*HS* 1:143, *HC*
5:104). To Robertson, however, this meant no more than that God
had wrought "that wonderful preparation of circumstances which
disposed the minds of men for receiving [the reformers'] doctrines"
(*HC* 5:104). These natural circumstances, not any supernatural
activities, were the exclusive focus of his actual analysis of the causes
of the Reformation (*HC* 5:134–60) and, when treating other past
events, he was more secular still—so fully secular, in fact, that through
all the centuries and nations that he wandered when telling his
famous story of the transformation of Europe "from the Subversion
of the Roman Empire to the Beginning of the Sixteenth Century,"
the operations of the hand of God were nowhere to be seen.[61]
Robertson's historical vision, like that of his fellow enlighteners,
constantly placed "man and not God . . . at the centre of the picture"

60. Which is to say that these works did not confine themselves exclusively to the
particular form of autonomy that is the focus of this study. On the history of
independence theme, see, in general, Skinner (1967, p. 18); on Hume, Forbes (1975*a*,
esp. pp. 369–99); on Millar, Forbes (1975*b*, pp. 198–200, 1977, p. 89), Lehmann
(1960, pp. 126–30), and Macfie (1961, p. 207); on Smith, Cropsey (1957), Forbes
(1975*b*, pp. 200–201), and Winch (1978, pp. 70–102). There has been no previous
commentary on this aspect of Robertson's work, but it can be seen quite clearly in
The Progress of Society in Europe. No secondary sources are mentioned at this point
for Ferguson because in his work—even, or perhaps especially, in his *Essay on the
History of Civil Society*—the historical development of autonomy was typically of less
concern than the vicissitudes of human virtue (see Kettler 1965, pp. 6, 165, 286).

61. The phrase quoted was part of Robertson's subtitle for *The Progress of Society
in Europe*, which was itself the introductory volume of his *History of the Reign of
Charles V*.

(Hay 1977, p. 183; see also Höpfl 1978, pp. 29, 31; cf. Horn 1956, p. 165; Meek 1976*b*, p. 136).

The measure of secularism that appeared in Scottish historical literature during the early eighteenth century had been of a wholly different sort, for it had always been harnessed to the unchallenged claims and partisan categories of established political groups. But the Scottish Enlightenment did not merely exchange the dependency and particularism of Calvinism for their more worldly equivalents. Rather, its independence and universalism came together in a historiography that was no longer governed by received political assumptions and distinctions. This aspect of the Enlightenment was as revolutionary as its break with traditional religious beliefs.

When the enlighteners' histories relinquished Scotland as their primary concern, they completely deserted the territory of Scottish patriotic and party history. By that single move, they abandoned the particularistic practices of celebrating Scotland's glorious past and of using it to vindicate the position of one or another Scottish political subgroup, and they shed the credulous attitude that had accompanied those practices. It is true that in his *History of Scotland,* Robertson remained on old, familiar soil. But from the outset, this work set itself apart from earlier histories of Scotland. Indeed, Robertson began by lamenting that the events of Scottish history

> gave rise to two parties, which were animated against each other with the fiercest political hatred, imbittered by religious zeal. Each of these produced historians of considerable merit, who adopted all their sentiments and defended all their actions. Truth was not the sole object of these authors. Blinded by prejudices, . . . they wrote an apology for a faction, rather than a history of their country. Succeeding historians have followed these guides almost implicitly, and have repeated their errors and misrepresentations. [*HS*, pp. cxxix–cxxx]

While similar observations had occasionally been offered by early eighteenth-century Scottish historians, what made Robertson unique was that he actually kept the promise to provide a "more impartial" treatment of Scotland's stormy past (*HS*, p. cxxx; see also *ER*, pp. 21–23). For it was his work that at last succeeded in going beyond subservience to the conventional programs of Scottish political factions and beyond their partisan standards for evaluating historical events to attain some measure of skepticism, detachment, and objectivity.[62]

The rest of the historical work of the Scottish Enlightenment preserved these qualities, even under the most adverse circumstances. For a variety of reasons, the enlightened intellectuals, especially Hume and Millar, channelled much of their historical attention to England. When they did so, they encountered a past more thoroughly politicized and controversial than Scotland's own. There were Whig renditions of English history and Tory renditions, and amid much talk in the eighteenth century about impartiality, it remained, as Adam Smith remarked, "the fate of all modern histories to be wrote in a party spirit" (*LRBL*, p. 112).[63] That, however, was not the spirit in which the enlighteners wrote their histories. As Forbes had carefully demonstrated, Millar's *Historical View of the English Government* consistently rose above the conflicting interpretations that different parties had given to England's past, while Hume's *History of England* was even more so "the non-party History," the history that went "beyond Whig principles and Tory prejudices . . . and [discovered] a guarantee of impartiality which is inherent in the structure of the story itself" (1954, p. 663, 1975*a*, pp. 263, 292). The same effect was accomplished when the Scottish Enlightenment followed Smith's example and extended its historical focus from the particulars of English history to the general processes by which all societies evolved. The broad historical-comparative approach set the events of England's past in the context of "analogous developments in the similar states of society in Europe and elsewhere [and thus] acted as a by-pass, taking the reader quickly and without fuss past learned controversies and the internecine opinions" that otherwise characterized the historiography of the day (Forbes 1954, pp. 665–66).[64] The fixed beliefs and paro-

---

62. See Black (1926, pp. 121–28), Gay (1969, p. 392), Horn (1956, p. 165), Pryde (1962, p. 111), and Stewart (1796, pp. 113–17).

63. Hume (*Essays*, p. 611) and Millar (*HV* 1:iii–iv) offered similar judgments, the essential accuracy of which has recently been corroborated by Forbes (1975*a*, pp. 233–67).

The "Whig" and "Tory" labels have been inserted in the text here only to make the discussion more concrete; they are in no sense offered as a description of the political divisions in eighteenth-century Britain (see chap. 1, note 31). It should also be noted that no differentiation is made in the current context between "party" and "faction," though ordinarily the analysis of the politics of this period requires that distinction.

64. See also Skinner (1967, p. 46). On the impartiality of Smith's historical analysis, see Forbes (1975*b*), Skinner (1975, p. 170), and Winch (1978, pp. 70–102). For

chial criteria of politics again went the way of their religious counterparts, displaced by the orientations that were the hallmarks of
the Scottish Enlightenment.[65]

The independence and universalism of the Enlightenment have
sometimes been regarded as fig leaves. Lucien Goldmann has, for
example, suggested that these orientations were a philosophical
translation of the workings of the "market economy" which made,
and time and again sought to make, everyone "an independent
element" enmeshed in exchange relations that disregarded the
"personal character," "convictions," and "qualities" of their partic-

further discussion of this aspect of the work of Hume and Millar, see Forbes (1975a,
pp. 260–307), and Robbins (1959, p. 215).

65. The detachment from political creeds and from their divisions and biases that
was exhibited in the historical work of the Scottish Enlightenment infused its political
theory more generally. The enlighteners were British subjects in an age when Britons
widely subscribed to components of the political ideology that Forbes has termed
"vulgar Whiggism" (the rubric "does not exclude commonwealthmen, republicans
or democratic radicals or even Tories, and . . . cuts deeper than any distinction
between 'court' and 'country' " [Forbes 1975b, p. 180]). Principally this ideology
asserted the matchless perfection of the English constitution, extolled its capacity
to procure the liberty of its subjects, and regarded other existing governments—
from France to Turkey—as illegitimate, absolutist, despotic forms that brought only
slavery, but it also propounded the contract theory of government, condemned the
practices of the Stuart kings, and justified the Glorious Revolution at the time that
it happened (Forbes 1975a, pp. 140–43, 1975b, pp. 180–81). The enlightened intellectuals were far too independent to accept these views uncritically, and far too
universalistic to embrace their provincial conclusions. For vulgar Whiggism, Smith
and particularly Hume substituted "skeptical Whiggism," the attitude that observed
"political phenomena with the cool detachment and neutrality of the impartial
spectator" and "attempt[ed] to rise above party and prejudice and friendship and
attachments, personal or public, altogether, and bring the . . . whole ethos of science
and 'philosophy' to bear on English politics in order to promote moderation" (Forbes
1975b, p. 180, 1975a, p. 136; these remarks pertain to Hume, but for comparable
assessments of Smith, see Forbes 1975b; Winch 1978; for more extended discussion
of this aspect of Hume's politics, see Forbes 1975a, pp. 125–92, 1977, 1978; Stewart
1963, pp. 6, 9, 196–255; note also Mossner 1965, p. 55; Robbins 1959, 218; for
evidence against the customary claim that Hume's political orientation changed
substantially as he grew older, see Forbes 1975a, esp. 125–39). As a result, Hume
and Smith typically rejected full-scale the cherished tenets of vulgar Whiggism and,
in so doing, they were joined (if less than completely) by Millar, Robertson, and to
some degree even Ferguson (on Millar, see Forbes 1954, pp. 660–67, 1975b, pp.
193–200; on Robertson, ER, p. 86, Progress, pp. 69, 131–33; cf. Ser; on Ferguson,
Kettler 1965, pp. 244, 276–77)—though Ferguson was frequently critical of much
of the emphasis on political detachment and moderation that was so basic to skeptical
Whiggism (Forbes 1966, pp. xxxv–xxxviii, 1967, p. 44; Kettler 1977, pp. 452–54,
1978, p. 209).

ipants (1968, pp. 18, 22). Behind this assertion is the venerable thesis that the intellectuals of the Enlightenment were "the philosophical exponents of bourgeois capitalism" (Mannheim 1927, p. 89),[66] and that Adam Smith in particular was "the champion of the claims and interests of competitive capitalism" (Pascal 1938, p. 168). The formulaic phrases here are an unfortunate camouflage: as Venturi has remarked, the "historical presupposition" of a relationship between the bourgeoisie and the Enlightenment only obfuscates the protean nature of that relationship (1971, pp. 10–12). With the exception of Hume, the Scottish enlighteners had grave reservations about the "commercial"—they did not themselves say "capitalist"—society developing around them.[67] Ferguson observed (to Marx's approval) that the division of labor can "contract and . . . limit the views of the mind" and judged "that the soul of man is of more value than his possessions, and that the happiness of individuals . . . depends more on the generosity, justice, and fortitude of their spirit, than on the trappings in which they are cloathed, or the quantity of merchandize they sell to their neighbor" (*EHCS*, p. 183, *HPM*, p. 179). Millar emphasized that the spread of "manufactures" robbed "the labouring people, who form the great body of the nation," of their "mental powers," converted them "into the mere instrument of labour," and made them "like machines, actuated by a regular weight, and performing certain movements with great celerity and exactness, but of small compass and unfitted for any other use" (*HV* 4:146, 152).[68] Smith similarly detailed the debilitating consequences "arising from a commercial spirit" (*LJB*, p. 255) and, in the following unequivocal terms, described the "oppressive inequality" of the modern world:

66. See also Anderson (1974, p. 57), and Therborn (1976, pp. 117, 132, 161, 213–14). Marx and Engels's classic statement of this position is contained in *The German Ideology* (1846, pp. 185–89). Marx's views on the "independence" and "universalism" of the capitalist economy are well discussed by Avineri (1968, pp. 162–68).

67. For Hume's views, see *Essays*, pp. 275–88; Forbes (1975a, pp. 87–88), and Winch (1978, pp. 73–74, 81). Robertson will not be specifically discussed at this juncture because of the relative scarcity of his commentary on his own times (see, however, Horn 1956, p. 164; Meek 1976b, p. 143).

68. For a fuller statement of Millar's position here, see *HV* 4:144–61; Forbes (1954, p. 650), Lehmann (1960, p. 128), Meek (1976b, pp. 171–72), and Schneider (1971–72, pp. 2093–94). On Ferguson's broader indictment of modern society, see *EHCS*, pp. 180–280, *RM*, pp. 8–12; Forbes (1966, 1967), and Kettler (1965, pp. 204–6). See Marx (1867, p. 123, note 1, p. 354) for the assessment of Ferguson referred to above.

In a Society of a hundred thousand families, there will perhaps be one hundred who don't labour at all, and who yet, either by violence, or by the more orderly oppression of law, employ a greater part of the labour of the society than any other ten thousand in it. The division of what remains too, after this enormous defalcation, is by no means made in proportion to the labour of each individual. On the contrary those who labour most get least. The opulent merchant, who spends a great part of his time in luxury and entertainments, enjoys a much greater proportion of the profits of his traffic, than all the Clerks and Accountants who do the business. These last, again, enjoying a great deal of leisure, and suffering scarce any other hardship besides the confinement of attendance, enjoy a much greater share of the produce, than three times an equal number of artizans, who, under their direction, labour much more severely and assiduously. The artizan again, tho' he works generally under cover protected from the injuuries of the weather, at his ease and assisted by the convenience of innumerable machines, enjoys a much greater share than the poor labourer who has the soil and the seasons to struggle with, and, who while he affords the materials for supplying the luxury of all the other members of the common wealth, and bears, as it were, upon his shoulders the whole fabric of human society, seems himself to be pressed down below ground by the weight, and to be buried out of sight in the lowest foundations of the building. [*ED*, pp. 327–28][69]

However trenchant their strictures against the social formation in which they found themselves, the intellectuals of the Scottish Enlightenment never advocated any sort of radical change. Millar

69. See also *LJB*, pp. 162–63, and *WN*, pp. 734–40. Smith's critique of the commercial society, and the inadequacies of the claim that Smith was the champion of competitive capitalism, have recently received extended attention (see particularly Cropsey 1957, pp. 88–92, 1963, pp. 152–53; Lindgren 1973, pp. 80–84, 106–7; Winch 1978, pp. 81–83, 88–90; contemporary radical scholarship has at last begun to reach similar conclusions, see Hunt 1975, p. 53). While Smith's economic views were fundamentally at odds with the positions of the principal social groups in his society (see Checkland 1967, pp. 73–79), it goes without saying that they still differed in basic ways from the nineteenth-century indictment of capitalism (see West 1969, 1975). Smith's reasons for preferring the commercial society despite its defects are analyzed in detail elsewhere (see Cropsey 1957, esp. pp. x, 98; Hirschman 1977, pp. 100–113; Lindgren 1973, pp. 84–132; Winch 1978, pp. 70–102; on the reasoning of other Scottish enlighteners here, see Hirschman 1977, pp. 56–66, 87–93).

and Smith, to be sure, refused to follow Ferguson and essentially to abandon the attempt to mitigate the adverse effects of the division of labor.[70] Both instead suggested that "as the circumstances of commercial society are unfavourable to the mental improvement of the populace, it ought to be the great aim of the public to counteract . . . the natural tendency of mechanical employments, and by the institution of schools and seminaries of education to communicate, as far as possible, to the most useful, but humble class of citizens, that knowledge which their way of life has, in some measure, prevented them from acquiring."[71] Endorsing Hume's belief that "every person, if possible, ought to enjoy the fruits of his labor, in full possession of all the necessaries, and many of the conveniences of life," Smith particularly urged also the "liberal reward of labour" and insisted that "it is but equity . . . that they who feed, cloath and lodge the whole body of the people, should have such a share of the produce of their own labour as to be themselves tolerably well fed, cloathed and lodged" (*Essays*, p. 271; *WN*, pp. 73, 70). He anticipated that economic growth would foster a "universal opulence which extends itself to the lowest ranks of the people" and proposed certain well-known changes in commercial policy to promote growth (*WN*, p. 11),[72] but like his fellow enlighteners was, as Viner has remarked, "only vestigially 'reformist' where social and political structure and property rights were involved" (1965, pp. 111–12). In the end, the Enlightenment lived by Ferguson's quaint maxim: "walls may be renewed or rebuilt in parts successively [but:] *Beware you take not away so much of your supports at once as that the roof may fall in*" (*PMPS* 2:497 [emphasis in original]). What made the latter possibility seem so immediate and threatening to enlighteners everywhere was "the overpowering presence of the illiterate masses and the absence [among them] of the habit of autonomy" (Gay 1969, p. 497). Millar's tolerance for "large bands of labourers" who, "by constant intercourse communicate all their sentiments and passions," call forth "leaders who

70. On this aspect of Ferguson's thought, see Kettler (1965, pp. 279–80, 284, 286); see also Hamowy (1968), and Mizuta (1980).

71. The statement is Millar's (*HV* 4:160), but Smith's opinions were similar (see *WN*, pp. 734–40). Smith's educational proposals, which Marx dismissed perhaps too quickly as "homeopathic doses" (1867, p. 362), have been the center of considerable recent controversy (see, e.g., Heilbroner 1975, pp. 535–36; Reisman 1976, pp. 155–61; West 1975, pp. 540, 552; Winch 1978, pp. 113–20).

72. Though well-known, these changes are still frequently misrepresented. Yet as Viner (1927) argued nearly a half-century ago, Smith's allegedly laissez-faire proposals actually assigned many essential functions to the state.

give a tone and direction to their companions," and "unite" or "riot
. . . in demanding a redress of grievances" was altogether singular
(*HV* 4:135; see also Hirschman 1977, pp. 89–92). Lehmann has
argued that Millar himself felt that the public needed some pro-
tection from "the irresponsible rule of the ignorant, the unthinking,
the easily excitable mob" (1960, p. 65); the other enlighteners provided the majority with still less of a real future. The objectivity
they achieved by transcending the customary religious and political
alignments of their age was always bounded by an avowed commitment—expressed even by the intellectuals who were deeply dis-
turbed by essential features in the existing order of things—to
uphold the basic economic and political arrangements of their society. Neither popular democracy, a fundamental redistribution of
economic resources, nor the eradication of social classes formed
any part of the program of the Scottish Enlightenment.[73]

These complex issues are introduced at this point to place the
cultural change that is the Scottish Enlightenment in perspective.
Perspective here will not be found, however, by treating independence and universalism as isomorphic with the principles of the
market economy. In Goldmann's account, the "independence" of
the market is an atomistic individualism that acknowledges no interpersonal bonds but those implied by the act of exchange; its
"universalism" a cool indifference to the many human attributes
that are irrelevant to, or interfere with, economic transactions (1968,
esp. pp. 18–22). Such notions were not those of the enlightened
intellectuals. Their brand of universalism disregarded personal attributes that were rooted in particularistic human divisions, not all
extraeconomic individual characteristics, and their assertion of independence was always conjoined with the belief that "the mutual
dependence of men is so great in all societies that scarce any human

73. The nonradical nature of the Scottish Enlightenment has been widely discussed: in general, see Campbell (1974, p. 69), Checkland (1967, p. 75), Kettler
(1965, p. 98), and Smout (1969*a*, p. 475); cf. Davie (1972), Emerson (1973, pp. 321–
22), and Phillipson (1973, 1974). On Ferguson, see Forbes (1966, pp. xl–xli), and
Kettler (1965, pp. 88–99, 154–63, 261); on Hume, Forbes (1975*a*, esp. pp. x, 91,
136, 219, 309), and Stewart (1963, pp. 174, 180, 319–20, 324); on Millar, Forbes
(1954, p. 667), Lehmann (1960, pp. 138, 169), Meek (1954, p. 44), Robbins (1959,
p. 217), and Schneider (1971–72, p. 2090); on Robertson, Gilbert (1972, p. xvi),
and Horn (1956, p. 160); on Smith, Campbell (1971, pp. 212–13, 1977, pp. 532–
34), Forbes (1975*b*), Gee (1968, p. 295), Heilbroner (1975, pp. 536–38), Lindgren
(1973, pp. 51–52, 58, 126, 131), Raphael (1973, p. 101), Skinner (1975, p. 178),
and Winch (1978, pp. 55, 157–58).

action is entirely complete in itself" (Hume *EHU,* p. 371).[74] Yet, for all this, the daring attitudes of the Scottish enlighteners can only strike us as extremely circumscribed. The Enlightenment encompassed by general standards those who had previously been particularistically divided and regarded, but did not challenge the existence of those tenacious class and status divisions that nullified universality in a thousand ways. It declared the autonomy of the human condition, but proposed little fundamental change for a world discovering ever more subtle and intractable forms of human bondage. To adopt formulation Marx (1852, p. 51) employed in a very different context: the intellectuals of the Scottish Enlightenment did not in these basic ways ultimately go beyond the practical limits of their situation. Within those limits, however, they had wrought a great transformation.

II

At the end of the eighteenth century, Immanuel Kant looked back and observed that the Age of the Enlightenment was not an enlightened age (1784, p. 388). This perceptive maxim has often been overlooked in descriptions of mid-eighteenth-century Scottish culture. Frequently, the Enlightenment has been regarded as the spirit of the entire age. Scottish Calvinism, however, was far too resilient to give way[75] to a cultural change as confined as the Scottish Enlightenment.[76]

The fundamental beliefs of earlier generations were so entrenched that they persisted even as the Church of Scotland was losing its previous role in Scottish life.[77] As the eighteenth century progressed, disputes that emerged within the Church increasingly

74. The ethical theories of the Scottish Enlightenment alone provide ample support for the first claim made in this sentence; the social conception of human nature is treated more fully in the literature cited in note 10 of this chapter.

75. The same is true of the traditional sort of Scottish historiography. The attitudes that the enlighteners brought to historical writing were, as Duncan has shown, "distinctively untypical of Scottish . . . historical thought in the eighteenth-century as a whole" (1965, p. 142); see also (Horn 1961, pp. 10–13).

76. Writing of the American situation, May has similarly remarked that the claim that the Enlightenment swamped orthodox religious culture "fails to fit [with the] actualities. Its main deficiencies are two: it makes it impossible to explain American nineteenth-century culture, and it leaves out most of the people of all periods" (1976*a*, p. 1406).

77. As the phrasing here should make clear, these remarks are concerned not with the continuity through the eighteenth century of every Calvinist theological doctrine, but with the persistence of the essential features of Scottish Calvinist culture that were discussed in chap. 1, sec. I.

drove dissident ministers and their flocks to depart from the religious establishment and to found the various Secession churches which, when combined with certain legislative changes, had the effect of placing many altogether beyond the Church's direct control. This organizational development was of far-reaching consequence for Scottish ecclesiastical history. Yet it actually did little to undermine the orthodox sentiments of the vast majority of mid-eighteenth-century Scots. Rather than advocating any sort of Enlightenment, the seceders upheld "the *Westminster Confession* as their doctrinal standard, and the Presbyterian polity as their form of government" (Taylor 1887, p. 23), and consistently remained more committed to strict Calvinist teachings than the Church itself. Nor did the establishment, which still retained the bulk of the Scottish people, relinquish the old faith. The Church had, to be sure, become divided into an Evangelical party and a more progressive, Moderate party. Throughout virtually all of Scotland, however, the Moderates were the minority voice. The staunchly Calvinist Evangelical ministers were always, as Sloan remarks, "closer to the actual life and thinking of the majority of congregations" (1971, p. 11), and they maintained loyal followings even in the heart of the professional world of Edinburgh. If its discipline was less rigorous in certain areas than it had once been, "the church was still," Ferguson has justly concluded, "a powerful social agency": freethinking eighteenth-century intellectuals, as Hume discovered firsthand, continually had their scrapes with the vigilant church courts and "large-scale heresy hunts" were prevented only by the skillful maneuvering of the Moderates (1968, pp. 209, 226).[78] But elephantine mechanisms for the suppression of heterodoxy were never the sole bulwarks against extensive change. Even if the abstruse works of the enlighteners were widely available (which is by no means certain), their message resonated little with the common experiences of great numbers of contemporaries and could scarcely compete with the orthodox creed that most churches and schools preached week after

78. On the continuing strength of the Church, see also Henderson (1957, pp. 146–47), Rae (1895, pp. 124–25), Reid (1960, pp. 110, 112), and Ross (1972, pp. 152–65); on discipline, see Withrington (1970*b*, pp. 99–104). On the popularity and the orthodoxy of the Evangelicals, see Burleigh (1960, pp. 292, 294), Henderson (1957, p. 139), and Mathieson (1910, pp. 229–30); on the minority status of the Moderates, Clark (1964, p. 4, 1970, p. 213). On the strict Calvinism of the Secession churches, see Graham (1899, pp. 374–76), Henderson (1957, p. 149), and Smout (1969*a*, p. 218); on their rise, Donaldson (1960, pp. 95–97), and Ferguson (1968, pp. 121–27); and on the legislative changes that enhanced their effectiveness, see chap. 1, sec. II.

week, year after year. Such a state of affairs ensured that through the Age of the Enlightenment Scottish culture "was deeply infused with Calvinistic . . . values" (Lehmann 1971, p. 159).

Between this traditional Calvinism and the Enlightenment there was in mid-eighteenth-century Scotland a broad range of possibilities. Scholarship that has either taken the meaning of the Enlightenment for granted, defined it by means of certain descriptive themes, or seen it as anything that transcended the most rigid orthodoxy has tended to regard all persons who occupied this intermediate range as one with the Scottish Enlightenment. The fact that these individuals are known principally as members of intellectual communities in which the enlighteners were deeply involved has greatly fostered this tendency. But although they often went beyond passages in *The Westminster Confession* and shared some of the views of Hume, Smith, and the other enlightened intellectuals, it is extremely misleading, in terms of the conception of the Scottish Enlightenment used in this study, to merge these communities en masse into the Enlightenment itself.[79] Scotland in the early eighteenth century had witnessed departures from the standard creed which nonetheless remained well within the bounds of Calvinism's elemental suppositions, and the deviations of the middle decades of the century, though more frequent, were of a similar sort. They are important not because they are part of the Scottish Enlightenment, but because they provided the Enlightenment with the half-converted audience that encouraged so many of its endeavors. This curious bridge from the orthodox Calvinist multitude to the enlighteners was formed primarily by three groups.[80]

79. This does not preclude the possibility that future research may discover that particular *individuals* from these communities were as committed to independence and universalism as the men classified here as constituting the Scottish Enlightenment. Except insofar as their thought has meshed with the ideas of the groups to which they belonged, the "lesser" figures of the period of the Enlightenment have been, as noted earlier, largely ignored in previous studies (for an exception, see Schmitz 1948). The following discussion reflects this deficiency: it treats the central tendencies of the groups surrounding the Enlightenment, rather than the range of attitudes that existed among their members.

80. Membership in these groups was not mutually exclusive; certain individuals belonged to all of them. Emerson (1973*b*) and Phillipson (1973, 1974) have identified the Scottish Enlightenment with the first of the groups; Kettler (1965, p. 33), McNeill (1954, p. 358), and Sher (1979) with the second; and Bryson (1945) and Schneider (1967) with the third.

The improvers were the first of these. Scotland's improvers provide an apt illustration of the intellectual mobilization process that Reinhard Bendix has found in several other "developing" areas: the emergence of an "educated minority or intelligentsia [that] sees its own country as backward [and then attempts to] mobilize forces which will be capable of effecting change[s]" that will end the backward condition (1978, p. 271). Although this process had been underway in Scotland long before the Enlightenment, it assumed its most defined forms during the mid-eighteenth century. For it was then that Scotland's ruling groups particularly set out, with the aid of modern science and English as well as Continental models, to modernize their society and, in so doing, they soon imparted— though with rather ambiguous results—a "new spirit of enterprise" to agriculture and trade, to manufacturing and mining, to communications and civic works, to medicine, the sciences, and the arts, and even to matters of language, taste, and morals.[81] Voluntary organizations designed to encourage improvement in these various fields quickly emerged as dominant forces in the social and cultural life of the age and absorbed the leisure hours of many of its leading figures, including the enlighteners (see Emerson 1973*b;* McElroy 1969, pp. 39–70; Phillipson 1974). The writings of the intellectuals of the Enlightenment, in fact, often manifest concern both with improving conditions in Scotland and with the same economic, political, and social issues that the associations for improvement debated in their campaign to apply scientific methods to human affairs (Emerson 1973*b,* p. 295; Rendall 1978, p. 14). But neither this commonality of interests between the enlightened intellectuals and their fellow improvers nor the sundry signs of universalism that can be detected in the form and content of the proceedings of improving societies mean that on the whole the improvers followed the enlighteners away from Calvinism's basic premises (on the signs of universalism, see Bell 1960, pp. 109–12; McElroy 1969, pp. 39–70). The belief that humans and their world are absolutely dependent upon God was, as Weber taught, anything but incompatible with the "spirit of enterprise." Indeed the two merged in the lives of many devout Calvinists, and the Scottish improvers were

81. See Campbell (1965, pp. 24–34), Emerson (1973*a,* p. 322), Smout (1969*a,* pp. 271–81) and, for the quoted expression, Hamilton (1932, p. 36). On analogous earlier developments, see Marshall (1980*a,* pp. 426–36), McElroy (1969, pp. 1–7, 26–31), Phillipson (1974, pp. 414–40, 1976*b,* pp. 110–11, 1980, pp. 751–52), and Smout (1963, p. 279).

frequently men of this breed,[82] even as they were unwitting allies of the Scottish Enlightenment.

The Enlightenment found a second set of supporters in the Moderates, the group of ministers generally associated with the Moderate party of the Church of Scotland. While several of its characteristic attitudes can be discerned much earlier, this group first organized formally in the midst of an esoteric controversy over lay patronage rights in 1752.[83] From then until around 1780, the Moderates were actively engaged in bringing Calvinism up-to-date by breaking down "the rigidity of the old Calvinist categories" and adjusting them to the new intellectual developments of the age (Clark 1970, p. 205; see also Clark 1964, p. 241). In the process, they revised the traditional view of the effects of the fall, presented a more promising picture of human capabilities, sought in nature evidence for the veracity of revelation (see Clark 1964, p. 204) and, above all, developed an extensive commitment to universalism. The influential Moderate divinity professor at Glasgow, William Leechman, for example, asserted that "wherever there was any one found, even in the Heathen world, . . . earnestly panting after light and purity, that god never did deny his grace to such a person." The "assurances from the great father of all, that he will be found of those who seek him, . . . exclude no one of whatever nation or country" (1743, p. 146). Nor were those of other faiths excluded. As Clark observes, "Moderate clergy boldly argued that all creeds and confessions, even that of Westminster, must necessarily be partial and incomplete. The Reformation [itself] was the product of a particular historical situation, and Luther and Calvin were no more likely to be infallible than their Roman Catholic contemporaries" (1970, p. 205). These universalistic sentiments had a practical side as well. The Moderates maintained an attitude of tolerance toward doctrinal differences within the Church of Scotland, supported religious freedom for those outside the establishment so long as they kept the peace, advocated the repeal of harsh laws against Catholics, and strongly opposed both the institution of slavery and

82. This is best seen in Marshall's (1980a, 1980b) research, though this focuses primarily upon an earlier generation of improvers and needs to be replicated systematically for those of the mid-eighteenth century. Although it is not possible to undertake this replication here, the following remarks do provide some indirect evidence insofar as they show that Calvinist assumptions characterized the Moderates—for, again, Moderates and improvers were often the same people.

83. On antecedent developments, see Henderson (1957, pp. 75–93), Mathieson (1910, pp. 187–89), and chap. 1, note 28. Cf. Clark (1964, p. 211).

the lucrative African slave-trade.[84] On topics such as these, the views of Moderates were virtually indistinguishable from those of the enlighteners, and this remains the case even when the ideas of those who were both Moderates and enlighteners, Ferguson and Robertson, are set aside. No other intellectual community in the mid-eighteenth century came nearly so close to the outlook of the Scottish Enlightenment.

Between the majority of the Moderates and the intellectuals of the Enlightenment, however, there was a cultural chasm. Though narrower in some places than others, and especially slender between Ferguson and Robertson and the most avant-garde of the remaining Moderates, this chasm was nonetheless deep. Quite apart from endorsing the bulk of the Westminster Confession, the Moderates continually affirmed the Calvinist orientation of dependency and the theological postulates that accompanied it.[85] If not as pessimistic about human nature as their ancestors and their Evangelical contemporaries, these liberal ministers still held that "the newborn infant" begins life in "guilt and error," and thereafter continues in a state of "ignorance, weakness, guilt, and danger," the victim of "irregular appetites and passions."[86] Above this sorry creature, the Moderates constantly placed "that great being who alone can bestow eternal happiness" (Gerald 1761, p. 325). Time and again they recounted "all his glorious perfections: his power and wisdom, his holiness, his justice, his truth" (Scotland c. 1776, p. 72). This truth, they insisted against the Enlightenment, was not to be found in the "airy schemes of philosophy," those "false and artificial remedies" that plunge mankind "into an unfathomable abyss of misery and despair" (Sommerville c. 1776, p. 103; see also Leechman 1758, p. 224). The word of God, rather, was the key. For the Moderates, the Bible ever remained "the rule of faith and life"; the evidence from nature that they were so willing to use "as a prop for bolstering the content of Revelation" was never conceived "as a critical standard by which Revelation itself was to be judged" (Clark 1964, pp.

84. Clark (1964, pp. 9, 17, 22, 203, 1970, pp. 201, 208). For other evidence of the universalism of the Moderates and their associates, see Price (1967, pp. 375–76), Robbins (1959, pp. 209–14), and Thornton (1968, p. 421). For a nicely balanced picture of the Moderates' universalistic and particularistic ideas, see Sher (1979).

85. On the affinities of Moderatism and orthodoxy, see Blaikie (1888, pp. 218–19), Cameron (1967, pp. 1948–49), Clark (1964, pp. viii, 191–99, 296–97), and Henderson (1951, p. 52, 1957, p. 139).

86. Blacklock (c. 1776, p. 133), Leechman (1743, p. 143). See also Finlayson (1787, p. 144), Leechman (1758, p. 229), and Scotland (c. 1776, p. 76).

197, 245). The Moderates had no desire to conceal the traditional message that underlay these familiar themes. Blair forthrightly announced that humans live in a "dependent state" (cited by Cameron 1967, p. 1948), Sommerville declared that they are "nothing . . . before the immensity of the Deity" (c. 1776, p. 101), and Leechman proclaimed that "we are in a dependent and indigent, a dark and uncertain state of being [and] feel in ourselves many marks of our dependence, our indigence and ignorance. . . . We are utterly insufficient for our own happiness [and] depend entirely upon our maker for all we possess here, or hope to enjoy hereafter" (1743, p. 140). With friends like these, do we wonder that the Scottish enlighteners were not always at ease with their world?

The third intellectual community that flanked the Scottish Enlightenment was composed of moral philosophers. In the eighteenth century, moral philosophy was the field that is now shared by the social sciences and the humanities, the field that, as Stewart explains, "treat[ed] of human action in private or in civil conduct, of human expression or production in the arts, and of the standards by which such action or expression is evaluated" (1963, p. 10; see also Schneider 1967, p. xiv). When speaking of the Scottish moral philosophers, one is referring to those who wrote in this field, not— as in the case of the improvers and the Moderates—to a formally organized social group. Ferguson, Hume, and Smith were moral philosophers in this sense, and many of the themes characteristic of their writings were part of the moral-philosophical equipage of mid-eighteenth-century Scotland. Thomas Reid (1710–96), father of the influential school of Common-sense philosophy,[87] for example, continually maintained that humans are social beings who must be studied scientifically, and James Burnett (1714–99), later Lord Monboddo, ordinarily the comically eccentric outcast of the Scottish intelligentsia, offered detailed speculations on the stages

87. The Common-sense school generally refers to a number of philosophers— particularly James Beattie, George Campbell, James Oswald, Dugald Stewart, William Hamilton, and James Ferrier—around and following after Reid who stood apart from the Scottish Enlightenment (see Grave 1960; Segerstedt 1935). Their "defensive philosophy" (to borrow May's [1976b, p. 347] apt term) is significant for the great impact it had on Scottish and American universities well into the nineteenth century (see Ahlstrom 1955; Hook 1975, pp. 73–92; Howe 1970, pp. 27–40; May 1976b, pp. 346–48; Meyer 1972, pp. 35–42; Olson 1971; Phillipson 1976a; Sloan 1971). Grave (1960) provides the best discussion of the characteristics of Common-sense philosophy.

of societal development (see Bryson 1945, pp. 19, 95–100, 165; Cloyd 1972, pp. 70–72).[88]

But whatever they had in common, the Scottish enlighteners and their philosophical contemporaries lived in different worlds. For the secularism and skepticism that were integral to the Enlightenment's belief in human independence, Monboddo substituted a condemnation of those who minimized the active role of Providence in earthly affairs, an account of human development that moved forward with supernatural assistance from demon kings, and a deliberately credulous attitude toward all things that had not been certainly disproven, including stories of mermaids, dogheaded men, and humans with tails.[89] Reid's ponderous work did not give Scottish intellectuals half so much amusement. It did, however, provide something of far greater appeal, "a philosophy of faith," as Laurie (1902, p. 134) calls it—a philosophy built on principles of human nature that could not ultimately be explained or proved, but were instead inspired by God (Bryson 1945, p. 146; Norton 1975, pp. 715–16; Stephen 1876, 1:63). As fervently as *The Westminster Confession,* Reid held that "no power in the creature can be independent of the Creator. His hook is in its nose; he can give it line as far as he sees fit, and when he pleases, can restrain it, or turn it withersoever he will" (1788, p. 262). Man the poor fish: the moving expressed image so freely evoked by one of the most liberal, informed, and penetrating minds of the age—and after virtually all the Scot-

88. Bryson (1945) and Schneider (1967) discuss in detail additional points of convergence between the enlighteners and the other moral philosophers of mid-eighteenth-century Scotland. Reid and Monboddo are mentioned here and below only as examples from the latter community, which was actually relatively extensive (Bryson [1945, pp. 11, 80–81, 206] identifies certain of its other important members). The moral philosopher who has received the most attention and is most frequently described as one of the figures of the Scottish Enlightenment is Henry Home (1696–1782), after 1752 Lord Kames (see Lehmann 1971; McGuinness 1970; Ross 1972; Stocking 1975). The conception of the Scottish Enlightenment used in this study requires, however, that Kames be viewed as beyond (though just beyond) the circle of enlighteners. While the similarities between his social theory and that of the intellectuals of the Enlightenment are numerous and fundamental, Kames nonetheless firmly retained the traditional commitment to human dependency and—despite his various departures from orthodox Calvinism—affirmed several of the essential theological notions that went with it (see esp. Lehmann 1971, pp. 131–41, 270–83; see also Bryson 1945, pp. 65, 95; Mossner 1954, p. 295; Schneider 1967, p. lxxi; Stocking 1975, pp. 70–71; Whitney 1934, pp. 277–81).

89. See Cloyd (1972, pp. 47, 62, 112–13, 144, 168, 173–74), Laurie (1902, pp. 197–98), Schneider (1967, p. lxxv), and Stephen (1876, 1:69).

tish enlighteners' works had appeared—underscores how little the spirit of the Enlightenment infected the Scotland of its day. The mystery is that it emerged at all.

3

Explaining the Scottish Enlightenment

Since Carlo Deanina's 1763 *Essay on the Progress of Learning among the Scots,* numerous studies have sought to account for the great transformation of eighteenth-century Scottish culture. A satisfactory explanation of the change is, however, still nowhere to be found. To demonstrate why this is the case, the first section of this chapter reviews the main social- and intellectual-historical explanations that have previously been offered for the Scottish Enlightenment; it then identifies the major limitations of those explanations and, by implication, of various explanations in the sociology of knowledge that take the same basic form when accounting for other instances of intellectual and cultural change. The second section proposes a rather different way of understanding fundamental transformations of cultural principles and beliefs, one designed not to supplant existing historical and sociological perspectives on the process but to overcome their central failings. How this general approach can actually be applied to the development of independence and universalism during the Scottish Enlightenment is then described as the prologue to the argument of the following four chapters.

I

There have been almost as many interpretations of the emergence of the Scottish Enlightenment as there have been interpreters. The multitude of conceptualizations of the Enlightenment and the plethora of features in its world that can be adduced as its cause have together generated explanations by the score. For all their diversity, however, these explanations exhibit a remarkably similar structure. In a manner that is formally identical with that utilized by the sociology of knowledge in the context of many other substantive problems, they account for the Scottish Enlightenment principally by citing important earlier changes in Scottish society or in European intellectual life. To illustrate the characteristics of this approach, it is sufficient here to examine the social and intellectual changes that, even as the meaning of "Enlightenment" has varied, have been most frequently identified as sources of the Scottish Enlightenment. The definition of the latter employed in this study only highlights the general problems that arise whenever these sorts of changes become the primary means for explaining cultural transformations (see Camic 1983a, pp. 155–64).[1]

Social-historical research has most commonly accounted for the development of the Scottish Enlightenment by referring to conspicuous features of eighteenth-century Scottish society, particularly to alterations in political and economic conditions. For modern historians the most dramatic political change was the official ending of the political independence of the Scottish nation. From at least the early seventeenth century onward, Scotland had been moving politically closer to England, and finally in 1707 the Scottish Parliament passed the Treaty of Union, the act that terminated the separate Scottish Parliament and incorporated it into the English Parliament at Westminster. Thereafter, although Scotland retained many of its own institutions, Scottish political life became more and more contingent upon the nature of English politics. Such was the political situation during the decades of the Enlightenment, and it has prompted many historians to contend that the Union was the "impetus" behind the Scottish Enlightenment.[2]

1. This point should be emphasized. The problems to be discussed have not surfaced only because this study uses a novel definition of the Scottish Enlightenment and thus confronts earlier accounts of the Scottish Enlightenment with something they never sought to explain. The general structure of previous explanations, as the text suggests, has *not* varied as definitions of the Scottish Enlightenment have varied and might easily be adapted to fit with the current conception of the Scottish Enlightenment (on this specious constancy, see Camic 1983a, pp. 166–67, note 9). There are, indeed, treatments of the European Enlightenment that have explained the Enlightenment in a manner very similar to that found in the research on the Scottish Enlightenment, even though they have defined "Enlightenment" as this study has (see esp. Gay 1966, 1969). For this reason, the discussion that follows in the text, although it simplifies the positions of particular scholars, does little injustice to the literature on the Enlightenment as a whole when it describes previous explanations of the Scottish Enlightenment without pausing to indicate that the development being explained is different from one scholar to another and is nowhere the emergence of independence and universalism (for a more faithful treatment of the diversity in previous scholarship, see Camic 1983a, pp. 146–53).

2. The quoted term is taken from Cain (1963, p. iii). On the incorporation of Scottish into English politics, see Ferguson (1968, pp. 113–65), Mathieson (1910,

The contention has several forms. Often it begins by suggesting that the Union produced a "crisis of Scottish identity": that the loss of political autonomy destroyed Scotland's previous self-image and left it "disorganized and disoriented," experiencing a "sense of inferiority" and "sense of guilt" over its own relatively backward ways, as well as a desire "to bury [its own] identity" and a "drive to emulate [the advanced example of] England"—all mixed with a "compensatory local pride" and the wish to assert "the value of the native [Scottish] inheritance."[3] This quandry, the argument continues, was the basis of the Scottish Enlightenment. As Phillipson maintains in a recent version of the thesis, by teaching "that in all societies man is determined by an external world operating according to discoverable secular mechanisms [the Scottish enlighteners created a] collective will to understand [that] was a substitute for the political action from which an earlier generation had derived its identity" (1974, pp. 447–48).[4]

The Scottish Enlightenment has also been seen as a product of the growth of political stability that the Union fostered. For much of Scottish history, civil disorder had been a chronic problem. As late as the closing decades of the seventeenth century, Highland clans plundered Lowland areas which retained their own traditions of violence. The Union, however, transferred the ultimate responsibility for the maintenance of law and order in Scotland to the more powerful and exacting English government. Although this step did not bring immediate results—Highland risings and urban riots continued long after the Union—it eventually combined with other policies and practices to make the eighteenth century an era

pp. 21–22), Riley (1964), Simpson (1970, p. 58), Smout (1969a, pp. 201–2), and chap. 7, sec. I. On the making of the Union, see Donaldson (1965, pp. 356–57), Riley (1964, pp. 1–23, 1978), and Smout (1969b).

3. The quotations are drawn, respectively, from Morrell (1971b, p. 159), Phillipson (1974, p. 410), Clive and Bailyn (1954, p. 211), Trevor-Roper (1967, p. 1635), Rendall (1978, p. 14), Clive (1970, p. 239), and Davie (1967, p. 25).

4. See also Phillipson (1973, 1980, 1981). Other variants of the Union–identity–crisis theory of the Scottish Enlightenment have been proposed by Clive and Bailyn (1954, pp. 207–13), Davie (1967), and Rendall (1978, pp. 12–14). Clive (1970) and Trevor-Roper (1967) also affirm something of this theory, although their more general claim is that Scottish Enlightenment was rooted in the social and cultural developments of the late seventeenth century. This claim will not be considered here, for, while the developments it identifies do differ from those described in most accounts of the Scottish Enlightenment, its logic of explanation is essentially the same (for a discussion of the substance of the claim, see chap. 1, note 19).

of unparalleled political stability.[5] In this way, historians hold, the Union provided a "background for the cultural achievement" of the Scottish Enlightenment, and "created conditions which . . . made [its] inquiries possible" (Rendall 1978, p. 7; Ferguson 1968, p. 210; see also Pryde 1962, p. 104).

Another popular explanation of the Scottish Enlightenment centers on the nature of the Scottish economy. Until the take-off of the agricultural and industrial revolutions in the 1780s and 1790s, capitalism—as a mode of production—was a very minor element in the overall economic life of the nation.[6] Wage laborers and factories did increase somewhat in numbers as the eighteenth century progressed, but their significance was long dwarfed by persisting feudal arrangements. Prior to the final years of the century, the enclosure movement advanced extremely slowly and the majority of the population was composed of peasants holding plots on farms leased from paternalistic landowners who extracted the rents and remained the economic and political leaders of the society. For most of the period, the "typical industrial unit," as Smout explains, "was still a single master working with an apprentice and a journeyman within the framework of craft regulations" (1969a, p. 229; cf. Marshall 1980b, pp. 134–39, 284–319). Even in the production of linen textiles, the premier industry before the Industrial Revolution, the age-old domestic system was only gradually giving way (see Hamilton 1932, pp. 76–103). But for all this underlying constancy, the eighteenth century brought heightened economic activity in numerous areas that had been carved out in the seventeenth century. The improvers vigorously pursued their campaign to modernize agriculture and manufacturing, and commercial development— "capitalism" in the lay sense[7]—dramatically accelerated. Trade had

5. On these developments, see Ferguson (1968, pp. 141–45), Hechter (1975, pp. 112–45), Phillipson and Mitchison (1970, pp. 1–2), Pryde (1960, pp. 9–10), Plumb (1967, pp. 179–82), Riley (1964, p. 289), and Smout (1969a, pp. 205–12, 321, 344–45).

6. Campbell (1964, 1965, pp. 18–75, 1967, 1974), Donaldson (1965, pp. 385–92), Ferguson (1968, pp. 70–101, 166–97), Flinn et al. (1977, p. 10), Hamilton (1932, 1959, 1963), Mitchison (1978, p. 41), Smout (1963, 1969a, pp. 111–70, 223–420, 1980), and Wallerstein (1980b) are the principal sources of the information presented in this paragraph. On the criteria that have been used for determining that capitalism was not the dominant form of economic organization in eighteenth-century Scotland, see Anderson (1974, pp. 15–42), Dobb (1963, pp. 1–254), and Marx (1867, pp. 336–480, 713–64, 1894, pp. 325–37). For a different assessment, see Foster (1973).

7. On the fundamental distinction between commercial activity and capitalism as a mode of production, see Dobb (1963, pp. 6–18) and Marx (1894, pp. 325–37).

been on a steep decline when the century began and, despite predictions to the contrary, the situation improved little in the decades immediately following the Union. From the 1740s onward, however, better access to English and colonial markets and related changes stimulated a substantial growth in the linen, cattle, and particularly the entrepot tobacco trade, and this trade in turn made way for the later and more radical transformation of the Scottish economy. Many scholars have recorded the bearing of such developments on the Scottish Enlightenment. Mizuta has suggested that "the Scottish Enlightenment was a product of the fast development of Scottish society . . . to the capitalist stage" (1976, p. 1461); Emerson has remarked that "a flourishing economy had something to do with" the Scottish Enlightenment (1973a, p. 104); Taylor has observed that "rapid change and increasing prosperity [form the] background [for understanding how] the Scottish Enlightenment occurred" (1965, p. 5); and Kettler, giving the argument a novel twist, has maintained that economic change wrought ambiguous effects which were a "source of perplexity" and a "stimulus" behind the Enlightenment's bold efforts to discover "the unifying and benevolent *logos* underlying the contradictory appearances" (1965, p. 39; see also Chitnis 1976, p. 91; Meek 1976b, p. 128; Therborn 1976, pp. 82, 157, 213–14).

These economic and political accounts of the development of the Scottish Enlightenment need not exclude one another. The most common social-historical strategy, in fact, has been to serve the Scottish Enlightenment up from a kettle containing both economic and political changes and various combinations of the numerous other factors—the distinctive social structure of the Scottish Highlands, the dynamic conditions in Edinburgh and Glasgow, the nature of urban social clubs, the altered role of the Church of Scotland, the availability of primary education, the intellectual awakening of the universities, the organization of the legal system and related social institutions, and the powerlessness of the intelligentsia—that have likewise been used to explain the cultural transformation of eighteenth-century Scotland.[8] Thus Robbins has stated that the Scottish Enlightenment "was hastened and immediately conditioned by the state of Scottish society in the largest sense" (1959, p. 177); Lehmann has claimed that the writings of the Enlightenment "can be seen to bear the marks, so far as they are not in fact a direct outgrowth of, practical problems of a judicial, political,

8. For a review of these additional explanations, see Camic (1983a, pp. 149–53).

economic, and social character emerging in the life of the nation in the period between the Union of the Parliaments in 1707 and the French Revolution of 1789" (1960, p. 96); and Swingewood has urged that "from within the Scottish environment, economic, political, religious, educational and social factors combined to produce the [Scottish Enlightenment which] reflects these changes and was indeed conditioned by them" (1969, p. 64).[9]

This social-historical approach to the Scottish Enlightenment has frequently been supplemented with intellectual-historical explanations which substitute the Union, the economy, and the rest with the ideas of figures whose writings preceded those of the intellectuals of the Scottish Enlightenment. The options here are plentiful for Ferguson, Hume, Millar, Robertson, and Smith were ravenous readers not only of one another's works and those of enlighteners outside of Scotland, but also of the classics of Western culture back to the "first Enlightenment" of the ancients. It is possible to ransack this enormous legacy and show that the themes, methods, and elemental attitudes of the Scottish enlighteners all had older roots, but ordinarily intellectual-historical accounts concentrate on the major thinkers in the period prior to the Scottish Enlightenment and suggest that these provided the basic materials with which the enlightened intellectuals forged their revolution, the foundation on which their great next step rested.[10] The Scottish Enlightenment's debt to Newton, Locke, and Montesquieu has particularly been emphasized in this context (see also chap. 2, note 12). The enlighteners regarded Newton's formulation of the laws of nature as "the greatest discovery that ever was made by man" (Smith *EPS*, p. 189) and time and again proposed to extend the scientific—analytical, inductive, observational, empirical, experimental—

9. See also Chitnis (1976), Emerson (1973*a*, pp. 103–4), Pryde (1962, p. 104), Rendall (1978, pp. 1–25), Smout (1969*a*, pp. 470–83), and Stewart (1963, pp. 1–7).

10. This, at least, is what the more reasonable versions of the intellectual-historical approach suggest. There are less penetrating variants that do not even begin to explain the Scottish Enlightenment, for they deny that the enlighteners represented any substantial break with previous intellectual tendencies and assert instead that they were simply perpetuating—with certain minor exceptions that are invariably lost in the telling—the achievement of a renowned foreign thinker whose work had reached Scotland (usually Newton or Locke), or of an innovative native (Stair, Simson, or particularly Hutcheson; for examples of this practice, see Camic 1979*a*, pp. 157–60). It should be clear at this point that the task of accounting for the Scottish Enlightenment cannot be so easily whisked away: the figures such explanations have adduced as progenitors of the Scottish Enlightenment did not in fact share its most fundamental beliefs (see chap. 1, sec. III).

methodology behind that achievement to their own field, the study of humans in society. For this reason, Newton has been widely seen as one of the "central intellectual influence[s] on the Scottish Enlightenment" (Chitnis 1976, p. 215). The impact of Locke was of a similar sort. The first to bring Newtonianism to the analysis of human beings, he developed an empirical psychology and epistemology that were at once scientific and practical, and in these matters the intellectuals of the Scottish Enlightenment were ever, as Bryson remarks, his loyal "followers" (1945, p. 146).[11] Historians have found that the comparative "political sociology" of Montesquieu's *Spirit of the Laws* had an even more "instantaneous effect" on the writings of the enlighteners (Trevor-Roper 1967, p. 1655). Skinner has suggested that "undoubtedly [their] chief source of inspiration was Montesquieu" (1967, p. 38), and Chitnis has maintained that "Montesquieu . . . was a most important influence in the generation . . . of the Scottish Enlightenment" (1976, p. 95).

There are many things wrong with previous explanations of the Scottish Enlightenment. They tend to overdraw the changes that were taking place in eighteenth-century Scottish society, to minimize the discrepancies between the work of the enlighteners and those who preceded them, to exaggerate the degree to which contemporaries were affected by developments that retrospectively seem so obviously consequential, and to ignore the vast time intervals that separated the Scottish Enlightenment from many of its alleged sources (see Camic 1983*a*, pp. 155–58, and note 16 below). These technical (and presumably correctable) difficulties fade, however, beside a far more fundamental problem. By themselves, the phenomena adduced in social- and intellectual-historical accounts are far too general and undifferentiated to explain a cultural transformation as circumscribed as the Scottish Enlightenment.[12] The combination of independence and universalism that defines the Scottish Enlightenment—or, for that matter, the Scottish Enlightenment as described in other formulations—was anything

11. See also Chitnis (1976, pp. 159–60), Gay (1969, pp. 176–80), Rendall (1978, pp. 21–22), and Smith (1941, pp. 62–68) on the impact of Locke; and on that of Newton, Bryson (1945), Campbell (1971), Gay (1969, pp. 128–40), Laurie (1902, pp. 4–5), Rendall (1978, pp. 19–21), Reisman (1976), Smith (1941, pp. 53–62), and Stewart (1963, pp. 11–12).

12. Note Karl Mannheim's objections to the practice of imposing an "artificial homogeneity" on the culture of a period, rather than undertaking its "proper differentiation" (1927, p. 76); see also Simonds (1978, p. 84).

but ubiquitous in mid-eighteenth-century Scotland. A nose count at any point in the Age of the Enlightenment would have given the victory, hands down, to traditional Calvinism, and its basic assumptions pervaded even the advanced circles of improvers, Moderates, and moral philosophers. But if the Enlightenment was a most limited change, the political, economic, and sundry other developments that have been taken as its causes were, both singly and jointly, extremely widespread. The Union and the economy were features in the environment of the entire Scottish people, and even factors relatively confined to the "middle class" of the enlightened intellectuals (certain educational institutions, urban clubs, and the like) were more or less common to all those with the same social location (on the Scottish "middle class," see Smout 1969a, pp. 338–65). The ideas of Newton, Locke, and Montesquieu were known no less widely. Newton and Locke, in fact, were already in vogue in the early eighteenth century, although then none of their talented admirers—not the Carmichaels, nor the Baxters, nor the Turnbulls—took the implied step into the Enlightenment. Montesquieu was immensely popular in mid-eighteenth-century Scotland, but this too did little to swell the enlightened population.[13] To understand a development as exceptional as the Scottish Enlightenment, something more is required than the social and intellectual conditions that thousands, and sometimes hundreds of thousands, of orthodox eighteenth-century Scots encountered quite as much as the enlighteners did.

A few existing studies have, to be sure, attempted to provide this something more.[14] They have abandoned the typical macroscopic approach to the whole Scottish Enlightenment for a microscopic investigation of social or intellectual factors that constitute the context for understanding specific elements in the writings of individual enlighteners. Charles Fay's (1956) research on Adam Smith provides the best illustration of the social-historical variant of this alternative. Rather than treating all of Smith's work, Fay concentrates on *The Wealth of Nations,* selects from it a number of concrete issues that Smith discussed, and then demonstrates how these issues were part of Smith's social world. Thus, when *The Wealth of Nations* mentions tobacco, Fay describes the details of the Glasgow tobacco

13. On Montesquieu's popularity in Scotland, see Brumfitt (1967, pp. 326–29), and Trevor-Roper (1967, p. 1655 and his note 30).

14. Or so they may be interpreted, although actually these studies were not developed to correct, nor do they claim to correct, the problem that has just been discussed.

trade that Smith witnessed firsthand and sets these next to the passages where Smith spoke of tobacco; when the book refers to nail-making, Fay observes that there were naileries in Pathhead, near Smith's native town of Kirkcaldy, and suggests that "we can say with confidence that he wrote with Pathhead in mind"; and when the work carefully considers the Navigation Act, Fay notices that Kirkcaldy was a seaport and remarks that a "man brought up on the sea front and watching day after day, as he wrote, the stream of shipping . . . would not lightly condemn the Act of Navigation" (1956, pp. 59–62, 43, 48). Although Glasgow's tobacco trade, Pathhead's naileries, and Kirkcaldy's sea front were seen by others beside Smith, by placing him at the center of a whole sequence of microlevel encounters, Fay successfully establishes a social environment that was virtually Smith's alone.[15]

A much more sophisticated, intellectual-historical version of this analysis has been developed by Duncan Forbes (1975a) in an examination of David Hume's politics. Instead of trying to explain Hume's position on all kinds of political matters by referring to the general ideas of the handful of earlier intellectual giants known to every college lad, Forbes investigates at great length hosts of writers, great and small, who had previously treated the multitude of specific topics that Hume addressed—the English journalists and pamphleteers who debated the monarchical and republican tendencies of the British government; the historians like Rapin, Bolingbroke, Lyttleton, Blackstone, Guthrie, and Hurd who explored the reigns of Elizabeth and the first Stuarts; and so on. Forbes regards these authors not as so many intellectual influences beyond which Hume took the next step, but as establishing the broader contexts of problems and assumptions in which to locate Hume's various political writings. By doing this, Forbes uncovers the intricate ways that those writings sometimes endorsed, sometimes modified, sometimes rejected, and sometimes deliberately ignored the claims of other political analysts, and, in the process, skillfully identifies "the uniquely and distinctively Humian thing in Hume's politics" (1975a, p. 136).[16]

15. This formulation, it will be noted, reads somewhat more into Fay's analysis than Fay explicitly states.

16. As will be clear to those familiar with current work on the methodology of intellectual history, Forbes's analysis is an expert application of the general approach to "classic" texts that has been advocated by Quentin Skinner (1966, 1969, 1972, 1974) and imported into sociology by Jones (1977) and Simonds (1978; for another application to the Scottish Enlightenment, see Winch 1978). For reasons illustrated by Forbes's research, this approach has rightly been critical of the notion of "intellectual influence." The concept covers over the different reactions that past thinkers

None of this, unfortunately, explains the Scottish Enlightenment. Inquiries of this sort provide historically appropriate interpretations of the work of various enlighteners and dispense with the objectionable practice of using overly global factors as the primary source of the Scottish Enlightenment. They do not, however, offer—nor do they claim to offer—an alternative explanation of even the narrow features of the Scottish Enlightenment with which they are concerned. Fay shows that Smith drew from his encounters with naileries and tobacco to illustrate his argument, but does not pretend that naileries and tobacco generated Smith's economics, let alone any of the more basic attributes of his writings. Those things constitute the givens. Similarly, Forbes places Hume against the background of the pamphleteers and historians of his age, but does so to indicate how Hume's protean reactions to their positions (accepting them, revising them, repudiating them, neglecting them) illuminate the distinguishing characteristics of his politics, not to suggest that these characteristics were produced by the work of the pamphleteers and historians. This, however, leaves the larger puzzle unsolved. Presumably, Hume's varying responses to all the specific arguments of his contemporaries and predecessors were not random. In fact, Forbes reveals the pattern underlying these responses when he demonstrates that Hume's political writings, unlike those of so many others, were consistently secular and nonpartisan. But on how these decisive qualities—or the independence and universalism of which they were part and parcel—developed, on the way that Hume acquired the novel attitudes that he displayed when reacting to political writers and constructing his own political (and nonpolitical) views, the microscopic approach to the Scottish Enlightenment is silent.

The macroscopic perspective is really no better, though it more effectively camouflages this silence. Naileries, tobacco, and long-

---

had to the writings of others, when the nature of those reactions, rather than the mere presence of the writings, is the factor relevant for understanding such thinkers and what set them apart from contemporaries who encountered the same influences. This argument pertains as well when the writings at issue are those of Newton, Locke, and Montesquieu as when they are those of little known journalists and historians. Recent scholarship has identified major areas where the Scottish enlighteners responded to their renowned predecessors in ways far less uniform—and less uniformly positive— than the typical assertion of influence implies (on Newton, see Forbes 1975a, pp. 3–18, 1977, p. 44; Grave 1960, p. 7; Lindgren 1973, pp. 1–19; Skinner 1974, pp. 181–82; Wightman 1975, pp. 59–64; on Montesquieu, see Camic 1983a, p. 158; Kettler 1965, pp. 7, 306, 1977, p. 452; Meek 1976b, p. 35; Rendall 1978, p. 124; Swingewood 1970b, p. 167).

forgotten political commentators are such humble little factors that they have never been offered up as explanations of the Scottish Enlightenment. Because the Union, the Scottish economy, Newton, Locke, and Montesquieu seem so much less prosaic, stronger—or at least more strongly intended—claims have been freely made on their behalf. It has been asserted that the Scottish Enlightenment was the "product," "direct outgrowth," and "reflection" of one or more of these weighty developments, and that these developments "influenced," "inspired," "stimulated," "hastened," "created conditions for," "provided the background for," and "had something to do with" the Scottish Enlightenment. Although the blunt early elements in this motley series of expressions may seem preferable to its increasingly vague, later components, analyses that have contained any of these terms have no more adequately explained the way in which the principal features of the Scottish Enlightenment developed out of the social and intellectual conditions of the eighteenth century than modest microlevel researches. Indeed, the most serious flaw in the traditional historical account of the Scottish Enlightenment is its studied neglect of the means by which all the alleged producing, reflecting, influencing, inspiring, stimulating, and hastening took place, its persistent failure to identify the processes or mechanisms by which various social or intellectual factors translated into the characteristic contents of the writings of the enlighteners, above all into that change in cultural orientations that defines the Scottish Enlightenment. The Union, the economy, Newtonian physics, Lockeian psychology, and the rest no more converted themselves into the attitudes of independence and universalism than did naileries, tobacco, and the controversies of obscure pamphleteers: in every case there is the same need to specify what intervened in the lives of the enlighteners to turn the baser metals to gold.[17] As C. Wright Mills argued nearly a half-century

17. It should be emphasized that this need is by no means reduced by pointing out that there were certain writings, notably the classics of antiquity and the work of Montesquieu, available in Scotland prior to the Enlightenment from which its fundamental themes *can* be extracted (on the Enlightenment of the ancients and of Montesquieu, see Gay 1966, 1969). Given on the one hand that the majority of the Scots who encountered these writings either never noticed such themes or retained their traditional attitudes in the face of them, and on the other hand that, as chapter 2 demonstrated, the intellectuals of the Enlightenment rejected religious beliefs that were far more frequently proclaimed and powerfully reinforced, the primary issue is not that the writings in question shaped the Scottish Enlightenment, but the reasons that the enlighteners reacted in so distinctive and favorable a way to the relevant portions of those writings. As Meek has remarked in a similar context,

ago, when we posit that social and intellectual changes "influence trends in intellectual work and belief we must ask *how* such influences are exerted." "That," he continued, "is a question to be answered by a social psychology" (1939, pp. 424–25; see also Merton 1945, p. 12, 32), something that all previous explanations of the Scottish Enlightenment have sadly lacked.

The apparent exceptions here have actually offered outlandish collective psychologizing rather than a credible social psychology. They have described how social conditions gave rise to the Scottish Enlightenment by summoning forth Scotland's identity crisis, its disorientation, its feelings of inferiority and guilt, its pride and envy, and its sense of perplexity. Can more elusive straws be imagined? Psychohistorians have shown the difficulties in establishing the presence of such psychological states and in employing them to explain even the autobiographical remarks of individuals for whom ample psychological information exists, and these difficulties are compounded a thousand times over when one moves to more momentous problems and to the psychological complexes of an entire nation. All of this, however, has been blithely ignored, as sufferings of the eighteenth-century Scottish psyche for which there is only the slimmest evidence have been used to account for the cultural transformation of mid-eighteenth-century Scotland. A convincing explanation of the Scottish Enlightenment requires a different procedure.

What seems to be necessary is an approach that focuses upon factors neither as pervasive as the Union nor as idiosyncratic as naileries and then examines, without lapsing into a specious mass psychology, the process by which those factors were related to the development of independence and universalism in eighteenth-century Scotland. An approach of this sort would complement existing accounts of the Scottish Enlightenment. The economic, political, and intellectual conditions identified in previous explanations, as well as such ubiquitous forces as the system of stratification, the church, and the Calvinist heritage, would still be required to someday tell the full story. These macrofactors may be insufficient to explain the Scottish Enlightenment, but without them much about that cultural change is hardly conceivable. It is difficult to imagine

---

if the enlightened intellectuals "were struck by these particular passages in the earlier literature they must have had a *predisposition* to be struck by them—a predisposition whose origin must up to a point be sought for outside the literature itself" (1976*b*, p. 35).

that such sustained and daring intellectual activity would have flourished had Scotland remained what it had been in an earlier age, a desparately poor and chaotic land, closely watched by a dour church with the power to put the heretical to death; that middle-class intellectuals in a precapitalist social formation could have advanced our more radical ideas of independence, universalism, and social reform; that the Enlightenment's commitment to independence, universalism, and social reform would have been as substantial as it was if Calvinism had not previously promoted some degree of libertarianism, eroded certain barriers within the human community, and promulgated the value of instrumental activism;[18] that the intellectuals of the Scottish Enlightenment could have seen the workings of the world in such a thoroughly secular fashion had Newton, for all his paeans to Providence, not discovered laws of nature that could later be severed from their Source; that the enlighteners could have wrought their revision of the Calvinist conception of human nature without guidance from the writings of the likes of Locke and Hutcheson; that the historiography of the Enlightenment would have assumed its characteristic shape except in reaction to the practices of earlier historians. Of course not every difficulty is an impossibility, and speculating about historical preconditions for changes like the Scottish Enlightenment can swiftly deteriorate into a meaningless exercise that mistakes untested and untestable hunches for a systematic explanation, a tedious listing that heaps one allegedly necessary antecedent upon another and, as Jones has lamented, leaves the "relative explanatory weight" of each wholly unspecified (1977, p. 294; see also Camic 1983a). Here there is no need to perpetuate this mechanical procedure. With the exceptions noted in the next section, it will suffice to treat the social- and intellectual-historical elements that this inquiry now by and large sets aside in a way similar to that used by the Marxist scholars who argue that "economic structures set limits on the possible forms of political and ideological structures, and make some of those possible forms more likely than others, but . . . within those limits . . . a fairly wide variety of . . . forms [can nonetheless] occur" (Wright 1978, p. 16). One can, in other words, regard the economic, political, religious, and intellectual developments as establishing the boundaries for the cultural life of mid-eighteenth-century Scot-

18. It is likely that considerations such as these prompted Weber's otherwise misleading claim (mentioned in the Introduction) that the Enlightenment was the "laughing heir" of Calvinism.

land.[19] They made numerous beliefs and values (including a few of our most cherished beliefs and values) inconceivable and made some (the passion for improvement, for example) far more probable than others. It should now be clear, however, that within these limits extremely diverse cultural orientations were expressed. The remainder of this study concerns the experiences that occurred within the wide boundaries of the time to foster the emergence of the distinctive orientations of the Scottish Enlightenment.

II

Were they seeking to explain the basic attitudes of members of their own society, most social scientists would before long inquire into the ways in which those persons had been socialized. Except for the very special case of psychohistorians, those attempting to account for historical transformations in beliefs and values have not shared this concern with socialization. At one level, this is not very surprising. Since socialization is usually regarded as the transmission to a new generation of the teachings of earlier generations, it appears of little relevance for understanding cultural change and how one generation comes to express orientations vastly different from those that it has inherited. Examining the socialization process seems to be a particularly curious means of constructing a fuller explanation for the Scottish Enlightenment. By their parents, teachers, and other significant others, Ferguson, Hume, Millar, Robertson, and Smith were taught the orthodox Calvinism that held sway in early eighteenth-century Scotland. The parents of the future intellectuals of the Enlightenment were, without exception, devout members of the Church of Scotland. The fathers of Ferguson, Millar, and Robertson were ministers themselves, continuously involved in spreading the church's doctrines; Hume and Smith,

19. This imagery is not intended to repudiate an "agency-structure duality" (see Giddens 1979, pp. 49–95) or to deny that eighteenth-century Scottish culture was itself consequential for the developments just enumerated. The remarks below on the role of macrofactors in structuring opportunities for the generalization of situationally acquired orientations and in shaping the experiences that go on in micro-level settings should be read as suggesting two little-known mechanisms by which these developments concretely set the limits for the cultural life of the period. In conjunction with the current observations in the text, those remarks should make it even clearer that this study regards macro- and microapproaches as counterparts rather than as contrarieties.

though fatherless, both had deeply religious mothers.[20] Other kin were of a similar breed. Outside of family circles, in the wider communities in which they were raised, the young enlighteners (and those around them) daily encountered the church's many devices for propagating the Calvinist's message and suppressing heterodoxy. At least four of the five lads also attended schools where lessons in Calvinism were a mainstay of the curriculum, and even Hume, whose early education probably took place exclusively at home, became "thoroughly indoctrinated with the Calvinist creed" (Smith 1948, p. 4; see also Letwin 1965, pp. 18–28; Mossner 1954, p. 34). Integral to this creed, of course, were the themes of dependency and particularism. But given that the concern here is with the development of independence and universalism, an analysis of the socialization process in which the enlighteners were enmeshed would seem like a most unpromising way of explaining the Scottish Enlightenment.[21]

The teachings that one generation passes on to the next are not, however, the whole of socialization. Social-psychological studies by Breer and Locke (1965) and Dreeben (1968), currently little known beyond the sociology of education, have shown that individuals can learn not only from what they are expressly taught, but also from their experiences, from the activities that they engage in and observe around them—in short, from what they and others actually

20. On the orthodoxy of Ferguson's home, see Anon. (1867, pp. 50–58), Fagg (1968, p. 9), Kettler (1965, p. 43), Small (1864, p. 600); on Hume's, Mossner (1954, p. 33); on Millar's, Lehmann (1960, p. 11); on Robertson's, Bower (1817–30, 3:24), Brougham (1845, pp. 256–58); on Smith's, Scott (1937, p. 20).

To avoid unduly cluttering the text, from this point onward specific citations to the sources from which the biographical information reported derives, whether directly or inferentially, will not ordinarily be given. Therefore, these sources should now be acknowledged: for Ferguson, Anon. (1867), Fagg (1968), Kettler (1965), Small (1864); for Hume, chiefly Mossner (1954; the 1980 edition of this source was not available at the time of this writing), and also Burton (1846), Hume (*Essays,* pp. 607–16), Greig (1931), Knight (1886); for Millar, principally Lehmann (1960), and also Craig (1801, 1806); for Robertson, Bower (1817–30), Brougham (1845), Carlyle (1910, 1973), Gleig (1819), Lynam (1824), Robinson (1949), Stewart (1818), Stewart (1796); for Smith, primarily Rae (1895), and also Fay (1956), Mossner (1969), Scott (1937), Stewart (1793), Viner (1968).

21. Unless, of course, it could be shown that the intellectuals of the Enlightenment were socialized in such a way that they later rebelled against parents and significant others, thus negatively reacting to what they had been taught and, in the process, rejecting dependency and particularism for independence and universalism. While an explanation of this sort could be compelling in many circumstances, almost everything that is known about the relationships of the enlighteners (in childhood, adolescence, and adulthood) with those who raised them belies the rebellion thesis.

do in the situations in which they find themselves. As Breer and Locke put it, social experiences are among "the raw materials out of which men construct their fundamental ideas" (1965, p. 6): by induction from the patterns of behavior going on about them, individuals can acquire basic cognitive and evaluative orientations. It has been found, for example, that those who participate in activities involving cooperation will infer or draw out[22] a principle of cooperation, even when there are no verbal references to it (see Breer and Locke 1965, esp. pp. 138–61). The last clause is extremely important. The kinds of experiences individuals receive vary with the nature of the particular microlevel setting (the workplace, schoolroom, and so on) where they are situated. The nature of such a setting is determined by a variety of interconnected factors—the setting's manifest and latent functions (making widgets, teaching Latin, reproducing class relations); its relationship to (including its degree of relative autonomy from) the many elements in its social and cultural environment; its internal structure (its size, scope, roles, concrete tasks, technical procedures for accomplishing tasks, etc.); the demographic, sociological, and psychological characteristics of its members; and the like.[23] Often these variables result in experiences through which humans derive principles congruent with the beliefs and values explicitly propagated in the setting in question. In a complex social world, however, there is no warrant for assuming this sort of integration. Empirically, it is quite possible for the factors just enumerated to generate experiences from which individuals can arrive by induction at orientations that no one has avowed, intended to teach them, or realized that they may someday advocate.

These considerations have far-reaching implications for cultural change. Experiences from which individuals can infer orientations that differ from preestablished attitudes and assumptions are rich seedbeds of new cultural orientations. Before cultural change emerges out of such experiences, however, three conditions must be met. First, at least some of the individuals who encounter the experiences must have the cognitive capacity actually to draw from

22. The references here and throughout to "inferring," "drawing out," and the like mean nothing more mysterious than that "people [tend to] make some kind of symbolic sense of their surroundings even if they don't necessarily put it into words" (Dreeben 1968, p. 53).

23. Dreeben (1968, pp. 7–49) offers instructive observations on these matters, but they are more fully treated throughout the extensive literature on the sociology of organizations.

them whatever principles they imply; and the more abstract the principles, the more this is the case (Bidwell 1972, p. 21; Breer and Locke 1965, p. 257; Dreeben 1968, pp. 53–56). Second, individuals must become positively attached or morally committed to the principles they have derived from their experiences. Commitment is a function of reinforcement (see, esp., Bidwell 1972). The more individuals are rewarded—with the intrinsic satisfactions that result from successful task mastery or with external positive sanctions—in a particular setting, the more they come to believe in and value the ideas they have formed by engaging in the activities that the setting provides. Conversely, a situation where individuals are unsuccessful promotes attachment to orientations that are the opposite of those inferred from the situation, provided that the opposite orientations have already been firmly acquired in some other way.[24] Third, individuals must generalize their orientations to fields outside of the setting in which they were constructed. If the beliefs and values that emerge from activities in a specific situation remain, as they often do, confined to that situation, they will have little consequence for cultural change. Generalization, Breer and Locke suggest, takes "the path of least resistance" (1965, p. 17); it does not extend to areas of certain and stable cultural orientations. Broader social and cultural conditions thus structure the possibilities for the generalization of commitments that derive from socialization experiences.

The following portions of this study apply this intentionally simplified theory of cultural change to the case of the Scottish Enlightenment, though it is important to realize that the theory might also be tailored to the analysis of other changes in ideas and attitudes in other times and places. The argument here is that the intellectuals of the Scottish Enlightenment were educated in a series of settings that offered them experiences through which they acquired and became committed to the orientations of independence and universalism that were later expressed in their writings. To demonstrate this, it is necessary to show either that Ferguson, Hume, Millar, Robertson, and Smith were generally presented with the kinds of experiences from which they could derive principles of independence and universalism and that they were on the whole

24. Breer and Locke offer the following illustration: "in a classroom situation which 'calls' for close co-operation, a student who is highly rewarded will become more positive in his attitudes toward cooperation, whereas the student who is punished (i.e., receives a failing grade) can be expected to change in the other direction" (1965, p. 52).

rewarded in the settings that offered these experiences, or that, having learned of independence and universalism, these figures were unsuccessful in situations where dependency and particularism were the operative standards. Variations among the five on these matters should be congruent with the differences in attitude that existed among them. If these hypotheses are found to be incorrect, the proposed explanation will be rejected. The discussion will assume throughout that the future enlighteners actually did infer the orientations that were suggested by the activities that they encountered. This assumption is amply justified by the fact that our subjects were not late bloomers. Their intellectual capacities stood out from their earliest years, and there can be little doubt that in fact each had the cognitive equipment to draw out the unstated lessons of his experience.

Of course, had the enlightened intellectuals found themselves in historical conditions that precluded the generalization of novel orientations acquired through situational experiences, these would have very limited relevance for the explanation of the cultural change produced by the Scottish Enlightenment. This investigation of social experiences proceeds only because opportunities for generalization were available to the enlighteners. In their age, men of ideas had attained some measure of security with which to develop new points of view (see Smout 1969a, pp. 478–81; p. 104 above). More significant, these men were for the most part involved in a variety of areas where consensus was, as the intellectuals of the Enlightenment recognized, anything but firmly established. David Hume doubtless exaggerated somewhat when he began his first book by announcing: "There is nothing which is not the subject of debate, and in which men of learning are not of contrary opinions. The most trivial question escapes not our controversy, and in the most momentous we are not able to give any certain decision. Disputes are multiplied; as if everything was uncertain" (*THN*, p. xiv). Nevertheless, in the Scotland of Hume's day, numerous theological, ethical, psychological, philosophical, historical, and economic topics were (relatively) wide open for discussion—witness the noisy theological quarrels within the Church, the steady influx of all manner of provocative foreign literature, the virulent tracts of controversial history, the ongoing debates of the improvers, and the rest. These developments had been underway decades before the Age of the Enlightenment and were felt by considerable numbers of eighteenth-century Scots, but in themselves entailed no abandonment of the basic assumptions of Scottish Calvinism and no shift toward the independence and universalism of the Scottish Enlightenment. They did, however, open channels for the expression of unorthodox beliefs and values,[25] if, when, and insofar as these emerged from elsewhere. Frequently contested economic, historical, philosophical, and related issues formed the path of least resistance for the generalization of the principles that Ferguson, Hume, Millar, Robertson, and Smith derived from their experiences. These areas were the fields where the Scottish enlighteners articulated and creatively applied orientations that, had these figures been placed in other social and cultural circumstances, might have remained situationally specific, or extended with different results to other intellectual matters or to more concrete forms of social action.

One additional link is now needed in the thesis about experience and Enlightenment. Before it is possible to determine whether or not the intellectuals of the Scottish Enlightenment were provided with experiences from which to infer the orientations of independence and universalism, it is necessary to specify the types of experiences that actually form the basis for these particular inferences. Contemporary social-psychological research has done much to identify these. It has demonstrated that individuals derive the principle of independence from experiences where, to a developmentally appropriate degree, they act on their own and decide for themselves: where they are, in a word, autonomous.[26] *Such experiences are made possible in social settings in which individuals are not enmeshed in strong relationships of dependency*—relationships where they receive essential kinds of material and emotional supports from persons with greater resources—*and* (more important) *in which their activities and decisions are not subject to direct and restrictive control*

25. This does not mean that these were the sole channels of this sort available in eighteenth-century Scotland. Opportunities for generalization were scarcely ubiquitous during this period, but were also to be found in natural philosophy and in some of the arts, areas that, for the reasons indicated in chap. 2, have been rather outside the bounds of this study. The question of why Ferguson, Hume, Millar, Robertson, and Smith not only became intellectuals, but became intellectuals interested in the fields under discussion in the text has generally been well treated (if often in somewhat different terms) by their biographers and need not detain us here. For an interesting sociological approach to the closely related issue of the efflorescence of intellectual achievement in eighteenth-centtury Scotland, see Bullough and Bullough (1971), Bullough (1970), and Bullough and Bullough (1973).

26. The qualification—"to a developmentally appropriate degree"—is inserted to reflect one of the most consistent findings of research of socialization: independence does not develop in children who are raised "permissively," that is, without a degree of control inversely proportional to their level of maturity (see Baumrind 1966, pp. 904–5; Clausen 1966, p. 13; Martin 1975, p. 508).

by others.[27] Experiences that supply the materials for inferring universalism are those "in which evident differences among [individuals] are subordinated to similarities in their characteristics and situation [and those individuals thus] have an opportunity to view each other and themselves as sharing common experiences, and being in the same boat despite the obvious personal differences among them" (Dreeben 1968, p. 22). *Experiences of this sort are generated in situations that subject a heterogeneous group of individuals to treatment by general standards:* situations that expose individuals "regularly and consistently to significant ranges of variation across several strata of humanity," while simultaneously handling them "very much alike"—not "identically," but by "the uniform [application] of standards and sanctions to many cases."[28] It goes almost without saying that situations are rarely as black and white as these generalizations suggest. Concrete social settings that offer individuals experiences for the drawing out of universalism and independence do so with different degrees of frequency, intensity, and consistency (see Camic, e.g., 1983*b*, pp. 62–63). The central tendency of any particular mix of experiences is not difficult to discern when the mix is placed in its historical context, but matters of degree make, as we shall see, their own contribution to understanding cultural change.

The remaining chapters of this book examine the social experiences that the Scottish enlighteners received in family, early ed-

27. Dreeben (1968, pp. 13, 21, 66, 67), and Loubser (1970, pp. 113–14). See also Baumrind (1966), Becker (1964), Clausen (1966), Elder (1965), Martin (1975), Watson (1957), and chap. 4, notes 13 and 21.

28. For the formulations quoted, see Loubser (1970, p. 111), Dreeben (1968, pp. 22, 82), and Bidwell (1972, p. 20). See also Breer and Locke (1965, p. 274), and Parsons (1959, pp. 136, 141–42).

It should be emphasized that the specification, that has just been given in the text, of the experiences that promote the development of independence and universalism has been tailored to correspond to the particular conceptions of independence and universalism that one finds in the Scottish Enlightenment. But given that these conceptions are only partially similar to the orientations Dreeben (1968, pp. 66–84) calls "independence" and "universalism," the argument here borrows only portions of his analysis of the experiences that underlie the acquisition of these orientations and supplements this with the work of scholars who view independence and universalism in ways better suited for the study of the Scottish Enlightenment. Sociologists of education should note that the independence and universalism of the Enlightenment resemble Loubser's (1970, pp. 109–14) "moral autonomy" and "moral universalism," or even Swidler's (1979, pp. 145–59) "autonomy" and "super universalism," more than the "independence" and "universalism" of Dreeben (see also, chap. 6, note 33).

ucational, university, and professional setings. The family no doubt seems like an odd starting point for an inquiry into the origins of independence and universalism. Dreeben's well-known observations, for example, portray the family as the cradle of dependency and particularism, an institution where the helpless young are inevitably bound by strong ties of dependency to their elders and where "behavior . . . is governed to a considerable extent by the unique personal characteristics of the members [and therefore] is weighted heavily on the side of special"—particularistic—"treatment" (1968, pp. 21, 81, 76).[29] While families may not be organized in quite this way in all places and periods, particularistic behaviors and relationships of dependency generally did pervade family life in eighteenth-century Scotland and, for this reason, the discussion of the family that follows in the next chapter concentrates neither upon the development of universalism nor on independence as it emerges from experiences little encumbered by bonds of dependency. The family cannot be wholly omitted, however, because a great deal of scholarship has shown that family arrangements that reduce authoritarian controls over the young provide experiences that are extremely important for the growth of independence (see note 27). This conclusion requires that an examination of the experiences that underlay the Scottish Enlightenment begin by considering the implications of authority relations in eighteenth-century Scottish homes for the early development of independence. This topic is the primary concern of chapter 4. Subsequent chapters are more broadly focused. Chapter 5 describes the fundamental role of certain early formal educational experiences in the initial acquisition of universalism and their more equivocal role in sustaining independence. Chapter 6 analyzes the changing university experiences that become decisive in reinforcing previously formed principles of independence and universalism. Chapter 7 discusses the significance of early professional experiences for consolidating commitments to both orientations. As this preview makes clear, the operations of homes, schools, and professions will be investigated only so far as they aid in understanding the development of independence and universalism. This does not exhaust what can be said about their operations, however, and those pursuing other problems would naturally want to consider additional things that the intellectuals of the Scottish Enlightenment and their contem-

29. Hagstrom has put the later point more simply: "Parent-child relations are everywhere particularistic" (1968, p. 274).

poraries learned from their experiences in familial, educational, and occupational institutions; the extent to which those institutions reproduced (and were structured by) the basic economic and political patterns of the epoch; and the like.

To treat the four settings just mentioned in separate chapters is not to erect boundaries between experiences that are intimately linked. The most blatant instance of such interconnection is the fact that youth in the eighteenth century often participated in the worlds of family, education, and profession concurrently. More important, however, are the developmental relationships among the learning experiences considered here. For better or worse, the social-psychological theory that this study has adopted does not yet include a stage-model of human development. But following virtually the entire socialization literature, it does insist that the impact of any particular kind of experience is contingent upon its place in a broader pattern and sequence of experiences. Everything else being equal, experiences that recur repeatedly across a range of settings (as well as within a given setting) are of greater consequence for the formation of beliefs and values than those that are rare. As Breer and Locke report, "the longer the period of time and the fewer the interruptions, the better will be the [learning] results" (1965, p. 261). Conversely, commitments tend to languish when they are not reaffirmed. Experiential learning is not, however, simply a matter of the frequency of a certain experience. Differently socialized individuals react differently to similar doses of new experiences, for the latter are received through the filter of previous experiences. The lessons of earlier experiences make some subsequent developments more likely than others and, unless a substantial amount of resocialization transpires, can preclude shifts to vastly contrary cultural orientations.[30]

These remarks can be viewed from a slightly different angle. Since not every experience that will be considered here tended in the same direction, a method is needed to explain how discrepant episodes in the socialization process combined to produce the learn-

30. Current research tends to indicate that when acquired early on, dependency is a particularly resilient orientation (see note 27 above). Particularism in contrast— or so Dreeben's (1968, pp. 74–84) work suggests—is (within limits) more likely to give way when individuals who have acquired it later encounter experiences from which to infer its opposite. It would seem, however, that this happens only among those whose cognitive capabilities have been previously well developed, for (relative to dependency, independence, or even particularism) universalism is an extremely abstract principle to learn by induction from ongoing social situations.

ing effects that appeared at the end of the process. Developmental considerations are valuable because they supply provisional guidance here, suggesting that certain experiences—those that start early and continue long and uninterrupted—weigh heavily, while others—those that are too late and too infrequent—can be discounted. The social psychology that underlies these suggestions is still too rudimentary, however, to be of much use in understanding the aggregate impact of a diverse stream of concrete experiences; early, long, and uninterrupted are relative terms whose applicability to many empirical cases is at least debatable, and then there are ambiguous instances of experiences that may, for example, begin early, proceed with little interruption, but last only a comparatively brief while. This lamentable situation thwarts the possibility of providing within this study a theoretically rigorous treatment either of the differential consequences of the various experiences of the individual enlighteners or of the experiential roots of the attitudinal differences among the several enlighteners. Lacking clear-cut rules for totaling up the joint ramifications of disparate activities, one can only offer ad hoc speculations for why some enlightened intellectuals were fully committed to orientations of the Enlightenment, while others were more partially committed; why this figure integrated Calvinist and Enlightenment beliefs, while that figure vacillated between the two; and so on. One can but hope that these speculations will someday be brought together with those that research on related issues will formulate in order thereby to enrich existing knowledge about the interplay of the elements in the intricate configuration that is human experience.

Because it concentrates upon the family, school, and professional experiences of the Scottish enlighteners during the first twenty-five years or so of their lives, this inquiry inevitably provides a rather selective treatment of the configuration of social experiences relevant to the emergence of independence and universalism. The intellectuals of the Scottish Enlightenment had innumerable experiences after turning twenty-five and they had many before that age beyond the few settings to be discussed, but everything is a bit much for a single study. Some narrowing down is essential and it is not difficult to determine for the problem at hand which years and settings are most appropriate. Quite apart from their general importance in a developmental perspective, the early years stand out because the enlighteners—except for Ferguson, whom the analysis follows until a somewhat older age—exhibited their commitment to independence and universalism in their very first intellectual productions, and these were works that they undertook either during or immediately after the period considered here. But once this period is selected, familial, educational, and professional situations are the logical next choice. Only in unusual circumstances has socialization research put other experiences on par with those that take place in these basic settings, and nothing that is now known about the early lives of the enlightened intellectuals suggests such circumstances or hints at decisive learning experiences beyond the confines of home, school, and profession, save for the above noted Calvinist influence of church and community. The experiences considered in the following chapters nevertheless should be seen as no more than strategic illustrations of the general thesis about the relationship between social experience and the orientations of the Scottish Enlightenment; they should not be construed as an argument that these particular experiences mattered while others did not. Thus, were one to establish that the enlighteners had experiences from which to acquire independence and universalism outside of the four settings to be described—or that inside these settings they had certain experiences of the same kind which go unmentioned in this investigation—one would confirm, rather than undermine, the proposed explanation of the Scottish Enlightenment.

A problem would, of course, arise if one discovered that the experiences excluded from the analysis were more conducive to the development of dependency and particularism than of their opposites. The results of this study might then be dismissed as a product of circular reasoning, of picking out from all of the experiences of the intellectuals of the Enlightenment the handful that was most suggestive of independence and universalism and using this misrepresentative lot as proof of the experiential foundation of the elemental commitments of the Scottish Enlightenment. None of the results, however, derive from reasoning of this type. Independence and universalism were chosen for their constitutive role in the Enlightenment's cultural revolution, while the enlighteners' home, school, and professional experiences were selected quite independently for the reasons indicated above long before it became clear that these generally were the sorts of experiences from which independence and universalism could be inferred—hardly a foregone conclusion in an age abounding in family, educational, and occupational experiences with vastly different implications. This does not deny that among the unmentioned experiences of the enlighteners were some that were incongruent with the orientations of the Enlightenment. As previously implied, it would be remarkable if this were not so, for in a complicated world the separate elements in the string of human experiences are never all bearers of identical messages. This observation in no way impugns the following interpretation. Individuals far more committed to independence and universalism than Scotland's enlightened intellectuals have no doubt occasionally been successful in situations whose activities constituted the raw materials for deriving principles of dependency and particularism. It has already been made clear that not every experience is of equal import; each derives its ultimate significance from its position in a whole sequenced pattern. In a developmental light, many experiences pale, though this is not the case for the bulk of those that are treated below. Obviously, however, since the light is still relatively weak, the conclusions to which it leads require corroboration from future social-psychological and historical research.

There is a still more serious impediment to a satisfactory analysis of the social experiences that the intellectuals of the Scottish Enlightenment encountered in family, school, and early professional situations: the data. The biographical scholarship on Ferguson, Hume, Millar, Robertson, and Smith varies widely in quality[31] and, even at its best, reveals extraordinarily little about the first two and a half decades of their lives.[32] By integrating various sources, it is possible to determine a few parental characteristics, the duration of the enlighteners' involvement with members of their families, the identity of the grammar schools and universities they attended, the approximate length of their stay and quality of their performance in these schools, and their initial fate on the professional job market. Sometimes a few other particulars are known, but never do the shreds of information add up to an adequate picture of the specific nature of the experiences of Ferguson, Hume, and the rest in the principal social settings in which they found themselves. This

31. On Hume, one has a thorough modern biography and certain informative older documents; on Smith, a dated full biography and several more narrowly focused discussions (Ross's long-promised *Life of Adam Smith* is still listed as forthcoming); on Ferguson, an adequate unpublished biography and several much shorter accounts, only one of which dates from this century; on Millar, one modern and two very old biographical treatments, all too brief; on Robertson, some half-dozen ancient and often elliptical sketches by authors with little historical training.

32. Less and less is known about the enlighteners the further back one goes within this twenty-five-year period, so that early childhood—the concern of so much developmental research—is the biggest mystery, save for infancy on which the biographical materials offer literally nothing (on the problems that result from the omission of infancy, see Demos 1973, esp. pp. 127–31).

is the very thing one would most like to have in order to discern whether or not the enlightened intellectuals were presented with experiences from which to infer the orientations of independence and universalism, but there is an alternative way of moving ahead. This is to turn from life histories to institutional histories and, through the latter, to identify pertinent characteristics of the social settings of interest during the periods when they involved the enlighteners: Did the settings impose or eliminate direct controls over individual decisions and actions? Did they foster or inhibit strong relationships of dependency? Did they contain a heterogeneous lot of individuals and treat it by general standards, or did they not? These characteristics are actually of decisive significance because, as suggested above, they are what shaped the degree to which the settings provided the kinds of experiences from which individuals could derive notions of independence and universalism. In principle, considerable information can thus be obtained about the experiences of the future intellectuals of the Scottish Enlightenment. Knowing the attributes of the settings in which the enlighteners were enmeshed, one knows (if one moves cautiously) a good deal about the general nature of the experiences they encountered, even though biographical materials make it impossible to ascertain all the particular permutations that those experiences underwent in the five cases.

But before this reasoning can be employed in practice, further obstacles must be confronted. Historical research on families, schools, and professions in eighteenth-century Scotland is remarkably thin, especially when it comes to the features of social settings most relevant for understanding the development of independence and universalism. Short of opting for one of the drastic suggestions considered in the Introduction, one must therefore proceed by slowly and systematically tying together bits and pieces from a great number of inquiries written for quite different purposes. The first section in each of the next four chapters attempts to do this; the second section in each then brings those who made the Scottish Enlightenment onto the scene. The difficulties entailed by the former task are compounded because, although some of the specific settings where the enlighteners were socialized have—however partially—been studied in their own right, others are knowable only by indirection. For example, while major institutions like the University of Glasgow have found their historians, the isolated little grammar schools that the enlightened intellectuals attended have not. Settings so mundane are barely mentioned in composite sketches of eighteenth-century primary and secondary education in Scotland and, for this reason, the early school experiences of the enlighteners can be described only at a level still further removed from their daily lives.

Here great care is required. In identifying the experiences of a handful of individuals from the characteristics of settings as reported in composite accounts, or even in singular institutional histories, one must not forget the old methodological lesson that what is true for an aggregate is not necessarily true for its component elements. After all, the particular settings that Ferguson, Hume, Millar, Robertson, and Smith encountered could have diverged from the norm and the lads themselves could have received experiences atypical in their settings. The remaining chapters therefore use the proposed method of determining the enlighteners' experiences only at junctures where these possibilities seem most unlikely. The simplest way of assessing this is to search such data as are obtainable on the early lives of the enlightened intellectuals and on the settings still wanting their own histories for any hints of the unusual—and, conveniently, these are something older sources note oftener than one might expect. Of course, on matters where there is a dearth of evidence to begin with, the absence of signs of atypicality is hardly conclusive proof of the reverse, but a sociologically surer step can also be taken in this context. The information that is available on aggregates can be utilized to establish the degree of uniformity that existed among their elements. From histories of the University of Glasgow, one can discover whether the organization of that institution required all students to undergo fairly identical experiences, or whether it instead allowed experiential diversity and the insulation of students or groups of students from activities relevant to the development of universalism and independence. Likewise, from materials on primary and secondary education in eighteenth-century Scotland, one can determine the extent of the variance between and within small town grammar schools. If, for inherent reasons, grammar schools in town after town exhibited substantially similar characteristics and if these imposed essentially uniform experiences upon the pupils in these schools, speculations about likely departures from the common pattern can be discounted. Since the inferences about the experiences of the enlightened intellectuals that are made here on the basis of institutional and composite histories are predicated on these types of precautionary measures, there would seem to be little reason to distrust the conclusions that derive from such inferences.

Yet even when the circuitous strategies are most effective in un-covering the enlighteners' experiences, the specific nature of those experiences does remain elusive. Although there are many places in the following analysis were the disparity between the general and the specific is not large, the former should never be regarded as more than a proxy indicator of the latter. Ideally, future historical research will make substantially refined indicators of the social ex-periences of the Scottish enlighteners possible. Still, for all its re-moteness from the ideal, the current stock of knowledge is at least sufficient to establish with a very high probability whether or not the intellectuals of the Scottish Enlightenment encountered the kinds of family, school, and early professional experiences from which to infer the orientations of independence and universalism—and this when all previous explanations of the Scottish Enlight-enment have been extremely improbable (see Camic 1983a, pp. 155–64), and in the sort of cultural-historical matter where a certain explanation is the greatest rarity.

If one can go some distance with the existing sources, they none-theless leave a big mystery unsolved. The thesis of this study is that Ferguson, Hume, Millar, Robertson, and Smith acquired a com-mitment to independence and universalism through their social experiences. During the period in their lives when they underwent these experiences, the five were also effectively socialized into the Calvinist creed of dependency and particularism through the in-structions of parents, teachers, and so many others. The two state-ments are not contradictory: psychology after psychology indicates that the developing personality can harbor widely divergent beliefs and values. This situation can actually last through adulthood, though in the areas of concern here, this generally was not the case for the enlighteners, not even Ferguson. In different ways, the enlightened intellectuals shed the dependency and particularism that they had been taught for the independence and universalism that they had simultaneously learned. Unfortunately, with one minor exception, it is not yet known when and in what circumstances they did so. This investigation will not pursue these questions; its general argument is independent of them and could in fact accommodate a variety of different answers. However, since the biographical ma-terials currently available do make it appear most unlikely that any of the Scottish enlighteners suddenly and dramatically converted from the world of Calvinism to that of the Enlightenment, it may be useful to offer for future research the alternative hypothesis that the transition from the former to the latter took place in a gradual, piecemeal manner as the five increasingly worked through, reflected upon, and then—usually in conjunction with planning and executing a first book—articulated their own views concerning certain of the hotly disputed psychological, philosophical, historical, economic, and other questions of the age. This speculation is consistent with the single bit of evidence at hand: the autobiographical remarks that show, as Mossner puts it, that Hume relinquished his belief in God "slowly and reluctantly, even against his will" while pondering the theological arguments of earlier philosophers (1954, p. 64; see also *HL* 1:154). It seems reasonable to suggest that, issue by issue, the same thing happened over and over again. Struggling with a fiercely contested topic here and a zealously debated problem there, the intellectuals of the Scottish Enlightenment variously and perhaps unwittingly brought to bear the orientations that had been most closely associated with their previous successes. The result in each case was not a mere assertion of the lessons of experience, but an elaborate development of those lessons in the context of a host of particular issues. The dynamics here may long remain obscure, but the fact that such dynamics occurred is in no way denied when one steps back from the particulars, sums across the range of issues, and speaks more generally of the emergence of independence and universalism and of the social experiences that underlay that development.

Insofar as it succeeds in establishing the claims stated above, this study will have at least partially filled the social-psychological void left by previous explanations of the Scottish Enlightenment: it will have demonstrated that experience was a primary mechanism or process by which social conditions in mid-eighteenth-century Scotland—specifically familial, educational, and professional conditions—translated into the orientations of independence and universalism. Initially, too, it may seem to have found in microlevel home, school, and occupational situations the mean between global developments like the Union and singular encounters with naileries. On this count, however, doubts soon arise. Surely other eighteenth-century Scots were found in the same family, school, and professional settings as Ferguson, Hume, Millar, Robertson, and Smith. Why then, one irresistibly wonders, were enlightened intellectuals so few and far between? The objection implied here is a poorly formulated one for three reasons.

First, it assumes that all those who received the same experiences as the enlighteners should have become enlighteners. But, as we have seen, it is most inappropriate to posit this simplistic kind of causal relationship. Not everyone who is presented with a social experience has the cognitive capabilities to draw out its unstated lessons; not everyone who infers such lessons is reinforced in a way that converts the lessons into moral commitments, into principles that are believed and valued; not everyone who acquires novel beliefs and values from experience is placed in a situation conducive to the generalization (or the same sort of generalization) of those orientations. Unless these points are fully taken into account, comparisons between the experiences of the intellectuals of the Scottish Enlightenment and their contemporaries are vacuous. The second problem with the above objection is the presumption that all those who encountered a situation that the enlighteners encountered received from it the same experiences. Such a supposition ignores matters of biography entirely. To be sure, it was suggested previously that there was little experiential diversity within several of the settings analyzed here and that, for this reason, institutional data can be substituted for certain kinds of biographical data without a serious loss of information. Substantial variations did exist in some situations, however, and in all events the need eventually to go beyond indirect indicators to the specifics of human experience remains. The enlightened intellectuals and the others of their age will inevitably seem far more alike in experience than they were if this is overlooked and one merely notes that large numbers of Scots passed through the same setting. As soon as even a few biographical facts are introduced—and the sparse materials now available at least reveal approximately how long the enlighteners were involved in particular settings and whether their involvement was continuous or interrupted—it becomes clear that not everyone encountered similar situations in an identical way. A third difficulty is that the objection disregards developmental considerations. Focusing upon the experiences that were presented to both the intellectuals of the Scottish Enlightenment and their fellows in individual situations, it forgets that experiential learning is a lengthy process that unfolds over a range of situations and that there is a vast difference between saying that the enlighteners had companions in this or that circumstance and demonstrating that a multitude met the same configuration of family *and* early educational *and* university *and* professional (*and* other) experiences as the enlightened few. This observation is not, however, independent of the previous remarks and if one were really bent on knowing the number of those who were socialized as Ferguson, Hume, Millar, Robertson, and Smith were it would be necessary to estimate how many eighteenth-century Scots went through the same pattern and sequence of situations, experienced these situations in a manner similar to the enlighteners, and had comparable inductive abilities, reinforcements, and opportunities to generalize the orientations born of experience.

The very phrasing of this requirement suggests that the number was small. Later chapters supply occasional bits of evidence to sustain this impression, though it would regrettably take years of research to compile the materials needed for an adequate treatment of the parts of the problem that can even be addressed at this remove from the eighteenth century. The only systematic alternative presently available is the analysis described in the Appendix of the Bullough data on intellectual achievement in eighteenth-century Scotland. These data offer biographical information on a fairly comprehensive listing of 222 Scottish intellectuals born between the late seventeenth century and 1750. That the listing excludes the many who wrote little or nothing[33] does not minimize its significance. It encompasses (or so one has every reason generally to assume) the figures who were not wanting in cognitive capacity and not cut off from that exposure to the age's intellectual controversies which made generalization a viable prospect—the figures, in short, who provide the best current basis for cogent comparisons between the experiences of the enlighteners and their contemporaries. The Bullough materials actually permit certain of these comparisons to be made, albeit in a rather tentative and mechanical way. Once the pool of 222 cases has been reduced by subtracting the five enlightened intellectuals and the 68 subjects for whom essential pieces of information are missing, it is possible to determine how many of the remaining 149 intellectuals encountered the same general kinds of university and early educational and family situations as the Scottish enlighteners experienced. Eight seem to have done so[34] and, had the data allowed one to take reinforcements, professional experiences, and the other factors discussed above into account, that number no doubt would have been

33. Unless, as in the case of inventors, architects, and painters, they made intellectual contributions that assumed nonwritten forms.

34. Had 68 subjects not been eliminated on the basis of missing information, this figure would perhaps be somewhat larger. The best estimate for how much larger is $8/149 \times 68$ or 3.65.

considerably smaller.[35] The exact calculations here are, of course, first shots in the dark. These hit so few bodies, however, that it is hard to believe a host will appear when the lights go on.

None of these remarks have been intended to suggest that the early lives of Adam Ferguson, David Hume, John Millar, William Robertson, and Adam Smith differed greatly from the lives of plenty of other lads who grew up in the early eighteenth century. In the Scottish enlighteners we will see a confluence of things—certain family, educational, and occupational experiences, intellectual capabilities, successes and failures, opportunities for generalization—that by themselves were quite familiar at the time, even if they usually were not the mode for the entire population. In fact, many of the basic ingredients—virtually all of those just mentioned save the last—can also be found in Scotland prior to the century of the Enlightenment, though insofar as they combined earlier they did so within macrohistorical boundaries unlike those that were laid subsequently (see pp. 109–10 above). The old elements acquired new potentialities as the various intellectual and social developments treated in previous explanations of the Scottish Enlightenment slowly reset the historical stage for individuals raised in roughly the first half of the eighteenth century—the enlightened intellectuals and those with whom they often enough shared something that will play a major role in the present interpretation. While in most of these cases the commonality was an item in a life package that was on the whole distinct from the ones the enlighteners received, there did exist individual combinations where the resemblances, although not perfect, were more numerous.[36] This state of affairs fits nicely with the distribution of cultural orientations in

35. It should be emphasized that a larger number would in no way undermine the central argument, unless it happened that those similar to the enlightened intellectuals in all the ways that are of concern here were individuals with radically different beliefs and values. After all, this inquiry contends only that Ferguson, Hume, Millar, Robertson, and Smith are the *known* enlighteners. This position allows that future research may uncover men of the same breed among the little studied figures of the age—and, as the text subsequently observes, the majority of those in the Bullough data set are still little studied figures. It is true that the small value reported above makes it unlikely that a multitude of others encountered the set of situations that fostered the independence and universalism of the five subjects of this study, but one must recognize that that set of situations was not necessarily the only one offering experiences for the development of the orientations of the Enlightenment (see pp. 232, 242–43 below).

36. This conclusion cannot be documented with a list of specific references but derives from indications sprinkled throughout the extensive biographical and social-

eighteenth-century Scotland: a mass of orthodox Calvinists, a handful of enlighteners, and a scattering at various points in between. Equally noteworthy in this connection is the fact that just as universalistic sentiments were more prevalent than the attitudes of independence, the developments that will be related to the growth of universalism were rather more widespread than those relevant to the emergence of independence. To confirm the existence of these speculative correlations would require not only the material wished for above on the experiences, abilities, and so on of a broad sample of eighteenth-century Scots, but also data on the breadth, depth, and consistency of their commitment to the postulates of the Scottish Enlightenment. But as chapter 2 demonstrated, discerning an individual's beliefs and values is a sufficiently arduous business when the individual wrote renowned volumes. For the rest, the problem is infinitely more intractable. While work at the frontiers of social history is at present time devising strategies for uncovering the opinions of history's silent types, such techniques have yet to be applied to eighteenth-century Scotland. Even for the intellectual population of the era, it is currently impossible to go beyond the impressionistic assessment of the relationship between experience and outlook. The fundamental orientations of the vast majority of Scotland's men of ideas are still shrouded in darkness, and this situation precludes adding pertinent attitudinal information to the biographical data set that is available on the Scottish intellectuals.[37] Gaps of this magnitude are a major hindrance to the incisive analysis of eighteenth-century Scottish culture at large, though fortunately they do not seriously affect our understanding

---

historical literatures cited in this and the following chapters and from examining the data discussed in the Appendix.

37. An inspection of the table presented in the Appendix will reveal, however, that a number of individuals who were prominent in groups (the improvers, the Moderates, the moral philosophers) that affirmed various aspects of the philosophy of the Enlightenment also seem to have had certain socialization experiences in common with the enlightened intellectuals. From the point of view of this study, this, of course, is a rather comforting finding, though it would be rash to make too much of it. As the text has just indicated, a great deal of precise information about the beliefs and the lives of other individuals in eighteenth-century Scotland is required in order to extend the kind of analysis of cultural orientations and social experiences that is developed here for the enlighteners. To connect mechanically a fact or two about the ideas of figures of the period with a few data on their experiences is no substitute for this.

of the intellectuals of the Scottish Enlightenment. Enough is known to make clear how their revolution was a union of circumstances that were integral features of their world.

4

Family Experiences

I

In this golden age of family historiography, knowledge of the Scottish family in times past is still extremely fragmentary. Recent demographic research has found that in the late seventeenth century the average size of Lowland families of the upper and middle strata[1] was approximately 4.5[2] and that these units were predominantly "two-generational, consisting of husband, wife and children" (Flinn et al. 1977, p. 196). The situation probably changed little by the first half of the next century, although average family size may have risen slightly by that century's end and nuclear families in Scotland long remained heavily involved in wider kinship networks.[3] To understand what actually went on inside the eighteenth-century Scottish family, flesh must be put on these skeletal facts about family

1. Families of this description are the principal focus of this section because its objective is to set the stage for an examination of the families of Ferguson, Hume, Millar, Robertson, and Smith, and with the partial exception of Ferguson (who was born in Logierait, Perthshire, at the entrance to the Highlands), these men were all from Lowland families of the middle or upper stratum. But since it is tedious to speak continually of the Lowland family from the middle and upper strata, from now on the text will abbreviate and use simpler terms such as the Scottish family and the eighteenth-century home. None of these expressions is intended to suggest an absence of variance among the many concrete families to which it refers, though it is also true that the difference between these family units and those not under discussion was generally much greater. For some instructive remarks on regional and class variation in family structure, see Carter (1973), Laslett (1972, p. 62), Flinn et al. (1977, p. 196), Marshall (1973, pp. 31–34), Plant (1952, p. 1), Stone (1977, p. 127), and Wood (1945, p. 99).

2. Household size was often considerably larger due to the presence of servants (see Flinn et al. 1977, p. 196; on servants in the eighteenth-century Scottish home, see also Lochhead 1948, pp. 181–89; Plant 1952, pp. 159–77).

3. See Flinn et al. (1977, p. 14), Marshall (1973, pp. 31–34), Somerville (1861, p. 368), and Stone (1977, pp. 86, 123).

size and structure, but unfortunately this has not yet been done in any detail. A few secondary sources and readily accessible primary documents do,[4] however, sketch the nature of authority relations within the Scottish home during the era when the future intellectuals of the Scottish Enlightenment were growing up, and conveniently this is the very issue that is of most importance in order to commence an analysis of family experiences and the development of independence. As previously noted, the family may typically be characterized by particularism and bonds of dependency, but insofar as it eliminates authoritarian restrictions over the actions of its members it can nonetheless provide an experiential foundation for an independent orientation. All the available evidence suggests that the eighteenth-century Scottish home ordinarily did not eliminate such restrictions. Patriarchy—autocratic control by the male head of the family over the activities and decisions of others in the family—rather was the norm.[5]

For so Calvinist a country, this was not surprising. In England and in New England, Calvinist teachings went hand in hand with patriarchal attitudes and the same was true in Scotland.[6] Here, as elsewhere, such attitudes were the faithful corollary of Calvinism's abiding conviction that families were the building blocks of the godly community. A Scottish minister writing anonymously in the early eighteenth century expressed the venerable position when he warned that "families being the seminaries or nurseries of a kingdom, the disorders thereof, at long run must affect and indanger the publick [and] bring Vengence and Judgement upon Church

4. The primary documents mentioned here consist of family memoirs, sermons, and other "literary" materials. In recent years, historians of the family have been sharply critical of the use of this kind of information. Laslett (1972, pp. 10–13) has argued that it conveys inaccurate impressions about household size and structure, and Shorter (1975, pp. 9–10) has maintained that it presents a misleading picture of family life among "the lower orders." But as the text indicates, the current study nowhere employs literary sources as guides to matters of these sorts. It goes without saying, however, that an adequate history of the Scottish family will require more and better literary materials, as well as more objective types of historical evidence.

5. Graham (1899, pp. 24, 75), Plant (1952, pp. 4, 7), and Smout (1969a, pp. 269–70) report some signs that, at the end of the eighteenth century, this pattern was beginning to change.

6. The writings of Schücking (1929, pp. 56–95) and especially Stone (1977, pp. 174–78) on the English situation and of Demos (1970, pp. 134–39), Morgan (1944, pp. 65–108), and above all Greven (1977, pp. 21–61) on its American counterpart offer illuminating treatments of the patriarchal beliefs and practices of Calvinism and, in so doing, throw considerable light on family life in Scotland during roughly the same period.

and State" (Anon. 1703, pp. 24–25). Several decades later William Dalrymple, a fellow cleric, put the familiar message as follows: "Families are divine plantations, settled by the Almighty himself; and intended to be the earliest and best nurseries of sound wisdom, and of every kind of excellence. These . . . being allowed to go into disorder, by neglect of cultivation, must give place to the rise and progress of ignorance, vice and all manner of future public distress" (1787, p. 56).

From the Reformation onward, stemming this dread calamity was the sacred duty of the father (see Stone 1977, p. 154). His great task was made inordinately difficult, however, by the poor quality soil on his divine plantation. Children, as the age heard time and again, entered the world marred by original sin and a willingness to succumb to the passions and attendant transgressions that were the lot of humankind. Drastic measures were therefore required. Calvinism taught that strict and absolute parental (ultimately paternal) control, exercised with all due sanctions from infancy through adulthood, was the only sure means to curb the "briars and thorns" sprouting in God's nurseries (Dalrymple 1787, p. 57; see Lochhead 1948, p. 225; Stone 1977, p. 406). Essential features of this view were repeated in one context after another. The clergy instructed their flocks: "You have Power and Authority in your hands, and if Intreaties and Admonition [to children] will not do, You can punish them in their Bodies, Portions, or Maintenance and, if need be, put them out of your houses" (Anon. 1703, p. 21). Popular books of etiquette spoke of the need for parents to "kill . . . the Seeds of Pride, Vanity and Self-conceit" in their young and to teach them of "their original Guilt, and natural Pollution, . . . and what their Sins deserve from God" (Petrie 1720, p. 4). while educational innovaters urged persistent parental vigilance and held that "rising [youthful] passions [must] be crushed" (James Barclay 1743, quoted in Hutchison 1976, pp. 235–36). And even Francis Hutcheson, who opposed "all unnecessary severity" within the family, regarded children as "rational agent[s], with rights valid against the parents," and was probably the most libertarian commentator on these matters in Scotland during the first half of the eighteenth century, insisted with Calvinism that "many restraints upon the . . . appetites [of children] are necessary," that "it is absolutely necessary that they should be governed a long time by others," and that for their "right education [their] parents [have the] right to an unlimited power of directing their actions" (*Works,* 6:188–92). John Witherspoon, a student of Hutcheson's and an ardent spokesman for progressive childrearing in America, captured the reformed tradition's central thesis on socialization more simply and directly when he insisted that parents establish "as soon as possible an entire and absolute authority" in order to guarantee the "absolute submission" of their children (1797, p. 88).

Of course as Goode (1963) remarked many years ago, attitudes about how the family ought to be do not always correspond to the way it actually is. A remarkable unity of theory and practice existed, however, in early eighteenth-century Scotland. Calvinist beliefs on childrearing, after all, were not some marginal set of ideas remote from ongoing affairs. This instead was a period when the Church of Scotland did everything in its enormous power to disseminate Calvinist views widely and to make sure that these were acted upon in the daily family life of the nation. In Scotland, moreover, one finds economic and political arrangements that closely resemble those that underlay the institutionalization of patriarchy in England, and with similar results.[7] Drawing on a variety of ethnographic materials, William Stephens has identified a pattern of outward behaviors that are reliable indicators of the patriarchal household the world over: "the father tends to get such traditional marks of deference as . . . the best food, the best or only chair, special deferential language; [and] father and child tend to be rather 'formal' and restrained in their intercourse" (1963, p. 318). Eighteenth-century Scotland knew precisely the same behavioral pattern. Writing at the end of the century on customs around 1730, Elizabeth Mure observed that "every master was revered by his family. . . . His hours of eating, sleeping, and amusement, were carefully attended by all his family. . . . He kept his own sete by the fire or at table with his hat on his head and often perticular dishes served up for himself, that nobody else shared off. Their [sic] children approached them with awe, and never spoke with any degree of freedom before them" (cited in Mure 1854, 1:260). Mure's

7. The English case is analyzed by Stone (1977, pp. 87–90, 151–59). Integral to the political arrangements he finds to be supportive of patriarchy was the system of patronage, the Scottish version of which is considered in chapter 7. Basic to the economic arrangements in question were the control of property and the rules (primogeniture, entail, and so on) that governed its transmission from generation to generation (on the relationship between paternal possession of land and patriarchalism in colonial America, see Greven 1970, esp. pp. 72–99; see also Smelser and Halpern 1978, pp. S293–94). Property relations similar in many respects also existed in eighteenth-century Scotland (see Farran 1958, pp. 135–80). For a different perspective on the connection between social conditions and patriarchal authority, see Hunt (1970, pp. 152–53).

contemporaries added that the fathers of the age continually kept "their children even when grown to mature years, at a great distance and exact[ed] from them a ceremonious attention to the forms of outward respect" (Somerville 1861, p. 348; see also Graham 1899, p. 25; Plant 1952, pp. 3–4; Tytler and Watson 1871, 2:182–83).

Behind these symbolic trappings of patriarchy, there was a great deal of substance. Aspect after aspect of children's lives was subject to close, thorough, and constant parental regulation, to which children responded with unquestioning obedience or paid the price. The patriarchal home in no sense offered its offspring experiences in autonomy. Plant has concluded that children in early eighteenth-century Scotland were "kept in complete subjection," and Lochhead has described their days of "thraldom" and "strictest discipline."[8] The presence of these traits does not mean that Scottish homes were bereft of positive sentiment. The sternest of Calvinist ministers recognized the deep love that parents had for their young, and feelings of this sort apparently were visible enough in eighteenth-century Scotland that the perceptive and cautious John Millar did not hesitate to speculate on the universality of "parental fondness" (Anon. 1703, p. 27; *Ranks,* p. 230).[9]

But such fondness, as Millar argued and might well have documented with Scottish illustrations, could all too easily coexist with deference, distance, and countless fatherly directives and restraints.[10] Mothers—"presumably because [of their own] frustrations and anxieties" under patriarchal domination, according to Lawrence Stone (1977, p. 170)—often willingly supported this regimen. Lady Balcarres, for example, punished her children's "little misdemeanors . . . as crimes," "structured everything . . . by authority and correction," made her household "a sort of little Bastile, in every closet of which was to be found a culprit,—some . . . sobbing and repeating verbs, others eating their bread and water—some preparing themselves to be whipped," and, by these methods, freed her husband to play the more benevolent despot.[11] In all events, authoritarian control in matters large and small left little room for

8. Plant (1952, p. 3), Lochhead (1948, p. 224). See also Graham (1899, pp. 24–25, 75), and Smout (1969a, pp. 92–93).

9. See also Dalrymple (1787, p. 69), Ferguson (*EHCS,* pp. 16, 19, 51, 53, 221), Graham (1899, p. 24), Robertson (*HA* 9:106–7), and Tytler and Watson (1871, 2:182).

10. See *Ranks,* p. 230. See also Greven (1977, pp. 22–24, 34), and Stone (1977, pp. 175, 193, 654).

11. Lindsay (1849, 2:303–4, 307). See also Dennistoun (1855, 1:309), Plant (1952, p. 5), and Tytler and Watson (1871, 2:182).

the initiatives of the children in the home, whatever their ages. Alexander Boswell, father of Samuel Johnson's famed biographer, did not appear unusual at his time when he demanded that his grown sons keep strict hours in the house, account for their various comings and goings, restrain their conversation in his presence, and submit to his decisions without reservation (Pottle 1966, pp. 56–57). In eighteenth-century Scotland, fathers—perhaps convinced with their colonial counterparts that one of the chief steps in successful childrearing was "to discipline the palate and to govern the stomach"—went to extreme lengths to regulate even the foods that their sons and daughters, whether young or old, consumed.[12] Parents seem to have been at least as active in fundamental decisions about the marriages and careers of their offspring, though this topic deserves much fuller study than it has yet received. The forward-looking Hutcheson taught that "children are sacredly bound to consult the inclinations of parents in such matters as are of high importance to the parents as well as to themselves; such is their marriage, from which those are to issue who must represent their parents, as well as themselves. . . . An high deference therefore to the parents in this matter must be due from the child even in mature years and judgment" (*Works*, 6:195). In an announcement in the *Edinburgh Courant* of 1758, one Robert M'Nair and his wife publicly specified the cost of intransigence: "if any of our children should propose or pretend to offer marriage to any without . . . our advice and consent, they in that case shall be banished from our family twelve months; and if they should go so far as to marry without our advice and consent, in that case they are to be banished from the family seven years" (quoted in Plant 1952, p. 18). Alexander Carlyle, a contemporary of the intellectuals of the Enlightenment, well reflected prevailing practices concerning life's other great choice when he remarked that, in selecting a career, he "yielded to parental wishes and advice, which in those days swayed the minds of young men" (1910, p. 58).

Families so wanting in experiences where children were able to decide for themselves and act on their own were not—as we now know both from contemporary social-psychological research and

12. See Dickinson (1952, p. 21), Fergusson (1882, p. 62), and Minto (1874, 1:22). The quotation on the colonial situation is from Greven (1977, p. 44). For another example of a Scottish patriarchial household in action, see Ross (1972).

from historical studies of authoritarian households[13]—settings for the formation of an orientation of independence. It must therefore seem strange that this orientation came to life in eighteenth-century Scotland. One has to realize, however, that because Scottish fathers were mortal and Scottish children mobile, patriarchal controls were not utterly inescapable. The death of a father with children still at home is a prospect in all societies and one that in past centuries was by no means as uncommon as today;[14] the departure of young children from their parents for service, apprenticeship, schooling, and the like was also formerly a routine occurrence.[15] Although it does not seem that middle and upper class eighteenth-century Scots generally sent their offspring away at quite the tender ages customary in fifteenth-century England and seventeenth-century America, it certainly was commonplace for boys from these strata to leave home by the early teens for several years at a distant college.[16] But whether occasioned by the death of the patriarch or the departure of his subjects, disruptions in familial autocracy cre-

13. See chap. 3, note 27 on the current social-psychological research. On pertinent historical studies, see Demos (1970, pp. 134–39, 1973, pp. 131–33), Greven (1977, pp. 21–109), and Hunt (1970, pp. 133–58). See also Hagan (1962, pp. 143–52) and, for the theory that underlies much of this work, Erickson (1950).

14. Bullough et al. estimate that in eighteenth-century Scotland "the median age at death of those who survived their first year was around 40 years" (1970, p. 117; see also Bullough and Bullough 1971, p. 1057). Comparable class- and sex-specific mortality figures, unfortunately, are not available. But it is interesting here to put together two other findings that Bullough and Bullough have reported: the fact that the majority of eighteenth-century Scottish intellectuals had, when they reached adulthood, two living parents and the fact that, while all classes produced a certain number of intellectuals, the bulk came from the "upper middle class" (1971, pp. 1054, 1056).

15. See Ariès (1962, pp. 154, 271–72, 364–70), Demos (1970, pp. 140–41), Herzog (1962), Morgan (1944, p. 77), Stone (1977, pp. 6, 29, 107, 167, 375, 379), and Trumbach (1978, pp. 238, 251–52, 255, 265).

The departure of a professionally or politically active father from his family for an extended period of time was another familiar event. The effects of this change deserve systematic study, though it apparently did not measurably alter the patriarchal arrangements of the home. It seems that the mother tended to keep things in good order for the return of the master, who was not hesitant to send her lengthy missives with interim commands (see, e.g., Dennistoun 1855, 1:309; Knight 1900, p. 3).

16. See Clarke (1959, p. 133), and Pottle (1966, p. 23). On the movement of younger children, see Beale (1953, p. 337), Boyd (1961, p. 77), Law (1965, pp. 60, 145), Simpson (1947, pp. 183–85), and the Appendix. On the leaving age in England, see Schücking (1929, p. 71); on the American case, see Demos (1970, p. 141).

ated the potential for new learning experiences.[17] To be sure, these were not necessarily any different from the old. A widow could ably tyrannize over a household or cede power to her father, brother, grown son, or next spouse, while the children who left home might wake up in another absolutist realm or confront a type of independence training that was too little and too late to reverse what had already been accomplished. All of these possibilities can be found in Scotland before, during, and after the early eighteenth century and were as congruent with the widespread commitment to dependency as the pervasive patriarchal pattern itself. Certain other possibilities remained, however, and at an apt point in social and cultural history these were encountered by five bright lads.

II

Not a great deal is known about the family lives of Adam Ferguson, David Hume, John Millar, William Robertson, and Adam Smith. There can be little doubt, however, that in varying degrees all of the Scottish enlighteners were liberated from the patriarchal home— liberated in ways that afforded experiences for the development of an orientation of independence.[18]

17. Psychologists have sometimes been wont to view familial disruption from an entirely different perspective, emphasizing in particular how separation from the father can deprive a son of a masculine role model, disrupt his superego development, and the like. One must be cautious with such notions. Not only have they been substantially revised by research on modern American society (see Clausen 1966, pp. 27–28; Yarrow 1964, p. 118), but their applicability to more patriarchal situations is extremely problematic. On the basis of a study of McClelland's (1961) famous need for achievement conducted among Turkish youth, Bradburn has reached a conclusion that is also relevant to independence in eighteenth-century Scotland: "In the United States, where the father may play a more encouraging role . . . loss of the father means the removal of a positive masculine model for achievement. In Turkey, on the other hand, where the father is a much more dominating figure, loss of the father represents an escape from restraining influences . . . and leaves the boy free to respond to any positive forces which may [promote his] achievement related behaviors" (1963, p. 197).

18. Three more standard pieces of information are also known about the family situation of the Scottish enlighteners and should be briefly noted. The first concerns family socioeconomic background. Hume was a son of a reasonably prosperous, minor landowner, or laird, Smith the son of a relatively wealthy government official, and Ferguson, Millar, and Robertson sons of Presbyterian ministers of modest means. In the social hierarchy of the time, lairds stood just below the nobility, while officers of the state and ministers belonged to what might be called the professional (upper-) middle class (see Smout 1969a, pp. 126–28, 338–40, 471–73; see also Bullough and Bullough 1971, p. 1054). Although the various experiences examined in this study were not, as we shall see, limited to youth from the upper and middle strata, a

Escape from the autocratic control of the father was most complete for Hume and Smith, the Enlightenment's staunchest proponents of independence. Hume's father died shortly after the second birthday of the future philosopher and with that single, effective step foreclosed the possibility that David's youth would, like that of so many of his contemporaries, revolve around a father's peculiar hours and meals and chairs and commands in all things great and small. The opportunity this created was not fleeting. David's four-year-old brother was too young to become a successful patriarch; his mother, Katherine Home, never remarried despite the offers that likely came her way; and no adult male relatives joined the household to fill the void. Nor did Katherine Home herself maintain an authoritarian regime. While not what one would now call a permissive parent, she established close and nurturant relations with David and his siblings and was very far from fathers and mothers who sternly regulated every aspect of their children's lives[19]—an interesting illustration of Stone's proposition that the passing of patriarchy brings "the liberation of maternal love" (1977, p. 449). David, as a result, was often permitted to pursue activities of his own liking with a minimum of rigid maternal directives. His childhood appears to have been full of hunting, shooting, fishing,

number of those experiences were more prevalent here than elsewhere in eighteenth-century Scotland. It must be remembered, however, that in terms of both the configuration of experiences they received and their basic beliefs and values, the Scottish enlighteners generally stood well apart from those with similar social backgrounds.

Data also exist on the size of the families of the intellectuals of the Scottish Enlightenment. Smith was an only child (though he had a distant half-brother), Hume had two siblings, Millar three, Ferguson eight (two of whom died during infancy or childhood), and Robertson ten (three of whom died before adulthood). Were one to apply to eighteenth-century Scotland the sociological generalization that parental authoritarianism increases as family size grows (see Clausen 1966, pp. 9–15), one would conclude that of the enlighteners, Robertson and Ferguson came from the most autocratic homes, Hume and Smith from the least—a speculation that converges nicely with the discussion that follows in the text.

Finally, there is information on the birth order of the enlightened intellectuals who had siblings. Millar and Robertson were the eldest children in their families, Ferguson the youngest, and Hume apparently the youngest (and certainly the youngest son). Bullough and Bullough (1971, p. 1056) have reported similar results for their larger pool of eighteenth-century Scottish intellectuals and have remarked that such results fit well with the social-psychological research that shows that oldest, youngest, and single children are especially inclined toward achievement, intellectual and otherwise.

19. See esp. Mossner (1954, pp. 26–34); see also Greig (1931, pp. 28–48), and Knight (1886, pp. 5–6).

fencing, and riding escapades with his brother which, while probably encouraged by the mother, nonetheless left her far behind (Mossner 1954, p. 22). Even in the weighty matter of his early education, David, though partly taught by professional instructors and by his mother, was something of a precocious autodidact, working his own way through the family's ample library (Mossner 1954, pp. 30–31). It is difficult to believe that the cultivated Katherine Home did not support her son's initiatives here, but to a lad who "from . . . earliest Infancy . . . found alwise a strong Inclination to Books & Letters," these certainly brought their own rewards (Hume *HL* 1:13; see also *Essays*, pp. 607–8). During adolescence, David was still more the master of his days. He continued to reside with his family for the bulk of this period, but became actively involved in a variety of gratifying intellectual and recreational pursuits with which his mother seems to have interfered little. She did want her son to take up a legal career and for a time he complied by studying law. To this, however, he soon formed "an insurmountable aversion" and resolved instead to undertake "an independent programme of philosophical and scholarly research directed toward the formulation of a new system of philosophy and criticism" (*Essays*, p. 608; Mossner 1954, p. 52). Parents far more tolerant than those in eighteenth-century Scotland would doubtless have some reservations about such a scheme from their eighteen-year-olds and Katherine Home was understandably unenthusiastic about David's grand plan, but she accepted it and allowed him years at home to follow his cherished ambition (for Hume's own commentary on this period, see *HL* 1:9–18). Acting on his own, deciding for himself: these are experiences from which independence is born.

The family setting in which Adam Smith grew up was no less free of the dependency-promoting experiences of patriarchalism. Young Adam actually spent not a day in a home dominated by his father, for his father died several months prior to his birth. The widowed Margaret Smith remained without a husband for the next sixty years of her life and no other family member ever moved into her household to become the surrogate despot. Whatever form it assumed, Margaret Smith's own method of childrearing did little to impose on her son's life the usual direct and restrictive controls. Though she did not cut the sickly boy off from the rigorous demands of the school, the church, and the other institutions of the day, she provided Adam with a rewarding home environment that was well supplied with tenderness and affection and suffered the "blame [of her contemporaries] for treating him with an unlimited indulgence" (Stewart 1793, pp. 5–6; see also Rae 1895, pp. 4, 24–25, 393; Scott 1937, p. 64). The contemporaries the poor woman had were, of course, the type to raise such a charge rather too quickly, but her son did not substantially disagree with their overall assessment when he later wrote—and in doing so he could scarcely have been thinking of the typical childrearing practices in his age or in most of the other ages that he knew—of loving and indulgent parents who set few harsh limitations on the natural inclinations of their offspring (*TMS,* pp. 96, 240–41, 244; see also *TMS,* pp. 360–62). Adam's emancipation from the Scottish family's standard restraints on independence continued in his adolescence. At the ripe age of fourteen, he left his mother and her community (and various little bonds of dependency between mother and son) far behind to go off by himself for a decade, first to the University of Glasgow, then to Oxford. What Adam learned during this lengthy sojourn carried forth his education in autonomy, as we shall see, while his relationship with his mother became a matter of casual and friendly letters that bear no trace of parental efforts to rule from afar (see *Corr,* pp. 1–3). For Smith as for Hume, death of the father had opened onto a new world.

The fathers of the other three enlighteners were made of sturdier stuff. They lived on until their famous sons were grown men and long provided their families with households that seem to have deviated little from the patriarchal pattern recommended in the Calvinist teachings that they so faithfully preached to their congregations. Although John Millar, William Robertson, and Adam Ferguson all lived years under these conditions, each also secured a release. The timing, duration, and character of these releases differed in ways that foreshadow the differences that these intellectuals later exhibited in their commitment to independence.

Millar was the only Scottish enlightener to write in detail about family life. Where Smith had dropped occasional references to parental indulgence, Millar discoursed at length, and with all the animation of a firsthand observer, on historical circumstances in which children are reduced to "a state of absolute slavery and subjection" and live "under the necessity of submitting to the severe and arbitrary will of their father [whose jurisdiction is] altogether supreme and unlimited" (*Ranks,* pp. 230, 235, 237). He then identified two developments as particularly effective antidotes to parental dominance: the intervention of kin and the going off to school. In so doing, Millar recapitulated the decisive episodes in his own rescue from patriarchy. At two years of age, John was separated, for obscure reasons that "might in some way have to do with his mother's estrangement from her brothers, or possibly with the law of entail" (Lehmann 1960, p. 11), from the home of his orthodox father and sent to live on the estate of the father's older brother. Here the boy stayed for five formative years, acquiring the rudiments from an amiable uncle who apparently—perhaps because as a bachelor he had never been forced to learn the patriarch's role—proved to be a lifelong abettor of the nephew's initiatives and undertakings (see Craig 1806, pp. v–vi). It is difficult indeed to believe that Millar subsequently would have offered the generalization that "the near relations of a family, who have a concern for the welfare of the children, and who have an opportunity of observing the manner in which they are treated, will naturally interpose by their good offices, and endeavour to screen them from [the father's] injustice and oppression" (*Ranks*, p. 238) had his own uncle not done likewise.[20] John's holiday from home did not last indefinitely, however. When he was seven and ready for the busy and arduous life of a grammar schoolboy, he moved to his father's community and for four years again took up residence with his family. A second and more permanent reprieve then allowed John's education to continue on the foundations laid during his original liberation. Having finished grammar schooling at age eleven, John went away to study for at least six years at the University of Glasgow, summered usually with his uncle, and thereafter commenced preparations in Glasgow and in distant Edinburgh for the legal career that he had chosen over his father's counsel to enter the ministry. These later and largely positive experiences will be considered in turn, but what is significant now is the early end that had for the most part come to John's days under the paternal roof and amid the controls and ties of dependency that accompanied it. Years afterwards, Millar put the consequences of this in general and approving terms. Sometimes, he wrote,

> children, at an early period of their life, are obliged to leave their home, in order to be instructed in those trades and professions by which it is proposed they should earn a livelihood, and afterwards to settle in those parts of the country which they find convenient for prosecuting their several employments. By this alteration of circumstances they are emancipated from their father's authority. . . . As they . . . are placed at such a distance from their father,

20. Greven (1977, pp. 155–56) has recently offered interesting support for Millar's generalization.

that he has no longer the opportunity of observing and controlling their behavior, it is natural . . . that their former habits [of submission and obedience] will be gradually laid aside and forgotten. [*Ranks,* p. 239]

Millar's argument is a remarkable anticipation of the conclusions modern scholarship has reached about the capacity of educational institutions that entail residential changes for the young to dissolve dependency and stimulate independence.[21] More than that, the argument provides privileged access to a phase in the experiential process through which Millar himself laid aside and forgot nearly as completely as Adam Smith, if not David Hume, the cultural habits of early eighteenth-century Scotland for the independence of the Enlightenment.

William Robertson never put quite so much of the habitual creed of dependency aside, but his deliverance from the traditional eighteenth-century Scottish family was longer in coming and quicker in going. By separation for the purpose of schooling, however, he too was granted an early respite from the experiences of the patriarchal setting. During his years at home, young William was, as his friend Carlyle remarked, "bred in all the Strictness of an Ecclesiastical Family at that Period" (1973, p. 277). The thoroughness of his father's policy of rigorous regulation can be seen in his demand that William was "never to dance, to attend the theatre, or to play cards" and in the fact that the boy was altogether "unacquainted with . . . Sports and Amusements" (Humphreys 1954, p. 7; Carlyle 1973, p. 277). For all this, William's father appears to have been the kindlier of his parents; his mother is one remembered as "more stern, and even severe" (Brougham 1845, p. 258). William's formal education conveniently removed him from this austere situation. After learning the basics in a small school in his father's parish, the boy was sent at around the age of seven for a classical education at a celebrated grammar school in a town some distance away. Here, except during a month or so of vacation annually, he remained for approximately five years, studying the Latin authors from whom he derived such satisfaction and presumably boarding with a number of other lads under the schoolmaster (Bower 1817–30, 3:25; see also Allardyce 1888, p. x). Given the nature of the educational institutions of the time, this period can hardly be

21. See Hagstrom (1968, pp. 265–66), Herzog (1962, pp. 324–34), Schücking (1929, p. 72), and esp. Trumbach (1978, pp. 238, 251, 265). Note also the relevant remarks of Adam Smith (*TMS,* pp. 363–64).

regarded as the ultimate escape. It did, however, bring William when still of tender years a greater control of his own actions, severing the boy from the perpetual supervision and the relationships of dependency that went hand in hand with daily membership in his dour family and transferring him to an environment where, for the most part, these could not be restored to their former levels (see chap. 5, sec. I)—additional support for the thesis about residential schooling and autonomy advanced by Millar and by more recent commentators. But William's experiences were to take another turn when, following the completion of grammar school, he moved at around his thirteenth year to live for a decade in Edinburgh. There he divided his days between two vastly different settings, resuming residence in the strict household of his parents and, at the same time, confronting the opportunities for autonomy that awaited undergraduate and graduate students at the university, opportunities designed to make good his previous lessons in independence. The implications of this odd experiential mix for the synthesis of Calvinist and Enlightenment themes that was the hallmark of Robertson's writings will be discussed at a later point in this study.

The family experiences of Adam Ferguson, the Scottish Enlightenment's most tepid exponent of independence, were a suitably modified version of those received by his enlightened fellows. Adam's redemption from patriarchy also began with leaving for a classical education, but this did not take place until a period of childhood longer than that found in the case of any of the other enlighteners had first been spent subject to a scrupulous father's awesome authority. It was, in fact, only in his tenth year that Adam, having outgrown the local parish school, departed from his orthodox home. At that time, he left for a successful stay at a renowned grammar school and lived under the charge of a townsman to whom he was related, a move that effectively distanced the youth from the parental armamentarium by which he had previously been kept in dependence and, by so doing, placed him in a relatively more autonomous position. It would be rash, however, to suggest that Adam was dramatically made over by this one change. The organization of eighteenth-century schools, the unlikelihood that Adam's forgotten kinsman was among the age's few indulgent caretakers, and particularly certain developmental considerations all militate against such a possibility. Independence emerges, after all, from experiences where individuals are on their own to a developmentally appropriate degree. While going away to school could have large consequences for a young child, especially a child who by early adolescence proceeded to a freer university life, its significance was less far-reaching for an older, more fully socialized lad like Adam, who would not go on to other new experiences until his sixteenth year. To be sure, because his departure from his parents' household commenced when it did and involved the intensive classical education, Adam's was not the empty emancipation of boys who, having remained in totalitarian confines until their teens, went off to college for seven or so months out of each of their next three or four years and then returned home to worship with their fathers. But in comparison with the rest of those who would make the Scottish Enlightenment, Adam's flight from the experiences of the authoritarian family had not started well. It did, however, continue on course. When Adam finished grammar school, he did not go back to his father, but moved further from him and the unknown kinsman to reside for four years at St. Leonard's College at St. Andrews, where annual sessions were generally longer than elsewhere in eighteenth-century Scotland. Subsequently, he studied divinity at St. Mary's College, St. Andrews and then continued this training at the University of Edinburgh. As we will see, it was only during this final phase of his education, when he was already a man, that Adam was genuinely on his own, and even then he was pursuing a clerical career in accordance with his father's wishes. Nevertheless, with each major step from the age of nine onward, Adam Ferguson was cut looser from the moorings of patriarchy, given increased scope over his daily activities, and thus prepared to profit from the later lessons that culminated, after the death of his father, in a sincere, though predictably ambivalent, commitment to independence.[22] His experiences in autonomy, like those of the other intellectuals of the Scottish Enlightenment, had their beginnings in an early escape from the enfeebling constraints of the patriarchal family—and in early eighteenth-century Scotland such beginnings could reach fruition.

22. Shortly after his father died, Ferguson also gave up his clerical activities, and Kettler speculates that it may actually have been "the death of his father [that] liberated [Ferguson] from the obligation to pursue such a career and gave him leave to try his fortune as a man of letters" (1965, p. 47). For the record, it should be further noted that Robertson's parents died before he composed any of his works. Millar, in contrast, was an established scholar of fifty at the death of his father.

5

Early Educational Experiences

I

Wherever they took hold, Calvinist teachings favored the growth of educational institutions to increase literacy and thereby to spread knowledge of the word of God as conveyed in the scriptures. But as Lawrence Stone has observed, it was in Scotland that this "zeal for a literate, moral, Bible-reading public found its fullest expression" (1969, p. 80). From the onset of the Scottish Reformation, John Knox and his fellow preachers had made their daring goals plain. Warning of the need to "be most careful for the virtuous education and godly upbringing of the youth of this Realm," the reformers' blueprint for the divine commonwealth boldly proposed a national educational system that included a teacher to instill the "first rudiments, and especially . . . the Catechism" in every rural parish and a school "to teach Grammar, and the Latin tongue [in every town] of any reputation" (*First Book of Discipline* 1560–61, pp. 130–31).

This sweeping recommendation was not quickly heeded, but ultimately it had its effect.[1] Governmental measures enacted in the seventeenth century made financial provisions to further the educational program of the leaders of the Reformation (see Knox 1953, pp. 4–7), and by the century's end visible progress had been made.[2] Throughout considerable portions of the Lowlands, local landowners did their duty and endowed schools in the rural par-

1. Except as noted, the sketch presented in this paragraph has been composed by drawing on Bain (1965), Beale (1953), Boyd (1961), Jessop (1931), Law (1965), Simpson (1947), Smout (1969a, pp. 82–83, 421–37), and Withrington (1962, 1965).

2. This progress obviously rested on far more than the recommendation of the reformers and a series of legislative enactments. For present purposes, however, there is no need to enter into the deeper economic, political, religious, and cultural factors that fostered and sustained the Scottish educational system.

ishes, while municipal councils, continuing a tradition that ante-
dated the Reformation, supported the town schools. Attendance
was not mandatory at any of these institutions, but to children of
parents duly persuaded by the insistent ministry of the importance
of formal instruction for the young, the extensive educational network offered the basic subjects of the age at small fees which were
often publicly defrayed for the indigent. A great deal remained to
be done, however. There were parishes still without a schoolmaster
when the century of the Enlightenment began and, although this
situation was largely corrected even in the Highlands by 1760,
problems of a more fundamental sort persisted as the reformers'
plan of one school in every town and country parish proved insufficient for the task of educating the nation. Too many parishes
were simply too spread out and too populous to be served adequately by a single schoolhouse, however spacious and well staffed.
The custom of providing children of the upper classes with in-
home tutors, the short and irregular school attendance of rural
youth from the lower classes, and the low expectations for female
education all lessened the load on parochial facilities, but these
were still far from enough.[3] In the eighteenth century, adventure
schools—a multiform welter of privately operated establishments
principally financed by student payments—and charity attempted
to fill the gaps in the publicly maintained educational system, and
their successes were halting. Yet it is nevertheless probable that,
when taken together, the various schools of the period achieved a
significant result. By the middle decades of the eighteenth century,
they had, in Christopher Smout's judgment, gone a long distance
toward creating among the men of the Lowlands the "literate peasant society" that had been envisaged at the start of the Scottish
Reformation (1969a, p. 431; on the distance that was still to go, see
Houston 1982).

Of these diverse educational arrangements, it is the publicly supported institutions that require fuller attention if we are to understand the schooling experiences of the intellectuals of the Scottish
Enlightenment. While all of these institutions were deeply involved
in religious instruction, they may be divided into several distinct

3. On upper-class arrangements, see Hans (1951, pp. 18, 23, 28), and Plant (1952,
p. 7). On female education, see Grant (1876, pp. 526–37), Morgan (1927, p. 87),
and Plant (1952, pp. 12–18), in addition to the general sources cited in note 1. It
is true that, despite the low expectations set for them, girls sometimes did attend
parish and small town schools. This chapter will, nevertheless, limit itself to a discussion of the primary recipients of instruction in these institutions: boys.

types according to their other curricular features. The reformers had operated with the simple dichotomy of country parish schools devoted to the basics and town Latin schools, but in the Lowlands there was a more complex, three-tier system. The broad base of this system was composed of rural parochial schools designed to provide children from the age of five to six onward with a thorough grounding in the "primary" subjects—reading the native English language and usually writing. Few parish schools actually stopped at this point, however, and at least by the eighteenth century many were putting certain of their older boys through the "secondary" course of Latin studies in preparation for the university.[4] Primary and secondary offerings also coexisted, though in very different proportions, in a majority of the small town grammar or (as they were often called) burgh schools that made up the second level of the system.[5] Here the principal objective was to take lads of about seven or eight, who had learned the basics of their own language, through an approximately five-year classical education that commenced with Latin grammar and then proceeded to the study of Roman authors, but schools of this sort likewise tended—either within the same building or in a neighboring facility—to give the beginners in the regions that they served training in the English rudiments.[6] In so doing, such schools diverged sharply from those of a third variety, the grammar schools of largest urban places like Aberdeen, Glasgow, and especially Edinburgh. These institutions were intended exclusively for youths pursuing classical studies and made no regular provision for teaching elementary subjects. City children who could not read and write had to learn at home or in

4. See Beale (1953, pp. 333–34), Boyd (1961, p. 57), Morgan (1927, pp. 73–74), Simpson (1947, p. 36), Smout (1969a, p. 438), and Withrington (1965, p. 125).

5. For convenience, the text speaks interchangeably of town schools and burgh schools, and uniformly treats these institutions as Latin grammar schools. To prevent misunderstanding, however, two comments are required. First, the equation of town and burgh schools abandons the awkward convention of withholding the "burgh school" designation from schools that were located in towns or burghs but maintained through parochial rather than municipal mechanisms (on this convention, see Beale 1953, pp. 9, 50; Grant 1876, pp. 98–99). Second, just as there were classical grammar schools in a few of the larger rural parishes (see Boyd 1961, p. 57), in some of the smaller or more backward places that were technically denominated "burghs" the study of Latin was no more common than in the typical country parochial school. Since it is not the aim of this chapter to construct a history of Scottish education, these complexities can be set aside in the present context.

6. See Bain (1965, pp. 131–32), Grant (1876, pp. 385–90), Morgan (1927, p. 87), and Strong (1909, pp. 141–42).

privately funded schools, or remain illiterate; the establishments at the pinnacle of the Scottish educational network were not for them.[7]

In outward form, these types of schools were none of them like our own. The closest eighteenth-century analogues to modern educational institutions were the city grammar schools, particularly Edinburgh High School, where students at each of the five levels of the classics curriculum were instructed in separate classrooms by different teachers (see Law 1965, pp. 22, 84).[8] But even here things were not what one might now expect, for while the school rector annually guided a different group of boys through the lessons of the fifth year, each of the remaining four schoolmasters stayed with the same cohort for four years—taking all of its members, however unequal in age and skill, from the first-year rudiments to the fourth-year authors—and only then passed it to the rector and started over with the school's new entering class. Outside of the greater urban centers, public schools attracted comparatively smaller pools of students and were organized still more simply and traditionally. The schools in the rural parishes often had only one instructor and those in the towns rarely more than two, one for the whole Latin course and another for English, and both subjects might well be taught within the same, spartan classroom (see Beale 1953, pp. 78–79, 87; Simpson 1947, p. 51). In either locale, schoolmasters were generally ill-paid and poorly prepared for the forbidding task of providing a variety of lessons to forty, fifty, sixty, or more pupils, ranging in age from five to fifteen,[9] and commentators have occasionally marvelled that Scottish youth learned anything at all (see Graham 1899, p. 433). But when the town and country schools of eighteenth-century Scotland are viewed more broadly, it becomes apparent that they had enormous potential as agencies of socialization, for they consumed huge portions of the

7. See Kerr (1910, p. 99), Law (1965, pp. 28–30), Morgan (1927, p. 87), and Strong (1909, pp. 140–41).

The preceding description has focused upon Latin and English since, along with Calvinist orthodoxies, these were the mainstays of the eighteenth-century curriculum. They were not, however, the only subjects offered. Arithmetic was widely taught (see, e.g., Beale 1953, p. 253), and a variety of more practical courses—navigation, geography, bookkeeping, geometry, French—was also made available at appropriate fees in many schools as the century of the Enlightenment progressed (see Withrington 1970a, pp. 170–84).

8. On similar arrangements in other city grammar schools, see Strong (1909, p. 143), and Withrington (1970a, pp. 174–75).

9. See Bain (1965, p. 118), Beale (1953, p. 87), Boyd (1961, pp. 46, 50), Graham (1899, pp. 420–34), and Smout (1969a, p. 425).

young lives of those who attended them regularly and exhibited striking similarities to what Goffman (1961) has called "total institutions."[10] Eighteenth-century students were required to put in seven-day weeks and for five days instruction generally ran eight long hours, from seven in the morning until six in the evening, with time out for meals. Saturdays brought a half-day in class and on Sundays children went to church services with their master and afterwards marched back to the schoolhouse for a detailed review of the sermon. Some burgh schools granted a one-month vacation each year, parochial schools often relaxed during periods when extra hands were needed in the fields, but for the most part the strenuous round recurred week after week, year after year.[11] In the process, schoolchildren, whatever they learned of their subjects, were inundated with experiences from which they could draw out lessons of a more basic sort, lessons sometimes at variance with the Calvinist creed that pervaded the schools of the age.

That variance was not very marked where dependency was concerned. Although Scottish schools did, as we will see, provide certain limited experiences in autonomy, on the whole they subjected their students to a world of direct and restrictive control where they had little range to act on their own. The chief source of this control was the schoolmaster, who bore the grave responsibility of carrying on the work of fathers and making something out of the ignorant and brazen babes that so threatened the godly. To this end, schoolmasters were not only to teach the standard subjects, but also to regulate carefully the behavior of their pupils in and out of class and—in the words of a typical eighteenth-century school code—"strictly to discharge all manner of immoralitie and incivilitie . . . establishing and maintaining good order and discipline and authority" (cited by Beale 1953, pp. 309, 313; see also Law 1965, pp. 198–99; Simpson 1947, p. 49). To expect all of this from men with large enrollments and families of their own was to demand the impossible. But while the masters were unable to reproduce the thorough domination of patriarchy, under the watchful eyes of their brethren most took seriously their principal moral obligations

10. Goffman defines a total institution as a place "where a large number of like-situated individuals, cut off from the wider society for an appreciable period of time, together lead an enclosed, formally administered round of life" (1961, p. xiii).

11. See Beale (1953, p. 308), Graham (1899, pp. 434–35), Grant (1876, p. 169), Kerr (1910, p. 87), and Morgan (1927, p. 84).

and devised intricate procedures by which to rein tightly the lives of their young charges. Grant reports that

> every school of importance had its . . . laws for governing the interesting little company assembled within its walls—a code so comprehensive as to embrace, if possible, the [pupils'] whole duties. . . . Great pains [were taken] that the little subjects who were required to obey it should be perfectly acquainted with its tenor. . . . The positive duties are few, but important and consist of injunctions to the scholars to seek God in the morning before they come abroad; to come to school with washed hands, combed hair, and neat clothes; and to obey and respect the masters. The negative duties are numerous enough—forbidding them to come late, to be absent or truant, . . . to sport or bargain, to throw stones or snowballs, to tease or nickname, to [wander] from place to place, [etc.] [Grant 1876, pp. 158, 194–95]

Primary and secondary schools have had their peculiar rules in other places, of course, but those in Scotland took uncommon measures to guarantee that children heeded the precepts. For times when their own vigilance gave out, schoolmasters were even wont to employ bands of student "captors" to monitor the doings of their peers and to bring the reprobate frequently to justice.[12] The routines of Kirkcaldy Burgh School were not unusual:

> That upon Munday and Saturday the catalogue [of rules] shall be read, and the captors examined what faults they have found in any of the scholars, that they may be duely corrected, and that there shall be a privy censor who is to take notice of the faithfulness of all the publick captors and privately to acquaint the Master who is . . . to chastise the faultie, after due examination of their faults, according to their demerits, and in caise any shall disobey their Masters, and not give them due defference; then the Magistrates and Minister or any of them shall come to the Schools, and see such scholars condingly punished for a terrour to others. [Cited in Beale 1953, p. 310]

"Terrour" it often was. A multitude of stiff penalties awaited those who violated regulations and there were no inhibitions about resorting to the leather strap when milder forms of punishment

12. See Bain (1965, p. 127), Graham (1899, p. 433), Jessop (1931, p. 172), and Kerr (1910, p. 167).

proved ineffectual.[13] Community authorities did restrain Scottish teachers from much of the classroom barbarity found elsewhere in times past, but, as Beale writes, "they also disapproved of over-indulgence" (1953, p. 90). Educational institutions were not to tolerate what patriarchal households prohibited. Homes and schools formed a solid alliance to keep independence well checked.

That objective was furthered by many of the teaching methods of the epoch. Burdened with an inordinate number of responsibilities, schoolmasters were not in the habit of trifling with the kinds of exercises that encourage youthful intellectual initiatives. In the basics, instruction was almost invariably mechanical, relying upon "a great deal of learning by rote" and resting content with "children repeating parrot-wise what they could not understand."[14] The state of affairs was rarely much improved in the advanced subjects. Stone's assessment that the post-Renaissance classical education "demanded effective repression of the will, the imagination, the emotions, and even intellectual curiosity" (1977, p. 166) may overstate the point, but it is the case that the study of Latin in Scotland required an astonishing amount of memorization—first of innumerable grammatical rules, later of the eloquent words of the Romans[15]—and at its very best attempted to instill the capacity to imitate the ancient models in writing and speech, not the ability to formulate any original views (Clarke 1959, pp. 3, 16). Instructional techniques of these sorts were not a potent solvent of dependency.

This is not, however, the complete story. Dreeben has argued that contemporary schools offer experiences essential for the development of an independent orientation because they remove children daily from the parents "with whom they have already formed strong relationships of dependency"; place those children in classroom situations that—since they contain a large number of other youngsters and are continually disrupted by yearly promotions to higher grades—limit "opportunities for establishing new relationships of dependency with adults and for receiving help from them"; and at the same time demand that each child work entirely by himself on an array of academic tasks (1968, pp. 10, 13, 21, 66–

13. See Beale (1953, p. 333), Boyd (1961, pp. 31–32), Grant (1876, pp. 196–97, 204–5), Kerr (1910, pp. 165–68), and Scotland (1969, 1:66).

14. Beale (1953, p. 88), Smout (1969a, p. 430). See also Bain (1965, p. 84), and Simpson (1947, pp. 24–26, 55–57).

15. On these aspects of the classical education, see Bain (1965, pp. 84–85), Duncan (1965, pp. 88–91), Fay (1956, pp. 49–50), Kenrick (1956, p. 35), Law (1965, p. 209), Simpson (1947, p. 38), and Somerville (1861, pp. 8–9).

67). In Scottish educational institutions of the eighteenth century, all of these arrangements, save for annual changes of teachers and classrooms, find dramatic parallels. When youth of that period entered the schoolhouse, they were cut off from parents and close familial ties of dependency for more hours, and days, and weeks of the year than their twentieth-century counterparts and supplied with even fewer chances to form those ties anew. Confronted with so many pupils, lessons, and other duties each day, parochial and small town schoolmasters ordinarily lacked the time and energy to provide ample help and support to more than a handful. Situational exigencies also forced these schoolmasters to make heavy use of assignments in which children were on their own for long periods of the schoolday. Where students at widely different levels of the curriculum shared the same unpartitioned space, the only effective way to cope was to divide students into groups by the level they had reached and then, as Beale explains, successively to require "all groups but one group [to] work away at tasks set by the master, while he instruct[ed] that one group" (1953, p. 87). These tasks may have been uninspiring, but school children had nonetheless to execute them independently. In England's grammar schools, the practice of pupils "prompting and helping one another," Vincent observes, was actually "more reprehensible and therefore to be more severely punished than failure to do well" (1969, p. 63) and, given how strongly these institutions resembled those in the north (see Clarke 1959, p. 134), it is not unlikely that a similar policy operated in Scotland. Scottish schools, in all events, clearly were not without the bulk of the organizational characteristics and the resulting experiences that make modern schools ideal settings for the acquisition of an attitude of independence. In the Scottish case, however, such experiences were embedded in an educational context where the dominant experiential motif was antithetical to independence; for this reason, they did not promote the same attitudinal outcome that they might today. For children who were growing up in authoritarian homes and going forth everyday to schools where their actions were ever under the control of powerful masters equipped with elaborate regulations, alert captors, and an abundance of painful sanctions, the chore of doing insipid exercises unaided was hardly enough to inaugurate a commitment to human autonomy. Lads whose family experiences had already sparked such a commitment and those whose school attendance entailed an early and prolonged separation from daily paternal commands and constraints were better prepared to benefit from the school's quiet instructions in independence, and such instructions would at least prevent a wholesale extirpation of the gains made elsewhere. Even on these lads, however, the pervasive behavioral and intellectual restraints that were the more pronounced characteristic of school life could not but take their toll, ineluctably driving in something of the age-old message of dependency.

In supplying this complex of experiences, primary and secondary educational institutions in Scotland were not entirely uniform. Instructors at poorly attended parochial establishments and city grammar school teachers attached to small classes were less constrained than their overworked colleagues to suppress relationships of dependency with their pupils, to rely on proxy devices to regulate student behavior, and to impose endless hours of busywork. Then too, from personal predilection or adherence to local customs, certain schoolmasters might punish youthful offenses more gently and infrequently than other masters, assign more difficult or interesting exercises, turn more often to student assistants, and the like (see Beale 1953, p. 88; Saunders 1950, p. 241; Simpson 1947, p. 50). Yet all of these developments were only so many limited variations around the familiar themes, not deviations that transformed some of Scotland's schools into settings that offered appreciably increased training in autonomy. In this and most other areas, public schools from the countryside to the metropolis were actually remarkably resistant to change throughout the whole dynamic eighteenth century. Long after the Enlightenment had come and gone, schoolroom organization, educational objectives, instructional methods, discipline, and the rest remained essentially as they had been back in the seventeenth century.[16] Some of these constant features of Scottish education deserve further consideration, however, because in the social and cultural circumstances of the eighteenth century they acquired a new significance. These features are the elements that made the schools breeding grounds of universalism.

A universalistic orientation is born of experiences in which a heterogeneous lot of individuals is treated by uniform standards. In the eighteenth century and before, the ability to provide experiences of this type was not found at all the tiers of the Scottish educational system. The differences in the curricular organization of each tier interacted with the differences in the social composition

16. See Bain (1965, pp. 12, 123), Beale (1953, pp. 156, 333), Gibson (1912, p. 60), Law (1965, p. 218), and Smout (1969a, pp. 429–30). Cf. note 7 of this chapter.

of the student population served at each level to make small town grammar schools, whatever their other dissimilarities, settings from which the young could derive a principle of universalism. In rural parish schools and large urban grammar schools, however, the structure of curricular activities combined with population characteristics in ways unfavorable to the same sort of learning opportunities.[17]

This is true despite the almost legendary heterogeneity of parish schools. In these humble little establishments, children of exceptionally diverse ages, aptitudes, and social strata all received an education. Against the backdrop of an era rigidly stratified at nearly every turn, the mixing of social classes is—and was to contemporaries—particularly striking. Parochial institutions gave instruction "to poor and wealthy alike" (Stone 1969, p. 80) and, side by side, sons of landed gentry, professionals, prosperous peasants and traders, minor craftsmen, and oppressed laborers passed their time in school, exposed for the same long days to the same schoolmasters, the same jejune theological lessons, the same behavioral regulations, punishments, and the like.[18] Laurance Saunders in fact contends that Scottish parish schools set up a world without traditional "artificial distinctions" and thereby "inculcated . . . universal standards" (1950, p. 242). But this view greatly idealizes the actual situation. The common experiences that parochial schoolchildren underwent took place in the midst of a process that manifestly failed to treat everyone uniformly. Even in the simple matter of attendance, there were conspicuous disparities among different types of students. While affluent pupils would march off to school regularly for several years, poorer youngsters, their supple bodies needed by the rural economy, their parents sometimes indifferent toward education, became chronic absentees who withdrew altogether (perhaps discharged by community officials reluctant to pay

17. As will become clear, these generalizations are based upon classifying the composition of parochial and small town schools as heterogeneous and that of large city schools as homogeneous. Although this simple classification is quite sufficient for the general discussion that follows, it is important to emphasize that heterogeneity is really a matter of degree, not an all-or-nothing affair. With fuller information than is currently available on the student populations of specific Scottish schools, one could presumably locate these institutions on a homogeneity-heterogeneity continuum and then, from this more subtle perspective, explore their varying implications for the growth of universalism (see Camic 1983b, pp. 62–63).

18. See Gibson (1912, p. 64), Kerr (1910, p. 165), Knox (1953, p. 10), and esp. Hans (1951, p. 26).

the fees of poor students for too long a time) after a few years of schooling had taught them to stumble their way through the Bible.[19]

Perfectly regular attendance by all would not, however, have mitigated a more fundamental divide that was inherent in parochial education: the dichotomy between English and Latin students.[20] The basics, not the classics, were the raison d'être of parish schools and in this respect they fulfilled expectations, providing Latin to only 5 percent or so of their pupils.[21] But this minority was unlike any of the groups that the master might have formed to facilitate teaching primary subjects to youth of unequal attainments. When their skills improved, children moved naturally in and out of the fluid groupings in reading and writing. Beyond the basics, however, the progression stopped abruptly for all but the few who, because of their status, or pocketbook, or exceptional talents, were granted entry into the advanced Latin course. This curricular double standard, even where it left no further traces on classroom life, suffused the parochial school experience by continually separating out a handful of lads for instruction in a language incomprehensible to the rest and, at the same time, labelling that handful as the elite who were destined for the universities and professions that, as every schoolboy knew, would nowise be the good fortune of students confined to English (see Morgan 1927, pp. 73–74; Saunders 1950, p. 242). That everyone was not on equal footing was frequently underscored by schoolmasters succumbing to "the temptation . . . to neglect the rank and file for the sake of the special few" (Morgan 1927, p. 74). Training youngsters in the classics was a long, drawn-out affair and, as Boyd has noted, in busy parish schools "attention could only be given to the boys studying Latin . . . at the expense of others" (1961, p. 70; see also Simpson 1947, p. 28). Latin classes, nevertheless, were something master after master, rejoicing "to see someone who owed everything to him go straight from his school to the university," eagerly provided (Simpson 1947, p. 51). "To prepare two or three pupils annually for the university," Morgan

19. See Bain (1965, pp. 112, 126), Beale (1953, pp. 338–39), Boyd (1961, p. 67), Jessop (1931, pp. 49–50, 100, 156), Simpson (1947, pp. 51, 55, 214), and Smout (1969a, pp. 428, 430).

20. Within this dichotomy, further divisions could be mentioned: some English students took writing and arithmetic, while others were taught only to read; some Latin boys studied Greek and French, while others did not (see Beale 1953, p. 335; Smout 1969a, p. 428). The following discussion will concentrate, however, on the division that was of overriding importance.

21. Smout (1969a, p. 428). See also Beale (1953, pp. 333–34), Boyd (1961, p. 70), and Simpson (1947, pp. 44–45).

observes, "was more attractive to the scholarly teacher than the laborious drilling of the mass of the children in the elements of education" (1927, p. 74; see also Boyd 1961, p. 68). The results of this ingrained preference were felt well into the nineteenth century: the "undue attention [accorded to the advanced] pupils had a bad effect on the general economy of the school [as] the junior classes (the most important in rural schools) were neglected in favour of the classes taking Latin" (Simpson 1947, p. 52). Such special treatment for special boys further undermined the capacity of Scotland's parochial establishments to offer their students the sort of experience from which to infer an orientation of universalism.

The grammar schools in the largest urban centers had limits of a wholly different kind. Pupils in these institutions—as well as at those in the smaller burghs—were removed from the incessant demands of rural life and thus differentiated themselves by few of the discrepancies in attendance that characterized country parish schools. Moreover, by specializing in the classics and sending the unlettered elsewhere, city grammar schools altogether abolished the radical distinction between English and Latin lads. At this level of the Scottish educational system, the curriculum was essentially "uniform for all pupils" (Gibson 1912, p. 67), and might look something like the following:

[First Year]	Vocables, Variae Loquendi Formulae Dicta Sapientum, Rudimenta Pietatis.
[Second Year]	Sulpitius de Moribus, Cato's Moral Distichs, Phaedri Fabulae.
[Third Year]	Poets—Phaedrus, Ovid's Epistles or Metamorphosis.
	Prose Authors—Cicero's Select Epistles, Cornelius Nepos.
[Fourth Year]	Poets—Virgil's Pastorals, Claudian, Ovid's Metamorphosis, Buchanan's Psalms.
	Prose Authors—Caesar's Commentaries, Velleius Paterculus, Justin, Curtius.
[Fifth year]	Poets—Terence, Virgil, Lucan, Horace, Juvenal, Buchanan's Psalms.
	Prose Authors—Cicero's Select Orations, Livy, Florus, Sallust, Suetonius, Vossius' little compend of Rhetoric. [Law 1965, p. 74]

Schoolmasters would break the list of works designated for each year down into day-to-day instructional agenda that presented to an entire group of boys the same classical passages, elements of grammar, vernacular translations, prose essays, verse compositions, and so on (see Bain 1965, pp. 84–85; on the various components of the classical education, see Clarke 1959, pp. 7–17). This mass assignment of similar tasks made possible a mass application of common performance criteria (see Bain 1965, p. 85), and urban grammar school youths were thus exposed not only to general procedural and disciplinary rules, but also to uniform standards of evaluation.

Yet, by and large, the universalistic message implicit in these arrangements was obfuscated by countervailing features of the classical education that the city schools offered. Urban Latin students, after all, were taught (except in their final year) by instructors who, because they interacted with the same class continuously for four years and were unencumbered by the arduous responsibility of supplying suitable lessons to a broad range of primary and secondary classes, had unparalleled opportunities to forge and exhibit personal attachments, both positive and negative, with many of their boys. These particularistic tendencies were strengthened whenever the instructors divided their pupils into ability groups (see Law 1965, p. 82) for, unlike reading and writing clusters in the rural parishes and classics classes in the small towns, these groups were not something through which children regularly progressed as their knowledge increased during their stay in school. In the city grammar schools where intraclass grouping was used, lads were typically kept in the same ability stratum year after year and repeatedly given a calibre of instruction that was reserved for that particular stratum (see Law 1965, p. 98)—a situation that recalls Dreeben's observation that teachers who "treat . . . segments of the class differently according to differences in capacity . . . partially recreate a [more particularistic] kinship-type of relationship with pupils" (1968, p. 77). But even without personalized teacher-student attachments and entrenched ability groups, the grammar schools in the largest burghs were not settings conducive to an efflorescence of universalistic sentiments. Not only were the children in these institutions generally closer in age to a majority of their classmates than rural schoolboys were, they were also a far more select, socially homogeneous lot. Edinburgh High School, for example, attracted youth from the nobility, the landed gentry, and the motley middle ranks (see Law 1965, pp. 59–60, 220), but not lads from the whole bottom range of the social structure, "the sons of labourers, chairmen, coalheavers, journeymen shoemakers, alehouse waiters, tan-house workers and caddies," and the rest (Smout 1969a, p. 444). Some of these youngsters might, with luck, acquire a few of the basics at one of Edinburgh's less elite educational establishments, though many were in fact foredoomed to illiteracy (see Law 1965, pp. 29, 220–21; Smout 1969a, pp. 438–39). In either case, the vast multitude of the children the city Latin boys saw on the streets before and after hours did not, and never would, accompany them into school. School was special, not a universal, experience.

In Scotland's small town grammar schools, it was otherwise. While not quite as encompassing of the social spectrum as public educational institutions in the rural parishes, the town schools drew students of the most disparate abilities and ages from widely separated levels of the class hierarchy and embraced "rich and poor alike."[22] Because these schools were principally classical seminaries, however, they did not follow the parochial practice of segregating a few privileged Latin boys off from the mass of English lads. Here most pupils studied the classics, though in a departure from the exclusionary policies of the large urban grammar schools, primary subjects were also provided for beginners. To manage the variegated groups before them, town schoolmasters were accustomed to divide students into several classes, one composed of novices, another of children starting the rudiments of Latin grammar, a third of youngsters who had passed through the first rudiments and were taking up the authors and parts of grammar specified for the second year of classical education, and so on. With these divisions in place, school life would then proceed much as it did at Kirkcaldy Burgh School in the 1730s:

> Commonly there are six classes in the school. The first four learn Latin, the fifth to read or have just begun the rudiments, the sixth is of the lectors or those who read English etc., to write and accompt only. Their school tasks or private from night to next morning as follows, the first class write a version. . . . This version is examined immediately after meeting in the morning, which done the boys take their paper in their hands and from the version of English they have made give the Latin of the author in the natural and constituted order of the words: the second, third and fourth classes repeat some part of the grammar of a poeticall author—to exercise their memorys and store their minds with vocables. They are also examined about what they

22. The quotation is from Grant (1876, p. 493). More generally, see Grant (1876, pp. 493–96), Hans (1951, p. 26), and Smout (1969a, pp. 438–39). See too note 27 of this chapter.

have repeated and helped to some understanding of it. The fifth get some vocables by heart or some part of the rudiments. And the sixth read a chapter or so in the bibles. Besides the first three classes have presented to them a certain number of vocables to employ and keep them busy while the masters are teaching the Lower classes, which these give account of immediately after these classes are taught. . . .

The work and exercise of the school classes in the forenoon as follows. The first and second classes write a theme. The third and fourth classes have prescribed to them some part of the rudiments and some vocables which they had learnt before . . . the fifth are taught for an hour to read a chapter then write and such as are more advanced in . . . writing are also to repeat some questions in the catechisms every forenoon till they have them perfectly. . . .

In the afternoon in school classes are employed as follows. The highest classes spend the whole afternoon in expounding authors. The two highest and sometimes the third have prescribed them a part of a poeticall author . . . and the fourth and sometimes the third class have some rules of the grammar together with some portion of an easy prose author. All these present and give account of their various prescriptions before the School is dismissed. The fifth are taught to read Latin or get some part of the rudiments; after which they prepare and get some vocables against next morning, the sixth read a chapter or two, then write and work some questions or example in arithmetic. [Cited in Fay 1956, pp. 49–50][23]

At first glance, this stratified little world hardly appears to be a scene for the development of universalism. That different classes worked at different tasks should not, however, obscure the fact that the heterogeneous lot of pupils that populated the town grammar schools repeatedly experienced treatment by uniform standards. Whatever their curricular level, or social status, or age, students kept the same basic schedule, shared the same set of facilities, and were governed by a behavioral code whose provisions and penalties applied to them all. Furthermore, whatever their social and per-

23. For a more general discussion of these instructional arrangements, see Grant (1876, pp. 330–73). Although the excerpt quoted makes no mention of classes for students interested in the age's auxiliary subjects (see note 7 above), presumably the masters in Kirkcaldy were like those in other small burghs and, without disrupting the ordinary routine, worked one or more of these subjects into the schedule from time to time.

sonal attributes, youth in the same school class grappled simultaneously with identical assignments and were afterward examined
and evaluated just as their peers. At the other two levels of the
Scottish educational system there were, as we have seen, analogues
to many of these experiences, but on both levels these were conjoined to grouping procedures with distinctly particularistic implications. The several classes found in the schoolrooms of the smaller
burghs differed markedly, however, from the chief classroom
groupings that existed elsewhere in the system. While the ability
groups in the city grammar schools and the Latin classes in the
rural parishes were exclusive arrangements, not for every student
even in principle, the various classes in the town schools were open
to all pupils in due course. Here in any particular year a student
would receive only some of the lessons that his master taught, but
in the following year he and his diverse classmates would advance
a level to undergo the instructions that the class a year their senior
had just completed, while handing down those they had finished
to the next junior class. The step-by-step progression would extend
to all the classes in the school and then (with the loss of the most
advanced class and the entry of new beginners) recur each year,
according different tasks in turn to different batches of boys on
the basis of a uniform organizational logic, not because they were
special. With great frequency, this process exposed children to the
"successive boundary crossings . . . from grade to grade" which,
Dreeben suggests, make it "possible for pupils to acquire [the] rel-
ativity of perspective [about] their own circumstances" that is integral to universalism (1968, pp. 76–77);[24] in Scotland's simple one-
or two-room schools, students not only themselves crossed the
boundaries between one class and the next annually, they directly
observed youngsters in other classes going through similar transitions, transitions then reenacted several times daily as each class
took up in public view the tasks that in previous years had fallen

24. The inclusion here and above of certain comments by Dreeben should not
be seen as implying that it is appropriate to transpose to the problem at hand his
entire analysis of the situational roots of universalism. Dreeben (1968, pp. 22–23,
76–77) argues that universalism is fostered when there is a parity of age and ability
among the students in a school class, and this claim is quite reasonable in light of
his particular conception of universalism. Intraclass age and ability homogeneity is,
however, the opposite of the sort of factor relevant to the development of the
Enlightenment's rather different brand of universalism (see Camic 1983b, p. 63,
note 11).

to other groups of lads.[25] It is doubtless true that through dealing season after season with many of the same children, encountering them and their families in various community settings, and receiving (by a Candlemas custom practiced throughout the educational network) financial gifts from pupils "in proportion to [their] parents' means" (Gibson 1912, p. 61), schoolmasters became personally acquainted with a number of their boys and developed likes and dislikes that were not always disguised. These, however, were scarcely enough to counterbalance the cumulative impact of all the homogenizing experiences that were built into town grammar schools; and particularly so since the masters, busy whirling from class to class and lesson to lesson, had comparatively little range to vent their preferences and were constrained to keep even their favorites more or less in step with youth at the same curricular level.[26] Lads who spent their childhood in institutions such as these were uniquely situated to draw out an orientation of universalism.[27]

25. The situation was quite different for pupils in large urban grammar schools. Isolated year after year in a classroom of their own with lads at the same place in the curriculum, these students neither saw other classes actually go through the inevitable progression, nor saw the process recreated on a daily basis. In fact, unless the demarcations between first, second, third, and fourth year lessons were particularly evident—which is rather unlikely when there was no change in instructor and, at the same time, no chance to compare one's own studies in any given year with those undertaken by more advanced classes during the same year of their education—boys in the city grammar school might scarcely be aware, until they were handed over to the rector in their final year, that they themselves had crossed a series of grade boundaries.

26. One wonders, though, whether a more complete suppression of the particularistic tendencies of schoolmasters might have supported the development of a more far-reaching universalism than that expressed by the Scottish Enlightenment.

27. It should be remarked that in arguing that small town grammar schools provided their students with experiences from which to construct a universalistic orientation, the preceding discussion has in no way intended to suggest that the workings of these institutions were universalistic from a macrosociological point of view. Research on contemporary societies has shown time and again that educational systems can eliminate all obvious classroom particularism while retaining massive inequalities of opportunity, generating attitudinal and behavioral outcomes that serve to reproduce unequal social relations, and upholding standards that—though uniformly applied—are inherently weighted in favor of children who act and communicate in the ways of the dominant social groups (see Bernstein 1961, 1971; Bourdieu and Passeron 1970; Bowles and Gintis 1976). It would be surprising if Scottish schools were radically different, but scholarship in the field has yet to investigate any of these possibilities. In fact, while there is considerable evidence for the social class heterogeneity of town grammar schools, currently one does not know even approximately the relative rates at which youth from different strata attended these schools and occupied their various English, Latin, and other

II

Adam Smith, John Millar, William Robertson, and Adam Ferguson were all products of the small town grammar schools of Scotland, Smith studying for five to seven years at Kirkcaldy Burgh School, Millar for four years at Hamilton Grammar School, Robertson for approximately five years at Dalkeith Grammar School, and Ferguson for roughly as long at Perth Grammar School.[28] Decades before their works declared their universalistic convictions to the world, these four Scottish enlighteners thus found themselves day after long day, week after lengthy week, in the type of formal educational setting that provided the experiences from which universalism could be inferred.

Paralleling the eventual differences in their commitment to universalism, Smith, Millar, Robertson, and Ferguson attended grammar school under somewhat different circumstances. There can be little doubt, however, that each encountered what experiences his school offered for the acquisition of universalism, for those experiences were rooted in general organizational attributes—the overall structure of curricular activities, the composition of the student population—from which no regular pupil could be effectively insulated. It is, moreover, highly unlikely, in terms of the organizational characteristics relevant to the development of a universalistic outlook, that the particular classical schools that the future enlightened intellectuals attended deviated markedly from the prototypical town grammar schools discussed in the previous section. The four little institutions may have had their idiosyncrasies, but Kirkcaldy Burgh School manifestly fitted the pattern of curricular activities presented above since the pattern was exemplified by citing arrangements at Kirkcaldy during the period when Adam Smith was its student; and the establishments in Hamilton, Dalkeith, and Perth would not have been styled grammar schools, or have had such widely admired masters at the time the young enlighteners

classes. Although information of this sort would be indispensable for any thorough analysis of the interrelationship between school and society in eighteenth-century Scotland, it can be set aside in the present context, for here it is the day-to-day experiences of young schoolboys, not the macrodevelopments that went on over their heads (and behind their backs), that are of paramount significance.

28. Gay (1969, pp. 501–6) has emphasized that, in their youth, *philosophes* all over Europe underwent a classical education. But in his view, it was the enlightened ideas of the ancient authors, not the unwritten lessons of the grammar school experience, that were decisive for the development of the Enlightenment (see esp. 1966, pp. 72–126; for reservations about this view, see chap. 3, note 17).

were enrolled, had they grievously violated prevailing norms about the structure of the classical education.[29]

There unfortunately are no measures of the heterogeneity of the student populations at these schools. The towns of Kirkcaldy and Hamilton diverged so inconsequentially from the lot of small Lowland burghs in size, location, social composition, religious, philanthropic and educational traditions, and the like,[30] however, that one has little reason even to suspect that their pupils were noticeably less diverse than those in other town grammar schools. The same cannot quite be said of schoolchildren in Dalkeith and Perth. During Robertson's stay, Dalkeith was "in the greatest Reputation of any School in the country" and drew lads—lads prosperous enough to afford the costly venture—"from all parts of Scotland."[31] Similarly, Ferguson's school at Perth "had a good reputation and attracted sons of the nobility and gentry" (Smart 1932, p. 55).[32] From this evidence one might well conclude that these two institutions were somewhat more exclusive than small burgh schools elsewhere, and then deduce that Robertson and Ferguson themselves were educated in surroundings less conducive to the growth of universalistic orientations than were Smith and Millar, a speculation that is certainly compatible with the fact that the universalism of Robertson

29. On the reputation of Millar's schoolmaster, see Craig (1806, p. ii); of Robertson's, Bower (1817–30, 3:24), Gleig (1819, p. vi), Lynam (1824, p. 6), Stewart (1818, p. i), and Stewart (1796, p. 103); of Ferguson's, Small (1864, p. 600), and Smart (1932, p. 59); and of Smith's, Fay (1956, p. 49), Rae (1895, p. 5), and Stewart (1793, p. 6).

The scattered observations on the enlighteners' schools by Grant (1876), Harvey and Sellar (1868, pp. 92, 233, 254), Sinclair (1791–99, 2:203, 12:24–25, 18:48–49, 538) and, for Perth alone, Smart (1932) also suggest nothing organizationally unusual (except as noted in note 32 below). For the most part, such observations do not, to be sure, pertain specifically to the period when the enlighteners were schoolboys, but since theirs was not an age during which educational institutions were undergoing major changes, the observations probably retain much of their value. Beale's (1953) extensive study of the schools in Fife confirms the judgment expressed above about Kirkcaldy Burgh School.

30. See esp. Sinclair (1791–99, 2:177–212, 18:1–61). Although compiled in the 1790s, Sinclair's materials offer considerable insight into conditions during the earlier decades of the eighteenth century.

31. Carlyle (1973, p. 277), Stewart (1796, p. 103). See also Hans (1951, p. 22), Law (1965, p. 59), and Sinclair (1791–99, 12:24).

32. That Perth had four instructors in the early eighteenth century (Grant 1876, p. 548; Smart 1932, pp. 58–59) instead of the usual one or two implies that it may have had certain other affinities with the classical seminaries in the largest urban centers, though Withrington's (1970a, p. 170) decision to include Perth among the small town grammar schools seems on the whole amply justified.

and Ferguson tended to be less far-reaching than that of either Smith or Millar.

But, in all likelihood, this deduction is an overinterpretation of the sketchy data on the composition of the schools at Dalkeith and Perth. There are actually more definite and fundamental variations in the enlighteners' early educational experiences that correspond with their later differences in the area of universalism, though these variations must also be kept in perspective; none of them would have meant much if anything had they not been subsequently reinforced by other experiential differences. In all events, in contrast to Smith and Millar, Robertson and Ferguson both spent the period before grammar school in the much less universalistic climate of the parish school. And while this period lasted for probably no more than two early years in Robertson's case, for Ferguson—the Enlightenment's most ambivalent apostle of universalism—it continued apparently for almost five years, ending only when Adam was already a relatively mature youth in his tenth year. Currently, Ferguson's school at Logierait and Robertson's at Borthwick are too little known to enable one to determine whether they were fully typical of institutions of their type, although it does appear that Logierait upheld the dichotomy between Latin and non-Latin boys that eroded the universalism of other parochial schools.[33] No knowledge of the inner workings of these two obscure old schools is even required, however, in order to understand why attending them placed Robertson and Ferguson in a position different than that of Millar and Smith. When at the insistence of their enterprising parents, William Robertson and Adam Ferguson left their parish schools to pursue the advanced course at a celebrated classical institution, they embarked upon an undertaking that set them apart from the majority of the children who had up to then been their classmates. In the new grammar school precincts, the two lads had greater opportunities than before to derive an orientation of

33. See Bower (1817–30, 3:7). Bower actually writes here of Logierait grammar school, which, in conjunction with Logierait's official burghal status (Pryde 1965, p. 74), may appear to invalidate the parish school label used in the text. But the fact that every other source describes the Logierait school as parochial (see Fagg 1968, p. 10; Kettler 1965, p. 43; Small 1864, p. 600; and esp. Sinclair 1791–99, 5:80–81), strongly suggests that this institution was one of those backward—here Highland—burghal schools that resembled the typical parish school by concentrating on the basics, while still providing some Latin instruction for advanced pupils (hence Bower's reference to grammar; see note 5 above). Had Logierait really offered the full classics course, Ferguson presumably would have gone on from it directly to the university, not to the grammar school at Perth.

universalism, but living for years away from their original schools and communities, they could scarcely forget that theirs was a rather special fate, a fate most of the youngsters back home never knew. The long shadow of the parish school did not fall upon Adam Smith and John Millar when they encountered the distinctive learning experiences of the small town grammar school.

Encountering such experiences and drawing out their universalistic message was not the same, of course, as coming to believe in and value that message. Grammar schoolboys who inferred universalistic principles from the activities going on about them, but found those activities extremely ungratifying, would not be expected to have become anything more than increasingly particularistic in attitude. The future enlighteners were schoolboys of another sort, however. This is not easy to establish firmly at this remove from the eighteenth century, and no doubt there were days when the four thought that classroom life was insufferably dull, days when they were harshly and unfairly chastised for their behavior and their work, and days far more unpleasant. Yet all existing signs indicate that on the whole school was a rewarding setting for these youngsters. The intellectuals of the Scottish Enlightenment had in their adult years such an impressive command of the classics[34] that it is very difficult to suppose that they failed in their youth to master the Latin rudiments and the skills of translation and composition. Their talents in these areas presumably earned them their share of commendations from the scholarly masters—perhaps even one of the occasional material prizes that this age without report cards sometimes used as incentives[35]—and such evidence on academic performance as biographers have uncovered certainly points unambiguously in this direction. Small reports that at Perth "Ferguson excelled in classical literature [and] his themes were not only praised at the time, but were long preserved, and shown with pride by [the rector] who declared that none of his pupils had ever surpassed the writer," while Stewart finds that Smith's exceptional abilities quickly "attracted notice" from his teacher and peers at Kirkcaldy.[36] But noticed or unnoticed, mastering the great works of the ancients—works they would cherish into old age—must surely

34. Gay (1966) provides the fullest treatment of the enlighteners' intimate knowledge of, and deep admiration for, the classical authors.

35. See Grant (1876, pp. 209–11), Kerr (1910, pp. 168–69), and Scotland (1969, 1:80).

36. Small (1864, p. 600), Stewart (1793, p. 6). See also Anon. (1867, p. 59), and Scott (1937, p. 26).

have been quite as intrinsically satisfying to the young enlighteners as effectively dealing with complex tasks is known to be for modern children (see Kohlberg 1969, pp. 433–37; White 1963, pp. 24–43). Even if the grammar school environment was less rewarding for Smith, Millar, Robertson, and Ferguson than it might have been, it thus was sufficiently gratifying to attach them in *some* positive degree to the universalistic principles implicit in that setting. Later experiences would solidify that commitment.

Two exceptions seem to mar the uniform pattern of support that the enlighteners' early school experiences lend to the claim for the experiential foundations of the basic orientations of the Scottish Enlightenment. The first is that David Hume did not attend one of Scotland's small town grammar schools. Instead, he apparently was educated at home by private tutors, an arrangement that was a common enough alternative at the time, though not one in which a variegated group of youngsters was treated by the same general standards.[37] The second exception is that, while in school, Smith, Millar, Robertson, and Ferguson were all exposed continually to social experiences antithetical to the independence that was at the root of their cultural revolution. But these findings appear incongruous only when viewed too narrowly. As soon as the two exceptions are placed in the context of other socialization experiences and of the attitudinal variations among the enlightened intellectuals, it becomes clear that both actually sustain the thesis about experience and enlightenment. It will be seen subsequently that Hume's experiences onward from the age of eleven, when he left his tutors for the university, were at least as conducive to the formation of a deep commitment to universalism as those encountered by his fellow enlighteners. That his campaign for universalism nonetheless differed from that of Smith, Millar, and Robertson by

37. On the particularism of the tutorial relationship, see Bidwell (1972, p. 20).

The nature of Hume's early education actually remains something of an open question. That he was tutored at home is the persuasively argued speculation of Mossner (1954, pp. 31–32), his most reliable biographer. Greig entertains the same possibility, but inclines for not very developed reasons to the alternative view that Hume attended a parochial school, most likely at Chirnside (1931, pp. 29–30, 33). Were this view correct, the argument in the text would require only slight modification for, as a parochial schoolboy, Hume would also have been removed from all the training in universalism that the grammar school offered. Furthermore, he would still have been less subject than the other enlighteners to the restraints on independence imposed by schools at all levels since, by Greig's own estimate, Hume spent only part of each year in the countryside, the area served by parish schools (1931, p. 28; see also Mossner 1954, p. 35).

stopping short of the lower orders is not a developmental anomaly, however, when it is realized that, for the whole first decade of his life, Hume experienced nothing of environs where children of strata both high and low were alike subject day after day to treatment by uniform standards.[38] What will also become evident is that there were smaller differences between Hume and the other enlightened intellectuals, particularly Smith and Millar, in family, university, and professional experiences than one might reasonably expect in light of the fact that Hume took up the cause of human independence in a more thoroughgoing way than any of the others. But this discrepancy in outlook no longer appears to be a curious aberration once it is understood that Hume alone was spared constant immersion in the straitening world of the school—the world that, even if it did not extinguish independence in lads who had otherwise acquired that orientation, did so little to foster its further growth. Consistently then, the early educational experiences of the intellectuals of the Scottish Enlightenment were of a piece with their ultimate convictions.

38. It is interesting to compare Hume's situation here with that of Ferguson, whose writings also treated those from different classes differently. Although Ferguson attended a grammar school, he did so only after likewise spending nearly a decade in other social circumstances. In his case, moreover, these other circumstances involved not simply remaining apart from the grammar school experience by staying at home, but actually going forth daily for several years to the more particularistic environment of the parochial school. This, as well as a number of Ferguson's post grammar school activities, set him apart in ways congruent with the fact that, in the end, his universalism was notably less extensive than Hume's.

6

University Experiences

I

The educational program of the Scottish reformers was not content with a national network of parish and town schools. It further proposed an intricate system of colleges and universities to provide upward of ten years of advanced instruction for all those who proved their intellectual mettle (*First Book of Discipline* 1560–61, p. 131; see also Strong 1909, pp. 58–61). The scheme was too grandiose to be actualized, but by the end of the sixteenth century supporters of the new religion had moved to reshape the existing establishments of Glasgow, St. Andrews, and Kings College, Aberdeen—each the legacy of a fifteenth-century papal bull—and had added to them the College of Edinburgh and Marischal College, Aberdeen.[1] The truculent religious controversies of the seventeenth century frequently disrupted the workings of these institutions, leading in turn to purges of Presbyterian and Episcopalian staffs, until the final ecclesiastical settlement of 1690 placed higher education under Presbyterian jurisdiction and installed principals and masters professing the Westminster Confession of Faith. This hard-won stability did not bring the ambitious educational vision of the reformers any closer to reality, however. For the entire eighteenth century, the colleges of Scotland continued as facilities composed chiefly of Arts students[2] in their early and middle teens and

1. The University of St. Andrews was composed of three separate colleges, St. Salvator's, St. Leonard's, and St. Mary's, and for this institution (as well as for Oxford) this chapter retains the traditional distinction between a university and a college. In all other cases, however, the two terms will be used interchangeably (see Cant 1967, p. 1956).

2. Students who completed the Arts sometimes stayed at the university to study divinity, law, and so on. Instruction in these areas will be discussed briefly at the end of the chapter. In this section, the concern is solely with the Arts course.

thus remained "glorified secondary schools" (Pares 1954, p. 240). Worse, despite their minimal admission standards (a smattering of Latin), low cost to prosperous youth, and scholarships and fee waivers for the poor, these establishments managed at best to reach only about one in every thousand Scots.[3] Of collegiate life, the vast majority of any generation knew nothing.

For most of the period from the Reformation to the early eighteenth century, Scotland's five universities, whatever their other differences, gave those who did attend an education that was highly traditional in both content and form.[4] Above and beyond Calvinist verities, the typical Arts curriculum of the age consisted of a year of Greek and a year of each of three branches—logic and rhetoric, moral philosophy, and natural philosophy—of an expurgated Aristotelian philosophy that absorbed modern intellectual developments very slowly.[5] In all of these fields, instruction was organized in a simple manner which outwardly resembles that used in city grammar schools and is customarily described as the regenting system. This system presupposed university faculties comprised of four "regents," men who were not academic specialists devoted to one of the four areas of the curriculum but rather in due course gave lessons in every subject. Under this arrangement, all the lads in the class beginning the Arts course in a particular year were assigned to the regent who had taught the graduating class of the previous year and then taken by him through the entire four-year sequence of studies, while each of the three other classes moved through the program with its own regent.

It was not the class as a whole, however, that was the ultimate pedagogical unit. Instead, from its outset, the regenting system set up a tutorial relationship between teacher and student, albeit not one composed exclusively of one-to-one encounters. For long por-

3. Bullough and Bullough (1973, p. 421); see also Smout (1969a, p. 449). Those who did attend the universities of the time were, without exception, males. Females had not yet gained admittance to the higher educational institutions in Scotland.

4. Since the principal sources of the general matters of fact that have been put together to construct the following sketch are too numerous to list at every turn, they should be formally acknowledged at the start: Cant (1952, 1967, 1970), Coutts (1909), Dalzel (1862), Dickinson (1952), Emerson (1977), Graham (1899, pp. 448–72), Grant (1884), Horn (1967), Kenrick (1956), Mackie (1954), Morgan (1933), Murray (1927), Rait (1895), Reid (1799), Scotland (1969), and Veitch (1877). Despite their titles, Bower (1817–30) and Herkless and Hannay (1905) were not particularly useful.

5. On the infiltration of such developments during the late seventeenth century, see Emerson (1977, pp. 464–70). See also chap. 1, sec. III.

tions of the average schoolday, the members of a cohort actually met together to grapple with their various exercises and to copy down ponderous sentences that the regent would read out at dictation speed from the works of the authorities under study.[6] Given the number of youngsters entrusted to each regent—classes of a hundred were not unknown, although those of fifty or less were more common—such aggregative practices were unavoidable. But apart from the most exceptional circumstances, these practices were interwoven with a good deal of individual supervision of pupils in and out of classroom hours and, in any case, the presumption of personalized instruction pervaded the process of higher education.[7] In the majority of Scottish universities during much of the sixteenth and seventeenth centuries, the tutorial system was conjoined with the requirement that students reside in college chambers and with a schedule nearly as demanding as that found in burghal and parochial schools. For the ten months of the academic year, the daily routine began at six in the morning and, between five or so hours in class, periods of supervised study and recreation, and meals in commons, lasted until the late afternoon, with a brief respite on Saturdays but hours of church services and doctrinal review sessions on Sundays. As the eighteenth century approached, the length of the schoolday and schoolyear gradually fell, and it increasingly became too costly to provide chambers for the growing undergraduate population. Several colleges, around the same time, confined their regents to the three-year round of philosophical subjects and established a separate Greek master to tutor every first-year class.[8] Even when they were in full swing, however, these changes were not of sufficient depth to alter fundamentally the nature of the socialization experiences that the world of regenting offered. True to the Calvinist heritage, Scottish universities remained set-

6. The custom of using class time for "dictates" developed in medieval universities to supply the want of printed textbooks. Scottish regents clung to this practice for more than two centuries after the invention of the printing press and, by so doing, spared themselves from preparing hours of lectures on a variety of subjects about which they often knew little (see Dickinson 1952, pp. xxviii–xxix; Morgan 1933, p. 71; Rait 1895, p. 154).

7. See Emerson (1977, p. 459), Grant (1884, 1:142, 147, 151), Kenrick (1956, p. 16), Laurie (1902, p. 12), Murray (1927, p. 22), Rait (1895, p. 201), and Veitch (1877, p. 82).

8. As the seventeenth century progressed, it also became common to appoint an additional master to improve the skills of those who were deficient in Latin when they arrived at the university. Students sometimes spent a year with this so-called professor of humanity before commencing the ordinary course of study.

tings organized to uphold orientations of dependency and partic- ularism and to arrest the growth of enlightened attitudes.

Experiences in autonomy were perhaps the utmost rarity in these institutions. A regent, etymologically, is a ruler, and the application of such a lofty title to university faculty members is a fitting tes- tament of the deep-seated Scottish belief that the surest means for perpetuating the regimen of control begun by the father and the schoolmaster lay in the opportunities for supervision that befell the college tutor.[9] Accordingly, well into the eighteenth century, the regent was given "emphatic and unquestioned" authority over his pupils (Cant 1952, p. lxx) and, as Thomas Reid observed, made responsible for "the whole Direction of their studies, the Training of their Minds, and the Oversight of their Manners" (cited in Rait 1895, p. 201). This broad license over both intellectual and moral matters left students formally with little chance to act on their own and decide for themselves, and seldom did they fare any better in practice. Under the careful watch of principals and the elect at large in the community, regents ordinarily discharged their duties with great diligence, superintending—with varying degrees of mal- evolence and benevolence—virtually "every aspect of the . . . daily life and conduct" of their young charges (Kenrick 1956, p. 13).[10] There was, to be sure, periodically an instructor given to laziness, drunkenness, and (in protest against imposed bachelorhood) pass- ing time with the enterprising ladies of the town (see Horn 1967, pp. 31–35). No more than such proclivities transform authoritarian fathers into egalitarian ones, however, did they mean a softening of the rule of the regents. Not only could a wayward master demand while on the job the strictest accounting of the interim activities of his boys, but the more assiduous regents enforced universitywide policies that were able to check the class of a dissolute colleague at the same time that they further restrained their own lads. When

9. For a discussion of the context in which the term regent entered the academic world and was extended to instructors, see Murray (1927, pp. 20–21). It is interesting to observe that, in at least one place, regents were accorded a type of deference that went well beyond anything given to fathers and schoolmasters to resemble the treatment often reserved for actual earthly rulers. By University of Glasgow reg- ulations of the seventeenth century, a student who encountered a regent in the streets was required "to avoid his glance on pain of corporal punishment; in very narrow lanes the student might cover his face with his hand, which was known as 'shirking' " (Scotland 1969, 1:151).

10. See also Cant (1970, pp. 33, 47), Donovan (1975, p. 8), Emerson (1977, p. 459), Graham (1899, pp. 458–61), Mackie (1954, p. 74), and Reid (1799, pp. 736, 739).

students of the period boarded in residence halls, they found themselves patrolled in even the wee hours as "the Regents in turn visited the chambers before six in the morning, and in the evening before nine to see that none . . . were 'playing, talking, or doing worse in their chambers, or wandering about the court, or going from chamber to chamber' " (Kerr 1910, pp. 122–23). "We need but look out of our windows to see them rise and when they go to bed," wrote regent Thomas Reid to a friend. "They are seen nine or ten times the day statedly by one or other of the masters, at publick prayers, school hours, meals, and in their rooms, besides occassional visits which we can make with little trouble to ourselves" (cited in Graham 1899, p. 459). Nor were nonresidents spared. Marischal College was not unusual in insisting that "those living without Academia shall never be found without it, except at the hours appointed for meals; if they sleep without, they must enter exactly at six . . . and not go out before nine . . . unless leave of play be given to all" (cited in Rait 1895, p. 257; see also Cant 1952, p. lxx; Rait 1895, p. 156).

Regulations of this sort were only the beginning. All Scottish universities went much further, devising a multitude of rules to cover, in rich detail, everything from praying, studying, and speaking to smoking and drinking, boxing, standing at the college gate, throwing snowballs, playing cards, dice, and billiards, and attending the theater. Compliance with such noble commandments was expected as a matter of course, but to ensure this outcome, college officials, borrowing the tactics of parish and town schoolmasters, employed networks of student captors to assist the policing efforts of the regents and then liberally inflicted penalties—fines, floggings, expulsion—on the culpable. This elaborate disciplinary machinery still had its limits, and episodes of youthful rowdiness did erupt from time to time, no doubt making the university a somewhat less tiresome place. A sprinkling of lively moments, however, was far from sufficient to undo the constant lessons in dependency that were conveyed by the long years of close and strict control by the regents.[11]

The techniques of instruction that prevailed in the colleges of Scotland tended to reinforce these lessons in the old orthodoxy.

11. On the extensity of university regulations, see Graham (1899, p. 458), Horn (1967, p. 34), Murray (1927, pp. 479–80), Rait (1895, p. 59), and Scotland (1969, 1:156). On methods of discipline, see Graham (1899, p. 458), Mackie (1954, p. 111), Murray (1927, pp. 152, 458, 484), Rait (1895, p. 155), and Scotland (1969, 1:157); and on their occasional breakdown, Dickinson (1952, p. lii, note 2), Henderson

For much of their time in class, pupils did little more than sit passively and transcribe lengthy passages dictated by the regent. Such an arrangement, Veitch remarks with understatement, was "not likely to promote the habit of original speculation," and things were scarcely improved when the hours of private study and tutoring were devoted, in the words of a standard syllabus of 1690, to "constant repetitions of what hath been formerly taught," and to themes and translations much like those forced upon grammar schoolchildren.[12] It is true that exercises that sound a bit more inspiring, daily oral examinations and weekly disputations where student philosophical theses were propounded and impugned, were also widely used. In fact, however, oral exams—"a continual stream of questions, mixed with exhortation and abuse," in Horn's judgment—were merely additional devices to force young lads to rehearse mechanically materials from previous days (Horn 1967, p. 23; Rait 1895, pp. 57, 288). The most stimulating disputations would have been a meager counterweight in such a situation, but generally even these came to naught. "The same subjects of disputation, the same arguments of attack and defense, were handed down among students" year after year, producing "conventionalism in phrase and argument and thus . . . a deadening rather than a quickening of intellectual effort" (Morgan 1933, p. 59; Veitch 1877, p. 213; see also Duncan 1965, p. 14).

With their stern governance of student actions and sterile teaching methods, Scottish universities essentially reproduced the dependency-sustaining structures of the primary and secondary schools of the era. In one important way, however, colleges went still further in foreclosing opportunities from which perceptive lads could derive an orientation of independence. Higher educational establishments were far less destructive than elementary institutions of bonds of dependency. Initially, this seems rather surprising. Universities, after all, kept youths out of the familial nest of dependency relations for a huge number of hours and days and weeks. When a college education entailed moving away from home and, on top of that, living in chambers, it actually effected the severance from family ties more completely than early schooling typically did. It is also the case that, like town and country schoolmasters, regents not only

---

(1957, p. 96), Horn (1967, pp. 32–35), Mackie (1954, pp. 130, 171–72), Murray (1927, pp. 487–88), and Rait (1895, p. 185). For an interesting account of some of the more acceptable types of student recreation, see Finlayson (1958).

12. Veitch (1877, p. 83), syllabus cited by Rait (1895, p. 288), and Grant (1884, 1:148–51).

assigned their pupils exercises to do by themselves, but had too many duties of their own to bestow on the boys the kind of solicitude that the family was able to provide. For all of this, however, relationships of dependency emerged again and again from the dynamics of university life. In making the college instructor responsible for carrying on the great childrearing project that had started in the home, the regenting system inevitably entrusted him with the task of attending to the legitimate needs of his young charges much as parents had done, and through the channels created by the tutorial linkages that were at the root of the system, the prospect of being personally cared for by the master was, in fact, continually realized (see Emerson 1977, p. 459). That the amount of care given to any particular lad was limited somewhat by the presence of his perhaps quite numerous classmates in no way affected the basic character of the situation here. Furthermore, one must recognize that, over the course of three or four years, the amount of help and support was itself not inconsiderable, especially since even the most harried regents had a far less consuming job—that of instructing a group whose membership turned over slowly and whose members were all at approximately the same curriculum level— than first impressions suggest. The bounds set by these circumstances were still sufficiently wide to accommodate various sorts of teacher-pupil bonds, but in all events, regenting meant tutelage and tutelage brought no release from dependency.

Particularism likewise went unchallenged, and this despite the heterogeneity of university students. Although the college population was probably at no point as variegated as that found at lower levels of the Scottish educational network, a degree of diversity was its hallmark from an early age. Not only were there certain differences in age, ability, and prior academic training among the boys in every school class, there was also, considering the period, a substantial range of variation in social class and nationality. In Scotland, attendance at seminaries of higher education was never the exclusive privilege of young nobles and gentry who could not go abroad to study. Low entry fees instead put college courses well within the reach of children of the prosperous middle ranks, while bursaries and free admission tickets issued by the faculty brought in somewhat poorer youth[13]—doubtless way too few by any principle of proportionality, but enough to lead sober contemporaries to fear

13. See Cant (1967, p. 1955), Horn (1967, pp. 22, 58, 60), Mackie (1954, pp. 127–28), and Rait (1895, p. 88).

an invasion by "the Mechanicks and poorer sort of People" and to lament that "one can make his Son what now passes for a Scholar, at a much cheaper Rate than he can breed him Shoe-maker or Weaver" (Andrew Fletcher 1704, quoted in Withrington 1970a, p. 172). Though each of Scotland's universities drew its undergraduates primarily from local environs, the larger establishments of Edinburgh and Glasgow also enrolled lads from other nations, especially England and Ireland, and in the process added a certain cosmopolitan flavoring to the already diverse mixture of college students.[14]

So motley a collection of pupils might seem, at first glance, to have offered the right makings of experiences for the development of universalism. But actually things were otherwise for, under the regenting system, a heterogeneous group of college youths would receive little of the uniformity of treatment that is the further prerequisite for experiences in universalism. This does not mean that students had nothing in common. The majority of the scholars in a given university all underwent the same basic course of philosophical studies, suffered through the same taxing schedule, and endured the same exhaustive regulations and exacting punishments. Typically too, at either the beginning or the end of every academic session, each boy was subjected to similar practices and standards of evaluation as he appeared before the entire faculty to be examined on lessons completed.[15] The pupils of any one regent shared still more: the full daily round of prayers, dictations, exercises, meals, study halls, recreational periods, and the like. One must, however, avoid the anachronism of tearing these various commonalities from their context and supposing that, in the days of regenting, their attitudinal consequences were what one would anticipate today. This sort of reasoning is extremely inappropriate given how the tutorial relationship that existed between a regent and his boys particularized the whole educational process in the old Scottish universities. All the while that lads moved in step with their classmates, they maintained the personal bonds that were the concomitant of individual moral and intellectual supervision by a master who, for his part, was under no obligation to suppress such bonds and thus bring instances of uniform treatment to the fore.

14. On localism in recruitment, see Horn (1967, p. 31), and Smart (1974, pp. 98–99). On international diversity at Glasgow and Edinburgh, see Coutts (1909, p. 173), and Horn (1967, p. 31).

15. For discussion of these examinations, see Dickinson (1952, pp. xxiii–xxxiii), Horn (1967, p. 25), and Murray (1927, pp. 79–81, 86).

The expectation, rather, was that the regent, as a tutor, would amply supply his charges with individualized attention and instruction. Often enough, as we have seen, this expectation was largely fulfilled; the various collective procedures that were used in enabling instructors to manage several dozen youngsters each day were generously intermixed with personalized regental monitoring and guidance. It is no doubt true that from the busyness, indolence, or indifference of their masters, a few pupils were slighted by this arrangement, but even in these lads the shared elements of the daily routine can scarcely have provoked much incipient universalistic sentiment. No matter how small the degree of personal attention he himself received, the college boy was in a pedagogical situation where different students fared differently in this regard, and where there was at the same time a wide field—the several-year span when the same regent and the same batch of youngsters interacted with one another for long hours in and out of class—upon which to display clearly the divers attachments that resulted from such differences.

The features of university life that went beyond the teacher-pupil relationship did little to alter this particularistic scene. The reverse, in fact, was more nearly the case, for when they accorded special privileges to students from the highest social strata upon the payment of additional fees, established separate tables to serve different quality meals to rich and poor undergraduates, and allowed those "whose circumstances permitted it, to be accompanied [while residing in chambers by their own private] tutors . . . as well as by their pages or personal servants" (Murray 1927, p. 21), the colleges of the period demonstrated in the most tangible of ways that the same standards were not for all.[16] The sole persistent indication to the contrary here was the fact that each scholar passed through fairly comparable courses and course materials at a similar stage in his academic career. But the reality of this uniform, step-by-step advancement over curricular boundaries was hardly accentuated during the time of the regenting system. Modern schoolchildren, Dreeben (1968, pp. 76, 83) contends, grasp that there is a standard progression for everyone as they are repeatedly promoted from the class of one teacher to the class of the next; the youngsters in the small town grammar schools of the Scotland of a past age, the previous chapter has suggested, could learn of the same point be-

16. On the practices just described, see Cant (1970, pp. 80, 84), Dickinson (1952, pp. xxvii–xxviii), Rait (1895, p. 204), and Scotland (1969, 1:165).

cause they constantly shared a schoolroom with pupils at various levels of the classical program. Regenting offered neither mechanism in developed form, nor any proper surrogate (see chap. 5, note 25). College lads were thus left with nearly as few opportunities to draw out a principle of universalism as they had to acquire an orientation of independence.[17]

The major alternative to regenting is a professorial system where different faculty members specialize in providing instruction in different academic fields. The idea of organizing university education in this manner was proposed in Scotland numerous times from the Reformation onward, and the plan was actually instituted in some colleges for several decades in the late sixteenth and early seventeenth centuries. In every case, regenting arrangements were ultimately restored for various pragmatic reasons, while advocates of the administrative and pedagogical advantages of an intellectual division of labor made do with the establishment of separate language masters and with the occasional appointment of a specialist periodically to lecture the whole college on a subject like mathematics.[18] By the early eighteenth century, however, University of Edinburgh Principal William Carstares, impressed by what he had seen of the professoriate at Leyden and Utrecht during his exile, was convinced that more thorough remodelling was again in order. Prodded by this politically powerful administrator and his band of regents, the Edinburgh Town Council, which had jurisdiction over university affairs, concurred in 1708 by converting each regent into a professor of one of the areas of the curriculum and assigning to him the task of offering the basic course in that area every year.[19]

17. To say that the universities of the period offered few experiences from which to derive a universalistic attitude is not to deny that the episodes of uniform treatment that were provided by these institutions may have been sufficiently evident in some instances to prevent the complete suppression of universalism in youngsters who had already acquired the orientation through their experiences in small town grammar schools. This possibility, it should be noted, is consonant with the fact that hints of universalism occasionally surfaced in Scotland prior to the Age of the Enlightenment (see chap. 1, sec. III).

18. This period also saw the creation of a number of specialized chairs outside of the Arts faculties (in divinity, law, and medicine).

19. As a result of this move, the Arts faculty subsequently consisted of a professor of Greek, a professor of logic, a professor of moral philosophy, and a professor of natural philosophy, in addition to the previously established professors of humanity and mathematics (see Grant 1884, 1:262–64). Professorships were slowly created in other fields as the eighteenth century progressed (see Cant 1967, pp. 1965–66).

In 1727, a royal commission of visitation, under the sway of the Edinburgh example, enjoined the faculty of the University of Glasgow to undergo a similar transformation.[20] In both places, professors, released from the responsibility of preparing lessons in vastly different fields each year, were finally able to devote more attention to specialized scholarship, and not a few soon built distinguished academic reputations for themselves and their institutions and began to attract a disproportionate share of college students. To stay afloat in this competitive situation, the other Scottish universities eventually decided to follow suit, although regenting was not abolished from its stronghold at Kings College until 1799 (see Withrington 1970a, pp. 184–91).

Standard histories of education in Scotland have frequently emphasized that the elimination of the regenting system at Edinburgh and Glasgow—the two establishments to fully install a professoriate prior to the start of the Scottish Enlightenment and therefore the chief concern in this discussion—wrought a revolution in the content of college courses and the methods by which they were conducted. Here it has been observed that as the specialist professors acquired expertise in their various subjects, they rapidly abandoned the antiquated Aristotelianism, insipid dictations, and mechanical assignments of the regents in favor of stimulating lectures on the novel philosophical developments of the age and thought-provoking oral and written exercises.[21] This is a bit too sweeping a generalization, however. Contemporary ideas did displace those of the ancients and dictating did give way to lecturing, but these changes occurred slowly and unevenly, while supposedly inspiring devices like the student essay and the hour of discussion following the day's lecture were, when used at all, generally little more then reincarnations of the themes, translations, disputation theses, and daily oral examinations of old.[22] Whether or not instruction became more stirring upon the cessation of regenting ultimately depended very

20. On the nature and the background of the changes at Edinburgh and Glasgow, see Coutts (1909, pp. 203–8), Grant (1884, 1:254–64), Kenrick (1956), and Mackie (1954, pp. 174–84).

21. See Davie (1961a, pp. 16–17), Kenrick (1956, p. 106), Murray (1927, p. 506), Sloan (1971, pp. 24–25), and Veitch (1877, pp. 83–84, 207–8).

22. See Cant (1967, pp. 1965–69), Coutts (1909, p. 196), Graham (1899, pp. 454–55), Henderson (1957, p. 170), Henderson (1741), Meek et al. (1978, p. 12, note 37), Mossner (1954, pp. 46–47), Reid (1799, pp. 733–36), Stewart (1818, pp. iv–v), Veitch (1877, pp. 216–17), and Wodrow (1789, p. 29). On the incidence of the procedures just enumerated, see Davie (1961a, pp. 24–25), and Morrell (1971b, p. 161).

much on the "character, capacity, and vigour" of individual professors (Veitch 1877, p. 208) and, in the eighteenth century, excellence in these matters was by no means the principal criterion for appointing and retaining members of the faculty (see chap. 7, sec. I). But to recognize this is not to suggest that the conventional wisdom errs in holding that the introduction of the professorial system revolutionized higher education in Scotland. The mistake has been to focus too narrowly on improvements at the discretion of particular instructors, while overlooking the far-reaching, if largely unanticipated, transformation that soon took place in the overall organization of university education and quietly altered the structure of the college experience even for pupils of the most old-fashioned of professors.

Central to this organizational transformation that followed the creation of the professoriate was a rearrangement of the schoolday and a concomitant growth in the number of college courses. The causes of these developments have not yet been thoroughly investigated, although currently it appears that faculty self-interest played a decisive role (see Horn 1967, pp. 58–60; Withrington 1970*a*, p. 184). Regents had derived a major share of their income from the fees they received from nonindigent scholars so that they had earned the most when they had the greatest quantity of students. A similar setup remained in effect when the professorial pattern was instituted, but during the backroom negotiations that accompanied and implemented this change, instructors at last succeeded in securing procedures by which they were able to draw in more pupils even without increases in total college enrollment. The idea here was to reduce the number of hours spent daily with any one teacher so that youngsters could take the classes—and be assessed the separate fees—of several teachers at the same time. Accordingly, in the early eighteenth century, the University of Glasgow arranged to offer each of its main subjects at a different hour to allow as many lads as possible to attend, and Edinburgh University adopted a schedule that went nearly as far in the same direction.[23] The advantages of such rescheduling would have been lost, of course, had there been a continuation of the regents' policy of making knowledge of one field the prerequisite for advancement to another. Professors were not about to give up their potential profits so easily, however: the Edinburgh faculty hastened to drop prerequisites on attendance

23. See Dalzel (1862, 2:307), Donovan (1975, p. 15), Murray (1927, p. 111), and Sharp (1946, p. 26).

almost entirely, while its Glasgow counterpart, though somewhat more cautious in this regard, softened a majority of the traditional requirements for course entry.[24] The plan still had one final loophole for, under the new arrangements, students could squeeze all the basic courses into a few sessions, instead of the usual four, and, in so doing, deprive professors of enough guineas over the long haul to erode their short-term gains. But to discourage this practice, the virtues of retaking the same classes were advertised with the pledge that admission would be free the third time around, a promotion that in fact induced numerous youngsters to pay twice for identical lessons (see Rae 1895, p. 50; Sharp 1946, p. 43). It was not long, however, before professors took even bolder steps to capitalize on their situation. Rather than confining themselves to the one basic course that they were assigned to teach annually, ambitious instructors began to promote and offer, for additional fees, courses on a whole variety of other topics included within their area of specialization.[25]

Henceforth, college life was no longer what it had been for either teachers or their charges. Regents had proffered a single subject per year, while devoting the better part of each schoolday to driving its truths home to a class whose composition changed only once in a three- or four-year period; professors taught an average of two or three classes a session to different, and ever rotating, groups and usually spent no more than an hour or two a day with any one.[26] For their part, students, previously limited to one main course a year[27] and to passing the bulk of their undergraduate days with the same master and set of schoolfellows, now might take—between the various courses of the half-dozen or so Arts professors, the

24. See Coutts (1909, pp. 208–9), Donovan (1975, p. 15), Horn (1967, p. 41), Grant (1884, 1:264–66, 277), Mackie (1954, p. 181), Morrell (1971*b*, p. 168), and Smith (*Corr*, p. 31). Cf. Henderson (1741, p. 372), and Mossner (1954, p. 617).

25. See Emerson (1977, p. 459), Henderson (1741), Horn (1967, pp. 41, 47), Kenrick (1956, p. 108), Meek et al. (1978, pp. 3–4), Mossner (1954, pp. 38–39), Murray (1927, pp. 111, 516), and Withrington (1970*a*, pp. 181–84).

26. These figures are drawn from Emerson (1977, p. 459). Cf. Carlyle (1910, p. 48), Dalzel (1862, 2:307), Henderson (1741), Smith (*Corr*, p. 31), and Somerville (1861, p. 2).

27. During the regenting period, some students might also attend the public lectures of the principal and the resident mathematician, or devote part of the time alloted for private study to advanced lessons from the language masters and to the esoteric classes of free-lance instructors outside of the college, but all of this still remained quite incidental to long hours of work in the area that the regent was covering in a particular year (see Dickinson 1952, p. xxii; Horn 1967, pp. 23, 35, 47; Rait 1895, p. 168).

additional selections made available in the college by part-time assistants, and the lessons provided in everything from elocution to dancing by educational entrepreneurs in the town—three to six subjects every year, each with a different instructor and group of classmates.[28] An early prototype of our own small colleges was suddenly a reality.

The consequences were radical. This whole reorganization happened to occur amid certain long-range trends that had first begun in the universities of Scotland in the era of regenting: a slow, but steady increase in the size of the collegiate population; a corresponding abandonment of the custom of residing in chambers; and a continual shrinking of the academic calendar, so that a year at Edinburgh and Glasgow in the eighteenth century ran for seven to eight months, with the schoolday starting later, and finishing earlier, than it had in the past.[29] In this complex of circumstances, the tutorial system could no longer be the heart of higher education. It is true that eliminating the tutorial relationship between teacher and pupil seems to have been no part of the intention of those who initially established the professoriate. Originally, it was envisaged that, apart from the fact that the student would have a new master every year, things would remain much as they had been (see Kenrick 1956, p. 108), and some traces of the old, individualized arrangements actually did linger on after the demise of regenting. Lads in small advanced classes where oral and written contributions were constantly demanded of pupils, lads who boarded in the homes of faculty members and paid for private lessons, and lads who hired special tutors from the town all had their moments of more or less intimate intellectual guidance. Such was the logic of the situation, however, that these moments were now unmistakably subsidiary aspects of undergraduate education, not unlike senior seminars and independent studies in modern colleges. The remodelled Scottish universities structured too few occasions over the full course of a student's career for the emergence and maintenance of the close, personal supervision that had once existed; tutorial instruction, though perfectly viable when regents were assigned to one

28. See Carlyle (1910, pp. 34–57), Macky (1723, p. 69), Smith (*Corr*, p. 31), and Somerville (1861, p. 10). On the courses available in the town and from part-time assistants within the college, see Coutts (1909, pp. 213, 230–31), Horn (1967, p. 92), and Law (1965, pp. 144–92).

29. On the waning of residence requirements, see Cant (1967, p. 1957), Knox (1953, p. 18), Mackie (1954, p. 213), Pryde (1962, p. 109), and Scotland (1969, 1:153). On changes in enrollment size, see Emerson (1977, p. 473, note 38).

cohort, morning, noon, and night, for several years, inevitably disappeared as the basis of academic life when professors encountered more, and sometimes larger, classes for time periods that were far briefer in both the short- and the long-run.[30] In the wake of this change and the developments that had brought it about, the universities of Edinburgh and Glasgow became agencies of socialization of a novel kind—agencies organized to promote in deed the principles that the intellectuals of the Scottish Enlightenment would eventually declare with their words.

One such principle was independence, for the new conditions presented college boys with unprecedented possibilities for autonomous actions and decisions. This was so even with respect to their program of studies, something that undergraduate institutions ordinarily fix with considerable precision. As the financial concerns of instructors undermined the practice of imposing a required sequence of subjects, eighteenth-century students found themselves with an astonishing degree of what Grant calls *Lernfreiheit* (1884, 1:264). From an ever growing list of course offerings, the lads at Glasgow and especially Edinburgh could, for the most part, choose classes "in whatever number and order best suited [their own] preferences and prospects . . . interests and aspirations," and this when they were still in their early teens.[31]

Faculties that withdrew so readily from these basic, but easily managed, academic matters did not long remain involved in strictly governing all the more intractable aspects of student life. Such governance was incompatible with the whole structure of Scottish universities in the age of the professoriate. The breakdown of the tutorial pattern meant the ineluctable dissolution of the primary mechanism through which college youths had previously been subjected to intensive and extensive control. Thereafter, the small amount of time that pupils spent per day in any one course and the short length of annual sessions allowed even professors with authoritarian dispositions (and classes of modest size) few real opportunities to exert the exhaustive intellectual and moral superintendence of the past. This in itself might have mattered little had the majority of the faculty united to enact restrictive policies in one

30. See Knox (1953, p. 18), Morrell (1974, p. 84), Murray (1927, p. 506), and Withrington (1970a, p. 182).

31. The quotation is from Morrell (1971b, p. 168). More generally, see Grant (1884, 1:277), Horn (1967, p. 41), Morrell (1971b, pp. 169–71, 1974, p. 84), Smout (1969a, p. 353), and Thornton (1968, p. 420).

class period after another and also during out-of-class hours. But, in fact, instructors were not on the whole inclined toward the tactics of the regents, not least because the role of the professor provided meager incentives to encourage such tactics. In eighteenth-century Scotland, professors gained scholarly recognition and attracted large classes of fee-paying students on the basis of their accomplishments in specialized academic fields, not their systematic repression of youthful initiatives (see Morrell 1974, p. 84; Scotland 1969, 1:144). The "free schools" and other libertarian educational institutions of the twentieth century are not yet upon us, of course.[32] Scottish undergraduates were still officially prohibited from partaking in all sorts of innocent pleasures; Glasgow boys were still taken to task every Saturday before the full staff for their lapses; and, unlike those in the progressive modern high schools that Swidler (1979) has described, no one then regarded teachers and pupils as equals.[33] The days of domination were nonetheless done. "Freedom from restraint," as well as from "the threat of corporal punishment for misconduct," became one of the stamps of an education at Edinburgh where, as early as the 1720s, scholars were released from the "strict Rules" that had confined prior generations; in Glasgow, the abolition of regenting ended, the loquacious Thomas Reid remarked, "the severity of the ancient discipline . . . by superseding many strict regulations, and of course rigorous penalties, which, in the former situation, had been thought necessary" (1799, p. 736).[34] It was also at this time that professors discontinued the custom of employing student captors to spy on the outside activities of their fellows, though (from one point of view) the fact that youngsters

32. It is not inappropriate to recall at this juncture—as well as in connection with the persistence, under the professoriate, of certain mechanical teaching techniques—that, from a twentieth-century standpoint, there are also definite limitations in the independence of the Scottish Enlightenment (see chap. 2, sec. I).

33. See Horn (1967, pp. 90–91), Murray (1927, pp. 479–80), and Reid (1799, pp. 736–37).

The contrast suggested here between Edinburgh and Glasgow in the eighteenth century and the schools that Swidler has discussed constitutes one of the main reasons why it would be inappropriate to employ her suggestion that "free schools" do *not* promote independence (and universalism) as evidence against the thesis of this chapter (see Swidler 1979, pp. 141–46). A further reason to consider is the fact that Swidler centers her argument around Dreeben's (1968) conception of "independence" (and "universalism"), not the conception used in this study.

34. The remarks quoted on the situation at Edinburgh are those of Horn (1967, pp. 47, 67), and Macky (1723, p. 69). On conditions at Glasgow, see also Mackie (1954, p. 213); and, for more general comment on the growth of student freedom, Graham (1899, p. 461), and Scotland (1969, 1:144, 153, 157).

could now schedule their courses to obtain an ample number of hours beyond the college gates each day increased more than ever the need for bands of roving detectives.[35] Other, and possibly more effective, monitoring devices certainly might have been substituted here. Characteristically, however, in Scotland's renovated universities no such devices were forthcoming.

Indeed, for all the controls that college officials now imposed, a student could, as Grant put it, "live . . . as his own master," both academically and otherwise (1884, 2:487),[36] which was an experience that had no parallel during the reign of the regents. If they attended the universities of Edinburgh or Glasgow, even boys whose schooldays most resembled those of their fathers—the boys who happened upon a disproportionate share of dull professors with archaic methods, the boys who enrolled in so many courses that they had little spare time, the boys who occupied the old residence halls which most teachers and pupils had deserted—passed their undergraduate years in a setting with structural properties that precluded the possibility of constant, direct, and thorough regulation by the faculty, and thus created the very type of environment where independence in action and attitude could prosper. The curiosity is that orthodox principals, preachers, and parents sat by while so potentially un-Calvinist an environment took shape. Although historians to date have not examined this question, it seems that the transformation of Scotland's chief seminaries of higher education was accepted because few either outside or inside the university noticed any danger afoot. Alarm there might well have been had student behavior visibly deteriorated, but, despite an occasional row (see Mackie 1954, pp. 213–14), this did not occur, at least not in the decades of interest here. The habits of good conduct that had been pounded into Scottish youths at home and in elementary school generally kept them on the straight and narrow during their stay in college (see Grant 1884, 2:480, 487; Reid 1799, p. 736; Thornton 1968, p. 420). As a result, rather than raising an outcry over the loss of regental supervision, the public patriotically applauded the intellectual achievements of its specialized professors and continually sent its sons to their universities. Without the benefit of modern social psychology, who then was to

35. On the demise of captors, see Horn (1967, p. 47), and Pryde (1962, p. 109). On the increase of unsupervised time, see Carlyle (1910, p. 54), and Withrington (1970a, pp. 181–82).

36. See also Morrell (1971b, pp. 168–71), Pottle (1966, p. 23), and Saunders (1950, pp. 353–54).

suspect what studying there would mean in the lives of a handful of budding intellectuals who were already on the path of autonomy?

There was yet another way in which the remodelled Scottish colleges became settings for the further development of an independent orientation. To eighteenth-century Scots, rigorously disciplining the young was always a far more pressing concern than providing them with material and emotional help and support. It is not surprising, therefore, that the universities that drastically cut back on essentials left little place for luxuries: the organizational alterations that made the controls of the past impossible simultaneously eroded the institutional foundation that had previously sustained relationships of dependency between teachers and pupils. With the decay of the tutorial system and the arrangements—the round-the-clock contacts, for years on end, between the regent and an unchanging batch of boys—that had allowed it to work, the faculty was no longer in a position to attend to student needs with parental care. More ephemeral bonds of dependency might still form now and then, as they do in complex organizations today. For the most part, however, Edinburgh and Glasgow professors had too little time (or alternative resources) with each of several different classes to keep up the old supportive ties. Consequently, as Morrell observes, undergraduates had to "learn . . . how to provide for themselves in the classrooms, lodgings, and taverns" of the great cities they inhabited (1971*b*, p. 169; see also Emerson 1977, p. 459; Withrington 1970*a*, p. 182). The university had again placed them on their own.

It also unwittingly exposed its students to fresh lessons in universalism. The social heterogeneity that had long characterized the collegiate population in Scotland persisted and, in some ways, increased further under the administration of the professors. Throughout the eighteenth century, the growing intellectual reputation of the Edinburgh and Glasgow faculties attracted more and more scholars from England, Ireland, Wales, the colonies, and elsewhere,[37] while local lads themselves remained a motley crew. It is, to be sure, rather misleading to claim, as William Ferguson has claimed, that the universities "opened their doors to all ranks of society" (1968, p. 97), for despite their low fees, bursaries, and fee waivers, Scottish higher educational institutions rarely encom-

37. See Emerson (1977, pp. 473–74), Horn (1967, pp. 64–65, 67), Mathew (1966, p. 75), Morrell (1971*b*, p. 167), and Smout (1969*a*, p. 354).

passed pupils so disparate in class backgrounds as those who attended the parochial schools of the age (see Smout 1969*a*, pp. 443–50). The degree of socioeconomic diversity at the college level, nonetheless, compared reasonably well with that found in small burgh schools and, in the eighteenth century, sons of nobles, gentry, professionals, merchants, urban artisans, and rural peasants all went on to study at Glasgow and Edinburgh.[38] Youngsters coming up from parish schools knew that this still left many behind, and the continual presence of laboring adolescents on the city streets probably drove the same point home even to grammar schoolboys who had watched a larger portion of their former classmates proceed to college in one place or another. For so highly stratified a society, however, the variety that the universities did comprehend was striking. This was especially so since, after the elimination of the regenting system, age and educational differences that were more pronounced than ever came to be superimposed upon the class and national differences among students. Although regents themselves had been quite willing to admit youths of various ages and academic attainments into the same entering class, the extent to which pupils diverged in these matters from those who were their classmates for the four-year program had always been limited—on the one hand because boys of the same age tended to enroll at the university within a few years of one another, and on the other because the regents generally put everyone in the cohort to which they were assigned through roughly the same lessons at the same time and, by so doing, kept all their charges more or less on par in terms of curricular training for the duration of their college stay. The introduction of the professoriate effectively disrupted this state of affairs, though without producing any known change in the age distribution of new undergraduates. The decisive factor, instead, seems to have been the increasingly prevalent policy of allowing students to take what subjects they wanted, whenever they wanted to take them. When put into practice, this policy meant that lads of all cohorts, and of all the varying ages and amounts of previous college preparation that these embraced, might easily end up in the same course. Moreover, they might easily end up there alongside the sundry "graduate" students in divinity, law, and medicine and the curious adults from the town whom profit-seeking

38. See esp. Hans (1951, pp. 27, 31), and Mathew (1966, pp. 78–80); see also Morrell (1971*b*, p. 167), Smart (1974, pp. 104–5), and Stone (1969, p. 136).

professors were starting to draw into the classroom.[39] The palpable result of such developments was, as Morrell has remarked in a slightly different context, that virtually "each university class showed marked variety not only in the provenance and rank of its members, but also in intellectual training and age" (1971*b*, p. 168).

Variety itself was no guarantee of experiences in universalism, however. What converted the restructured Scottish universities into breeding grounds for that orientation was the great frequency with which they subjected the heterogeneous undergraduate population to uniform treatment. To a casual observer, it may, of course, appear that the new conditions meant much less uniformity than the old since they no longer imposed on all lads the same sequence of courses, the same schedule, and the same ubiquitous regulations, but rather left students more to their own, often dissimilar, devices. Yet behind the discrepancies that were thus created in programs of study, periods of time spent in and out of the college, and the like was the fact that the university provided the same basic alternatives in these areas to every scholar in attendance, regardless of age, or capability, or country, or class.[40] There were no special privileges here to becloud the universalistic message that was conveyed more directly by other features of college life as it was during the years of the professoriate. The disintegration of the tutorial pattern that followed the termination of regenting was, after all, the disintegration of the system of individual instruction that had previously personalized the entire process of higher education. And, although a comparable result could no doubt have been accomplished through other means, at the universities of Edinburgh and Glasgow in the eighteenth century, organizational procedures were weighted heavily in favor of an outcome of a very different sort. Under the arrangements then coming into being, collegiate training involved taking a series of courses with a succession of professors who were sometimes too burdened even to be personally acquainted with their pupils. In one course, a youngster would move, with diverse sorts of classmates, through one particular subject and the various exercises that were used to assess academic progress in that field; in a second course, he and another variegated

39. See Graham (1899, pp. 467–68), Horn (1967, p. 91), Lehmann (1960, p. 16), Morrell (1971*b*, p. 168), and Murray (1927, p. 113).

40. One should, however, keep in mind the issue that historians have yet to investigate: the unequal resources of diffferent social classes may have affected the rates at which the various academic alternatives were actually used by youths from different strata.

lot of fellows—some known from before, some not—would take up another subject and an additional set of exercises; in a third course, there would be other faces, along with new lessons and new tasks for all; and so it went, so that the manifold external differences among students were subordinated, over and over again, because they were in the same boat, enrolled in the same class at the same time. Eighteenth-century college boys were, in other words, presented with an experience much like that encountered by contemporary high school students who, as they "move from classroom to classroom, in each one receiving instruction in a different subject area by a different teacher, . . . discover . . . over a range of activities . . . relatively uniform demands and criteria of evaluation" and thereby grow increasingly universalistic (Dreeben 1968, pp. 77–78).

Naturally, like instructors today, Scottish professors might still have their biases. Mackie remarks on certain members of the Glasgow faculty with a "partiality . . . for students who boarded with them and whose families they knew" (1954, p. 213), and Alexander Carlyle, a friend of the enlighteners, long remembered the Edinburgh Latin master who "was very partial to his scholars of rank, and having two lords at his class . . . took great pains to make them . . . appear among the best scholars" (1910, pp. 35–36; see also Horn 1967, p. 67). That favoritism now stood out for such commentary—that Carlyle could blandly assert that it "would not do, and served only to make [an instructor look] ridiculous" (1910, p. 36)—is, however, itself no small sign that prevailing practices had changed, that the pervasive particularism of the regents was a thing of the past. Required to cover entire fields in a short schoolyear that was made up of daily sessions of only an hour or so, professors actually had, especially in comparison with their predecessors, relatively few opportunities even to air personal predilections (see chap. 5, note 26). Set over against such preferences as instructors did manifest, moreover, were all the common lessons and assignments that students went through each year in one class after another, all the similar curricular options they had simply because they were attending the same institution, and, on top of this, an academic situation where lads were also being treated more evenhandedly outside their courses. Universitywide examinations and scholastic contests had always been organized and judged fairly impartially, and this continued to be the case under the professorial system where, as Thomas Reid explains, elaborate procedures were established "to correct the common defects and irregularities in the distribution of prizes, and to render the competition fair and equal" (1799, p. 738; see also Mossner 1954, pp. 46–48; Murray 1927, pp. 79–81, 86). In addition, with a smaller and smaller number of youngsters boarding in the college, administrators no longer bothered to keep up the different accommodations that they had formerly provided for boys of different strata. It made little sense, for example, to serve meals in residence halls, let alone to maintain separate tables for rich and poor, when so few were left to dine in chambers. Of course, as undergraduates dispersed to seek food, lodgings, and the rest in the towns of Edinburgh or Glasgow, the influence of unequal pocketbooks was again sorely felt (see Horn 1967, p. 61; Murray 1927, pp. 458–60). The reorganization of the universities did not abolish stratification in the larger society. Within the school precincts, however, young scholars of all varieties were now treated in a remarkably uniform way. The materials for the development of a universalistic orientation were at hand.[41]

One should not suppose that every Edinburgh and Glasgow lad was similarly affected by his college experiences. Youths embarked upon higher education with very different formative experiences already behind them, and the renovated universities were not structured to force all pupils to adopt the same beliefs and values. The total institutions of the regents were gone; with briefer academic years, shorter schooldays, and fewer demands on students throughout, colleges in the age of the professoriate stopped well short of the rigorous, protracted, and uninterrupted training that would have rendered them powerful mechanisms for remaking the ultimate convictions of their young clients (see McPherson 1973, pp. 170–71)—a fact particularly significant in view of the incorrigibility of human dependency. There must have been many instances, therefore, where the experiential messages of collegiate life fell upon deaf ears. As it happened, however, some boys who arrived at the university were rather well prepared to learn what it subtly taught.

II

Although Scotland contained five universities, to David Hume's family, which lived south of Edinburgh, kept a house in the capital, and had patronized the local college in earlier generations, Edin-

41. The important qualification entered in chap. 5, note 27 is, however, also relevant at this point.

burgh was the logical place to educate a son. It was also the obvious choice in the Robertson household, for the senior William Robertson was assigned to minister in one of Edinburgh's churches at the same time that his namesake was ready to leave grammar school for a more advanced course of studies. In contrast, the Millar family lived within the Glasgow area, and John, like his father, was consequently sent to college in that city. Adam Smith was from a town that was close to both St. Andrews and Edinburgh, but, following a parental plan to seek a lucrative fellowship to Oxford only available to Glasgow students, instead enrolled at the University of Glasgow. In each of these cases, the years spent in college fell after the elimination of the regenting system and the distinctive methods of socialization that accompanied it. Four of the future Scottish enlighteners, as a result, grew up in the world of the professoriate.

What this meant in practical terms is that, for an average of four school years, Hume, Millar, Robertson, and Smith were face-to-face with experiences that ran counter to the dependency and particularism of the age. Extremely little, to be sure, is known about the collegiate careers of the four. The information that has surfaced indicates that the lads probably had a few more stimulating than fossilized professors, but otherwise reveals nothing particularly outstanding about their college training.[42] Although this is not proof

42. On Hume, see Mossner (1954, pp. 38–51); on Millar, Lehmann (1960, pp. 13–16); on Robertson, Stewart (1818, pp. iv–v), and Stewart (1796, pp. 104–7); on Smith, Rae (1895, pp. 8–17), and Scott (1937, pp. 28–37).

These sources can also be consulted for a discussion of the various intellectual currents to which the enlighteners were exposed by their professors. Much of this literature, it is worth noting, advocates a slight variant of the intellectual-historical approach to explaining the Scottish Enlightenment that was discussed in chap. 3, viz., the claim that the Scottish Enlightenment emerged, not from ideas in writings that the enlightened intellectuals read, but from ideas in lectures that they heard while in college. Although the research that has put forth this claim has generated a number of important insights, to date it has faltered as an explanation of the Scottish Enlightenment for reasons analogous to those identified earlier: such research either has failed to consider the paramount issue here, the process that transformed pre-Enlightenment lectures into the constitutive attitudes of the Enlightenment, or has unjustifiably dissolved this issue by obliterating the fundamental differences between the enlighteners and their predecessors.

There might seem, however, to be a way of salvaging something from this research and bringing it to bear on the problem of this study. Previous interpretations of the Scottish Enlightenment have repeatedly emphasized that Adam Smith was a student of Francis Hutcheson and that John Millar was a student of Adam Smith; and these pieces of information take on additional significance given the earlier remarks on the universalism of Hutcheson and the independence and universalism of Smith. One might wonder, in fact, if it would not be reasonable to set experience aside

that these youngsters were prototypical, here there is no need to advance such a claim. In the eighteenth century, the universities of Edinburgh and Glasgow presented scholars, both typical and not, with experiences in independence and universalism, for these experiences derived neither from the whims of specific faculty members nor from structural arrangements that encompassed only certain groups of pupils, but from organizational characteristics— the social composition of the student body, the number of college courses, the mechanics of the schoolday, the decline of tutorial instruction, and so on—that framed the lives of the entire undergraduate population. It is difficult, to say the least, to imagine that the enlighteners were in biographical circumstances so bizarre that they became exceptions to the rule.

Excluding this possibility, Millar, Robertson, and Smith accordingly found themselves in a position where previously formed commitments to independence and universalism could solidify, while the precocious and discerning David Hume was situated to draw out a universalistic attitude and to grow further attached to the idea of independence (see chap. 3, note 30). That such developments actually materialized under these conditions was by no means inevitable, of course, since college might well have been a most unrewarding affair. By and large, however, it was an affair of another sort for the intellectuals of the Scottish Enlightenment. Hume,

---

and propose that Smith and Millar acquired their enlightened opinions directly from their teachers. The major difficulty with this speculation is the tacit assumption that bright adolescents accept everything they hear. Such a supposition, dubious in all events, is especially problematic when applied to figures like the enlighteners who did not ordinarily just go along with the views of teachers and significant others, but instead abandoned some of the most basic beliefs of their time. It is true that the lectures of Hutcheson and Smith have the reputation for having been more persuasive than those of other instructors of the period. But this point does not obviate the problem at issue, since there certainly were limits to the persuasiveness of these lectures—witness Adam Smith's rejection of Hutcheson's belief in human dependency and, more important, witness the mass of those who remained orthodox Calvinists after studying with Hutcheson and Smith. For the fact that Smith and Millar deviated from this mass, which is the real puzzle here, lectures that everyone heard are obviously an insufficient explanation. Indeed, it is not until taking into account the family, grammar school, and college experiences that Smith and Millar carried with them when they entered the classes of their renowned professors, that one can begin to understand why Smith was in a position to take favorable notice of Hutcheson's universalism, and why Millar was prepared to respond similarly to the independence and universalism of Smith. This argument does not mean, however, that the impact of Hutcheson on Smith and of Smith on Millar should be discounted; simply that the ideas of those teachers cannot be the primary basis for an explanation of the Scottish Enlightenment.

who was not given to boast or hyperbole, recalled unto the final year of his life passing through "the course of education with success" and "excelling his schoolfellows," and his biographer has argued that, if anything, Hume's comments probably understate the extent of his college accomplishments (*Essays,* p. 601; Mossner 1954, pp. 48, 50). Of the positive reinforcements that Smith received during his undergraduate days, the historical record speaks more clearly still. Young Adam succeeded so well at his studies that he was graduated with great distinction and unanimously awarded the Snell Exhibition to Oxford, "the prize of the best student of Glasgow College" (Rae 1895, p. 16; Scott 1937, pp. 36, 137). John Millar, though not quite as fortunate, likewise earned his share of commendation by the faculty and, at the same time, stood out "among his companions for . . . the extent of his knowledge, and his powers of argument" (Craig 1806, pp. iii–iv). Among the enlighteners, only William Robertson, in fact, seems to have been rather unappreciated by peers and professors. Lynam observes that "no feats of . . . excellence, early depth of understanding, no sallies presaying an unusual brilliancy of imagination are recorded" of the boy (1824, pp. 6–7), whose "genius," Stewart delicately remarks, "was not of that forward and irregular growth which forces itself prematurely on public notice" (1796, p. 104). Such notice was not essential, however; hurling himself "with indefatigable zeal" into his education,[43] proclaiming at the start of every notebook that "Vita sine literis mors est," William plainly derived his own satisfactions from university life and the intellectual challenges that it posed. And, in this, one should not assume that he was alone, for confronting all the philosophical issues that were broached in the college courses of the period must certainly have been intrinsically gratifying to lads with the exceptional passion for literature and for learning that Hume, Millar, and Smith are known to have had even in their adolescence.[44] To those who would make the Scottish Enlightenment, therefore, the university setting offered ample rewards amid experiences in independence and universalism, a combination most propitious for creating commitment to the fundamental principles of the Enlightenment.

43. The quoted remark is from Brougham (1845, p. 254). See also Lynam (1824, p. 7), Stewart (1818, pp. ii–viii), and Stewart (1796, p. 104).

44. On Hume, see *Essays,* pp. 607–8, *HL* 1:13; and Mossner (1954, pp. 30–31, 40, 50–51); on Millar, see Lehmann (1960, pp. 16–17); and on Smith, Stewart (1793, pp. 7–9).

In the case of Adam Ferguson, the combination was different. Adam had his collegiate successes, so much so that he "finished his curriculum in arts with the reputation of being one of the best classical scholars and perhaps the ablest mathematician and meta-physician of his time at the University" (Small 1864, p. 600; see also Anon. 1867, p. 59; Fagg 1968, p. 12). That university, however, was St. Andrews, where the talented youth had been attracted by a bursary to St. Leonard's College, an institution that was then a curious blend of the new and the old. Here the traditional regenting system, though not entirely and officially abolished until a later date, was in actuality largely eclipsed. In Ferguson's undergraduate days, St. Leonard's students no longer proceeded through the four-year round of subjects under one regent; instead, they were as-signed to a regent only in their second and third years since there were now separate professors of Latin and Greek for the first year and a specialized professor of natural philosophy for the fourth year, in addition to a mathematics professor providing optional lessons to boys in various cohorts (see Cant 1970, pp. 69–70, 83, 91; Emerson 1977, pp. 461–62). The information that Small (1864, p. 600) presents strongly suggests that Ferguson studied with all five members of this faculty, but makes clear in any event that the future enlightener received his college education from multiple instructors. His situation, consequently, diverged in no small way from the situation of those who passed the bulk of their college career with a single tutor and with the prolonged relationships of dependency and extended supervision that were fostered by such tutorship. Furthermore, because pupils at St. Leonard's during this period were handed over to a different teacher with nearly every advancement through the major stages of the curriculum, Ferguson found himself in a setting containing—as regenting arrangements did not—a mechanism to underscore systematically the fact that there was a uniform academic progression for scholars of all the ages, capabilities, and strata then attending St. Andrews (on the heterogeneity issue, see Smart 1974, pp. 104–5).

But these beginnings of an education in independence and uni-versalism never precipitated the sweeping experiential turnabout that occurred at Edinburgh and Glasgow. In the mid-eighteenth century, St. Leonard's still retained too much from the past to hasten toward the Enlightenment even those who arrived with the proper leanings. As a result, although the college was no longer so well equipped to eradicate these leanings as the universities of the regents, one can scarcely imagine that Ferguson would have become an enlightener had this been the final phase in his cognitive and moral development. The situational impediment in this instance was that a majority of the decisive organizational changes that elsewhere accompanied the introduction of the professoriate failed to take place at St. Leonard's, which was then too financially troubled to respond to the competitive challenge posed by Scotland's other higher educational institutions (see Cant 1970, p. 78; Withrington 1970*a*, p. 185). The undergraduate population thus remained extremely small, with entire cohorts sometimes consisting (as Ferguson's did) of fewer than fifteen youths; students, particularly bursars like Ferguson, continued to reside in chambers; the number of course offerings stayed essentially constant; and neither the schoolday nor the schoolyear underwent significant restructuring.[45] In these conditions, there was nothing to jeopardize the system of tutorial instruction that was so admirably suited to sustain the creed of dependency and particularism: young scholars may have been assigned to a new teacher nearly every year, but during their long hours with the master they had for any one academic session, their circumstances were no different from those that befell college boys when regenting was the rule. It is true that the long hours with the master did not extend quite as far as they once had. By the eighteenth century, the members of the St. Leonard's faculty had generally ceased to live in residence halls, and this restricted their ability to provide the degree of control, care, and individualized attention that had previously existed. They compensated, however, as Cant explains, with a weekly rotational scheme by which instructors in turn "lodged in the college, presided at meals, and carried through the morning and evening inspections of students' rooms" (1970, p. 90)—all the while maintaining different meals and facilities for lads in different social classes and imposing strict discipline on residents and nonresidents alike.[46] After pausing for four years in a setting such as this, is it a wonder that when Ferguson came to the Enlightenment he came with hesitations the other enlighteners knew not of?[47]

45. See Cant (1952, p. lxxi, 1970, pp. 75–97), Dickinson (1952, pp. xv–xxxv), and Smart (1974, p. 95).

46. See Cant (1952, pp. lxx–lxxi, 1970, pp. 84, 98). For evidence that the stratified practices at St. Leonard's directly implicated Ferguson, see Fagg (1968, p. 12).

47. Again in accordance with the general policy stated in chap. 3, though, it is important not to divorce Ferguson's college experiences from the context of what preceded them and of what was to follow.

Upon leaving college, lads in eighteenth-century Scotland went in diverse directions that reflect the different resources and aspirations of their parents. Some returned to the ancestral estates that they would someday rule or awaited their inheritance by going off to the Continent for study and travel; some took humble positions as assistant parish schoolmasters or tutors in households of modest means, or sailed away to the colonies for a new beginning; and others, probably the majority, pursued a middle course, eventually entering commerce, the army, the navy, the state bureaucracy, or, with luck, one of the professions, particularly law or the church (see Graham 1899, pp. 32–34; Mathew 1966, p. 85). Accordingly, it was in no way unusual that Adam Ferguson, John Millar, William Robertson, and Adam Smith, who were themselves children of professional families, and David Hume, who was the second son of a minor landowner and not therefore heir to any substantial property holdings, had their sights directed to the professions at least from early adolescence. What they experienced as they looked out upon the professional scene and made their first attempts to break onto it is the subject of the following chapter. Here, however, it is necessary to take note of the enlighteners' more concrete activities during this period when they were waiting for the real start of their professional lives.

Except for the fact that all five youths spent some portion of this period in postgraduate professional training, these activities seem initially to have little in common. After graduating from St. Leonard's, Ferguson enrolled briefly at St. Mary's College, St. Andrews and then continued his theological education at the University of Edinburgh until, some two and a half years later, he was appointed deputy-chaplain to a well-known military regiment and set on what he hoped was the route to a prosperous clerical career. Hume, upon finishing college courses, studied law for three years and subsequently devoted five years at home and three additional years in the countryside of France to the private research and writing that culminated, by the end of the sojourn, in his first work, *A Treatise of Human Nature*. Millar, when his undergraduate days were over, remained in Glasgow for up to seven years, originally as an auditor in the classes of Adam Smith, who had recently joined the Arts faculty, but shortly thereafter as a law student at the university and presumably in an advocate's office as well. He completed this training in Edinburgh under Lord Kames, whose son he tutored for the two years that preceded the start of the law practice that he then quickly abandoned to accept the chair of civil law at Glasgow and to develop the speculations that would soon establish him as one of the enlighteners. Following the conclusion of the Arts course at the University of Edinburgh, William Robertson undertook approximately four years of study in divinity at the same institution. Two years later, he was appointed minister for the parish of Gladsmuir, where he assumed his duties the next year and promptly commenced the inquiries that eventually became *The History of Scotland*. Smith, after garnering the prestigious fellowship from Glasgow to Oxford, spent six years at Balliol College, officially heading for the clergy, although it seems that an academic position already loomed as a more suitable destination. From England, he returned home, first to live in Kirkcaldy for two years with his mother, next to offer in Edinburgh for three years a series of public lectures that adumbrated a number of his seminal ideas, and finally to occupy the chair of logic and then of moral philosophy at the University of Glasgow.

Beneath this quite varied assortment of comings and goings, there is nonetheless a pattern. In each of the five cases, the years after college brought a moratorium,[48] a time apart from the full demands and responsibilities of a regular professional career: a time to be on one's own still more completely than during the undergraduate period.[49] This interval of enhanced independence included even the years of professional training, for in eighteenth-century Scotland such training was not a very rigorous matter. For young Scots who did not flee to universities abroad like Groningen, Leyden, and Utrecht, preparation for a legal career was, for example, an exceedingly haphazard process of periodically attending university or private law lectures, participating in the workings of

48. From a perspective different from the current one, Erikson (1958, pp. 43–44, 99–104) provides the classic discussion of the role of moratoria in cultural change.

49. It is interesting to observe that the differing degrees of commitment to independence that existed among the enlightened intellectuals are consonant also with the differing lengths of this interval: approximately two years for Ferguson, six for Robertson, nine for Millar, and eleven for Smith. The text suggests an eleven year figure for Hume as well, since it leaves off when the bulk of the *Treatise of Human Nature* had been composed and one can thus be certain that Hume had formed his enlightened ideas. Yet Hume's moratorium actually continued long after this time—in some senses for the rest of his life, but at least for nine additional years, at which point he worked in various military missions for two years in the eventually lucrative position of secretary. In Hume's own words: "These two years were almost the only interruptions which my studies have received in the course of my life [and they enabled] me [to] reach a fortune, which I called independent" (*Essays*, p. 609).

an established law practice, or striking some balance among these alternatives.[50] What balance Hume and Millar struck in their days as law students is not known, but it is clear in all events that neither was much deflected from intellectual and recreational pursuits of his own choosing. In correspondence from this period, Hume reported reading almost everything save his law books and remarked: "I live like a King pretty much by my self; Neither full of Action . . . nor perturbation" (*HL* 1:10)—an assessment that needs to be modified only enough to make room for all the nights of conviviality that Hume shared with his companions in the oyster cellars, taverns, and coffeehouses that the literary circles of Edinburgh then frequented (Mossner 1954, pp. 57–62; see also *Essays*, p. 608, *HL* 1:13). And "Time & Leisure," "Study & Idleness," "Study & Diversion" were no less the themes of the young philosopher's letters and life during the years after he formally gave up legal studies for independent research and reflection at home and then, entirely alone, in France (*HL* 1:16, 17, 22; see Mossner 1954, pp. 66–104). John Millar was never granted so extended a holiday. But in the course of his own long program of training for admission to the bar, he too found himself freed sufficiently from mundane obligations to pursue privately many of his own intellectual interests and then to gather repeatedly with his friends for lively displays of "wit and [of] argumentative powers."[51]

If legal studies were unexacting, education for the ministry was a virtual cipher. During the period when Robertson and Ferguson took part in it, the regular divinity course at the University of Edinburgh in its entirety consumed a mere four or so months out of each of four years—the six-year irregular course, which was popular and still less demanding, is not of concern here—and consisted of only three classes, two where attendance was wholly optional, and one where it was laxly enforced. This is not something one expects to find in a staunchly Calvinist country, though it apparently resulted, at least in part, from the church's desire to keep its ranks open to the poorer theology students who had to support themselves in an age when university towns offered little part-time

50. See Graham (1899, pp. 465–66), Grant (1884, 1:283–90), Greig (1931, pp. 64–65), Mossner (1954, p. 54), Murray (1927, pp. 215–21), and Ross (1972, pp. 20–23).

51. The comment quoted is one that was later made by Millar's friend at this time, James Watt. It is cited by Lehmann (1960, p. 17). For some more general remarks on this period in Millar's life, see Craig (1806, p. iii), and Lehmann (1960, pp. 16–18).

employment so that many were compelled to work considerable distances away.[52] Minimal training requirements provided a means to accommodate aspirants to the clergy such as these, but at the same time had the unintended consequence of creating an extended respite for those like Robertson and Ferguson who were not in immediate need of holding down a job. What the two did instead during their long hours outside of the lecture halls was not only to follow systematically their personal plans of study, but also to form with their peers intense and vigorous debating societies which irreverently canvassed the hot topics of the day.[53]

It goes almost without saying that the various intellectual and social experiences in which they decided to engage at this time were a source of gratification for Hume, Millar, Robertson, and Ferguson. These, after all, were young men who thrived on scholarly endeavors, and it is highly unlikely that they would have so willingly kept up their self-imposed schedules of reading and socializing had this not meant ample intrinsic, if not extrinsic, rewards. The next chapter will indicate that there was a decidedly negative side to the enlighteners' lives during these years, but this derived from the nature of the eighteenth-century professional world, not from the activities that these aspiring intellectuals had chosen for themselves. One may therefore safely conclude that in the period after college Hume, Millar, and Robertson were for a prolonged interval in circumstances well organized to consolidate attachment to independence, while Ferguson was, however briefly, at last presented with comparable circumstances in unadulterated form. Of course, even for the halting commitment to autonomy that Ferguson's writings express, this may still seem to be a weak experiential foundation, but then it is important to remember that Ferguson was not finally to take up his pen on behalf of the Enlightenment until many additional years of experience had elapsed.

52. Pertinent aspects of this situation are discussed by Mathew (1966, pp. 82–83, 85, 92), Morgan (1933, p. 94), and Saunders (1950, pp. 348–49). On the Edinburgh divinity program, see Carlyle (1910, pp. 63–69), Grant (1951, p. 30), Grant (1884, 1:334–36), and Somerville (1861, pp. 17–19).

53. On Robertson, see Bower (1817–30, 3:29), Gleig (1818, pp. ix–x), Stewart (1818, pp. vii–viii), and Stewart (1796, pp. 106–7). On Ferguson, see Anon. (1867, p. 60), Kettler (1965, p. 44), and chap. 7, note 29.

Although Robertson completed his divinity training a year before Ferguson arrived at the University of Edinburgh, there is some evidence that Ferguson joined the same debating society where Robertson was still an active participant (see Anon. 1867, p. 60; Kettler 1965, p. 44). Several other members of this group of divinity students also went on to become notable Moderates (see McElroy 1969, p. 106).

Through all of this, William Robertson was in a particularly interesting position. Robertson, as we have seen, was alone among the enlightened intellectuals in integrating the basic postulates of the Enlightenment with those of Calvinism, in combining, without Fergusonian vacillations, a bold declaration of human independence with an ardent affirmation of man's ultimate dependence on God. The fusion of these disparate beliefs has a remarkable parallel in experience for, all the while that he was involved with friends and private study as a divinity student and in the interlude immediately afterwards, Robertson lived under his father's roof, which was also the arrangement during his undergraduate days. The experiences in autonomy that he encountered in college and in the time of moratorium—the experiences that dovetailed so neatly with those promoted by his earlier separation from his family— were thus constantly and directly conjoined with and encircled by the contrasting experiences of patriarchy. In this, Robertson was again unique. Hume resided with his family all through his college years and the period prior to departing for France and Smith lived at home after returning from Oxford, but neither was from a patriarchal household; on the other hand, Millar and Ferguson, who were from households of this sort, remained (except for occasional visits) altogether apart from them after the first decade of life. However little guidance contemporary social psychology offers here and however much caution is in order, it is difficult, nevertheless, to doubt that the distinctive conditions in which Robertson was placed made their mark: that a full ten years of moving back and forth, day after day, between hard lessons in dependency and forceful lessons in independence at least strongly inclined him toward the synthesis of cultural orientations that was his peculiar contribution to the Enlightenment. If we set out intentionally to devise a set of experiences that would promote such a synthesis, could we really improve upon this?

Adam Smith has been left for the last here because, in one important respect, his situation appears to contradict the claim that all of the intellectuals of the Scottish Enlightenment had a time out for independence at the conclusion of their undergraduate education. Although Smith's years in Kirkcaldy and Edinburgh after leaving Oxford conform to the pattern of self-directed research and socializing well enough (see Rae 1895, pp. 30–41; Scott 1937, pp. 46–65; Viner 1968, p. 322), the Oxford period itself may seem rather suspect. During Smith's stay in the 1740s, training at Oxford was, as before and since, organized on the basis of a tutorial system that officially required college instructors to regulate assiduously the conduct and intellectual progress of their charges, which in outline is an arrangement that sounds a lot like regenting and would seem far more conducive to dependency than its opposite. But, in fact, these and other official requirements were widely in abeyance at Oxford in the first half of the eighteenth century, especially at beleaguered Balliol College, where Smith's scholarship was tenable. This is not to say that the university was on the whole the utter academic wasteland depicted by earlier generations of historians. Tutors did teach and pupils did work far more regularly than is often supposed and, by the latter part of the century, Balliol itself was undergoing a respectable recovery.[54] Even when it was most scrupulous about upholding its standards, however, the Oxford of Smith's day left young scholars very much on their own. In the best of circumstances, the student spent "his morning from 9.30 to 1.0 on college work, and the rest of the day on his avocations" (Sutherland 1973, p. 22), though more generally he was allowed, as Green remarks, to "read what he liked, indulge in scholarly study when the inclination suited him or merely pass the time in recreation" (1974, p. 116).[55] That Adam Smith encountered these opportunities firsthand is clear from his own testimony. His correspondence from Balliol is sprinkled with references not only to long spells of lounging in his elbow-chair, but also to the fact that "it will be his own fault if any one should endanger his health at Oxford by excessive Study, our only business here being to go to prayers twice a day, and to lecture twice a week" (*Corr*, pp. 1, 3; see also *WN*, p. 718). All the remaining hours were his, for reading, for "company," or for quiet reflection as he saw fit,[56] which was a freedom of choice that Smith seems to have relished quite as much as the activities to which it led (see *Corr*, pp. 1–3), and this despite his avowed dislike of Balliol on other grounds that will soon emerge. The moratorium for rewarding experiences in autonomy that the

54. For discussion of how the Oxford tutorial system was intended to work, see Mallet (1924–28, 3:58–59). For evidence that tutors and pupils did work at academic matters, see Green (1961, pp. 33, 36), and Sutherland (1973, pp. 21–23); see also the revisionist research of Green (1974, pp. 85–120), and Hans (1951, pp. 41–51). On the decay of Balliol in the early eighteenth century, see Davis (1899, pp. 150–72), Godley (1908, p. 60), and Mallet (1924–28, 3:55–86); on its subsequent recovery, see Hunt (1963).

55. See also Clarke (1959, p. 68), Godley (1908, pp. 67, 154), and Sutherland (1973, pp. 24–25).

56. On company and quietude, see *Corr*, pp. 2–3; on Smith's probable readings, see Rae (1895, pp. 22–23), Scott (1937, pp. 40, 51), and Stewart (1796, p. 9).

other enlightened intellectuals enjoyed was no less a part of Adam Smith's socialization for the Enlightenment.

The period in the enlighteners' lives that is now being considered had implications not only for independence, but also for universalism. For the most part, however, it is best to postpone examination of these implications until the next chapter, since in eighteenth-century Scotland the realities of the larger professional world had far greater salience to men training for the professions than the properties of the specific settings where they occasionally attended law or divinity lectures, above all because these settings were themselves continually pervaded by the larger realities. Adam Smith's years at Oxford create the one exception here, for these distanced the young intellectual temporarily from the Scottish professional scene and immersed him in an educational environment with its own ramifications for the growth of universalism. Whatever else it may have been, eighteenth-century Oxford was not an institution that imposed uniform standards on a socially heterogeneous group of individuals. The student population, while encompassing a sundry mixture of ages and abilities and more socioeconomic diversity than once believed, still consisted primarily of English and Welsh lads from a relatively narrow, upper range of the social hierarchy. Nor would increased variety have meant great changes, since even those pupils who knew nothing of the particularism that emerged when and where the tutorial system was operative witnessed little uniformity of treatment. The colleges of Oxford instead maintained markedly different privileges, requirements, rules, accommodations, meal tables, and dress codes for scholars from different social classes and, in so doing, backed the natural predilections of a majority of faculty and students with considerable organizational force. Balliol went even further. Having become, through the terms of scholarships set up in an earlier era, the destination for the handful of Scots who made it to Oxford by receiving such assistance, it proceeded to subject its sojourners from the north to all manner of harsh discrimination; and when young Scots on the Snell foundation launched in 1744 a formal protest "complaining that their treatment was uncivil and that they were habitually allotted the worse rooms" the master of Balliol characteristically responded that, if the petitioners were unhappy, they could leave the college for good (Davis 1899, p. 141).[57] As one

57. On the fact that Oxford was more heterogeneous than the conventional wisdom has taught, yet still limited in its makeup, see Green (1974, p. 109), Hans (1951, pp. 45–46), and esp. Stone (1974, pp. 20, 37, 57–58). On the existence of

of the four Snell fellows at the time, Smith was presumably involved directly in this affair. But even if this was not the case, he can scarcely have avoided coming up against the prejudices that others encountered, and, in fact, he eventually did leave Oxford "in disgust"—as his close friend John Callander put it when recounting the story—almost certainly to escape the climate of intolerance (Scott 1937, pp. 43–44).

First impressions notwithstanding, one should not regard this side of Smith's Oxford experiences as an impediment to the development of a fuller commitment to universalism. Beyond doubt, Balliol was short on episodes from which universalistic principles could be inferred; it was also long on ways in which attachment to particularism could be reinforced, since many students inevitably benefited from the prevailing discriminatory practices. But, as we have just seen, Smith was by no means one of these students, and this is a circumstance that takes on considerable significance in view of the educational experiences he had undergone during his pre-Oxford years. In other words, if Smith fared poorly under Balliol's particularistic procedures, he had already been rewarded in both a grammar school and a university that were characterized by activities that carried the message of universalism. Here one might recall that social-psychological research has shown that when individuals who have once acquired a particular orientation are subsequently unsuccessful in settings that exemplify its opposite, their commitment to the original orientation is enhanced (see chap. 3, sec. II). For it requires nothing more than a straightforward application of this principle to make clear that, whatever it meant to youths with different previous experiences, life at Oxford could only have confirmed the universalism of Adam Smith. In spite of itself, the ancient English university thus kept the budding enlightener on course once again. This was not to be the last instance where conditions that portend traditional attitudes played their part in preparing the Scottish intellectuals for their cultural revolution.

different collegiate arrangements for the members of different classes, see Davis (1899, p. 169), Godley (1908, pp. 160–61), Green (1974, pp. 117–19), Hans (1951, p. 47), Mallet (1924–28, 3:65), Stone (1974, pp. 42–43), and Sutherland (1973, pp. 5–10); on the particularism of the Oxford tutorial system, see Godley (1908, p. 67), and Mallet (1924–28, 3:59–61). On the anti-Scottish ways of Balliol, see Davis (1899, pp. 138, 141, 154–55, 164), and Rae (1895, pp. 25–26).

7

Early Professional Experiences

I

As a group, sons of professional families and younger sons of landed families were, in centuries past, often in a predicament. Seeking a way of maintaining their accustomed style of life, they turned time and again to the professions only to find themselves frequently in competition with one another for the quite limited number of professional places available in peasant societies (see Darnton 1971a, p. 97; Stone 1971, p. 25). The problem was especially severe in circumstances where relatively open educational systems greatly expanded the pool of young men in quest of professional employment by giving those who otherwise would have worked the fields many years of formal schooling (see Stone 1969, p. 75). Such circumstances assumed an extreme form in Scotland before and, even more so, during the eighteenth century. For all its deficiencies, the nation's network of schools and universities was, as Richard Pares has remarked, "several sizes too large for it," with the result that "all of the professions were overcrowded" and a multitude of ungratified aspirants still remained (1954, p. 244). At the beginning of the century of the Enlightenment, the University of Edinburgh faculty expressed alarm that candidates for the "professions are so numerous that the one halfe can hardly make bread" (cited in Christie 1974, p. 124) and, as succeeding decades brought increases in school attendance, the situation worsened. "Always," as Smout justly observes, "there were more educated men than there were openings for them" (1969a, p. 341).[1] The general rule held firm for each of the fields that the young enlighteners hoped to enter.

1. See also Chitnis (1976, p. 44), Graham (1899, pp. 32–34), and Mathew (1966, p. 88).

The shortage of positions was, in fact, probably most acute in the Church, for the ministry was an exceptionally alluring prospect to those not born in the upper class. Divinity training, after all, was neither difficult nor expensive, and clerical appointments meant considerable prestige along with at least a fair amount of material prosperity.[2] Unfortunately, the Church provided only some nine hundred benefices and, once filled, a benefice might well remain out of circulation for the lifetime of its incumbent. In the years immediately following the disestablishment of episcopacy in 1690, Presbyterian preachers were much sought after, but parochial organization and finance precluded, for the rest of the eighteenth century, any more lasting increases in the demand for ministers. Reflecting on the 1730s and 1740s, Alexander Carlyle deplored the fact that "preferment is so difficult to be obtained in our Church" (1910, p. 211), and pamphleteers from the same period lamented that "at present we are overstocked with young clergymen [because too] many people out of vanity . . . will educate a son in this way to push him into a rank in the world above his birth and condition" (cited in Graham 1899, p. 351, note 1)—a state of affairs that scarcely improved as the century progressed.[3] Many would-be ministers were thus forced to wait years for assignment to a parish, while others had to give up altogether and permanently resign themselves to ill-paid and wearisome jobs as schoolmasters or private tutors.[4] Decade after decade, a few legendary success stories continued, nonetheless, to attract an excess of candidates for the clergy.

In law, there was also a surfeit of ambitious young men. The numbers involved here were probably at no point as large as they were for the Church, but then legal credentials were costlier and

2. On the earthly benefits of the clerical life, see Bullough (1970, p. 97), Graham (1899, pp. 281–82, 359–60), Mathieson (1910, p. 149), and chap. 4, note 18. On the accessibility of divinity training, see Mathew (1966, p. 83), and chap. 6, sec. II.

3. See Clark (1964, p. 146), Pares (1954, p. 244), and Reid (1960, p. 114).

4. See Carlyle (1910, p. 62), Clark (1964, p. 146), and Plant (1952, pp. 9–10).

It is worth observing here that, in eighteenth-century Scotland, private tutors on the whole "occupied a very lowly position" and, apart from sometimes enjoying a good deal of spare time, were virtually on par with servants (Plant 1952, pp. 9–10). Tutorships with young noblemen constituted the one marked deviation from this pattern. These were high-status, if inevitably temporary, jobs that "had none of the [ordinary] servility" attaching to them (Fay 1956, p. 14), and typically offered generous salaries, pensions, and other advantages (see Rae 1895, pp. 165–66). But, as Fay has observed, "of necessity tutorships of this grade were only for the few" (1956, p. 15)—and rarely were the few, young unemployed professionals.

career opportunities hundreds fewer. Openings for advocates were not, to be sure, as rigidly fixed as openings for ministers.[5] After going through an unexacting sequence of courses in philosophy and jurisprudence, an apprenticeship of highly uncertain rigor, or some hazy combination of the two, a prospective lawyer wrote or commissioned a thesis, underwent examination by committees from the Faculty of Advocates[6]—the guildlike association of the two hundred or so members of the patrician legal profession—and, if successful, was then admitted to the Faculty upon payment of a hefty fee.[7] He was thereafter entitled to plead cases before Scotland's principal courts and could directly go about building up his own legal practice; no biding time until an established position became available was necessary. It happened, however, that unless one was sufficiently well connected to draw an ample clientele early on, the private practice of law in so small a country did not generally bring adequate financial and social returns for many hard years.[8] To compensate, a majority of advocates, novices and veterans alike, attempted to obtain appointive offices as judges, sheriffs, prosecutors for the Crown, and so on. But here, as Stocking comments, the "competition was keen" indeed (1975, p. 66). Not only did the official places total less than a hundred (Chitnis 1976, p. 77) and commonly carry life terms, even those who achieved such places kept up the search—either for something better or merely for something more, since several positions imposed limited responsibilities and could be held in conjunction with one or more other lucrative positions. Under these conditions, there were never nearly

5. This discussion focuses on advocates since advocates constituted the branch of the Scottish legal profession that was the intended destination for both Hume and Millar. A similar analysis could, however, be developed for the smaller, lower level of the profession, the Writers to the Signet (see Ross 1972, pp. 11–17; Smout 1969a, pp. 351–52). The difference between advocates and writers was roughly comparable to the English distinction between barristers and solicitors (Lehmann 1971, p. 8).

6. "Faculty" in this connection has no academic connotation. The Faculty of Advocates was a private corporate body, not a group of university professors. For a good discussion of the Faculty's role and composition during the eighteenth century, see Phillipson (1976b).

7. See Carswell (1967, p. 46), Graham (1899, pp. 465–66), Lehmann (1971, pp. 8–12), Mathew (1966, p. 89), Ross (1972, pp. 20–26), Saunders (1950, pp. 343–48), and Wilson (1968, pp. 237, 254).

8. See Clive (1970, p. 228), Lehmann (1971, p. 21), and Ross (1972, p. 26). Apparently in reference to conditions in eighteenth-century Scotland, Adam Smith remarked: "Among the lawyers there is not one among twenty that [manages even] to get back the expenses of his education" (LJB, p. 175).

enough legal employments to go around (see Clive 1970, p. 228; and more generally, Lehmann 1971; Ross 1972).

Nor did the universities and other traditional havens for aspiring professionals close the gap. In the eighteenth century, the arts, divinity, law, and medicine faculties of the five Scottish universities together offered fewer than fourscore academic jobs, all with slow turnover and many with meager salaries. So slim were the pickings that young Scots rarely planned in advance to make a career of college teaching; in practice, they did not even need to do so because, apart from the fact that professors of divinity, law, and medicine were expected to have studied their particular field, no specialized postgraduate training was required of faculty members. A man applied for a university position if suitable vacancies chanced to occur during the time that he was casting about for a stable professional niche and, in an age of fluid interdisciplinary boundaries, the same man might become a credible candidate for chairs in areas as disparate as ethics, mathematics, and rhetoric, whether or not he had pursued any of these subjects since his undergraduate days. This unrestrictive arrangement guaranteed perpetual overcrowding in the tiny academic job market and did little to change the gloomy forecast for success on the professional scene. Since the scant employment opportunities available at home in medicine, science, and the administrative and military branches of the state likewise provided little respite, many of the enterprising actually deserted Scotland for good and attempted to make a go of it elsewhere. Eighteenth-century Scots thus surfaced in Jamaica and in the North American colonies, in India and in Russia, and at innumerable stops in between. Above all, they flocked in droves to London, hoping to find in the metropolis that was now their capital a stage worthy of their earnest ambitions. Here some floundered and some flourished, yet on the whole the exodus barely dented the glut of young professionals still frantically chasing careers in Scotland.[9]

9. The number of academic positions reported at the outset of this paragraph was arrived at by adding up figures taken from Cant (1952, p. lxxi), Dalzel (1862, 2: 329), Graham (1899, p. 470), Henderson (1741, pp. 371–74), Mackie (1954, p. 196), and Rait (1895). On the minimal credentials required for becoming a candidate for an academic post, see Christie (1974, p. 127), and Graham (1901, p. 110). On the shortage of jobs in medicine, science, and the like, see Christie (1974), Donovan (1975, pp. 67–70), Emerson (1973a, pp. 106–8), and Shapin (1974a, pp. 96–98,

For those with intellectual inclinations, the embryotic profession of letters was no help either. Peter Gay speculates that the independence of the Enlightenment had roots in "the growing independence of the literary profession," a development made viable by the formation of "a wide reading public" during the eighteenth century (1969, pp. 57–58; cf. Darnton 1971a, pp. 85, 97–98). In eighteenth-century Scotland, however, the possibility of securing an adequate livelihood as "an author by profession" was virtually nonexistent. The market of readers of anything other than religious, pseudo-historical, and journalistic pulp was minuscule at the century's start and, despite gradual expansion, could not sustain even a small cadre of professional writers until the Age of the Enlightenment was approaching its close. For various religious and financial reasons, moreover, the nobility and gentry of Scotland never really upheld the European aristocratic custom of serving as generous patrons of literature, philosophy, and the like.[10] Both Allan Ramsay and Thomas Ruddiman, the prolific titans of the Scottish literary firmament in the period prior to the Enlightenment, got by only by undertaking an assortment of menial jobs (see Duncan 1965; Martin 1931), and the plight of the litterateur was not lost on contemporaries. During the youth of the enlighteners, "there was," John Ramsay wrote, "little prospect of any suitable reward" for men of letters (1888, 1:2), and thus, Dugald Stewart reported with regret, "the trade of authorship was unknown in Scotland" (1796, p. 104). Of course since Scotsmen wrote in English they could always try—through migrating southward or simply sending their wares to London booksellers—to establish themselves as professional authors by tapping England's more extensive audience for books.[11] This was a strategy that became increasingly popular as the eighteenth century advanced, and Hume and Robertson were, in fact, among those for whom it eventually netted a tidy fortune. But for young men starting out, the odds against

1974b). On emigration beyond the British Isles, see Pares (1954, p. 244), and Smout (1969a, p. 341); and on the influx to London, Cochrane (1964, pp. 4–5), Emerson (1973b, p. 320), Fay (1956, p. 6), Ferguson (1968, pp. 225–26), Graham (1899, pp. 65–66), Grant (1951, p. 36), and Smith (1970, p. 108).

10. On the inadequacy of the Scottish reading public, see esp. Craig (1961, pp. 127–29, 198–205). See also Clive (1970, pp. 227–28), Graham (1899, p. 112, 1901, pp. 1–6), Grant (1951, p. 32), Lamont (1975, p. 18), and McDougall (1978, pp. 17–18). On the dearth of literary patronage, see Craig (1961, p. 131), Graham (1899, p. 112), Lamont (1975, p. 17), and Ross and Scobie (1974, p. 96).

11. For good reviews of the literature on the growth of this audience, see Coser (1965, pp. 37–49), and Watt (1957, pp. 35–59).

making it in this way were overwhelming; the sums that Hume and Robertson earned in middle age from book sales came as windfalls and after they had sensibly pursued career lines that were less risky than the profession of letters. Not only was the much-touted English reading public itself still extremely circumscribed, particularly in the first half of the century, but the literary outpourings of everyone from country parsons to Grub Street hacks vied desperately for such buyers as there were (see Collins 1928, p. 19; Saunders 1964, pp. 123–24; Watt 1957, pp. 35–37). In this situation, "security for the writer was," as Saunders has rightly concluded, "hard to find, and security with a proper measure of independence harder still" (1964, p. 124). Their limited openings notwithstanding, the Church, the law, and the universities ordinarily seemed good gambles by comparison.

When occupational opportunities are in short supply, the means by which existing positions can be had tends to assume overarching importance in the lives of place-seekers, and Scotland in the eighteenth century provides no exception to the rule. The means in this case, as in many traditional and early modern societies, was what men of the time matter-of-factly referred to as patronage.[12] The term was their shorthand for an elaborate allocational system whose intricate workings became a familiar and omnipresent reality for young Scots from the time that their families began shaping them for professional careers. The system had three salient aspects.

The first of these was the curious institution of formal patronage rights. For each of Scotland's established professional positions— each clerical benefice, each appointive legal office, each university chair—there was a patron, an individual or corporate body legally empowered to choose a successor for the position upon the death or resignation of its previous occupant. Who the patron would be in any given instance is a knotty question that involved the seignorial privileges of those who had originally endowed the particular post and the subsequent transferral, hereditary transmission, or forfeiture of those privileges. As a result of historical twists and turns

12. In recent years, social scientists have shown a renewed interest in the general subject of patronage and have insightfully viewed its dynamics from a variety of theoretical perspectives: see, for example, Aminzade (1977), Eisenstadt and Roniger (1980; this is the best current review of the large literature on patronage), Kaufman (1974), Shefter (1977), Weingrod (1968), and Wolf (1966). Unfortunately for present purposes, much of this work treats separately aspects of patronage that were closely intertwined in eighteenth-century Scotland.

that made perfect sense in the eighteenth century, more than half of all Church benefices had various members of the Scottish nobility and gentry as their patrons, while the Crown controlled the bulk of the remaining clerical assignments; the Crown and the Faculty of Advocates were the patrons for the majority of choice legal places; the Edinburgh Town Council the patron for most of the chairs at the University of Edinburgh; the Crown the patron for about half of the University of Glasgow professorships, the Glasgow faculty itself the patron for the rest; and so it went.[13] What these arrangements meant in practical terms was that, to obtain a professional opening, a man needed to be officially named to fill the vacancy by whoever its patron happened to be. After that, the job was his, unless unusual circumstances, which are of no concern here, developed (as they periodically did regarding Church appointments). Conversely, without support from the appropriate patron, the aspirant for a position had no option but to give up the dream of getting the place at issue and to try on another occasion for something else.

As pivotal figures in the high-stakes game of securing professional employment, patrons were not wont to distribute the careers at their disposal randomly. Rather, they typically proceeded according to an iron logic that contemporaries understood only too well. That logic, the second prominent characteristic of the Scottish patronage system, entailed the awarding of positions to professional hopefuls with the right connections: those related by kinship or friendship to the patron; those who conformed with the patron's political and religious views; those whom the patron was rewarding for past services or counting on for future favors; or those tied in one or more of these ways not to the patron, but to an interested third party whom the patron was seeking to repay, to placate, or to ingratiate himself with. Applying the criterion of connections was not, it is true, always a simple matter. Holders of patronage rights frequently had to juggle the conflicting claims of nephews, sons-in-law, dependable old allies, and friends of powerful new friends, and the complications involved here were multiplied many times over when patrons were corporate bodies whose members were pushed and pulled in all sorts of different directions and could marshal a majority behind a particular candidate only by unwieldy compromises. But the problems that arose in weighing

13. See Chitnis (1976, p. 77), Lehmann (1960, p. 43), Mathieson (1910, pp. 145–56, note 1), and Morrell (1971*b*, pp. 162–63).

incommensurate connections were not enough to encourage the use of alternative selection principles. Reader's analysis of eighteenth-century England is valid for Scotland during the same period: "A patron who preferred an able candidate, simply on grounds of his ability, to one [with the proper connections was widely seen to be] behaving improperly," not only in terms of his own interests and the interests of those around him, but even with regard to the offices under his control. The men put forward on the basis of family, friendship, loyalty, and the like were, or so it was sometimes argued, men who had established their personal, moral, and ideological suitablility for responsible professional places far more convincingly than those notable merely for technical expertise (1966, pp. 5, 88–89; see also Riley 1964, p. 53). This is not to say that judgments about job performance capacities had no role in the allotment of positions. For posts that were not absolute sinecures, such judgments might enter the picture quite often, especially when patrons stood to gain economically, politically, or socially from having highly competent professionals in strategic locations (see, e.g., Morrell 1976). By and large, however, ability was no more than a subsidiary factor for further differentiating those who already met the prerequisite of good connections. It was not a means of circumventing the main requirement of the age.[14]

In eighteenth-century Scotland, the connections requirement was in no sense unique to the world of the traditional professions. On the contrary, having the right links to the right people could bring lucky Scots everything from college bursaries, library privileges, and backing for new cultural ventures to fulsome introductions to potential benefactors, lucrative tutorships with young noblemen, and lifelong pensions. The path to virtually all the benefits and honors at the bestowal of the state was precisely the same, and even for procuring purchasable military commissions and building up solid clienteles in law, medicine, and trade—matters that have occasionally been treated as if they were somehow removed from the vagaries of patronage—ties to men of influence were vital assets.[15]

14. To date, there has been no systematic examination of the matters treated in this paragraph. The main sources for the argument are the authorities referred to in the next paragraph and the notes that accompany it, but the preceding analysis is really a summing up of a state of affairs that, fragment by fragment, has emerged over and over again from virtually all of the biographical and social-historical materials cited in the list of references.

15. For illustration and discussion of the situation summarized in the preceding two sentences, see Carlyle (1910, pp. 57, 69), Emerson (1973b, pp. 303, 311, 318, 320), Fay (1956, pp. 14–15), Lamont (1975, p. 18), Mossner (1954, p. 56), Phillipson

Naturally, however, of greatest concern to those hoping for professional employment was the way this basic fact of life actually manifested itself in the allocation of legal, clerical, and academic positions. Behind career advancement in law, nepotism (so long as it produced choices politically acceptable to the king's ministers) was probably the most common factor. Generation after generation, judges and other high-level legal appointees were drawn disproportionately from a few dozen aristocratic families, and it was not atypical for sheriffs to constitute nothing but "a list of sons, sons-in-law, and alliances of the gentlemen" already in office.[16] In the Church, the standard procedure was for patrons to fill the humbler vacancies either with young kinsmen of magnates with whom they traded favors or with sons of clergymen who had served them well in the past; clerical charges with larger stipends and more eminent parishioners were generally reserved for established ministers endorsed by a broad constellation of friends and relations with pull.[17] For university appointments, candidates' "family relationships, . . . religious views," and "political influence [with] chancellors, rectors, the crown and its servants, local gentlemen, merchants or ministers" all came into play on various occasions in the eighteenth century, the contribution of each element to the final decision varying with patrons, colleges, and periods (Rendall 1978, p. 40; Emerson 1977, p. 456; see also Mackie 1954, pp. 163–64, 185–95). Here as elsewhere, however, it was the man with multiple connections who stood the best chance of making it through the professional maze (Emerson 1977, p. 457).

If one wished to summarize all of this in simplest terms, few words would do as poorly as universalism and independence. It is difficult to imagine a method of distributing professional places better designed to accentuate particularism and dependency than the Scottish patronage system. Under universalistic arrangements, Parsons has observed, the position a person obtains is unaffected by the specific social relationships in which he or she is involved

---

(1973, p. 130), Plumb (1967, p. 75), Rae (1895, pp. 165–66), Reader (1966, p. 75), Shapin (1974a, p. 101, 1974b, p. 6), Smith (1972, pp. 30–32), and the remarks below on British politics.

16. The comment quoted was one made in the 1730s by Andrew Mitchell and is cited by Ferguson (1968, p. 143). See also Emerson (1973b, pp. 303–5), Phillipson (1974, p. 130), and esp. Wilson (1968, pp. 250–55). On the earlier history of the Scottish legal aristocracy, see Donaldson (1976, pp. 10–11).

17. See Carlyle (1910, pp. 211–13), Cater (1970, p. 69), Emerson (1973b, pp. 307–8), Sefton (1966, pp. 5–6), and Somerville (1861, p. 167).

(1951, pp. 62, 182–83; see also Parsons and Shils 1951, pp. 81–82). But in eighteenth-century Scotland, a would-be professional's specific relationships, whether derived from birth into a certain family or social group or earned through performing special favors for particular individuals, were nothing less than the major determinant of his occupational destiny. When openings occurred for clergymen, lawyers, or professors, patrons time and again tended to give priority to those from their own exclusive kinship, friendship, religious, and political circles, while leaving by the wayside equally capable or needy men who did not belong to the preferred groupings, all exactly as in the particularistic patronage networks that have been uncovered by research on other societies (see Eisenstadt and Roniger 1980, p. 49; Kaufman 1974, pp. 285, 297, 301; Shefter 1977, pp. 410, 411; Stone 1977, p. 90).

The Scottish system also carried a blunt announcement of human dependency. Where professional men could obtain a station in life only with the assistance and support of powerful individuals and groups, they were, by definition, in a relationship of dependency on others, and unequivocally so. It was impossible for an eighteenth-century Scot to make it in the Church, the university, or the middle and upper levels of the law alone and by his own devices. To break in or get ahead, he at least needed the official backing of the illustrious patron of the office he was seeking, and, with few exceptions, this was an outcome that hinged directly on whether or not he received help from as many connections as he could mobilize. What one actually sees here is the incarnation in the realm of the professions of ties of dependency strikingly similar to those that are ordinarily associated with the serfs and lords of feudalism and, in the eighteenth century, still lingered on among some of the peasants and landowners in the Scottish countryside—a similarity that the phraseology of the age readily acknowledged when it aptly designated both peasants and place-hunters as the "dependents" of their social superiors.[18] Contemporaries did more, however, than simply recognize that those in pursuit of positions depended on a benefactor's goodwill. From time to time, they asserted that this situation led to dependency of another sort, the suspension of independent decision and action on the part of appointees. Francis Hutcheson, for example, claimed that disbursing Church benefices through patronage induced the "servile compliance [of ministers]

18. For a recent and more general discussion of patron-client relations as relationships of dependency, see Aminzade (1977).

with the humor of . . . great [lords] whether that humor be virtuous or vitious" (1735, p. 7), and John Bisset described the erosion of "the dignity and character [of officeholders as a result of their] sneaking and slavish dependence on great men" (pamphlet of 1732, cited by Henderson 1957, p. 129). Such charges somewhat overstate the issue, of course. Patrons usually had better things to do than to direct assiduously the daily activities of the various clerics, judges, and faculty members that they had helped along, and posts that (barring grievous offenses) conferred life tenure allowed their incumbents to deviate with a degree of impunity from the expectations that patrons did impose. In the long run, however, behavior so daring was the surest way of undoing one's prospects of advancing to loftier professional positions, acquiring certain of the sundry other benefits that flowed through patronage channels, and accumulating enough obligations from influential parties to redeem on behalf of family and friends. When professionals were so numerous, so in need of the support of patrons, and so inclined to keep in their good favor, why reward a man who insisted on having matters his own way?[19] Independence was as out of place in the world of patronage as universalism.

The day-to-day dynamics of British politics vividly underscored this point. These dynamics can be seen as the third dimension of the Scottish patronage system, for, particularly in the wake of the Union of the English and Scottish Parliaments in 1707, that system became enveloped by and entangled with the affairs of the Crown and the Parliament at Westminster. In the eighteenth century, the British monarch and his chief ministers of state had an enormous array of alluring prizes at their disposal: peerages, knighthoods, pensions, contracts, official decorations, and, above all, positions by the hundreds—in the royal household, the army, the navy, the diplomatic service, the colonies, the Church, the higher reaches of the law, and the various administrative branches of the government, with posts scattered throughout England, Ireland, and Scotland. But for all this abundance, there were never enough offices and honors to satisfy the endless queue of those dependent on favors from the state and, in this situation, familiar allocative procedures

19. The relative ease with which patrons could have things their way, and thus maintain their economic, political, and social dominance, when professionals were oversupplied was a factor that no doubt did its part to perpetuate the arrangements under which the educational institutions of Scotland continually turned out more educated men than there were positions for them to fill.

came to the fore.[20] Many ministers simply retained the best plums for themselves or handed them over to loyal friends and kinsmen (see Plumb 1961, pp. 92–100; Simpson 1970, p. 53; Smith 1972, p. 91). After these were taken care of, members of the Lords and the Commons who were willing to vote in accord with the ministry were given their due rewards. Once ministers mastered this way of influencing Parliament, such rewards actually emerged, as Plumb has argued, as "the dominant theme in [the] political life" of the nation and one of the primary mechanisms that "cemented the political system [and] held it together" (1956, p. 78, 1967, p. 189). In an age when the executive had few means of enlisting parliamentary support, the careful meting out of places, pensions, and the like served to bend a sizable and often decisive bloc of pliant legislators toward the king's policies and to "keep [its members] in dependence on the Court."[21] When their turn came, the men who captured the spoils of office in this manner distributed them by the same particularistic standards that the ministers used, reserving the real prizes for their own benefit or for family and associates, and passing the remainder on to the constituents back home in exchange for their votes at election time (see Plumb 1967, p. 92; Smith 1972, p. 79).[22] Electors caught on quickly, as Plumb comments: "The letter-bag of every M.P. with the slightest pretensions to influence was stuffed with pleas and demands from voters [for jobs and other favors] for themselves, their relatives or their dependents. . . . These [benefits] were the true coin of politics, the solvent that diminished or obliterated principle. . . . This was apparent to the meanest intelligence" (1968, p. 6).

It was no less apparent that Scotsmen were as forceably pulled into the whirlpool of political patronage as Englishmen. This development had roots far back in the seventeenth century, but it crystallized more and more as the eighteenth century progressed. The Crown had long been the patron for scores of places in Scotland and, following the Union and the extension into Scotland of

20. For discussion of the many state offices and honors that were available, as well as of their ultimate scarcity, see Owen (1974, pp. 100–146), Plumb (1967, pp. 107–26, 1968, p. 6), and Smith (1972, pp. 15–16, 23–24, 31–32, 79–81, 85).

21. The quotation is from Plumb (1956, p. 73). For more general support of this position, see Plumb (1950, pp. 42–51, 1967), Smith (1972, pp. 31–32, 73–74), and Speck (1977, pp. 211–12). Cf. Owen (1972, 1974, pp. 100–107).

22. Literary men willing to serve as political propagandists for the right parties might also profit as rewards filtered down from the top. For discussion of this issue, and the relationship between political and literary patronage in eighteenth-century England, see Collins (1927, pp. 114–221), and Saunders (1964, pp. 113–14, 123).

various English administrative agencies, the number of offices in the hands of the state grew substantially and came under increasingly tight control by the king's ministers and their generally subservient Scottish intermediaries. By means of this control, the ministers were able to ensure that the Union worked toward their benefit. Through offers of positions and other valuables dispensed by the state, Scottish members of the British Parliament who might have voted with the opposition and Scottish administrators who might have undermined the government's plans for its northern provinces could all be lined up behind the ministry. And so the English patronage system was foisted upon Scotland—with government appointments and honors going to the well-behaved political allies of the men in power at any given time, or to the relatives and other connections of those allies—and, as Kettler remarks, Scottish " 'politics' in the eighteenth century [was reduced to a search for] the jobs, force, and favors at the disposal of the British Crown" (1965, p. 20). The Scots who sat in the Lords and the Commons were particularly notorious as the docile props of successive ministries; decade after decade, they eagerly "traded their votes in return for advantages for their particular constituencies, and for themselves [and] their friends" (Pares 1954, p. 234).[23] Many of the legal, clerical, and academic positions for which the Crown was the patron were inevitably drawn into the wheeling and dealing that resulted, but these were by no means the only professional posts in Scotland implicated in the vicissitudes of national politics. For fear of cutting themselves off from the king's treasury of gifts, the individuals and groups who were the patrons for other places in the Church, the law, and the universities frequently filled vacancies by considering the particularistic preferences of the English ministers and their Scottish deputies in addition to their own political, religious, and familiar biases. Writing of the mid-eighteenth century, for example, Thomas Somerville, a young contemporary of the enlighteners, observed that "all the subaltern stations and executive offices were dealt out in conformity with [the] advice and recommendation [of the ministry's deputy for Scotland]. Nor was his influence restricted to the disposal of places at the nomination

23. See also Brady (1965, pp. 4–7), Mathieson (1910, pp. 21–22), Plumb (1967, p. 156), Pryde (1960, pp. 10–11), and Smout (1969a, p. 201). On the extension of the centrally controlled English patronage system into Scotland and the resultant scramble for places on the part of the Scots, see Donaldson (1965, p. 215), Ferguson (1968, pp. 137–47), Murray (1974, p. 54), Plumb (1967, pp. 180–82), Riley (1964), and Simpson (1970).

of Government. He often had an initiative, and always a controlling power in appointments which were nominally in the gift of corporate bodies and of individuals, by virtue of their official or patrimonial privileges. . . . To such an extreme was this scheme of universal patronage stretched, that it was always deemed prudent to obtain [the deputy's] goodwill before making any application even for places of the most inconsiderable emolument and importance" (1861, pp. 379–80; see also Cater 1970, pp. 68–70; Clark 1964, pp. 54–60, 158–61; Wilson 1968, p. 247). The infiltration of British politics into Scotland did not need to go nearly this far, however, to provide on the national level a dramatic confirmation of the commonplace fact that scarce places were not alloted impartially to independent men.

That patronage loomed so large in the process of securing such professional positions as were available in eighteenth-century Scotland did not mean the same thing to every career-minded young man. Under patronage arrangements, sons of certain upper-class families, as Emerson points out, "could expect office almost as a right of birth" (1973b, p. 304; see also Smout 1969a, pp. 473–74), and there was always a lucky handful of youths of humbler origin whose connections brought them an ideal appointment as soon as they completed their professional training. Most job-seekers were far less fortunate, however, and had to wait, in an anxious and crowded field of competitors, until whatever ties the could claim or cultivate finally did the trick. The extent to which this everyday occurrence had further consequences depended on the prior learning experiences of the men involved. For those who had been thoroughly steeped in the beliefs of earlier generations before arriving on the professional scene, the scramble for place was a personally trying experience, sometimes extremely so, but not a harbinger of any great cultural transformation. It was otherwise, however, for those who had already had the opportunity to acquire a commitment to principles at variance with the standards that were in evidence throughout the whole patronage system.

II

Had the intellectuals of the Scottish Enlightenment made promising starts on the professional job market, had they succeeded as much in the climate of particularism and dependency as they had done earlier in social settings where experiences in universalism and independence were the norm, their commitment to the fundamental orientations of the Enlightenment may well have been an extremely equivocal one. With the predictable exception of Adam Ferguson, however, none of these men initially were successes in the professional world that was so much a part of their lives from the time they began training to participate in that world. William Robertson, John Millar, Adam Smith, and David Hume, instead, all waited years for a position in the professions to come their way.[24] And although these years did prolong their moratorium for independent study and recreation, this pleasant side effect could not conceal the fact that this was hardly a time of good fortune in the areas of life that were governed by patronage. But the enlighteners' employment problems are in no way inconsistent with the general thesis about the experiential basis of the Enlightenment. As previously argued, being unsuccessful in circumstances where dependency and particularism are the operative principles is actually the sort of experience that increases attachment to independence and universalism on the part of those who have already learned these alternative orientations.

William Robertson's troubles were typical of young candidates for the ministry. He completed both his undergraduate education and his graduate training in divinity in the normal length of time, but two long years later was still without any position in the Church. Since his father earned a fairly adequate living, Robertson was not immediately required to take some menial job in order to get by. That things might eventually come to this, however, was a prospect that apparently weighed heavily on his mind. Carlyle recalls the "abhorence" that he, Robertson and their unemployed friends had for the traditional option of becoming a "Domestick Tutor" for a local gentleman: "We thought we had observed [how] tutors had contracted a certain obsequiousness or *bassese*, which alarmed us for ourselves" (1910, p. 70, 1973, p. 277; see also note 4 above).

24. The reasons why any particular man happened to suffer such a wait were various: he might not only lack connections, but fail—for want of knowledge, interpersonal savvy, or the like—to court the connections he had in an appropriate way, or otherwise make poor career moves; enter the market when openings were particularly limited in his field, or when better-connected professional hopefuls were especially numerous; and so on. For purposes of the argument of this section, however, there is no need to explore the specific situational factors that were responsible for the unemployment of each of the enlightened intellectuals. And that the following discussion indirectly speaks to this matter at several points should not obscure the fact that its principal objective is simply to indicate that, for whatever reasons, all of the enlighteners had an unsuccessful period in their professional lives.

After his two years in limbo, Robertson was saved from this possibility or worse by finally securing a clerical appointment, albeit one where, according to Stewart, "the income was but inconsiderable" (1796, p. 107)—and this when, shortly following the appointment, Robertson's parents died and left him to support all seven of his younger siblings. He did not obtain a more satisfactory assignment for over a decade.

John Millar fared no better in the legal profession. When his college days were at an end, Millar diligently underwent approximately six years of training in law, but his admission to the Faculty of Advocates—the last step before he could practice—was then delayed for two additional years. Although his biographers offer no explicit reason for this rather unusual delay, presumably it was tied in with the fact that, having studied in Glasgow, Millar as yet had little standing with the Edinburgh-based Faculty. In any case, the young enlightener spent his next years in Edinburgh and took temporary employment as a tutor for Lord Kames's son, a post well beneath both his aspirations and his credentials.[25] The association with Kames did, nonetheless, acquaint Millar with the ins and outs of Edinburgh's legal establishment and ultimately he gained entry to the Faculty. Thereafter, he began his legal practice and was, as his nephew John Craig put it, "universally considered as a very rising young lawyer" (1806, p. ix). Unfortunately, with lawyers as plentiful as they were in mid-eighteenth-century Scotland, many a rising star never rose at all, and Millar's few connections were a meager basis upon which to build hopes for either the large clientele or the appointive office that meant professional security. To complicate matters further, Millar was now a married man with a growing family.[26] He accordingly felt compelled, within a year of launching his long-planned law career, to give it all up and assume the professorship of civil law at the University of Glasgow. Given that Glasgow housed none of Scotland's higher courts, however, this position was "hardly a chair of distinction" (Lehmann 1960, p. 19); in an age when faculty members relied heavily on fees from

25. The post appears, in fact, to have been little more than the typical private tutorship of the period (see note 4 above). Neither Kames nor his son were noblemen—Kames's lordly title was merely a complimentary accompaniment of his judgeship—and there are no indications that Millar reaped appreciable financial benefits from this stint as a tutor.

26. Millar was the only enlightener to marry so early in his career. Robertson postponed marriage for eight years after securing his first appointment, Ferguson delayed well into middle age, and Hume and Smith were lifelong bachelors.

pupils to augment their low salaries, Millar's predecessors had been lucky to attract four or five law students a year. But Craig recounts the rationale for his uncle's decision as follows: "He saw that it was impossible for a young lawyer, whatever his abilities and diligence might be, to maintain a family, even with the most rigid oeconomy; and [while the] emoluments of a Professor of Law were not, indeed, very great; . . . they were much superior to what, for many years, he could expect to reach at the bar" (1806, p. x). To Millar's friends, it "seemed . . . an extraordinary want of ambition [to abandon the legal profession and] sit down contented with the moderate revenue, and the less brilliant reputation of a Teacher of Law" (Craig 1806, p. ix). Professional advancement in law being the risky and convoluted business that it was, however, one could only grab when a stable job presented itself and bear the disapprobation of friends. A second-rate compromise was preferable to penury.

Adam Smith was forced to wait still longer before securing a permanent professional place. After his wounded departure from Oxford prior to completing his intended course of study, he returned to Scotland and, in Stewart's words, immediately confronted "the uncertain prospect of obtaining . . . one of those moderate preferments, to which [exclusively] literary attainments lead" (1793, p. 9). Smith hoped eventually to join the faculty of one of the universities, but in the interim was willing apparently to accept a tutorship with a young nobleman. Two years later, however, he was no further professionally than when he started. Neither a professorship, a tutorship of any kind, nor another sort of position had materialized or seemed very likely to do so. To prevent his career from ending before it began, Smith decided to seek more of the limelight and offer to the public in Edinburgh a year-long series of lectures on literary topics, even though free-lance lecturers were then figures of little distinction. By the mid-eighteenth century, it had become customary for men who otherwise had no source of livelihood to set themselves up to instruct the public in one or more popular fields, and the Edinburgh papers were full of advertisements from teachers and lecturers on the make (see Law 1965, pp. 144–92; Scott 1937, pp. 48–49). Luckily, Smith's series was sponsored by some of the leading citizens of Edinburgh and, as a result, it managed to attract considerable notice and to pay off financially. It did not, however, bring the desideratum of a job offer and so Smith gave a second series of lectures, and then a third. Only in the midst of the latter, after almost five years of hanging on, was Smith at last nominated for a professorship. And to his great relief, the Glasgow faculty upheld the nomination, appointing the university's scholarly alumnus to the modest position of professor of logic.[27]

If Robertson, Millar, and Smith had a rough entry onto the professional scene, Hume was a fiasco. In the entire eight-year interval between ending his legal studies and completing the main portions of the *Treatise,* Hume simply had no job at all, save for a clerkship with a Bristol sugar merchant from which he was discharged after some four months for correcting the style of his incensed employer's letters.[28] One could argue, to be sure, that because Hume was born into a higher social stratum than his fellow enlighteners and even possessed a small patrimony, protracted unemployment, though an alarming event in the lives of men less established, was actually something about which he was fairly indifferent. Occasions when he was off enjoying his literary pursuits and indulging his philosophical inclinations, rather than working in one way or another to advance in the professions, could duly be adduced in support of this interpretation. In fact, however, as Mossner has made clear, achieving an adequate place was a matter that concerned Hume deeply time and time again from the period when he first finished his formal education until years after the *Treatise* had been published (see 1954, pp. 71, 109, 133, 149, 170, 187–88, 205). In his autobiography, Hume explained that while preferring to devote himself wholly to "philosophy and general learning," he realized early on that in the long run his "very slender fortune [was] unsuitable to this plan of life" (*Essays,* p. 608). But what to do instead, when openings were so few and so contingent on connections, was an intractable problem. Hume speaks in one of his first surviving letters of "a bashful Temper" and of lacking "Confidence & Knowledge enough of the World to push my Fortune"; somewhat later, he complains that obtaining "any Office [is] uncertain, and precarious," and then adds "I am not a good Courtier, or very capable of pushing my Fortune by Intrigue or Insinuation" (*HL* 1:18, *NHL,* p. 26). In this situation, his studies provided solace, but these were even interrupted during four of the years of interest

27. For a subject more to his liking, but only a very small salary advantage, Smith transferred one year later to the newly vacated chair of moral philosophy.

28. This account stops at the end of this eight-year interval for the reason stated in chap. 6, note 49. But Hume actually was to remain wholly jobless for another eight years, at which time he took on a tutorship from which he was dismissed within a year. In the following year, he was appointed to the secretarial position mentioned in the note just cited.

here by a mild mental and physical breakdown which, Mossner convincingly argues, was at least partially fostered by "the problem of reconciling his literary ambitions with a practical career" (1954, p. 71). Perhaps, as Greig speculates, Hume's family made matters worse by constantly worrying about his professional future (see 1931, pp. 65–66, 78, 88); certainly the young man's unemployment acutely embarrassed him before his friends. At the end of the eight-year interlude, he wrote from London to Henry Home in Edinburgh: "I have a great Inclination to go down to Scotland this Spring to see my Friends, . . . but cannot over-come a certain Shamefacedness I have to appear among you at my Years without having yet a Settlement. . . . How happens it that we Philosophers cannot as heartily despise the World as it despises us?" (*NHL*, p. 2; see also *HL* 1:28). Whatever else he may have been, David Hume was not a man coolly unaffected by his sorry occupational fate.

A situation in marked contrast to that of Hume and the others befell Adam Ferguson, whose education in independence and universalism was already lagging behind. Here one initially sees nothing of the familiar floundering in the arena of patronage, nothing of the kind of professional experience that was structured to further the development of enlightened attitudes. Indeed, rather than undergoing a long, agonizing period of delay between the conclusion of professional training and the acquisition of a position, Ferguson succeeded in breaking into his chosen profession when he was little more than half way through the prescribed course of study for the ministry.[29] The appointment that he obtained at that time was a deputy-chaplaincy in a military regiment headed by a nobleman from the powerful house of Athole—a house with which Ferguson's father had maintained friendly ties for decades—and, within months of this first appointment, Athole influence induced the General Assembly to waive its ordinary requirements for admission to the clergy so that Ferguson could be ordained a minister and hence promoted to the higher office of chaplain. This was an auspicious beginning and one that Ferguson had every reason to regard as a sure stepping-stone to a well-endowed benefice. More-

29. Although Fagg (1968, p. 35) is probably right to doubt the episode, it should be noted that there is some suggestion that, at an even earlier date shortly after beginning the Edinburgh divinity course, Ferguson occupied for a brief time (which is not inconsistent with the approximately two-year moratorium previously discussed) the post of secretary to Lord Milton, one of the most influential men in mid-eighteenth-century Scotland (see *Dictionary of National Biography* 1885–90, 6:1201; Small 1864, p. 605, note †).

over, in view of the overall balance of his experiences to this point, it is nowise surprising that when his first work, *A Sermon Preached in the Ersh Language,* appeared the next year, it revealed a man who still was plainly within the bounds of Calvinism.

But in the years that followed, Ferguson ineluctably confronted far less welcome professional experiences. These could not, of course, eradicate what had gone before and transform his prior professional, educational, and familial experiences into the more thoroughly and consistently enlightening variety that Hume, Millar, Robertson, and Smith encountered. They could, nevertheless, resuscitate and make good the various lessons in universalism and independence that he had previously received and thus change the total configuration of his experiences in favor of the Enlightenment, though such a development by no means precluded future equivocations and harkings back to the orthodox beliefs that had been transmitted during the alternate phases of his socialization. The earliest sign of an alteration in Ferguson's occupational prognosis appeared within a few years of this assignment as a chaplain. Hoping at this time to advance to a more established position in the Church, he requested and was then denied a benefice for which the Duke of Athole was himself the patron. To keep going, Ferguson decided to remain with his regiment some while longer. Eventually, however, perhaps because the unit was slated to sail for America, he abandoned military life, aspiring no doubt to make his much-awaited move up the career ladder. His plan was quickly frustrated. Having evaded the lamentable lot of the unemployed professional for nine years, Ferguson now at the mature age of thirty-one entered upon a five-year period of "unpleasant makeshifts and unsuccessful schemes to [achieve] financial security" (Kettler 1965, p. 49; see also Fagg 1968, p. 31).

The first big setback came when the Duke of Athole failed to name Ferguson to fill the opening in the Church that was created by his father's death. Shortly thereafter, he took on a travelling, quasi-tutorial position with little stature and probably quite minimal monetary compensation.[30] Kettler (1965, p. 49) goes so far as to claim that Ferguson "had no source of income at all" during this

30. For the known details of this position, see Ferguson's early letter to Adam Smith (*Corr,* pp. 14–16). From the forms of address used in this letter and the editorial notes appended to it, it is clear that Ferguson's charge was not a young nobleman and, therefore, that his was not among the few high-status tutorships of the age. If surnames are any evidence here, the tutee was simply a kinsman of Ferguson's mother.

stage of his career and during its sequel—when he was back in Edinburgh as a sort of glorified errand boy—and Fagg (1968, pp. 31–45) draws a picture that is nearly as grim. Not for some two and a half years after relinquishing his chaplaincy did Ferguson finally obtain another stable position, and this was nothing more distinguished than the keepership of the Faculty of Advocates' Library, an office whose salary was "pitiful . . . for even those frugal times" (Kettler 1965, p. 49). Approximately a year later, Ferguson left this post for a second tutorship, this time with the sons of the Earl of Bute. Since Bute was then among the leading Scottish nobles, this would seem at first glance to be one of the age's rare choice tutorships. Yet Ferguson hesitated before accepting Bute's offer, ostensibly because it entailed superintending two youngsters instead of the usual one. But for a man in his circumstances, this was a peculiar cavil, as the ordinarily sympathetic David Hume observed (see *HL* 1:263), and one suspects the objection to be a cover for a more serious grievance: perhaps Bute paid below the going rate for tutoring young noblemen on a part-time basis, or neglected to promise the pension that ideally accompanied this rather short-lived type of work. In all events, Ferguson's financial outlook remained bleak after a year in Bute's employment,[31] by which point he was again casting about for a more permanent resolution to his professional predicament.

His sights were now set on a professorship in the law of nature and nations at the University of Edinburgh, but here he was once more unsuccessful. An effort to secure the Glasgow chair in church history—the office Hume hoped "would prevent a new Dissappointment to [Ferguson], after so many he has undergone" (*NHL,* p. 56)—likewise collapsed the following year, and reprieve did not arrive until the Edinburgh Town Council elected him professor of natural philosophy later the same year. Though natural philosophy was a field remote from Ferguson's own interests, he understandably was in no mood to quibble this time around and promptly accepted the opportunity to have a foothold in the professions at long last; "I who never had a home till now must prepare to go to Edinburgh" is how Ferguson recounted the course of events to a friend (letter cited by Fagg 1968, p. 58). It was, however, just before this opportunity materialized, when he was still in the midst of what those who knew him described as "a cruel & distressful Situation"

31. See *HL* 1:287, *NHL,* p. 56; and Ferguson's letter to Milton, cited by Fagg (1968, p. 53).

(*NHL*, p. 57), that Ferguson circulated among his friends a revised manuscript which he had recently completed. The manuscript was a draft of the great—if appropriately ambivalent—declaration of enlightened principles that was published several years later as *An Essay on the History of Civil Society*, a draft which no less an enlightener than Hume preferred to the final product in both form and content (see *NHL*, pp. 52, 57, *HL* 2:12, 133).[32] For Ferguson, as for our other intellectuals, travails in the precincts of patronage, particularism, and dependency had, when combined with earlier successes in circumstances that conveyed the message of independence and universalism, culminated in the Enlightenment.

The enlighteners' professional impasse, as previously noted, was not a permanent one. What radicals they may have become had they been continually spurned by those with power and patronage privileges and forever denied the means of prosperity will, consequently, never be known. None of the enlightened intellectuals had actually ever been entirely without helpful connections and, however insufficient these were in the short run, eventually they grew in number and brought respectable results—a benefice for Robertson, professorships for Ferguson, Millar, and Smith, even a government post for poor Hume. Except for Millar (who voluntarily remained where he was), much greater rewards lay ahead: more attractive professorships and a pension for Ferguson; a promotion in the Church, a trio of sinecures, a pension, and the principalship of the University of Edinburgh for Robertson; a substantial pension and a pair of well-paid government administrative appointments for Smith; and several pensions and undemanding public offices for Hume, to mention only the highlights. These were men who thoroughly understood how the game worked. Their letters are, for example, both a running commentary on newly vacated professional positions and the patrons of those positions, and a vast storehouse of appeals and schemes for places and other benefits for themselves and their worthy relatives and friends. There were, to be sure, some expected differences here. Hume had, as Mossner

32. Previously, when still only halfway through the period of makeshifts, Ferguson had published two pamphlets, *Reflections Previous to the Establishment of a Militia* and *The Morality of Stage-Plays Seriously Considered*, which—as far as one can judge the matter from some brief topical remarks on a pair of not particularly revealing subjects—appear to be transitional works. In these documents, the orthodoxy of the early *Sermon in Ersh* has faded, but has yet to be replaced by what will come in the *Essay*.

has observed, a "deep-set aversion to soliciting favours from the great [which at times became] almost a mania" (1954, p. 403; see also Forbes 1975a, pp. 132, 188–89); Ferguson, on the other extreme, repeatedly penned "requests for favors, occasionally phrased in almost abject terms" (Kettler 1965, p. 47). By middle age, however, all had profited very handsomely through their high-placed connections, and without coming close to selling their souls in the deal.[33]

Yet this turn of events did not extinguish their bitterness over the ways in which the professional world operated. It is no small measure of how severely the enlightened intellectuals had been bruised early on that, even when their fortunes were on the upswing, they disdained the accoutrements of the patronage system nearly every time these cropped up in their writings. This, of course, does not mean that, in their program for their own society, these men sought fundamental alterations in the system. Millar was alone among the enlighteners in putting forth an all-out indictment of the behemoth that patronage had become in British political life. Discoursing on the insidious ramifications of the Crown's ability to make or break careers "in all the departments of government" as well as "in the army, in the church, at the bar, in the republic of letters, in finance," and in other domains simply with the device of patronage, Millar averred:

> With what a powerful charm does it operate in regulating opinions, in healing grievances, in stifling clamours [and] the most furious opposition! It is the great opiate which inspires political courage, and lulls the reflection. . . . All who enjoy, or who expect offices, or places of emolument . . . and even in some degree their kindred and connexions [are wont] to court, and to support that interest upon which they depend [and to form] the correspondent habits of dependence. [*HV* 4:78–79, 83, 95–96][34]

33. How the enlighteners ultimately achieved this unlikely victory is the story of the next decades of their lives and well beyond the scope of this study. For the details of the story, the standard biographical sources (see chap. 3, note 20) may be consulted and supplemented in Robertson's case with the more recent work of Cater (1970) and McKelvey (1969). On the important issue of Robertson's refusal to make concessions to his backers, see Clark (1964, pp. 95–96, 1970, pp. 210–11), Mathieson (1910, p. 170), and McKelvey (1969, p. 238).

34. See also *Ranks*, p. 289, and the passages from Millar's *Letters of Crito*, cited in Lehmann (1960, pp. 391–92).

The substance of Millar's attack on patronage was not novel. English political commentators had been saying much the same thing at least from the mid-seven-

Hume and Smith, examining the same topic several decades earlier, were more restrained. Anticipating the modern historical claim that Crown patronage was among the principal sources of political stability in eighteenth-century Britain, Hume argued that, a certain amount of "corruption and dependence" notwithstanding, the influence that the king and his councilors commanded by virtue of "the offices and honours . . . at [their] disposal" was "necessary to the preservation of our . . . government," and Smith held a similarly sober view of the consequences of the numberless "prizes which sometimes come from the wheel of the great state lottery of British politics" (*Essays*, pp. 45–46; *WN*, p. 587).[35] On the issue of whether ministers of the Church should be selected by patrons—the only aspect of patronage arrangements, apart from the growth of Crown influence, to stir controversy at the time and to receive some systematic attention in the documents of the Enlightenment—the Scottish intellectuals again endorsed the status quo, insisting that existing appointment procedures were a surer guarantee of an able and independent clergy than the popular alternative of allowing each congregation to elect its own minister.[36]

Despite their reluctance to countenance social structural reforms, however, all of the enlighteners remained, in the face of professional success, personally as antipathetic as Millar to life as it had to be under the stranglehold of patronage. Ferguson maintained that when men are drawn into a chase for positions and other favors from the powerful—a chase he scornfully likened to a petty scramble after "caps, ribbons and petticoats for the maids, sugar-plumbs for the children, and luncheons for the clerks"—principle is overthrown and "magnanimity, courage, and the love of mankind, are sacrificed to avarice and vanity, or suppressed under a sense of dependence" (*HPM*, p. 138, *EHCS*, p. 238). Hume derisively characterized his age as one in which even magnates of "Sense & Learning" reserved all their "Favours [for] Voters, & Cabballers, & Declaimers, & Spies, & such other useful People" (*HL* 1:113). Rob-

---

teenth century onward: see Owen (1972, p. 373, 1974, p. 286), Plumb (1967, pp. 129–30, 140–44, 151), Pocock (1975, p. 478), Robbins (1959, p. 8), Speck (1977, pp. 5, 22, 222–23), and Winch (1978, p. 32). On attitudes toward patronage in Scotland, see Ferguson (1968, pp. 242, 247).

35. On Hume's views, see also *Essays*, pp. 128, 509; Forbes (1975a, pp. 211, 216–17), and Plumb (1956, pp. 61–62). On Smith's position, see *WN*, p. 583; Forbes (1975b, p. 183), and Winch (1978, pp. 62–63, 102, 152–53, 156).

36. For Hume's stand on this issue, see Mossner (1954, p. 278); for Robertson's, see Clark (1964, p. 30), Henderson (1957, p. 168), and Stewart (1796, pp. 234–35); and for Smith's views, *WN*, pp. 760–62.

ertson, while ordinarily too much the historian to state opinions on contemporary affairs, betrayed underlying sentiments of a very similar sort when he described the quest for offices and honors at the bestowal of superiors as a primary means by which the subjects of the Roman empire came to lose "not only the habit but even the capacity of deciding for themselves, or of acting from the impulse of their own minds" (*Progress,* p. 8). And Adam Smith made the verdict unanimous. To him, it was wholly reprehensible that professional men—whose odds against ever making it were "ten to one" to begin with—should have their destinies determined "in the drawing-rooms of the great" where "flattery and falsehood too often prevail over merit and abilities," "where success and preferment depend . . . upon the fanciful and foolish favour of ignorant, presumptuous, and proud superiors" (*LJB,* p. 175, *TMS,* p. 129). A hungry spaniel, Smith declared, can only "gain the favour of those whose service it requires . . . by every servile and fawning attention," but such "arts" do not become a man (*WN,* pp. 13–14). These petulant outbursts against patronage are a recurrent reminder that the early professional experiences that became the men of the Enlightenment had left palpable scars, though they had left as well men of Enlightenment.

Conclusion

When they emerged from the series of experiences traced in the preceding chapters, the enlighteners were on the threshold of a revolutionary rift with the culture that had held sway in Scotland since the Reformation. Hume was, in fact, already a published author who had announced to the world that the particularism and dependency of the past must give way to universalism and to independence, and as Ferguson, Millar, Robertson, and Smith brought out during the next decade or so of their lives the works they had begun while waiting for a professional opening or shortly after securing one, the same bold commitments were affirmed again and again. Additional works followed in later years and, by the time these had all appeared, the five Scottish intellectuals had variously extended their novel orientations to fields ranging from philosophy and history to psychology and economics, and forged a great moment in the advance toward modern culture.

It was a moment for which, we now know, they were well prepared. Although the men of the Enlightenment had grown up amid continual repetitions of the traditional Calvinist creed, they had simultaneously confronted social experiences with vastly different cultural implications. Told over and over of human dependency, they were repeatedly provided with rewarding opportunities for autonomy, opportunities to decide and to act on their own. For David Hume, Adam Smith, and John Millar, these began in earliest childhood with liberation—lasting liberation, save in the instance of Millar—from the shackles of the patriarchal family, continued through mid-adolescence with attendance at those universities where restrictive controls and ties of dependency were least in evidence, and persisted long afterwards in a moratorium for study and recreation which allowed them full scope to be masters of themselves. Each of these developments had its counterpart in the early life of

William Robertson, if always with something of a hitch. Robertson also escaped the confines of the patriarchal household, but not until he was an older lad; he too received his undergraduate and post-graduate education in circumstances organized to foster independence, though all through this education he once more lived under patriarchy. The same developments were further attenuated in the case of Adam Ferguson, for his release from paternal domination was still longer in coming, his college better equipped to regulate students and ensnare them in relationships of dependency, his moratorium for self-governance much briefer than that undergone by any of his enlightened fellows. These variations and those evident in Robertson's case coalesced into patterns of socialization that differed from the pattern encountered by the other members of the Scottish Enlightenment, and the discrepancies were subsequently displayed in their respective writings: while Robertson fused his belief in independence with the venerable theme of dependency and Ferguson habitually vacillated on the matter, Millar, Smith, and, even more so, Hume avowed autonomy without equivocation. But leaving the variations aside, all of the enlightened intellectuals were presented in their youth with practical lessons in independence, and on the whole they all succeeded in the various settings where the lessons were offered. Their latter professional disappointments, their protracted failure to obtain decent jobs in the dependency-saturated domain of patronage after having done so well in situations of the opposite sort, then supplied the materials to confirm their commitment to independence and to bring their previous training for cultural change to fruition. The enlighteners could now embark upon the Enlightenment. Familial, educational, and occupational experiences had subtly combined to carry them beyond the age-old assumption of human dependency.

The path to universalism was a parallel one. At the same time as they heard all about the divergent destinies of the different social groups into which Scottish culture divided the world, in their daily lives the young enlighteners met success under conditions where individuals ostensibly very different from one another were treated the same way, and failure where more particularistic policies were the rule. These experiences in universalism commenced for Smith, Millar, and Robertson, and then more belatedly for Ferguson, during their rewarding years as grammar schoolboys, for in the small grammar schools of their era, pupils of highly diverse sorts were routinely subjected to treatment by uniform standards. Such an edifying scene was not something that Hume witnessed in his childhood, though, by receiving his early education outside of a grammar school, he alone among the enlightened intellectuals managed to avoid the school's sundry impediments to the growth of autonomy. Hume's departure here from the general pattern foreshadows not only his singularly far-reaching pronouncement of independence, but also the limits that appear when his otherwise vigorous universalism is compared with that of Smith, Millar, and Robertson. For the next major phase of his education, moreover, Hume was, along with Smith, Millar and Robertson, in a setting structured to convey the message of universalism. While the Enlightenment's most inconstant universalist, Ferguson, spent his undergraduate years at a university where the customary particularistic procedures were only in partial abeyance, the four remaining enlighteners attended the very colleges in which heterogeneous groups of students were time and again treated uniformly. In the course of doing so, all of them also garnered their share of successes and satisfactions, which was the reverse of the fate they subsequently encountered in that great realm of favoritism that was the professional job market. But in light of how the budding intellectuals of the Enlightenment had been socialized by that point, the professional hardships that assailed them were really ideal vehicles to solidify firmly their commitment to the option of universalism. So armed by experience, Ferguson, Hume, Millar, Robertson, and Smith would soon fissure the cultural foundations upon which they had been raised.

It took more than experience, of course, to bring the transformation about. Able young persons may be offered opportunities to draw out new moral principles and reinforced in ways that lead them to value such principles, but these may then remain forever concealed in the far recesses of their being. Had Ferguson, Hume, Millar, Robertson, and Smith been born a century earlier, they might easily have undergone (at least outside of the university) many of the same experiences that they received during their own century, and yet they could scarcely have become enlighteners as we know them. To the extent that the economic, political, religious, and intellectual conditions of preceding periods made it even possible to generalize experientially-derived ideas beyond the specific settings where they originated, they circumscribed the process within limits unfavorable to much that is characteristic of the Enlightenment. By the time Ferguson, Hume, and the others came on the scene, however, the numerous historical changes that have been emphasized in previous accounts of the Scottish Enlightenment—

commercial expansion, Isaac Newton, and the rest—altered the parameters for the cultural life of the mid-eighteenth century and, as part of this development, opened avenues for the expression of novel attitudes in areas like philosophy, psychology, economics, and history. The Scottish enlighteners, accordingly, could extend and work out their orientations of universalism and independence through accessible cultural channels, thereby making use of the potentialities that were contained within the boundaries of their age. To put the point simply: enlightening experiences could culminate in the Enlightenment because they fell, in eighteenth-century Scotland, on a particular type of fertile soil.

But the independence and universalism that define the Enlightenment were by no means the only beliefs that might have taken hold here. Among the huge majority of eighteenth-century Scots, including those in such fields as philosophy and history, dependency and particularism actually thrived nearly as well as they had during previous generations, and infinitely better than the modern attitudes that animated the program of the enlightened intellectuals. The origin of these attitudes does not become comprehensible until one moves systematically beyond the broader social and cultural context in which these intellectuals and all of their contemporaries were embedded to identify what worked to set the enlighteners apart and how this, in turn, specifically gave rise to universalism and to independence. And on the basis of the evidence of this study, it seems not only that sequenced patterns of experience in microlevel social settings were the differentia, but also that the particular experiential pattern encountered by Ferguson, Hume, Millar, Robertson, and Smith constituted the concrete process through which their distinctive orientations came into being. It is true that, at the present time, this statement cannot be regarded as definitive for there remain limitations both in the underlying theory and, more seriously, in the accompanying documentation. Handicapped by a deficiency of information on the day-to-day experiences of the young enlighteners, the analysis has relied heavily on proxy indicators that, although selected and used cautiously enough to render the steps in the argument highly probable, nonetheless tend to mask large segments of experiential reality. The overall results must therefore be corroborated by more fine-grained research. Pending this, however, the preparative series of family, educational, and professional experiences summarized in the preceding paragraphs provides such consistent confirmation of the thesis advanced at the outset of this investigation that we may tentatively conclude that it was through this series of experiences that the individuals who would make the Scottish Enlightenment initially acquired and became committed to the orientations of independence and universalism. Apparently, in other words, the elemental components of the Scottish Enlightenment, the principles that did so much to distinguish it, give it shape, and make it a cultural revolution, were first born of experience.

Experience was not the unmoved mover. Experiences are a function of the nature of the setting where they occur and this is a factor that itself has causes. In eighteenth-century Scotland, the family, the school, the university, and the professional marketplace were all deeply affected by larger sociohistorical conditions. From the point of view of Great Divide theories of the genesis of modern culture, this fact is a very convenient one. It was observed earlier that Great Divide approaches have long overlooked the cultural transformation that was the Enlightenment, but one can readily see how these approaches could attempt to assimilate the Scottish Enlightenment and the evidence for its experiential basis. Starting, for example, with that watershed of watersheds, the Reformation, one might emphasize all that Calvinism did to mold the salient features of the eighteenth-century Scottish family, the several ways that the reformed church encouraged the establishment, maintenance, and utilization of schools and universities, and the means by which the extensive educational network that resulted produced the overcrowding that was such a decisive aspect of the professional world, and then suggest that the particular socialization experiences received by the enlightened intellectuals were no more than the inexorable unfolding of possibilities implicit in this fecund situation. Other popular candidates for the Great Divide might similarly be pressed into yeoman service; historical sociology is well supplied with models one might follow here.

Ultimately, however, glosses of this kind do not suffice. The familial, educational, and professional experiences that were significant in the lives of the Scottish enlighteners cannot be so facilely reduced to renowned historical turning points, except by a reasoning so tortuous that it would even deny that any genuine changes followed from the Calvinist Reformation or various contending landmarks. To some extent, the operations of microlevel socialization settings in eighteenth-century Scotland can be traced back to one or more Great Divides, but in differing degrees these operations were also shaped by a host of humbler considerations.

Chief among these were internal structural properties, like the ratio of teachers to students, the type of curriculum, and the duration of the schoolday and the schoolyear in the case of elementary schools, and the amount of tutorial instruction, the presence or absence of prerequisites on course attendance, and the nature of residential arrangements in the case of universities; such characteristics of the participants in social settings as the longevity of fathers, the child-rearing practices of widowed young mothers, the class and national diversity of pupils, the financial self-interest of faculty members, and the political self-interest of patrons; and the logistics of mundane organizational functions, of teaching several Latin classes in one place at one time, of offering multiple college courses to the same students on the same day, of training impecunious men for the ministry in cities with few part-time jobs, and so on. Experience emerged from the conjunction of factors from all of these categories as well as from the wider social and cultural environment, and within the shadows of the same great historical events, that conjunction frequently assumed drastically different forms, as is evident from the coexistence throughout the eighteenth century of universities staffed by professors and by regents, and of rural parochial schools, small town grammar schools, and large urban grammar schools. Given its capacity to convey basic normative orientations, experience in any case introduced contingencies of a new order into the historical process, contingencies that are altogether missed when the situational dynamics that structured experience are regarded as the simple derivatives of lofty developments at work above and beyond the situational level. Sometimes, to be sure, these contingencies served merely to reinforce prevailing cultural standards: in Scotland during the early eighteenth century, many social settings imparted a thoroughly traditional experiential message. In addition, even when the message was otherwise, it often failed to seize those who were exposed to it because it arrived too late developmentally, was weakly reaffirmed by subsequent experience, was attended with an inappropriate combination of rewards and punishments, or was not drawn out in the first place. In the instances of Ferguson, Hume, Millar, Robertson, and Smith, however, where experiences bearing principles of a heterodox type began early and then repeatedly recurred along with suitable reinforcements and in the presence of inferential abilities, the eventual precipitate was a sweeping departure from existing cultural patterns and one whose substance was far more than the long-

gestated aftereffect of some previous watershed like the Reformation. That precipitate was the Scottish Enlightenment.

There is no reason, of course, to restrict this perspective on
experience exclusively to the study of the Scottish enlighteners.
Experience is a reality in all historical circumstances and, outside
of social formations so highly integrated that a perfect correspondence obtains between formally taught beliefs and values and those
arising from ongoing activities in concrete settings, it constitutes a
vital source of new cultural orientations which can then become—
insofar as cognitive, gratificational, and developmental considerations are conducive and relevant opportunities for generalization
are accessible—elements in the general cultural life of the particular
social group. In order to determine how often this occurs or has
occurred, how broadly, and with what results, the strategy used in
this inquiry needs to be extended and adapted to other episodes
of cultural change. To the degree that these episodes resemble the
Scottish Enlightenment by consisting primarily of small numbers
of intellectuals, they are developments of a sort conventionally relegated to the sociology of knowledge; the point, however, would
be to analyze intellectual transformations without complacently
stopping with the macrosocial and -cultural variables that have left
so many explanations in the sociology of knowledge as poorly differentiated and as social-psychologically wanting as previous explanations of the Enlightenment in Scotland. But intellectuals are
by no means the only persons whose commitments can be altered
in the course of experience and later vented. With appropriately
specific data, one could investigate the experiential roots of attitudinal shifts in the most varied types of social groupings.

The obvious place to begin the task of extension and refinement
is in Scotland itself. In the process of exploring the makings of the
Scottish Enlightenment, this study has put aside questions that now
deserve detailed scrutiny about the reception of enlightened ideas
and about their vicissitudes in succeeding generations. It seems,
from bits and pieces of information of the Age of the Enlightenment and the decades immediately afterwards, that independence
consistently failed to take hold in Scotland, though universalism
may have fared somewhat better. Whether or not this proves to be
a correct characterization of the cultural scene during the latter
part of the eighteenth century and the early years of the nineteenth
century, however, the beliefs and values of the period were held
by individuals who had undergone many learning experiences, and

the issues that require examination are the extent to which these were enlightening experiences, and how the prevalence of such experiences among intellectuals and nonintellectuals alike affected the diffusion or the demise of the revolutionary principles of the men of the Scottish Enlightenment. In addition to confronting the problem of what eventually became of these principles, one might look beyond Ferguson, Hume, Millar, Robertson, and Smith and systematically investigate the relationship between experience and attitude for other early and mid-eighteenth-century Scots, drawing here from the Calvinist multitude, those who occupied the cultural waystations between Calvinism and the Enlightenment, and any further enlighteners who turn up.

Another ready field for research is offered by the Enlightenment in other countries, both Calvinist and not. In the eighteenth century, the French, the English, the Italians, the Germans, the Spanish, the Polish, and the Americans all had their versions of Enlightenment. How similar these were to their counterpart in Scotland is, to be sure, still an open question. Where independence and universalism were once more the main innovations, employing the approach proposed in this study would in principle be fairly straightforward; on the other hand, for cases that involved an efflorescence of fundamental orientations of a different kind, it would be necessary to identify the experiential arrangements that promote these orientations before venturing to determine if the Enlightenment was again formed of social experience. But in none of these instances, including those pertaining to Scotland, do the particular organizational structures and processes and the particular settings that have been stressed in the preceding chapters necessarily provide benchmarks for research. Familial, formal educational, and professional settings may well supply enlightening experiences— even experiences in universalism and independence, in fact— through ways other than those that have surfaced in the analysis of the five Scottish enlighteners (see pp. 242–43), and in the lives of certain men and women, these settings may themselves pale in importance before other arenas of socialization. Only when such possibilities are fully appreciated can the thesis about experience and Enlightenment be meaningfully applied and evaluated in diverse studies of the rise and fall of enlightened ideas.

The Enlightenment is not the end of the matter, however. At least as it occurred in Scotland, it is but an epochal illustration of the emergence of cultural orientations of one variety from the midst of circumstances suffused by attitudes and assumptions of a disparate variety—a process that is not confined to any special time and place or to any specific set of orientations, but one that is ever actualized by individuals who have lived through an assortment of instructive experiences. This proposition does not mean that experience is always the decisive ingredient in the process. Its role, no doubt, is protean, and as its dynamics are examined on a wider scale, it should become possible to specify the conditions under which cultural change commences in experience, as it apparently did in the case of the Scottish Enlightenment, and when its sources lie elsewhere. Instead of new simplisms for old, we might then have a realistic understanding of how modern cultures have come to be as they are.

Appendix

The argument of chapters 4–7 raises a nagging doubt. The thesis about experience and Enlightenment, one could easily contend, works only so long as enlightening experiences were as rare as enlighteners were in Scotland during the early and middle decades of the eighteenth century. But, the objection might continue, this was by no means the case. For while there may have been only a handful of enlightened intellectuals, many of their contemporaries were also separated from their fathers, educated in the appropriate schools, forced to confront the overcrowded professions, and so on. Previously this issue was discussed in analytical terms and the mistaken assumptions that underlie the whole manner in which it is posed were identified; it was suggested that the only sensible strategy for grappling with the question of how many others were prepared for the Enlightenment in the same way Ferguson, Hume, Millar, Robertson, and Smith were would be to determine the number of those, with the capacity to infer general principles from concrete social settings, who encountered the same total configuration of experiences as the enlighteners, under the same conditions (that is, starting at the same age, continuing for the same length of time, etc.), with the same pattern of reinforcements, and then were likewise situated in fields where the generalization of experientially acquired attitudes was a viable prospect (see chap. 3, sec. II). Currently, the data necessary for this ambitious task do not exist, and the most adequate data available are so short of the ideal that one almost hesitates to introduce them. All things considered, however, presenting what is known seems preferable to giving the entire problem up to groundless speculation.

The extant data best suited to the present purposes were originally collected by Vern Bullough and his associates in the course of a comparative study on intellectual achievement (see Bullough and Bullough 1971; Bullough 1970; Bullough and Bullough 1973; Bullough et al. 1970) and consist of selected biographical information on 375 Scots educated during the eighteenth century or in the decades immediately preceding it. The 375 comprise a listing, assembled by surveying histories of various spheres of culture and the *Dictionary of National Biography*, of men and women who made at least modest contributions to fields such as philosophy, history, theology, natural science, literature, architecture, and painting. While excluding persons recognized chiefly for political, military, or administrative accomplishments, the listing more or less comprehensively embraces the age's known "intellectual achievers"—to use Bullough's expression, which is abbreviated below as "intellectuals"—and this emphasis is quite apt in the current context. Not only do these figures constitute, apart from the achiever here and there overlooked in Bullough's researches, the effective population of those in eighteenth-century Scotland who were either in or in close proximity to the areas where attitudinal generalization was a definite possibility, but taking intellectual achievement as a fair indicator of general cognitive capacity, one can be confident that on the whole these were individuals well able actually to learn the lessons of experience. What one has here, in other words, is a good approximation of the total, currently accessible pool about which it is meaningful to ask how many encountered the same package of experiences and rewards as the intellectuals of the Enlightenment. Were such a package commonplace among the early and mid-eighteenth-century Scots in this group, one might indeed wonder why enlightened attitudes were not considerably more widespread at the time than they were and fault the foregoing account of the Scottish Enlightenment as inconsistent with the experiences and ideas of all the intellectuals who were not of the Enlightenment. Let us therefore see, by going as far as possible with the information coded on the Bullough data set, just how prevalent the enlighteners' experiences were.

In order to do this, it is first necessary to select from among the 375 subjects those who were born either before or during the same period as the enlightened intellectuals. Men and women born at a later time might have perpetuated or diffused the cultural change wrought by Ferguson, Hume, Millar, Robertson, and Smith, but they could not have been part of the cohort that effected the change and, for this reason, they are outside the scope of this particular study (see chap. 2, sec. I). Of course, in fixing a precise date at which this "later time" begins, there is a certain degree of arbitrariness. Given that Hume was born in 1711, Ferguson, Robertson, and Smith in the early 1720s, and Millar in 1735, 1740 might seem to be the most reasonable dividing point; persons born in 1740 or afterwards would not generally have been engaged in the fields where they might have expressed their situationally acquired orientations until at least the mid-1760s, by which time all the enlightened intellectuals were active participants on the Scottish cultural scene, with the result that the creed of dependency and particularism was already decisively breached. One might argue, however, that eliminating everyone born from 1740 onward biases the investigation too much in favor of the conclusion that is most obviously consonant with the proposed explanation of the Enlightenment—viz., that the enlighteners' pattern of experiences was not widely shared. In conformity with the wise methodological rule that, in doubtful procedural matters, one should opt for the alternative that is less likely to demonstrate what one hopes to demonstrate, it is better to draw the line between the period of the birth of the enlightened intellectuals and succeeding periods at a later date, even if this leads to an overstatement of the number who were actually in the same boat as the men of the Enlightenment. To be as inclusive as possible here without altogether forgetting that the concern is with the generations that produced the cultural change embodied in the Scottish Enlightenment, 1750 was taken as the cutoff year. The men and women in the Bullough data were accordingly divided into the two groups shown in the two tables below. The latter table consists of the 153 figures who were born in 1750 or after and thus not subjected to further analysis; their names are listed out to make clear exactly which eighteenth-century Scots were excluded from consideration on this basis. The former table is composed of the 222 remaining subjects, five of whom (numbered as cases 218–22) are the enlighteners themselves.[1] The 217 others are the focus of the following discussion.

The data enable one to compare these figures with Ferguson, Hume, Millar, Robertson, and Smith in terms of three general kinds of experiences.

1. *Family Experiences.* Chapter 4 emphasized the significance of early separation from the father for all of the Scottish enlighteners, and the first two columns in the table below record the incidence

1. In order not to underreport the number of persons similar in experience to the enlighteners, this table also includes those subjects whose date of birth was not provided in the Bullough materials. It likewise, where appropriate, classifies the college years of these subjects as falling during the period of the professoriate.

of this development in the lives of their contemporaries. While "separation from father" was not itself an item included in Bullough's study, the data provide two ways of assessing whether or not separation occurred. The two could be combined to produce an overall measure for this factor, but this has not been done in the table in order to preserve the previous distinction between Ferguson and Robertson, who left their fathers to go off to school, and Hume, Millar, and Smith, who were parted from patriarchy by paternal death and miscellaneous other causes. Separation for all "noneducational reasons" was determined by an item that specified the principal party or parties who raised each subject before the age of twelve. Those raised either by their parents or by their fathers are assigned a minus in the first column of the table, while those raised by mothers, grandparents, aunts and uncles, and so on are assigned a plus. Separation for "educational reasons" was determined by comparing the identity of the parish that contained the school where the subject chiefly received his early education with the identity of the parish in which he was born or reared. In instances where the identities were the same, a minus is entered in the second column below; otherwise a plus is recorded. It is true that the measures for both the educational and noneducational reasons for separation are fallible. A subject might have been educated in a parish different from the one he was born in not because he had left his father and the rest of his family behind to go off to school, but because together they had moved to a new location. More seriously, a subject raised by someone other than his father was not necessarily liberated from patriarchy. In the cases of Hume, Millar, and Smith, one has tangible evidence to rule out the possibility that a surrogate patriarch materialized in the figure of a stepfather, an older brother, a grandfather, or the like, but the Bullough data do not speak to this basic issue for the other intellectuals of the period. The number of plus signs in the first two columns, therefore, tends to exaggerate the amount of similarity between these intellectuals and those of the Enlightenment. This should not be the source of much concern, however, since it works against rather than for the larger argument of this inquiry.

2. *Early Educational Experiences.* The third column of the table examines the matter of early formal education. Figures assigned a plus are those principally educated either, like Ferguson, Millar, Robertson, and Smith, in one of Scotland's small grammar schools or, like Hume, at home. Home education, coded as such in the data, was a simple item to determine, but deciding which schools

were grammar schools posed a somewhat greater problem. Because schools were identified in the original research by the name of the parish to which they belonged, rather than in terms of their curricular offerings, it was necessary to obtain the required information elsewhere and then add it onto the data set. Here, however, there was only one strategy that was at all feasible and appropriate. On the basis of Pryde's (1965) complete listing of Scottish burghs, parishes that were burghs in the eighteenth century were first distinguished from nonburghal parishes. Then, capitalizing on the fact that the majority of burgh schools were grammar schools (see chap. 5, sec. I), schools situated in burghal parishes were classified as grammar schools. The same designation, finally, was given to schools in rural (nonburghal) parishes known—from a second data set that Bullough compiled, but we otherwise need not draw upon— to have contained a Latin seminary. To the extent that these procedures erred, they did so by overstating the number of grammar schools in eighteenth-century Scotland. Since such an overstatement was by no means favorable to the claims of this study, it was an acceptable approximation for current purposes. Persons assigned a minus in the column for early education are those who were educated either outside of Scotland, in Scotland's large urban grammar schools (Edinburgh, Glasgow, Aberdeen), in rural parishes that were without grammar schools, or in some other way not paralleled in the lives of the intellectuals of the Scottish Enlightenment.

3. *University Experiences.* An item in the original data conveniently specified where subjects received their college education, and this made it very easy to determine who, with the enlighteners, attended the universities of Edinburgh, Glasgow, and St. Andrews. A difficulty arose, however, from the absence of information on the year in which individuals entered the college where they studied. What one wants to know is not the number of intellectuals who went to Edinburgh, Glasgow, and St. Andrews at any time from the late seventeenth century onward, but the number who attended Edinburgh and Glasgow after the elimination of regenting and St. Andrews after the inauguration of the modified professorial system that Ferguson found in place when he arrived. The dates for these developments were 1708, 1727, and 1727, respectively, and persons born either subsequently or only a few years earlier naturally met such developments when they entered college. Since not everyone born earlier could have done likewise, however, some means of differentiating those who did and those who did not was clearly

needed. Had lads uniformly started college upon attaining a fixed number of years, one would know immediately that all those born up to that number of years prior to the initiation of the relevant changes actually encountered those changes. Unfortunately, there was no such uniformity. Scots of the seventeenth and eighteenth centuries might well begin university training at any point in early adolescence, and first-year students as young as eleven and as old as eighteen were not unknown. Including everyone born as much as twenty years before the onset of the changes would probably have captured all the subjects who experienced the same university conditions as the enlighteners, but to reduce even further the chance of passing over cases that might undermine the position one would like to establish here, everyone born up to twenty-two years before was included. In other words, figures with a plus in the fourth column of the table either attended the University of Edinburgh and were born after 1685, or attended the universities of Glasgow or St. Andrews and were born after 1704. The figures with a minus are those who went to the same colleges as the enlightened intellectuals but were born too early to avoid the regenting system, went to altogether different colleges, or received no sort of university education.

Due to inevitable gaps in the historical record, some desired pieces of information were missing for certain subjects. In these instances, as well as in a few cases of apparent errors and inconsistencies in the coding of the original data, blank spaces appear in the table. It is not necessary, however, to exclude from further consideration everyone about whom there are some indeterminable biographical facts. Doing so would actually sacrifice a great deal of information: for all that may not be known about them, one does know that those intellectuals with a minus either in the first *and* second columns, or in the third column, or in the fourth column were not presented with the same configuration of learning experiences as the men of the Enlightenment. Only when missing data prevent making the decision about whether or not a match with the enlighteners occurred must eliminations be made. By this criterion, the 68 figures whose names and dates are in italics are removed from the final step of this analysis.[2]

2. The figures whose *numbers* have been italicized are those for whom the information recorded in the table does not necessarily correspond to what is reported in the Bullough data. While investigating sundry issues that arose in the course of this study, I had occasion to consult biographical scholarship by Pottle (1966) on Boswell, Henderson (1957, pp. 163–79) on Gerald, Cloyd (1972) and Knight (1900)

For the 149 who remain, one can at last ask how many received the same general family, early educational, and university experiences as the five enlightened intellectuals. The answer is simply the number of those with pluses in the third, the fourth, and either the first or the second columns, or eight—the eight men identified with asterisks. Considering particularly that the data were handled in ways that tended to exaggerate the frequency of the commonalities between the enlightened intellectuals and their contemporaries, this is a strikingly small number (but see chap. 3, note 34). It would, no doubt, be smaller still had the data set allowed a broadening of the comparison not only to postgraduate and early professional experiences, but also to factors like the timing and duration of such experiences as school attendance and separation from the father, and above all to the matter of reinforcements. Subjects unsuccessful in settings where Hume, Smith, and the others were rewarded and successful in settings where the young enlighteners floundered would obviously have been educated very differently from the men who made the Enlightenment. And, in the materials that happen to be available on the early life of Thomas Somerville (case 194), one of the eight experientially matched figures, one does, in fact, see a vivid example of a grammar school education that, in a reversal of the enlighteners' situation, brought frustration and ridicule far more than reward (see Somerville 1861, pp. 8–9). Even without taking all the pertinent variables into account, however, it is clear that relatively few early and mid-eighteenth-century Scottish intellectuals were socialized as Ferguson, Hume, Millar, Robertson, and Smith were along the way to the Enlightenment.

The eight intellectuals who appear from the table to be closest in experience to the Scottish enlighteners have an interesting thing in common. Insofar as one can judge the issue with a source like the *Dictionary of National Biography* and a general knowledge of eighteenth-century culture, none seem to have been a part of the age's great mass of orthodox Calvinists. Possibly some were even kindred spirits with at least certain members of the Enlightenment; the enlighteners discussed in this book are, after all, merely the

---

on Monboddo, Fraser (1898) and Stewart (1802) on Reid, and so on, along with standard reference works like the *Dictionary of National Biography* (1885–90) and Chambers's *Biographical Dictionary of Eminent Scotsmen* (1870) on various other Scottish intellectuals, and the facts uncovered in the process sometimes entailed slight modifications in the classifications that resulted when working simply from the original data set.

known enlighteners. Without intellectual biographies of a type that has yet to be attempted on a majority of these figures—presumably because biographers favor luminaries and James Thomson (case 203) alone has measured up here, albeit almost exclusively for his accomplishments as a poet—it now, however, is impossible to characterize their commitment to universalism and independence. Only for Somerville and Robert Wallace (case 208) does some specific attitudinal information currently exist, and the picture that emerges from this is not inconsistent with the available picture of the general socialization experiences of these two intellectuals. Somerville was something of a Moderate and Wallace was arguably the most enlightened of all pre-Enlightenment Scottish thinkers (see chap. 1, note 28, and chap. 2, sec. II; for fuller discussion of Somerville's experiences see Somerville 1861; for Wallace, see Sefton 1966). What is ultimately needed to carry the argument about experience and attitude beyond Ferguson, Hume, Millar, Robertson, and Smith to others in eighteenth-century Scotland, however, is not this sort of glib speculation on the basis of a few facts, but the kind of detailed case-by-case analysis of both ideas and experiences that this study has tried to offer for its five subjects.

The table requires one last qualification. Although the main point of this foray beyond the known boundaries of the Enlightenment is to show the comparative distinctiveness of the package of experiences that the enlightened intellectuals received, it is important to keep in mind the possibility of other, quite different means of acquiring the orientations of independence and universalism. When minuses appear in the table, one is tempted to infer the presence of experiences antithetical to those that befell the enlighteners— unbroken residence in a patriarchal household, education in a rural parochial school, and then at a college like Kings or Marischal where regenting was still the practice. While such an inference would be correct in many cases, it fails to do justice to the early life of someone like the younger Allan Ramsay (case 166), the painter who may also have been a man of the Enlightenment (see chap. 2, note 7). Behind Ramsay's several minus signs are experiences of an entirely unexpected variety: upbringing by a father who, though no enlightener, was notorious for deviating from Calvinist standards, followed by specialized training at art schools in Edinburgh, London, and Rome, in lieu of attendance at more conventional educational institutions (see Smart 1952, pp. 1–36; on Ramsay's father [case 165], see also Martin 1931). Perhaps these art schools offered enlightening lessons, and perhaps Ramsay was prepared to learn these lessons because he had been raised in the home of a rebel. One does not know, of course, for neither art academies nor households that directly taught a creed other than orthodox Calvinism have been examined. The analysis here and throughout has, of necessity, been organized around the pattern of experiences that Ferguson, Hume, Millar, Robertson, and Smith encountered, rather than in terms of the various additional ways in which a commitment to the ideas of the Enlightenment might conceivably be fostered. The results, therefore, are scarcely the final word on who had enlightening experiences and who did not.

Eighteenth-Century Scottish Intellectuals Born before 1750	Separation from Father			
	Non-educational Reasons	Educational Reasons	Early Education	University Education
1. Abercrombie, John (1726–1806)		−	−	−
2. *Abercromby, Alexander (1745–95)*	−			+
3. Abercromby, Patrick (1656–1716)		−	+	−
4. Adam, Alexander (1741–1809)		−	−	+
5. Adam, Jean (1710–65)	+	−	+	−
6. Adam, Robert (1728–92)	−	−	−	+
7. Aikin, John (1747–1822)	−	+	−	+
8. Aikman, William (1682–1731)				−
9. Akenside, Mark (1721–70)		−	−	+
10. Allen, David (1744–96)	−	−	+	−
11. Anderson, James (1662–1728)				−
12. *Anderson, James (1739–1808)*				+
*13. Anderson, John (1726–96)	+	−	+	+
14. *Armstrong, John (1709–79)*		−	+	+
15. *Arnot, Hugo (1749–86)*				

Eighteenth-Century Scottish Intellectuals Born before 1750	Separation from Father		Early Education	University Education
	Non-educational Reasons	Educational Reasons		
16. Arthur, Archibald (1744–97)		−	+	+
17. Baine, James (1710–90)	−			+
18. Balfour, James (1705–95)				+
19. Bannatyne, William (1743–1833)				
20. Barclay, John (1734–98)				+
21. Barry, George (1748–1805)				+
22. Beattie, James (1735–1803)	+	−	+	−
23. Bell, John (1691–1780)				
24. Bissett, Charles (1717–91)				+
25. Black, Joseph (1728–99)	−	−	−	+
26. Blacklock, Thomas (1721–91)	−	+	−	+
27. Blackwell, Thomas (1701–57)		−	−	−
28. Blair, Hugh (1718–1800)	−	−	−	+
29. Blair, John (d. 1782)		−	−	+
30. Blair, Robert (1699–1746)	+			+
31. Blane, Gilbert (1749–1834)				+
32. Boswell, James (1740–95)	−	−	−	+
33. Brown, John (1735–88)	+	−	−	+
34. Bruce, James (1730–94)	−	+	−	+
35. Buchan, William (1729–1805)				
36. Buchanan, Andrew (1690–1759)	−			
37. Buchanan, Dugald (1716–68)		−	−	+

Eighteenth-Century Scottish Intellectuals Born before 1750	Separation from Father		Early Education	University Education
	Non-educational Reasons	Educational Reasons		
38. *Burgh, James* *(1714–75)*		−	+	+
39. Burnett, James (Lord Monboddo) (1714–99)	−	+	−	−
40. Burnett, John (1729–84)		−	−	
41. Cameron, Hugh (1705–1817)		−	−	−
42. *Cameron, John* *(1724–99)*				+
43. *Campbell, John* *(1708–75)*	+			
44. Carlyle, Alexander (1722–1805)	−	−	+	+
45. Chalmers, George (1742–1825)		−	−	
46. Cheyne, George (1671–1743)	−			−
47. *Clark, John* *(1744–1805)*				+
48. *Cleghorn, George* *(1716–89)*		−	+	+
49. Clerk, John (1684–1755)	−	−	−	+
50. *Cochran, William* *(1738–85)*		+	−	−
51. Cockburn, Alison Rutherford (1712–94)	−	−	+	−
52. Colden, Cacwallador (1688–1776)	−	−	+	+
53. Colquhoun, Patrick (1745–1820)		−	+	−
54. Copland, Patrick (1749–1822)	−	−	−	
55. *Craig, William* *(1745–1813)*	−			+
56. *Creech, William* *(1745–1815)*		−	+	+
57. *Cruikshank, William* *(1745–1800)*				+
58. Cullen, William (1710–90)	−	−	+	+

APPENDIX

Eighteenth-Century Scottish Intellectuals Born before 1750	Separation from Father			
	Non-educational Reasons	Educational Reasons	Early Education	University Education
59. Dale, David (1739–1806)		−	−	−
60. Dalrymple, Alexander (1737–1808)	−	+	+	−
61. Dalrymple, David (Lord Hailes) (1726–92)	−	+	−	+
62. Dalzell, Andrew (1742–1806)	−	−	+	+
63. Denham, James (1712–80)	−		+	+
64. Dick, Alexander (1703–85)	−	−	+	+
65. Doig, David (1719–1800)	+	−	−	+
66. *Douglas, Francis (1710–90?)*				
67. Drummond, George (1687–1766)		−	−	−
68. Duncan, Andrew (1744–1828)	−	−	+	+
69. Duncan, William (1717–60)		+	−	−
70. Dundas, Henry (Viscount Melville) (1742–1811)	−	+	−	+
**71*. Elliott, Gilbert (1722–77)	−	+	+	+
72. Elliot, Jane (1727–1805)	−	−	+	−
73. Elphinstone, George (Viscount Keith) (1746–1823)	−	−	+	−
74. Erskine, David (Earl of Buchan) (1742–1829)	−	−	+	+
75. Erskine, Ebenezer (1680–1754)	−	−	+	+
76. *Erskine, Henry (1746–1817)*	−			+
77. *Erskine, John (1695–1768)*				+
78. Erskine, John (1721–1803)	−	−		+

APPENDIX

Eighteenth-Century Scottish Intellectuals Born before 1750	Separation from Father		Early Education	University Education
	Non-educational Reasons	Educational Reasons		
79. Ewen, John (1741–1821)		−	+	−
80. Falconer, William (1732–69)	−			−
81. Ferguson, James (1710–76)	−	+	−	+
82. *Fletcher, Archibald (1746–1828)*	−	+	+	
83. Forbes, William (1739–1806)	+	−		−
84. Fordyce, Alexander (d. 1789)	+	−	−	−
85. Fordyce, David (1711–51)	−	−	−	−
86. Fordyce, George (1736–1802)	+	−	−	+
87. Fordyce, William (1722–92)	−	−	−	+
88. *Forsyth, William (1737–1804)*				
89. *Foulis, Andrew (1712–75)*	−	−	+	+
90. Foulis, Robert (1707–76)	−	−	+	+
91. Garden, Alexander (1730–91)		−	−	+
92. *Garthshore, Maxwell (1732–1812)*		−	+	+
93. *Ged, William (1690–1749)*				
94. Geddes, Alexander (1737–1802)		−	+	−
95. *Gerard, Alexander (1728–95)*	+	+	−	−
96. Gibbs, James (1692–1754)	−	−	−	+
97. *Gilchrist, Ebenezer (1707–74)*				+
98. *Gillespie, Thomas (1708–74)*	+	+	−	−
99. Gillies, John (1747–1836)	−	−	+	+
100. Goodall, Walter (1706–66)				−

Eighteenth-Century Scottish Intellectuals Born before 1750	Separation from Father		Early Education	University Education
	Non-educational Reasons	Educational Reasons		
101. Gow, Neil (1727–1807)	−	−	+	−
102. *Grainger, James (1721–66)*	+	+	+	
103. Gregory, John (1724–73)	−	−		−
104. Guthrie, William (1708–70)		−	+	−
105. *Hamilton, Alexander (1739–1802)*				+
106. *Hamilton, Gavin (1723–98)*				+
107. Hamilton, James (1749–1835)	−	−	−	+
108. Hamilton, Robert (1743–1829)	−	−		+
109. Hamilton, William (1730–1803)	−	−		−
*110. Henry, Robert (1718–90)		+	+	+
111. Herd, David (1732–1810)				−
112. Home, Henry (Lord Kames) (1696–1782)	−	−	−	−
113. *Home, John (1722–1808)*		−	+	+
*114. Hope, John (1725–86)		+	+	+
115. Howie, John (1735–91)	+	+	+	−
116. Hunter, Alexander (1729–1809)		−	−	+
117. Hunter, John (1728–93)	−	−	+	−
118. *Hunter, John (1745–1837)*				+
119. Hunter, William (1718–83)	−	−	+	+
120. Hutcheson, Francis (1694–1746)	+	+	−	−
121. Hutton, James (1726–97)	+	−	−	+
122. *Johnstone, James (1730–1802)*				

Eighteenth-Century Scottish Intellectuals Born before 1750	Separation from Father		Early Education	University Education
	Non-educational Reasons	Educational Reasons		
123. Jones, John Paul *(1747–92)*	−	−	+	−
124. Keith, Francis (1696–1758)	−	−	+	+
125. Keith, Robert (1681–1757)		+	−	−
126. *Keith, Robert* *(d. 1774)*				
127. *Keith, Robert* *(1730–95)*				
128. Leechman, William (1706–85)		−	−	+
129. Lind, James (1716–94)		−	−	+
130. Lothian, William (1740–83)		−	−	+
131. *Low, George* *(1746–95)*				
132. Macdonald, Alexander (1700–1780)	−	−	+	−
133. *Macfarlan, Walter* *(1700–1767)*				
134. *M'Gill, James* *(1744–1813)*	−			+
135. Macintyre, Duncan (1724–1812)		−	−	−
136. MacKay, Robert (1714–78)	−	−	−	−
137. Mackenzie, Henry (1745–1831)		−	−	+
138. Maclaurin, Colin (1698–1746)	+			−
139. Maclaurin, John (Lord Dreghorn) (1734–96)	−	−	−	+
140. Macneill, Hector (1746–1818)	−	+	+	−
141. Macpherson, David (1746–1816)		−	−	+
142. *Macpherson, James* *(1738–96)*		+	+	
143. Macqueen, Robert (Lord Braxfield) (1722–99)	−	−	+	+

Eighteenth-Century Scottish Intellectuals Born before 1750	Separation from Father		Early Education	University Education
	Non-educational Reasons	Educational Reasons		
144. Main, James (1700–1761)		−	−	−
145. Martin, David (1737–98)				−
146. Meikle, Andrew (1719–1811)				−
147. *Mickle, William (1735–88)*	+	+		
148. Miller, Patrick (1731–1815)				−
149. *Miller, Thomas (Lord Glenlee) (1717–89)*	−			+
150. *Milne, Colin (1743–1815)*				
151. Monro, Alexander (1697–1767)	−	−	+	+
152. Monro, Alexander (1733–1817)	−	−	−	+
153. Monro, Donald (1727–1802)	−	−	+	+
154. Moor, James (1712–79)		−	−	+
155. Moore, John (1729–1802)	+	−	−	+
156. *Mure, William (1718–76)*			+	+
157. Murray, William (Earl of Mansfield) (1705–93)	−	−	+	−
158. Mylne, Robert (1734–1811)	−	−	−	−
159. Orr, Hugh (1717–98)		−	−	−
160. Oswald, James (1715–69)	+	+	+	−
161. Park, Mungo (?)	−	−	+	+
162. Pitcairne, Archibald (1652–1713)		+	+	−
163. Playfair, John (1748–1819)	−	−	+	+
164. *Pringle, John (1707–1782)*		−	+	+

Eighteenth-Century Scottish Intellectuals Born before 1750	Separation from Father		Early Education	University Education
	Non-educational Reasons	Educational Reasons		
165. Ramsay, Allan (1686–1758)	+	−	+	−
166. Ramsay, Allan, Jr. (1713–84)	−	−	−	−
167. *Ramsay, James (1733–89)*		−	+	+
168. *Reid, John (1721–1807)*	−			+
169. *Reid, Thomas (1710–96)*	−	+	−	−
170. *Richardson, William (1743–1814)*		−	+	+
171. Robinson, John (1739–94)		+	−	+
172. *Roebuck, John (1718–94)*		−	−	+
173. *Roy, William (1726–90)*		−	+	
174. Ruddiman, Thomas (1674–1757)	−	−	−	−
175. Runciman, Alexander (1736–85)	−	+	−	
176. Russell, Alexander (1715–68)	−	−	−	+
177. *Russell, Patrick (1727–1805)*				+
178. *Russell, William (1741–93)*		−	+	+
179. *Rutherford, Daniel (1749–1819)*	−	+	−	+
180. *Rutherford, John (1695–1779)*		−	+	+
181. Sanders, Robert (1727–83)		−	−	−
182. Scot, David (d.1834)		−	−	+
183. Schanck, John (1740–1823)	−			−
184. *Short, James (1710–68)*	+	−	−	+
185. Short, Thomas (1680–1772)				−
186. Sibbald, James (1747–1803)		+	+	−

Eighteenth-Century Scottish Intellectuals Born before 1750	Separation from Father		Early Education	University Education
	Non-educational Reasons	Educational Reasons		
187. Simpson, John (1668–1740)				−
188. Skinner, John (1721–1807)		−	+	−
189. Smellie, William (1697–1763)	−	+	+	−
190. Smellie, William (1740–95)	−	−	−	+
191. Smith, John (1747–1807)				+
192. Smollett, Tobias (1721–71)	+	−	+	
193. Smyth, James (1741–1821)				+
*194. Somerville, Thomas (1741–1830)	−	+	+	+
195. Stewart, Matthew (1717–85)		−	+	+
196. Stone, Edmund (d. 1768)		−	+	−
197. Strahan, William (1715–85)		−	−	−
198. Strange, Robert (1721–92)	−	+	+	−
199. Stuart, Gilbert (1742–86)	−	−	−	+
200. Stuart, John (1743–1821)				+
201. Swinton, John (1720–99)				
202. Tassie, James (1735–99)	−	+	−	−
*203. Thomson, James (1700–1748)	−	+	+	+
*204. Thomson, William (1746–1817)		+	+	+
205. Tytler, Alexander (Lord Woodhouselee) (1747–1813)	−	+	−	+
206. Tytler, James (1747–1804)		−	+	+
207. Tytler, William (1711–92)		+	−	+
*208. Wallace, Robert (1697–1771)	−	+	+	+

Eighteenth-Century Scottish Intellectuals Born before 1750	Separation from Father			
	Non-educational Reasons	Educational Reasons	Early Education	University Education
209. Watt, James (1736–1819)	−	−	+	−
210. Webster, Alexander (1707–84)		−	−	+
211. Whitefoord, Caleb (1734–1810)	+	−	−	+
212. *Whytt, Robert (1714–66)*	+			+
213. *Wilkie, William (1721–72)*		−	+	+
214. *Wilson, Alexander (1714–86)*		−	+	+
215. Wilson, James (1742–98)	+	−	−	+
216. *Wilson, Peter (1746–1825)*				+
217. Wodrow, Robert (1679–1734)	−			−
218. Ferguson, Adam (1723–1816)	−	+	+	+
219. Hume, David (1711–76)	+	−	+	+
220. Millar, John (1735–1801)	+	−	+	+
221. Robertson, William (1721–93)	−	+	+	+
222. Smith, Adam (1723–90)	+	−	+	+

Eighteenth-Century
Scottish Intellectuals
Born 1750 and After

223. Abercrombie, John   (1780–1844)
224. Adam, William   (1751–1839)
225. Allan, Thomas   (1777–1833)
226. Anderson, Robert   (1750–1830)
227. Baillie, Joanna   (1762–1851)
228. Baillie, Matthew   (1761–1823)
229. Baird, George   (1761–1840)

230. Ballantyne, James   (1772–1833)
231. Barclay, John   (1758–1826)
232. Bell, Andrew   (1753–1832)
233. Bell, Charles   (1774–1842)
234. Bell, Henry   (1767–1830)
235. Bell, James   (1769–1833)
236. Bell, John   (1763–1820)
237. Blackwood, William   (1776–1834)
238. Boswell, Alexander   (1775–1822)
239. Brougham, Henry   (1778–1868)
240. Brown, Robert   (1757–1831)
241. Brown, Robert   (1773–1858)
242. Brown, Thomas   (1778–1820)
243. Bruce, Thomas (Earl of Elgin)   (1766–1841)
244. Buchanan, Claudius   (1766–1815)
245. Buchanan, Francis   (1762–1829)
246. Burns, John   (1774–1850)
247. Burns, Robert   (1759–96)
248. Campbell, Alexander   (1764–1824)
249. Campbell, Thomas   (1777–1844)
250. Chalmers, Alexander   (1759–1834)
251. Chalmers, Thomas   (1780–1847)
252. Christie, Thomas   (1761–1796)
253. Constable, Archibald   (1774–1827)
254. Couper, Robert   (1750–1818)
255. Currie, James   (1756–1805)
256. Dalyell, John   (1776–1851)
257. Dick, Thomas   (1774–1857)
258. Douglas, Howard   (1776–1861)
259. Douglas, Thomas (Earl of Selkirk)   (1771–1820)
260. Duncan, Andrew, Jr.   (1773–1832)
261. Duncan, Henry   (1774–1846)
262. Erskine, David   (1772–1837)
263. Erskine, Thomas   (1750–1823)
264. Ewing, Greville   (1767–1841)
265. Fergusson, Robert   (1750–74)
266. Finlay, Kirkman   (1773–1842)
267. Finlayson, James   (1758–1803)
268. Fletcher, Eliza Dawson   (1770–1858)
269. Forbes, Charles   (1774–1849)
270. Fraser, Robert   (1760–1831)
271. Fulton, George   (1752–1831)
272. Gall, Richard   (1776–1801)
273. Galt, John   (1779–1839)
274. Gerard, Gilbert   (1760–95)
275. Gibb, John   (1776–1850)
276. Gibson, Patrick   (1782–1829)
277. Gilchrist, John   (1759–1841)
278. Glenie, James   (1750–1817)
279. Gow, Nathaniel   (1766–1807)

280. Grahame, James   (1765–1811)
281. Graham, John   (1754–1817)
282. Grant, Anne   (1755–1838)
283. Grant, William   (1752–1832)
284. Gregory, James   (1753–1812)
285. Haldane, James   (1768–1857)
286. Hall, James (Baronet of Dunglass)   (1761–1832)
287. Hall, Robert   (1763–1824)
288. Hamilton, Archibald   (1769–1827)
289. Hamilton, William   (1751–1801)
290. Hamilton, William   (1758–90)
291. Hill, George   (1750–1819)
292. Hogg, James   (1770–1835)
293. Hope, Thomas   (1766–1844)
294. Horsburgh, James   (1762–1836)
295. Hume, David   (1757–1838)
296. Hume, Joseph   (1777–1855)
297. Irving, David   (1778–1860)
298. Jameson, Robert   (1774–1860)
299. Jeffrey, Francis   (1773–1850)
300. Johnstone, Christian Isabel   (1781–1857)
301. Keith, George   (1752–1823)
302. Kemp, John   (1763–1812)
303. Kerr, Robert   (1755–1813)
304. Laing, Malcolm   (1762–1818)
305. Leslie, John   (1766–1832)
306. Leyden, John   (1755–1811)
307. Lindsay, Anne   (1750–1825)
308. Lizars, John   (1783–1860)
309. Lumsden, Matthew   (1777–1835)
310. McAdam, John   (1756–1836)
311. Macaulay, Aulay   (1758–1819)
312. Macaulay, Zachary   (1768–1838)
313. Macculloch, John   (1773–1835)
314. M'Diarmid, John   (1779–1808)
315. Macdonald, John   (1759–1831)
316. MacFarland, Duncan   (1771–1857)
317. Macgill, Stevenson   (1765–1840)
318. Macintosh, Charles   (1766–1843)
319. Mackenzie, Alexander   (1755–1820)
320. Mackintosh, James   (1765–1832)
321. Maclachlan, Ewen   (1755–1822)
322. Maclaren, Charles   (1782–1866)
323. Maclean, John   (1771–1814)
324. Mavor, William   (1758–1837)
325. Melish, John   (1771–1822)
326. Mill, James   (1773–1836)
327. Minto, Walter   (1753–1796)
328. Mitchell, David   (1766–1837)
329. Monro, Alexander   (1773–1850)

330. Montgomery, James   (1771–1854)
331. Moore, John   (1761–1809)
332. Mudie, Robert   (1777–1842)
333. Murray, Alexander   (1775–1813)
334. Mushet, David   (1772–1847)
335. Nairne, Carolina Oliphant   (1766–1845)
336. Napier, Macvey   (1776–1847)
337. Nasmyth, Alexander   (1757–1840)
338. Nicholson, Peter   (1765–1844)
339. Nimmo, Alexander   (1783–1832)
340. Neilson, John   (1778–1839)
341. Pasley, Charles   (1780–1861)
342. Picken, Ebenezer   (1769–1816)
343. Pinkerton, John   (1758–1826)
344. Playfair, William   (1759–1823)
345. Raeburn, Henry   (1756–1823)
346. Reddie, James   (1775–1852)
347. Reid, Robert   (1773–1865)
348. Rennie, John   (1761–1821)
349. Ross, John   (1777–1856)
350. Roxburgh, William   (1751–1815)
351. Scott, Walter   (1771–1832)
352. Shaw, James   (1764–1843)
353. Sinclair, John   (1754–1835)
354. Somerville, Mary Fairfax   (1780–1872)
355. Steuart, Henry   (1759–1836)
356. Stevenson, Robert   (1772–1850)
357. Stewart, Dugald   (1753–1828)
358. Stewart, Helen Cranstoun   (1765–1838)
359. Symington, William   (1763–1831)
360. Tannahill, Robert   (1774–1810)
361. Taylor, James   (1753–1825)
362. Telford, Thomas   (1757–1834)
363. Thomson, Anthony   (1778–1849)
364. Thomson, John   (1778–1840)
365. Thomson, Thomas   (1768–1852)
366. Thomson, Thomas   (1773–1852)
367. Trotter, Thomas   (1760–1832)
368. Wallace, William   (1768–1843)
369. Watson, George   (1767–1837)
370. Watt, Robert   (1774–1819)
371. Wilkie, David   (1785–1841)
372. Wilson, Alexander   (1766–1813)
373. Wilson, John   (1774–1855)
374. Wilson, John   (1785–1854)
375. Wylie, James   (1768–1854)

Matters of Abbreviation

To make citations less cumbersome, two simplifying procedures are used throughout this book. The first involves the dating of cited materials. For many sources, there is a difference between the year of original publication, or the year of known completion in the case of long-unpublished documents, and the year of the particular edition to which reference is made. Information on the latter date, however, is generally provided only in the bibliography; ordinarily, the date given in the course of the book is simply the original date.

The second shortcut taken is to designate the writings of the men of the Scottish Enlightenment, as well as a few frequently quoted pre-Enlightenment documents, by abbreviated titles. The abbreviations employed are listed below, along with the original date of each work. In a few instances where conformity with scholarly conventions has dictated the use of a specific later edition, the year and number of that edition are also indicated.

For the Writings of Adam Ferguson

SPE	*A Sermon Preached in the Ersh Language* (1746)
RM	*Reflections Previous to the Establishment of a Militia* (1756)
MSP	*The Morality of Stage-Plays Seriously Considered* (1757)
HPM	*The History of the Proceedings in the Case of Margaret, Commonly Called Peg, Only Lawful Sister to John Bull, Esq.* (1761)
EHCS	*An Essay on the History of Civil Society* (1767)
IMP	*Institutes of Moral Philosophy* (1769)
PMPS	*Principles of Moral and Political Science* (1792)

For the Writings of David Hume

HL	*The Letters of David Hume*
NHL	*New Letters of David Hume*
EC	"An Historical Essay on Chivalry and Modern Honour" (c. 1726)
HEM	"Hume's Early Memoranda, 1729–1740: The Complete Text"
THN	*A Treatise of Human Nature* (1739–40)

Abst	An Abstract of a Treatise of Human Nature (1740)
Essays	Essays: Moral, Political, and Literary (1741–77)
EHU	An Enquiry Concerning Human Understanding (1748)
IPM	An Inquiry Concerning the Principles of Morals (1751)
Dialogue	"A Dialogue" (1751)
HE	The History of England (1754–62)
NHR	The Natural History of Religion (1757)
DNR	Dialogues Concerning Natural Religion (1779)

FOR THE WRITINGS OF FRANCIS HUTCHESON

| Works | Collected Works (1725–55) |

FOR THE WRITINGS OF JOHN MILLAR

| Ranks | The Origin of the Distinction of Ranks (1771; 3d ed., 1779) |
| HV | An Historical View of the English Government (1787–1803) |

FOR THE WRITINGS OF WILLIAM ROBERTSON

SW	"The Situation of the World at the Time of Christ's Appearance" (1755)
ER	Miscellaneous Book Reviews, Edinburgh Review (1755–56)
HS	The History of Scotland (1759)
Progress	The Progress of Society in Europe (1769)
HC	The History of the Reign of the Emperor Charles V (1769)
HA	The History of America (1777)
Ser	Sermon (1788)
India	An Historical Disquisition Concerning the Knowledge Which the Ancients Had of India (1791)

FOR THE WRITINGS OF ADAM SMITH[1]

Corr	The Correspondence of Adam Smith
AN	The Anderson Notes (early 1750s; published in Meek 1976a)
Letter	"A Letter to the Authors of the Edinburgh Review" (1756)
TMS	The Theory of Moral Sentiments (1759; 6th ed., 1790)
LJA	Lectures on Jurisprudence (1762–63)
LRBL	Lectures on Rhetoric and Belles Lettres (1762–63)
ED	"An Early Draft of the Wealth of Nations" (c. 1763)
LJB	Lectures on Justice, Police, Revenue, and Arms (1763–64)
WN	An Inquiry into the Nature and Causes of the Wealth of Nations (1776; 5th ed., 1789)
EPS	Essays on Philosophical Subjects (1795)

1. As the bibliography will make clear, more popular and more accessible editions of Smith's works have generally been preferred to the great, recent *Glasgow Edition of the Works of Adam Smith,* which is likely to remain primarily a tool for specialized Smithian scholars. *LJB* has been used instead of *LJA* for the same reason.

MATTERS OF ABBREVIATION

CF   *The Westminster Confession of Faith* (1647)
LC   *The Larger Catechism* (1647)
SC   *The Shorter Catechism* (1647)

2. These documents are collected together in the volume listed in the references as *The Westminster Confession of Faith; The Larger and Shorter Catechisms.*

References

Ahlstrom, Sydney E. 1955. "The Scottish Philosophy and American Theology." *Church History* 24:257–72.

Allardyce, Alexander. 1888. "Introduction." In John Ramsay, *Scotland and Scotsmen in the Eighteenth Century*, vol. 1, pp. vii–xxiv. Edinburgh: William Blackwood & Sons.

Aminzade, Ronald. 1977. "Breaking the Chains of Dependency: From Patronage to Class Politics, Toulouse, France, 1830–1872." *Journal of Urban History* 3:485–506.

Anderson, Perry. 1974. *Lineages of the Absolutist State.* London: New Left Books.

Anonymous. 1703. *Family Religion Explained and Inforc'd With Proper Arguments, Motives, and Directions; Whereby It's Prov'd to be the Indispensable Duty of Parents and Other Heads of Families, in a Letter from a Minister to His Parishioners.* Edinburgh: Symson.

Anonymous. 1867. "Adam Ferguson." *Edinburgh Review* 125:48–85.

Anspach, Ralph. 1972. "The Implications of the *Theory of Moral Sentiments* for Adam Smith's Economic Thought." *History of Political Economy* 4:176–206.

Ariès, Philippe. 1962. *Centuries of Childhood.* Translated by Robert Baldick. New York: Knopf.

Avineri, Shlomo. 1968. *The Social and Political Thought of Karl Marx.* Cambridge: Cambridge University Press.

Bain, Andrew. 1965. *Education in Stirlingshire from the Reformation to the Act of 1872.* London: University of London Press.

Barnard, F. M. 1965. *Herder's Social and Political Thought.* Oxford: Clarendon.

Battersby, Christine. 1980. "An Enquiry Concerning the Humean Woman." *Studies on Voltaire and the Eighteenth Century* 193:1964–67.

Baumrind, Diana. 1966. "Effects of Authoritative Parental Control on Child Behavior." *Child Development* 37:887–907.

Beale, J. M. 1953. "A History of the Burgh and Parochial Schools of Fife from the Reformation to 1872." Ph.D. diss., University of Edinburgh.

Beattie, William. 1949. *The Scottish Tradition in Printed Books*. Edinburgh: Thomas Nelson.

Becker, Carl L. 1932. *The Heavenly City of the Eighteenth-Century Philosophers*. New Haven: Yale University Press.

Becker, Wesley C. 1964. "Consequences of Different Kinds of Parental Discipline." In Martin L. Hoffman and Lois Wladis Hoffman (eds.), *Review of Child Development Research*, vol. 1, pp. 169–208. New York: Russell Sage Foundation.

Bell, J. F. 1960. "Adam Smith, Clubman." *Scottish Journal of Political Economy* 7:108–16.

Bellah, Robert N. 1965. "Epilogue." In Robert N. Bellah (ed.), *Religion and Progress in Modern Asia*, pp. 168–229. New York: Free Press.

———. (1968) 1970. "Meaning and Modernization." In Robert N. Bellah, *Beyond Belief*, pp. 64–75. New York: Harper.

———. 1970. "Between Religion and Social Science." In Robert N. Bellah, *Beyond Belief*, pp. 237–59. New York: Harper.

Bendix, Reinhard. 1978. *Kings or People*. Berkeley: University of California Press.

Bernstein, Basil. 1961. "Social Class and Linguistic Development: A Theory of Social Learning." In A. H. Halsey, Jean Floud, and C. Arnold Anderson (eds.), *Education, Economy, and Society*, pp. 288–314. New York: Free Press.

———. 1971. *Class, Codes and Control*. Vol. 1: *Theoretical Studies toward a Sociology of Language*. London: Routledge & Kegan Paul.

Bernstein, John Andrew. 1978. "Adam Ferguson and the Idea of Progress." *Studies in Burke and His Time* 19:99–118.

Bidwell, Charles E. 1972. "Schooling and Socialization for Moral Commitment." *Interchange* 3 (no. 4):1–27.

Bierstedt, Robert. 1978. "Sociological Thought in the Eighteenth Century." In Tom Bottomore and Robert Nisbet (eds.), *A History of Sociological Analysis*, pp. 3–38. New York: Basic Books.

Birley, Robert. 1962. *Sunk without Trace: Some Forgotten Masterpieces Reconsidered*. London: Hart-Davis.

Black, J. B. (1926) 1965. *The Art of History: A Study of Four Great Historians of the Eighteenth Century*. New York: Russell & Russell.

Blacklock, Thomas (c. 1776) 1789. "Concerning the Necessity of Death, and Its No Less Necessary Effects." In *The Scotch Preacher: or, A Collection of Sermons, by Some of the Most Eminent Clergymen of the Church of Scotland*, vol. 2, pp. 104–35. Edinburgh: Dickson.

Blackstone, William T. 1965. *Francis Hutcheson and Contemporary Ethical Theory*. Athens: University of Georgia Press.

Blaikie, William Garden. 1888. *The Preachers of Scotland from the Sixth to the Nineteenth Century*. Edinburgh: T & T Clark.

Boswell, James. (1791) 1934. *Boswell's Life of Johnson*, vol. 2. Edited by George Birkbeck Hill. Rev. ed. of L. F. Powell. Oxford: Clarendon.

Bourdieu, Pierre, and Jean-Claude Passeron. (1970) 1977. *Reproduction in Education, Society and Culture.* Translated by Richard Nice. London: Sage.

Bower, Alexander. 1817–30. *The History of the University of Edinburgh.* 3 vols. Edinburgh: Smellie.

Bowles, Samuel, and Herbert Gintis. 1976. *Schooling in Capitalist America.* New York: Basic Books.

Boyd, William. 1961. *Education in Ayrshire through Seven Centuries.* London: University of London Press.

Brackenridge, R. Douglas. 1969. "The Enforcement of Sunday Observance in Post-Revolution Scotland, 1689–1733." *Records of the Scottish Church History Society* 17:33–45.

Bradburn, Norman. (1963) 1968. "When Is a Father a Liability to a Son?" In H. Kent Geiger (ed.), *Comparative Perspectives on Marriage and the Family,* pp. 191–98. Boston: Little, Brown & Co.

Brady, Frank. 1965. *Boswell's Political Career.* New Haven: Yale University Press.

Breer, Paul E., and Edwin A. Locke. 1965. *Task Experience as a Source of Attitudes.* Homewood: Dorsey.

Brissenden, R. F. 1969. "Authority, Guilt, and Anxiety in *The Theory of Moral Sentiments.*" *Texas Studies in Literature and Language* 11:945–62.

Brougham, Henry. 1845. *Lives of Men of Letters and Science Who Flourished in the Time of George III,* vol. 1. London: Charles Knight & Co.

Brumfitt, J. H. 1967. "Scotland and the French Enlightenment." In W. H. Barber et al. (eds.), *The Age of the Enlightenment,* pp. 318–29. Edinburgh: Oliver & Boyd.

Bryson, Gladys. 1945. *Man and Society: The Scottish Inquiry of the Eighteenth Century.* Princeton: Princeton University Press.

Buckle, Henry Thomas. (1861) 1970. *On Scotland and the Scotch Intellect.* Edited by H. J. Hanham. Chicago: University of Chicago Press.

Bullough, Bonnie, and Vern L. Bullough. 1971. "Intellectual Achievers: A Study of Eighteenth-Century Scotland." *American Journal of Sociology* 76:1048–63.

Bullough, Vern L. 1970. "Intellectual Achievement in Eighteenth-Century Scotland: A Computer Study of Importance of Education." *Comparative Education Review* 14:90–102.

Bullough, Vern L., and Bonnie Bullough. 1973. "Historical Sociology: Intellectual Achievement in Eighteenth-Century Scotland." *British Journal of Sociology* 24:418–30.

Bullough, Vern L., Bonnie Bullough, Martha Voght, and Lucy Kluckholm. 1970. "Longevity and Achievement in Eighteenth-Century Scotland." *Omega* 1:115–19.

Burke, Peter, 1980. "Scottish Historians and the Feudal System: The Conceptualization of Social Change." *Studies on Voltaire and the Eighteenth Century* 191:537–39.

Burleigh, J. H. S. 1960. *A Church History of Scotland.* London: Oxford University Press.

Burrell, Sidney A. (1960) 1968. "Calvinism, Capitalism, and the Middle Classes: Some Afterthougths on an Old Problem." In S. N. Eisenstadt (ed.), *The Protestant Ethic and Modernization: A Comparative View,* pp. 135–54. New York: Basic Books.

Burrow, J. W. 1966. *Evolution and Society.* Cambridge: Cambridge University Press.

Burton, John Hill. 1846. *Life and Correspondence of David Hume.* 2 vols. Edinburgh: William Tait.

Cain, Roy Edward. 1963. "David Hume and Adam Smith: A Study in Intellectual Kinship." Ph.D. diss., University of Texas.

Cameron, James K. 1967. "The Church of Scotland in the Age of Reason." *Studies on Voltaire and the Eighteenth Century* 58:1939–51.

Camic, Charles. 1979*a.* "Social Experience and Cultural Change: Family, Schooling, and Professions in Eighteenth-Century Scotland." Ph.D. diss., University of Chicago.

———. 1979*b.* "The Utilitarians Revisited." *American Journal of Sociology* 85:516–50.

———. 1983*a.* "The Enlightenment and Its Environment: A Cautionary Tale." In Robert Alun Jones and Henrika Kuklick (eds.), *Knowledge and Society,* vol. 4, pp. 143–72. Greenwich, Conn.: JAI Press.

———. 1983*b.* "Experience and Ideas: Education for Universalism in Eighteenth-Century Scotland." *Comparative Studies in Society and History* 25:50–82.

Campbell, R. H. 1964. "An Economic History of Scotland in the Eighteenth Century." *Scottish Journal of Political Economy* 11:17–24.

———. 1965. *Scotland Since 1707: The Rise of an Industrial Society.* Oxford: Basil Blackwell.

———. 1967. "The Industrial Revolution: A Revision Article." *Scottish Historical Review* 46:37–55.

———. 1974. "The Union and Economic Growth." In T. I. Rae (ed.), *The Union of 1707: Its Impact on Scotland,* pp. 58–74. Glasgow: Blackie & Son.

Campbell, R. H., and R. G. Wilson. 1975. *Entrepreneurship in Britain 1750–1939.* London: Black.

Campbell, T. D. 1971. *Adam Smith's Science of Morals.* London: Allen & Unwin.

———. 1975. "Scientific Explanation and Ethical Justification in the *Moral Sentiments.*" In Andrew S. Skinner and Thomas Wilson (eds.), *Essays on Adam Smith,* pp. 68–82. Oxford: Clarendon.

———. 1977. "Adam Smith and Natural Liberty." *Political Studies* 25:523–34.

Cant, Ronald Gordon. 1952. "The Constitution of the University in the Early Eighteenth Century." In William Croft Dickinson (ed.), *Two Students at St. Andrews, 1711–1716,* pp. lxviii–lxxii. Edinburgh: Oliver & Boyd.

_____. 1967. "The Scottish Universities and Scottish Society in the Eighteenth Century." *Studies on Voltaire and the Eighteenth Century* 58:1953–66.

_____. 1970. *The University of St. Andrews: A Short History.* Rev. ed. Edinburgh: Scottish Academic Press.

Carlyle, Alexander. 1910. *The Autobiography of Dr. Alexander Carlyle of Inveresk, 1722–1805.* Edited by John Hill Burton. Edinburgh: Foulis.

_____. 1973. *Anecdotes and Characters of the Times.* Edited by James Kingsley. London: Oxford University Press.

Carswell, R. D. 1967. "The Origins of the Legal Profession in Scotland." *American Journal of Legal History* 11:44–56.

Carter, Ian. 1973. "Marriage Patterns and Social Sectors in Scotland before the Eighteenth Century." *Scottish Studies* 17:51–60.

Cassirer, Ernst. (1932) 1951. *The Philosophy of the Enlightenment.* Translated by Fritz C. A. Koelln and James P. Pettegrove. Princeton: Princeton University Press.

Cater, Jeremy J. 1970. "The Making of Principal Robertson in 1762: Politics and the University of Edinburgh in the Second Half of the Eighteenth Century." *Scottish Historical Review* 49:60–84.

Chambers, Robert (revised by Thomas Thomson). (1870) 1971. *A Biographical Dictionary of Eminent Scotsmen.* Rev. ed. 3 vols. Hildesheim: Georg Olms Verlag.

Chamley, Paul E. 1975. "The Conflict between Montesquieu and Hume: A Study of the Origins of Adam Smith's Universalism." In Andrew S. Skinner and Thomas Wilson (eds.), *Essays on Adam Smith,* pp. 274–305. Oxford: Clarendon.

Checkland, S. G. 1967. "Adam Smith and the Biographer." *Scottish Journal of Political Economy* 14:70–79.

Chitnis, Anand C. 1976. *The Scottish Enlightenment: A Social History.* London: Croom Helm.

Christie, John R. R. 1974. "The Origins and Development of the Scottish Scientific Community, 1680–1760." *History of Science* 12:122–41.

Clark, Ian D. L. 1964. "Moderatism and the Moderate Party in the Church of Scotland 1752–1805." Ph.D. diss., Kings College, Cambridge.

_____. 1970. "From Protest to Reaction: The Moderate Regime in the Church of Scotland, 1752–1805." In N. T. Phillipson and Rosalind Mitchison (eds.), *Scotland in the Age of Improvement,* pp. 200–224. Edinburgh: Edinburgh University Press.

Clarke, M. L. 1959. *Classical Education in Britain, 1500–1900.* Cambridge: Cambridge University Press.

Clausen, John A. 1966. "Family Structure, Socialization and Personality." In Lois Wladis Hoffman and Martin L. Hoffman (eds.), *Review of Child Development Research,* vol. 2, pp. 1–53. New York: Russell Sage Foundation.

Clive, John. 1970. "The Social Background of the Scottish Renaissance." In N. T. Phillipson and Rosalind Mitchison (eds.), *Scotland in the Age of Improvement*, pp. 225–44. Edinburgh: Edinburgh University Press.

Clive, John, and Bernard Bailyn. 1954. "England's Cultural Provinces: Scotland and America." *William and Mary Quarterly* 3d series 11:200–213.

Cloyd, E. L. 1972. *James Burnett, Lord Monboddo.* Oxford: Clarendon.

Cochrane, J. A. 1964. *Dr. Johnson's Printer: The Life of William Strahan.* Cambridge, Mass.: Harvard University Press.

Collins, A. S. 1927. *Authorship in the Days of Johnson: Being a Study of the Relation between Author, Patron, Publisher and Public, 1726–1780.* London: Robert Halden & Co.

————. 1928. *The Profession of Letters: A Study of the Relation of Author to Patron, Publisher, and Public, 1780–1832.* London: Routledge & Sons.

Comte, Auguste. (1822) 1974. "Plan of the Scientific Operations Necessary for Reorganizing Society." In Auguste Comte, *The Crisis of Industrial Civilization*, pp. 111–81. Edited by Ronald Fletcher. London: Heinemann.

Coser, Lewis A. 1965. *Men of Ideas: A Sociologist's View.* New York: Free Press.

Coutts, James. 1909. *A History of the University of Glasgow from Its Foundation in 1451 to 1909.* Glasgow: James Maclehose & Sons.

Craig, David. 1961. *Scottish Literature and the Scottish People, 1680–1830.* London: Chatto & Windus.

Craig, John. 1801. "The Character of the Late Professor Millar." *Scots Magazine* 63:527–28.

————. 1806. "Account of the Life and Writings of John Millar, Esq." In John Millar, *The Origin of the Distinction of Ranks*, pp. i–cxxxiv. 4th ed. Edinburgh: Blackwood.

Cropsey, Joseph. 1957. *Polity and Economy.* The Hague: Martinus Nijhoff.

————. (1963) 1975. "Adam Smith and Political Philosophy." In Andrew S. Skinner and Thomas Wilson (eds.), *Essays on Adam Smith*, pp. 132–53. Oxford: Clarendon.

Cunningham, W. 1914. *Christianity and Economic Science.* London: John Murray.

Dalrymple, William. 1787. *Family Worship Explained and Recommended in Four Sermons.* Kilmarnock: Wilson.

Dalzel, Andrew. 1862. *History of the University of Edinburgh from Its Foundation.* 2 vols. Edinburgh: Edmonston & Douglas.

Darnton, Robert. 1971*a*. "The High Enlightenment and the Low-Life of Literature in Pre-Revolutionary France." *Past and Present* 51:81–115.

————. 1971*b*. "In Search of the Enlightenment: Recent Attempts to Create a Social History of Ideas." *Journal of Modern History* 43:113–32.

———. 1971*c*. "Reading, Writing, and Publishing in Eighteenth-Century France: A Case Study in the Sociology of Literature." *Daedalus* 100:214–56.

Davie, George Elder. 1961*a*. *The Democratic Intellect: Scotland and Her Universities in the Nineteenth Century.* Edinburgh: Edinburgh University Press.

———. 1961*b*. "Hume in His Contemporary Setting." In *David Hume: University of Edinburgh 250th Anniversary of the Birth of David Hume 1711: 1961. A Record of the Commemoration Published as a Supplement to the University Gazette,* pp. 11–15. Edinburgh: Edinburgh University Press.

———. 1967. "Hume, Reid, and the Passion for Ideas." In *Edinburgh in the Age of Reason: A Commemoration,* pp. 23–39. Edinburgh: Edinburgh University Press.

———. 1972. *The Social Significance of the Scottish Philsophy of Common Sense.* Dow Lecture, the University of Dundee, 30 Nov. 1972. Printed 1973.

Davis, H. W. Carless. (1899) 1963. *A History of Balliol College.* Rev. ed. of R. H. C. Davis and Richard Hunt. Oxford: Basil Blackwell.

Deanina [Denina], Carlo. 1763. Extract from *An Essay on the Progress of Learning among the Scots.* No publication information.

Demos, John. 1970. *A Little Commonwealth: Family Life in Plymouth Colony.* London: Oxford University Press.

——. 1973. "Developmental Perspectives on the History of Childhood." In Theodore K. Rabb and Robert I. Rotberg (eds.), *The Family in History: Interdisciplinary Essays,* pp. 127–39. New York: Harper & Row.

Dennistoun, James. 1855. *Memoirs of Sir Robert Strange.* 2 vols. London: Longman.

Dickinson. William Croft (ed.). 1952. *Two Students at St. Andrews, 1711–1716.* Edinburgh: Oliver & Boyd.

Dictionary of National Biography. (1885–90) 1937–38. Edited by Leslie Stephen. 21 vols. London: Oxford University Press.

Dobb, Maurice. 1963. *Studies in the Development of Capitalism.* New York: International Publishers.

Donaldson, Gordon. (1960) 1972. *Scotland: Church and Nation through Sixteen Centuries.* Edinburgh: Scottish Academic Press.

———. (1965) 1966. *Scotland: James V to James VII.* New York: Praeger.

———. 1976. "The Legal Profession in Scottish Society in the Sixteenth and Seventeenth Centuries." *Juridical Review,* pp. 1–19.

Donovan, A. L. 1975. *Philosophical Chemistry in the Scottish Enlightenment: The Doctrines and Discoveries of William Cullen and Joseph Black.* Edinburgh: Edinburgh University Press.

Dreeben, Robert. 1968. *On What Is Learned in School.* Reading: Addison-Wesley.

Drummond, Andrew L., and James Bulloch. 1973. *The Scottish Church, 1688–1843: The Age of the Moderates.* Edinburgh: Saint Andrew Press.

Duncan, Douglas. 1965. *Thomas Ruddiman: A Study in Scottish Scholarship of the Eighteenth Century.* Edinburgh: Oliver & Boyd.

Durkheim, Emile. (1892–1901) 1965. *Montesquieu and Rousseau.* Ann Arbor: University of Michigan Press.

Eisenstadt, S. N. 1968. "The Protestant Ethic Thesis in an Analytical and Comparative Framework." In S. N. Eisenstadt (ed.), *The Protestant Ethic and Modernization: A Comparative View,* pp. 3–45. New York: Basic Books.

Eisenstadt, S. N., and Louis Roniger. 1980. "Patron-Client Relations as a Model of Structuring Social Exchange." *Comparative Studies in Society and History* 22:42–77.

Elder, Glen H. 1965. "Family Structure and Educational Attainment: A Cross-National Analysis." *American Sociological Review* 30:81–95.

Emerson, Roger L. 1973*a*. "The Enlightenment and Social Structures." In Paul Fritz and David Williams (eds.), *City and Society in the Eighteenth Century,* pp. 99–124. Toronto: Hakkert.

———. 1973*b*. "The Social Composition of Enlightened Scotland: The Select Society of Edinburgh, 1754–1764." *Studies on Voltaire and the Eighteenth Century* 114:291–329.

———. 1977. "Scottish Universities in the Eighteenth Century, 1690–1800." *Studies on Voltaire and the Eighteenth Century* 167:453–74.

Erikson, Erik H. (1950) 1963. *Childhood and Society.* 2d ed. New York: Norton.

———. 1958. *Young Man Luther.* New York: Norton.

Fagg, Jane Bush. 1968. "Adam Ferguson: Scottish Cato." Ph.D. diss., University of North Carolina, Chapel Hill.

Farran, C. D'Oliver. 1958. *The Principles of Scots and English Land Law: A Historical Comparison.* Edinburgh: W. Green & Son.

Fay, C. R. 1956. *Adam Smith and the Scotland of His Day.* Cambridge: Cambridge University Press.

Ferguson, Adam. 1746. *A Sermon Preached in the Ersh Language.* London: Millar.

———. 1756. *Reflections Previous to the Establishment of a Militia.* London: Dodsley.

———. 1757. *The Morality of Stage-Plays Seriously Considered.* Edinburgh.

———. 1761. *The History of the Proceedings in the Case of Margaret, Commonly Called Peg, Only Lawful Sister to John Bull, Esq.* 2d. ed. London: Owen.

———. (1767) 1966. *An Essay on the History of Civil Society.* Edited by Duncan Forbes. Edinburgh: Edinburgh University Press.

———. 1769. *Institutes of Moral Philosophy.* Edinburgh: A. Kincaid & Bell.

———. (1792) 1975. *Principles of Moral and Political Science.* 2 vols. New York: Georg Olms Verlag.

Ferguson, William. 1968. *Scotland: 1689 to the Present.* Edinburgh: Oliver & Boyd.

Fergusson, Alexander. 1882. *The Honorable Henry Erskine, Lord Advocate for Scotland.* Edinburgh: Blackwood.

Finlayson, C. P. 1958. "Illustrations of Games by a Seventeenth-Century Edinburgh Student." *Scottish Historical Review* 37:1–10.

Finlayson, James. (1787) 1789. "The Reputation of the Righteous." In *The Scotch Preacher: or, A Collection of Sermons, by Some of the Most Eminent Clergymen of the Church of Scotland,* vol. 4, pp. 140–55. Edinburgh: Dickson.

First Book of Discipline. (1560–61) 1970. In Gordon Donaldson (ed.), *Scottish Historical Documents,* pp. 126–34. Edinburgh: Scottish Academic Press.

Flinn, Michael, Judith Gillespie, Nancy Hill, Alisce Maxwell, Rosalind Mitchison, and Christopher Smout. 1977. *Scottish Population History: From the 17th Century to the 1930s.* Cambridge: Cambridge University Press.

Forbes, Duncan. 1951. "James Mill and India." *Cambridge Journal* 5:19–33.

———. 1954. " 'Scientific' Whiggism: Adam Smith and John Millar." *Cambridge Journal* 7:643–70.

———. 1966. "Introduction." In Adam Ferguson, *An Essay on the History of Civil Society,* pp. xiii–xli. Edited by Duncan Forbes. Edinburgh: Edinburgh University Press.

———. 1967. "Adam Ferguson and the Idea of Community." In *Edinburgh in the Age of Reason: A Commemoration,* pp. 40–47. Edinburgh: Edinburgh University Press.

———. 1975*a.* *Hume's Philosophical Politics.* Cambridge: Cambridge University Press.

———. 1975*b.* "Sceptical Whiggism, Commerce, and Liberty." In Andrew S. Skinner and Thomas Wilson (eds.), *Essays on Adam Smith,* pp. 179–201. Oxford: Clarendon.

———. 1977. "Hume's Science of Politics." In G. P. Morice (ed.), *David Hume: Bicentenary Papers,* pp. 39–50. Austin: University of Texas Press.

———. 1978. "The European, or Cosmopolitan, Dimension in Hume's Science of Politics." *British Journal for Eighteenth-Century Studies* 1:57–60.

Ford, Franklin L. 1968. "The Enlightenment: Towards a Useful Redefinition." In R. F. Brissenden (ed.), *Studies in the Eighteenth Century,* pp. 17–29. Toronto: University of Toronto Press.

Foster, John. (1973) 1975. "Capitalism and the Scottish Nation." In Gordon Brown (ed.), *Red Paper on Scotland,* pp. 141–52. Nottingham: Russell.

Fraser, A. Campbell. 1898. *Thomas Reid.* Edinburgh: Oliphant Anderson & Ferrier.

Gay, Peter. (1957) 1964. "Carl Becker's Heavenly City." In Peter Gay, *The Party of Humanity,* pp. 188–210. New York: Knopf.

———. 1966. *The Enlightenment: An Interpretation.* Vol. 1: *The Rise of Modern Paganism.* New York: Knopf.

———. 1969. *The Enlightenment: An Interpretation.* Vol. 2: *The Science of Freedom.* New York: Knopf.

———. 1970. *The Bridge of Criticism.* New York: Harper & Row.

———. 1973. "Introduction." In Peter Gay (ed.), *The Enlightenment: A Comprehensive Anthology,* pp. 13–26. New York: Simon & Schuster.

Gee, J. M. A. 1968. "Adam Smith's Social Welfare Function." *Scottish Journal of Political Economy* 15:283–99.

Gerald, Alexander. (1761) 1789. "The Influence of Piety on the Public Good." In *The Scotch Preacher: or, A Collection of Sermons, by Some of the Most Eminent Clergymen of the Church of Scotland*, vol. 2, pp. 307–27. Edinburgh: Dickson.

Gibson, John S. 1978. "How Did the Enlightenment Seem to the Edinburgh Enlightened?" *British Journal for Eighteenth-Century Studies* 1:46–50.

Gibson, W. J. 1912. *Education in Scotland: A Sketch of the Past and Present*. London: Longman.

Giddens, Anthony. 1979. *Central Problems in Social Theory*. Berkeley: University of California Press.

Gilbert, Felix. 1972. "Editor's Introduction." In William Robertson, *The Progress of Society in Europe*, pp. xi–xxiv. Edited by Felix Gilbert. Chicago: University of Chicago Press.

Ginsberg, Robert. 1972. "David Hume versus the Enlightenment." *Studies on Voltaire and the Eighteenth Century* 88:599–650.

Gleig, George. 1819. "The Life of Dr. Robertson." In William Robertson, *The History of Scotland*, pp. v–xcviii. Edinburgh: Stirling.

Godley, A. D. 1908. *Oxford in the Eighteenth Century*. London: Methuen.

Goffman, Erving. 1961. *Asylums*. Garden City, N.Y.: Doubleday Anchor.

Goldmann, Lucien. (1968) 1973. *The Philosophy of the Enlightenment*. Translated by Henry Maas. London: Routledge & Kegan Paul.

Goode, William J. 1963. *World Revolution and Family Patterns*. New York: Free Press.

Goody, Jack. 1977. *The Domestication of the Savage Mind*. Cambridge: Cambridge University Press.

Graham, Henry Grey. (1899) 1969. *The Social Life of Scotland in the Eighteenth Century*. London: Black.

———. 1901. *Scottish Men of Letters in the Eighteenth Century*. London: Black.

Grant, Alexander. 1884. *The Story of the University of Edinburgh during Its First Three Hundred Years*. 2 vols. London: Longmans.

Grant, Douglas. 1951. *James Thomson: Poet of 'The Seasons.'* London: Cresset.

Grant, James. 1876. *History of the Burgh and Parish Schools of Scotland*. Vol. 1: *Burgh Schools*. Glasgow: Collins.

Grave, S. A. 1960. *The Scottish Philosophy of Common Sense*. Oxford: Clarendon.

Gray, Andrew. 1789. *The Whole Works of the Reverend and Pious Mr. Andrew Gray*. Falkirk: Mitchell.

Green, V. H. H. 1961. *The Young Mr. Wesley: A Study of John Wesley and Oxford*. New York: St. Martin's Press.

———. 1974. *A History of Oxford University*. London: B. T. Batsford.

Greig, J. Y. T. (1931) 1934. *David Hume*. London: Jonathan Cape.

Greven, Philip J., Jr. 1970. *Four Generations: Population, Land, and Family in Colonial Andover, Massachusetts*. Ithaca: Cornell University Press.

———. 1977. *The Protestant Temperament: Patterns of Child-Rearing, Religious Experience, and Self in Early America*. New York: New American Library.

Hagen, Everett E. 1962. *On the Theory of Social Change: How Economic Growth Begins*. Homewood: Dorsey.

Hagstrom, Warren O. 1968. "Deliberate Instruction Within Family Units." In Andreas M. Kazamias and Erwin H. Epstein (eds.), *Schools in Transition: Essays in Comparative Education*, pp. 262–79. Boston: Allyn & Bacon.

Hall, Roland. 1978. *Fifty Years of Hume Scholarship: A Bibliographical Guide*. Edinburgh: Edinburgh University Press.

Hamilton, Henry. 1932. *The Industrial Revolution in Scotland*. Oxford: Clarendon.

———. 1959. "Economic Growth in Scotland, 1720–1770." *Scottish Journal of Political Economy* 6:85–98.

———. 1963. *An Economic History of Scotland in the Eighteenth Century*. Oxford: Clarendon.

Hamowy, Ronald. 1968. "Adam Smith, Adam Ferguson, and the Division of Labour." *Economica* n.s. 35:249–59.

———. 1969. "The Social and Political Philosophy of Adam Ferguson." Ph.D. diss., University of Chicago.

Hampson, Norman. (1968) 1976. *The Enlightenment*. Harmondsworth: Penguin.

Hans, Nicholas. 1951. *New Trends in Education in the Eighteenth Century*. London: Routledge & Kegan Paul.

Harvey, Thomas, and A. C. Sellar. 1868. *Report on the State of Education in the Burgh and Middle-Class Schools in Scotland*. Vol. 2: *Special Reports*. Edinburgh: Constable.

Hawthorn, Geoffrey. 1976. *Enlightenment and Despair*. Cambridge: Cambridge University Press.

Hay, Denys. 1977. *Annalists and Historians*. London: Methuen.

Hechter, Michael. (1975) 1977. *Internal Colonialism: The Celtic Fringe in British National Development, 1536–1966*. Berkeley: University of California Press.

Heilbroner, Robert L. 1975. "The Paradox of Progress: Decline and Decay in *The Wealth of Nations*." In Andrew S. Skinner and Thomas Wilson (eds.), *Essays on Adam Smith*, pp. 524–39. Oxford: Clarendon.

Henderson, G. D. 1935. *The Scottish Ruling Elder*. London: James Clarke.

———. 1937. *Religious Life in Seventeenth-Century Scotland*. Cambridge: Cambridge University Press.

———. 1951. *The Claims of the Church of Scotland*. Warrick: Hodder.

———. 1957. *The Burning Bush: Studies in Scottish Church History*. Edinburgh: Saint Andrew Press.

Henderson, Robert. 1741. "A Short Account of the University of Edinburgh, the Present Professors in It, and the Several Parts of Learning Taught by Them." *Scots Magazine* 3:371–74.

Herkless, John, and Robert Kerr Hannay. 1905. *The College of St. Leonard*. Edinburgh: William Blackwood & Sons.

Herzog, John D. 1962. "Deliberate Instruction and Household Structures: A Cross-Cultural Study." *Harvard Educational Review* 32:301–42.

Hill, Christopher. 1961. "Protestantism and the Rise of Capitalism." In F. J. Fisher (ed.), *Essays in the Economic and Social History of Tudor and Stuart England*, pp. 15–39. Cambridge: Cambridge University Press.

———. (1967) 1969. *Reformation to Industrial Revolution*. Harmondsworth: Penguin.

Hirschman, Albert O. 1977. *The Passions and the Interests: Political Arguments for Capitalism before Its Triumph*. Princeton: Princeton University Press.

Hook, Andrew. 1975. *Scotland and America: A Study of Cultural Relations, 1750–1835*. Glasgow: Blackie.

Höpfl, H. M. 1978. "From Savage to Scotsman: Conjectural History in the Scottish Enlightenment." *Journal of British Studies* 17:19–40.

Horn, D. B. 1956. "Principal William Robertson, D. D., Historian." *University of Edinburgh Journal*, Autumn, 155–68.

———. 1961. "Some Scottish Writers of History in the Eighteenth Century." *Scottish Historical Review* 40:1–18.

———. 1967. *A Short History of the University of Edinburgh, 1556–1889*. Edinburgh: Edinburgh University Press.

Houston, Rab. 1982. "The Literacy Myth? Illiteracy in Scotland 1630–1760." *Past and Present* 96:81–102.

Howe, Daniel Walker. 1970. *The Unitarian Conscience: Harvard Moral Philosophy, 1805–1861*. Cambridge, Mass.: Harvard University Press.

Hume, David. (1726) 1947. "An Historical Essay on Chivalry and Modern Honour." Edited by Ernest Campbell Mossner. *Modern Philology* 45:54–60.

———. (1729–40) 1948. "Hume's Early Memoranda, 1729–1740: The Complete Text." Edited by Ernest Campbell Mossner. *Journal of the History of Ideas* 9:492–518.

———. (1739–40) 1975. *A Treatise of Human Nature*. Oxford: Clarendon.

———. (1740) 1938. *An Abstract of a Treatise of Human Nature*. Cambridge: Cambridge University Press.

———. (1741–77) 1963. *Essays: Moral, Political, and Literary*. Oxford: Oxford University Press.

———. (1748) 1974. *An Enquiry Concerning Human Understanding*. In *The Empiricists*, pp. 307–430. New York: Doubleday Anchor.

———. (1751a) 1957. "A Dialogue." In David Hume, *An Inquiry Concerning the Principles of Morals*, pp. 141–58. Edited by Charles W. Hendel. Indianapolis: Bobbs-Merrill.

———. (1751b) 1957. *An Inquiry Concerning the Principles of Morals*. Edited by Charles W. Hendel. Indianapolis: Bobbs-Merrill.

———. (1754–62) 1965. Selections from *The History of England*. In David Fate Norton and Richard H. Popkin (eds.), *David Hume: Philosophical Historian*, pp. 109–376. Indianapolis: Bobbs-Merrill.

———. (1757) 1956. *The Natural History of Religion*. Edited by H. E. Root. Stanford: Stanford University Press.

———. (1779) 1974. *Dialogues Concerning Natural Religion*. In *The Empiricists*, pp. 431–517. New York: Doubleday Anchor.

———. 1932. *The Letters of David Hume*. Edited by J. Y. T. Greig. 2 vols. Oxford: Clarendon.

———. 1954. *New Letters of David Hume*. Edited by Raymond Klibansky and Ernest C. Mossner. Oxford: Clarendon.

Humphreys, R. A. 1954. *William Robertson and His History of America*. London: Hispanic and Luso-Brazilian Councils.

Hunt, David. 1970. *Parents and Children in History: The Psychology of Family Life in Early Modern France*. New York: Basic Books.

Hunt, E. K. 1975. *Property and Prophets: The Evolution of Economic Institutions and Ideologies*. 2d ed. New York: Harper & Row.

Hunt, R. W. 1963. "The College in the Second Half of the Eighteenth Century." In H. W. Carless Davis, *A History of Balliol College*, pp. 272–84. Rev. ed. Oxford: Basil Blackwell.

Hutcheson, Francis. (1725–55) 1969–71. *Collected Works*. 6 vols. Hildesheim: Georg Olms Verlag.

———. (1735) 1773. *Considerations on Patronages Addressed to the Gentlemen of Scotland*. Glasgow.

Hutchison, Henry. 1976. "An Eighteenth-Century Insight into Religious and Moral Education." *British Journal of Educational Studies* 24:233–41.

Jensen, Henning. 1971. *Motivation and the Moral Sense in Francis Hutcheson's Ethical Theory*. The Hague: Martinus Nijhoff.

Jessop, J. C. 1931. *Education in Angus*. London: University of London Press.

Jessop, T. E. 1938. *A Bibliography of David Hume and of Scottish Philosophy from Francis Hutcheson to Lord Balfour*. London: A. Brown.

Jones, Robert Alun. 1977. "On Understanding a Sociological Classic." *American Journal of Sociology* 83:279–319.

Kant, Immanuel. (1784) 1973. "What Is Enlightenment?" In Peter Gay (ed.), *The Enlightenment: A Comprehensive Anthology*, pp. 383–90. New York: Simon & Schuster.

Kaufman, Robert R. 1974. "The Patron-Client Concept and Macro-Politics: Prospects and Problems." *Comparative Studies in Society and History* 16:284–308.

Kenrick, Isabel. 1956. "The University of Edinburgh: 1660–1715." Ph.D. thesis, Bryn Mawr.

Kerr, John. 1910. *Scottish Education: School and University*. Cambridge: Cambridge University Press.

Kettler, David. 1965. *The Social and Political Thought of Adam Ferguson*. Columbus: Ohio State University Press.

———. 1977. "History and Theory in Ferguson's *Essay on the History of Civil Society:* A Reconsideration." *Political Theory* 5:437–60.

————. 1978. "Ferguson's *Principles:* Constitution in Permanence." *Studies in Burke and His Time* 19:208–22.

Kluckhohn, Clyde. 1951. "Values and Value Orientations in the Theory of Action: An Exploration in Definition and Classification." In Talcott Parsons and Edward Shils (eds.), *Toward a General Theory of Action,* pp. 338–433. New York: Harper & Row.

Knight, William. (1886) 1970. *Hume.* Port Washington, N.Y.: Kennikat Press.

————. 1900. *Lord Monboddo and Some of His Contemporaries.* London: John Murray.

Knox, H. M. 1953. *Two Hundred and Fifty Years of Scottish Education, 1696–1946.* Edinburgh: Oliver & Boyd.

Kohlberg, Lawrence. 1969. "Stage and Sequence: The Cognitive-Developmental Approach to Socialization." In David A. Goslin (ed.), *Handbook of Socialization Theory and Research,* pp. 347–480. Chicago: Rand McNally.

Krieger, Leonard. 1970. *Kings and Philosophers, 1689–1789.* New York: Norton.

Kuhn, Thomas S. (1962) 1970. *The Structure of Scientific Revolutions.* 2d ed. Chicago: University of Chicago Press.

Lamont, Claire. 1975. "Literary Patronage in Late Eighteenth-Century Edinburgh." *Scottish Literary Journal* 2:17–26.

Laslett, Peter. 1972. "Introduction: The History of the Family." In Peter Laslett and Richard Wall (eds.), *Household and Family in Past Time,* pp. 1–89. Cambridge: Cambridge University Press.

Laurie, Henry. 1902. *Scottish Philosophy in Its National Development.* Glasgow: James Maclehose & Sons.

Law, Alexander. 1965. *Education in Edinburgh in the Eighteenth Century.* London: University of London Press.

Leechman, William. (1743) 1789. "The Nature, Reasonableness, and Advantages of Prayer; with an Attempt to Answer Objections Against It." In *The Scotch Preacher: or, A Collection of Sermons, by Some of the Most Eminent Clergymen of the Church of Scotland,* vol. 1, pp. 138–206. Edinburgh: Dickson.

————. (1758) 1789. "The Wisdom of God in the Gospel-Revelation." In *The Scotch Preacher: or, A Collection of Sermons, by Some of the Most Eminent Clergymen of the Church of Scotland,* vol. 2, pp. 215–80. Edinburgh: Dickson.

Lehmann, William C. 1930. *Adam Ferguson and the Beginnings of Modern Sociology.* New York: Columbia University Press.

————. 1960. *John Millar of Glasgow, 1735–1801.* Cambridge: Cambridge University Press.

————. 1970. "Some Observations on the Law Lectures of Professor Millar of the University of Glasgow (1761–1801)." *Juridical Review* 15:56–77.

————. 1971. *Henry Home, Lord Kames and the Scottish Enlightenment.* The Hague: Martinus Nijhoff.

———. 1971–72. "Comment on Louis Schneider, 'Tension in the Thought of John Millar.'" *Studies in Burke and His Time* 13:2099–2110.

✗ ———. 1978. *Scottish and Scotch-Irish Contributions to Early American Life and Culture.* Port Washington, N.Y.: Kennikat Press.   *10, 45*

Letwin, Shirley Robin. 1965. *The Pursuit of Certainty.* Cambridge: Cambridge University Press.

Lindgren, J. Ralph. 1973. *The Social Philosophy of Adam Smith.* The Hague: Martinus Nijhoff.

Lindsey, Lord (Alexander William Crawford). 1849. *Lives of the Lindsays.* 3 vols. London: John Murray.

Lochhead, Marion. 1948. *The Scots Household in the Eighteenth Century.* Edinburgh: Moray Press.

Loubser, Jan J. 1970. "The Contribution of Schools to Moral Development: A Working Paper in the Theory of Action." *Interchange* 1 (no. 1):99–117.

Lynam, Robert. 1824. "The Life of Dr. Robertson." In William Robertson, *The Works of William Robertson,* pp. 5–75. London: Baynes.

McClelland, David C. 1961. *The Achieving Society.* New York: Free Press.

McCosh, James. 1875. *The Scottish Philosophy.* New York: Robert Carter & Bros.

McDougall, Warren. 1978. "Gavin Hamilton, Bookseller in Edinburgh." *British Journal for Eighteenth-Century Studies* 1:1–19.

McElroy, Davis D. 1969. *Scotland's Age of Improvement: A Survey of Eighteenth-Century Literary Clubs and Societies.* Pullman: Washington State University Press.

Macfie, A. L. 1955. "The Scottish Tradition in Economic Thought." *Scottish Journal of Political Economy* 2:81–103.

———. 1961. "John Millar: A Bridge between Adam Smith and Nineteenth Century Social Thinkers?" *Scottish Journal of Political Economy* 8:200–210.

———. 1967. *The Individual in Society.* London: Allen & Unwin.

McGuinness, Arthur E. 1970. *Henry Home, Lord Kames.* New York: Twayne.

McKelvey, James L. 1969. "William Robertson and Lord Bute." *Studies in Scottish Literature* 6:238–47.

Mackie, J. D. 1954. *The University of Glasgow, 1451–1951: A Short History.* Glasgow: Jackson, Son & Co.

Macky, John. 1723. *A Journey through Scotland.* London: Pemberton.

Macleod. John. (1943) 1946. *Scottish Theology in Relation to Church History Since the Reformation.* Edinburgh: Knox.

McNeill, John T. (1954) 1967. *The History and Character of Calvinism.* London: Oxford University Press.

McPherson, Andrew. 1973. "Selections and Survivals: A Sociology of the Ancient Scottish Universities." In Richard Brown (ed.), *Knowledge, Education, and Cultural Change,* pp. 163–201. London: Travistock.

MacRae, Donald G. 1961. *Ideology and Society.* London: Heinemann.

———. 1969. "Adam Ferguson." In Timothy Raison (ed.), *The Founding Fathers of Social Science,* pp. 17–26. Harmondsworth: Penguin.

Mallet, Charles Edward. 1924–28. *A History of the University of Oxford.* 3 vols. New York: Longmans, Green & Co.

Mannheim, Karl. (1927) 1953. "Conservative Thought." In Karl Mannheim, *Essays on Sociology and Social Psychology,* pp. 74–164. London: Routledge & Kegan Paul.

Marshall, Gordon. 1980a. "The Dark Side of the Weber Thesis: The Case of Scotland." *British Journal of Sociology* 31:419–40.

———. 1980b. *Presbyteries and Profits: Calvinism and the Development of Capitalism in Scotland, 1560–1707.* Oxford: Oxford University Press.

Marshall, Rosalind K. 1973. *The Days of Duchess Anne.* London: Collins.

Martin, Barclay. 1975. "Parent-Child Relations." In Frances Degen Horowitz (ed.), *Review of Child Development Research,* vol. 4, pp. 463–540. Chicago: University of Chicago Press.

Martin, Burns. 1931. *Allan Ramsay.* Cambridge, Mass.: Harvard University Press.

Marx, Karl. (1852) 1963. *The Eighteenth Brumaire of Louis Bonaparte.* New York: International Publishers.

———. (1867) 1967. *Capital: A Critique of Political Economy,* vol. 1. New York: International Publishers.

———. (1894) 1967. *Capital: A Critique of Political Economy,* vol. 3. New York: International Publishers.

Marx, Karl, and Frederick Engels. (1846) 1977. Selections from *The German Ideology.* In David McLellan (ed.), *Karl Marx: Selected Writings,* pp. 159–91. Oxford: Oxford University Press.

Mathew, W. M. 1966. "The Origins and Occupations of Glasgow Students, 1740–1839." *Past and Present* 33:74–94.

Mathieson, William Law. 1902. *Politics and Religion: A Study in Scottish History from the Reformation to the Revolution.* 2 vols. Glasgow: James Maclehose & Sons.

———. 1905. *Scotland and the Union: A History of Scotland from 1695 to 1747.* Glasgow: James Maclehose & Sons.

———. 1910. *The Awakening of Scotland; A History from 1747 to 1797.* Glasgow: James Maclehose & Sons.

May, Henry F. 1976a. "The Decline of Providence?" *Studies on Voltaire and the Eighteenth Century* 154:1401–16.

———. 1976b. *The Enlightenment in America.* New York: Oxford University Press.

Mechie, Stewart. 1967. "The Theological Climate in Early Eighteenth-Century Scotland." In Duncan Shaw (ed.), *Reformation and Revolution,* pp. 258–72. Edinburgh: The Saint Andrew Press.

Meek, Ronald L. (1954) 1967. "The Scottish Contribution to Marxist Sociology." In Ronald L. Meek, *Economics and Ideology and Other Essays,* pp. 34–50. London: Chapman & Hall.

———. 1971. "Smith, Turgot, and the 'Four Stages' Theory." *History of Political Economy* 3:9–27.

———. 1976*a*. "New Light on Adam Smith's Glasgow Lectures on Jurisprudence." *History of Political Economy* 8:439–77.

———. 1976*b*. *Social Science and the Ignoble Savage*. Cambridge: Cambridge University Press.

Meek, Ronald L., D. D. Raphael, and P. G. Stein. 1978. "Introduction." In Adam Smith, *Lectures on Jurisprudence*, pp. 1–42. Edited by R. L. Meek, D. D. Raphael, and P. G. Stein. Oxford: Clarendon.

Meek, Ronald L., and Andrew S. Skinner. 1973. "The Development of Adam Smith's Ideas on the Division of Labour." *Economic Journal* 83:1094–1116.

Meikle, Henry W. 1947. *Some Aspects of Later Seventeenth-Century Scotland*. Glasgow: Jackson, Son & Co.

Meldrum, George. 1704. *A Sermon Preached Before the Lord Ross, Her Majestie's Commissioner, and the General Assembly of the Church of Scotland*. Edinburgh: Mosman.

Merton, Robert K. (1938) 1970. *Science, Technology, and Society in Seventeenth-Century England*. New York: Howard Fertig.

———. (1942) 1973. "The Normative Structure of Science." In Robert K. Merton, *The Sociology of Science*, pp. 267–78. Chicago: University of Chicago Press.

———. (1945) 1973. "Paradigm for the Sociology of Knowledge." In Robert K. Merton, *The Sociology of Science*, pp. 7–40. Chicago: University of Chicago Press.

Meyer, D. H. 1972. *The Instructed Conscience: The Shaping of the American Ethic*. Philadelphia: University of Pennsylvania Press.

Millar, John. (1771; 3d ed. 1779) 1960. *The Origin of the Distinction of Ranks*. Reprinted in William C. Lehmann, *John Millar of Glasgow, 1735–1801*. Cambridge: Cambridge University Press.

———. (1787–1803) 1818. *An Historical View of the English Government*. 4 vols. London: Mawman.

Millar, John Hepburn. 1903. *A Literary History of Scotland*. New York: Scribner's.

———. 1912. *Scottish Prose of the Seventeenth and Eighteenth Centuries*. Glasgow: James Maclehose & Sons.

Mills, C. Wright. (1939) 1963. "Language, Logic and Culture." In C. Wright Mills, *Power, Politics, and People*, pp. 423–38. London: Oxford University Press.

Minto, Countess of. 1874. *Life and Letters of Sir Gilbert Elliot, First Earl of Minto, from 1751 to 1806*. 3 vols. London: Longmans.

Mitchison, Rosalind. 1978. "Scottish Landowners and Communal Responsibility in the Eighteenth Century." *British Journal for Eighteenth-Century Studies* 1:41–45.

Mizuta, Hiroshi. 1975. "Moral Philosophy and Civil Society." In Andrew S. Skinner and Thomas Wilson (eds.), *Essays on Adam Smith*, pp. 114–31. Oxford: Clarendon.

————. 1976. "Towards a Definition of the Scottish Enlightenment." *Studies on Voltaire and the Eighteenth Century* 154:1459–64.

————. 1980. "Two Adams in the Scottish Enlightenment: Adam Smith and Adam Ferguson on Progress." *Studies on Voltaire and the Eighteenth Century* 191:812–19.

Moore, Barrington, Jr. 1966. *Social Origins of Dictatorship and Democracy.* Boston: Beacon.

Morgan, Alexander. 1927. *Rise and Progress of Scottish Education.* Edinburgh: Oliver & Boyd.

————. 1933. *Scottish University Studies.* London: Oxford University Press.

Morgan, Edmund S. (1944) 1966. *The Puritan Family: Religion and Domestic Relations in Seventeenth-Century New England.* Rev. ed. New York: Harper & Row.

Morrell, J. B. 1971*a*. "Professors Robinson and Playfair, and the *Theophobia Gallica*: Natural Philosophy, Religion, and Politics in Edinburgh, 1789–1815." *Notes and Records of the Royal Society of London* 26:43–62.

————. 1971*b*. "The University of Edinburgh in the Late Eighteenth Century: Its Scientific Eminence and Academic Structure." *Isis* 62:158–71.

————.1974. "Reflections on the History of Scottish Science." *History of Science* 12:81–94.

————. 1976. "The Edinburgh Town Council and Its University, 1717–1766." In R. G. W. Anderson and A. D. C. Simpson (eds.), *The Early Years of Edinburgh Medical School*, pp. 46–65. Edinburgh: Royal Scottish Museum.

Morrow, Glenn R. 1923. *The Ethical and Economic Theories of Adam Smith.* New York: Longmans.

Mosse, George L. 1960. "Puritan Radicalism and the Enlightenment." *Church History* 29:424–39.

Mossner, Ernest Campbell. 1943. *The Forgotten Hume: Le bon David.* New York: Columbia University Press.

————. 1954. *The Life of David Hume.* Edinburgh: Thomas Nelson.

————. 1965. "The Enlightenment of David Hume." In Robert Mollenauer (ed.), *Introduction to Modernity*, pp. 43–62. Austin: University of Texas Press.

————. 1969. *Adam Smith: The Biographical Approach.* Glasgow: George Outram & Co.

Mure, William (ed.). 1854. *Selections from Family Papers Preserved at Caldwell.* 3 vols. Glasgow: Maitland Club.

Murray, Athol L. 1974. "Administration and Law." In T. I. Rae (ed.), *The Union of 1707: Its Impact on Scotland*, pp. 30–57. Glasgow: Blackie & Son.

Murray, David. 1927. *Memories of the Old College of Glasgow.* Glasgow: Jackson, Wylie & Co.

National Library of Scotland. 1958. *Four Hundred and Fifty Years of Scottish Printing.* Edinburgh: Morrison & Gibb.

Nelson, Benjamin. 1973. "Weber's Protestant Ethic: Its Origins, Wanderings and Foreseeable Futures." In Charles Y. Glock and Philip E. Hammond (eds.), *Beyond the Classics? Essays in the Scientific Study of Religion*, p. 71–130. New York: Harper & Row.

Nisbet, Robert. 1969. *Social Change and History*. New York: Oxford University Press.

———. 1980. *History of the Idea of Progress*. New York: Basic Books.

Norton, David Fate. 1975. "George Turnbull and the Furniture of the Mind." *Journal of the History of Ideas* 36:701–16.

Noxon, James. 1973. *Hume's Philosophical Development*. Oxford: Clarendon.

Nybakken, Elizabeth I. 1980. "The Enlightenment and Calvinism: Mutual Support Systems for the Eighteenth-Century American Wilderness." *Studies on Voltaire and the Eighteenth Century* 192:1126–35.

Olson, Richard. 1971. "Scottish Philosophy and Mathematics, 1750–1830." *Journal of the History of Ideas* 32:29–44.

Owen, J. B. 1972. "Political Patronage in Eighteenth-Century England." In Paul Fritz and David Williams (eds.), *The Triumph of Culture: Eighteenth Century Perspectives*, pp. 369–87. Toronto: Hakkert.

———. 1974. *The Eighteenth Century, 1714–1815*. New York: Norton.

Pares, Richard. 1954. "A Quarter of a Millennium of Anglo-Scottish Union." *History* n.s. 39:233–48.

Parsons, Talcott. (1951) 1964. *The Social System*. New York: Free Press.

———. (1959) 1970. "The School Class as a Social System." In Talcott Parsons, *Social Structure and Personality*, pp. 129–54. London: Free Press.

———. 1968. "Christianity." In David L. Sills (ed.), *International Encyclopedia of the Social Sciences*, vol. 2, pp. 425–47. New York: Free Press.

———. 1971. *The System of Modern Societies*. Englewood Cliffs: Prentice-Hall.

Parsons, Talcott, and Edward Shils. 1951. "Values, Motives, and Systems of Action." In Talcott Parsons and Edward Shils (eds.), *Toward a General Theory of Action*, pp. 47–243. New York: Harper & Row.

Pascal, Roy. 1938. "Property and Society: The Scottish Historical School of the Eighteenth Century." *Modern Quarterly* 1:167–79.

Patterson, Orlando. 1977. *Ethnic Chauvinism: The Reactionary Impulse*. New York: Stein & Day.

Peardon, Thomas Preston. 1933. *The Transition in English Historical Writing, 1760–1830*. New York: Columbia University Press.

Petrie, Adam. (1720) 1877. *Rules of Good Deportment, or of Good Breeding, for the Use of Youth*. In Adam Petrie, *The Works of Adam Petrie*, pp. 1–136. Edinburgh.

Phillipson, Nicholas T. 1973. "Toward a Definition of the Scottish Enlightenment." In P. Fritz and D. Williams (eds.), *City and Society in the Eighteenth Century*, pp. 125–47. Toronto: Hakkert.

———. 1974. "Culture and Society in the Eighteenth-Century Province: The Case of Edinburgh and the Scottish Enlightenment." In Lawrence

Stone (ed.), *The University in Society,* vol. 2, pp. 407–48. Princeton: Princeton University Press.

———. 1976*a*. "The Export of Enlightenment." *Times Literary Supplement,* July 2, 823–24.

———. 1976*b*. "Lawyers, Landowners, and the Civic Leadership of Post-Union Scotland." *Juridical Review,* pp. 97–120.

———. 1980. "Virtue, Commerce, and the Science of Man in Early Eighteenth-Century Scotland." *Studies on Voltaire and the Eighteenth Century* 191:750–53.

———. 1981. "The Scottish Enlightenment." In Roy Porter and Mikulas Teich (eds.), *The Enlightenment in National Context,* pp. 19–40. Cambridge: Cambridge University Press.

Phillipson, Nicholas T., and Rosalind Mitchison. 1970. "Introduction." In N. T. Phillipson and Rosalind Mitchison (eds.), *Scotland in the Age of Improvement,* pp. 1–4. Edinburgh: Edinburgh University Press.

Plant, Marjorie. 1952. *The Domestic Life of Scotland in the Eighteenth Century.* Edinburgh: Edinburgh University Press.

Plumb, J. H. (1950) 1963. *England in the Eighteenth Century.* Harmondsworth: Penguin.

———. 1956. *Sir Robert Walpole: The Making of a Statesman.* London: Cresset.

———. 1961. *Sir Robert Walpole: The King's Minister.* Boston: Houghton Mifflin.

———. 1967. *The Origins of Political Stability: England, 1675–1725.* Boston: Houghton Mifflin.

———. 1968. "Political Man." In James L. Clifford (ed.), *Man Versus Society in Eighteenth-Century Britain,* pp. 1–21. New York: Norton.

Pocock, J. G. A. 1965. "Machiavelli, Harrington, and English Political Ideologies in the Eighteenth Century." *William and Mary Quarterly* 3d series 22:549–83.

———. 1975. *The Machiavellian Moment.* Princeton: Princeton University Press.

Popkin, Richard H. 1965. "Skepticism and the Study of History." In David Fate Norton and Richard H. Popkin (eds.), *David Hume: Philosophical Historian,* pp. ix–xxxi. Indianapolis: Bobbs-Merrill.

Pottle, Frederick A. 1966. *James Boswell: The Earlier Years, 1740–1769.* New York: McGraw-Hill.

Price, John Vladimir. 1967. "Concepts of Enlightenment in Eighteenth-Century Scottish Literature." *Texas Studies in Literature and Language* 9:371–79.

Pryde, George S. 1960. *Central and Local Government in Scotland since 1707.* London: Routledge & Kegan Paul.

———. 1962. *Scotland from 1603 to the Present Day.* London: Thomas Nelson.

———. 1965. *The Burghs of Scotland.* London: Oxford University Press.

Rae, John. (1895) 1965. *Life of Adam Smith.* New York: Augustus M. Kelley.

Rae, Thomas I. 1973. "Historical Scepticism in Scotland before David Hume." In R. F. Brissenden (ed.), *Studies in the Eighteenth Century,* vol. 2, pp. 205–21. Toronto: University of Toronto Press.

Rait, Robert Sangster. 1895. *The Universities of Aberdeen: A History.* Aberdeen: James Gordon Bisset.

Ramsay, John. 1888. *Scotland and Scotsmen in the Eighteenth Century.* Edited by Alexander Allardyce. 2 vols. Edinburgh: William Blackwood & Sons.

Raphael, D. Daiches. 1947. *The Moral Sense.* London: Oxford University Press.

———. 1969. "Adam Smith and 'The Infection of David Hume's Society.' " *Journal of the History of Ideas* 30:225–48.

———. 1973. "Hume and Adam Smith on Justice and Utility." *Proceedings of the Aristotelian Society* n.s. 73:87–103.

———. 1975. "The Impartial Spectator." In Andrew S. Skinner and Thomas Wilson (eds.), *Essays on Adam Smith,* pp. 83–99. Oxford: Clarendon.

Raphael, D. Daiches, and A. L. Macfie. 1976. "Introduction." In Adam Smith, *The Theory of Moral Sentiments,* pp. 1–52. Edited by D. D. Raphael and A. L. Macfie. Oxford: Clarendon.

Reader, W. J. 1966. *Professional Men: The Rise of the Professional Classes in Nineteenth-Century England.* New York: Basic Books.

Reid, J. M. 1960. *Kirk and Nation: The Story of the Reformed Church of Scotland.* London: Skeffington.

Reid, Thomas. (1788) 1969. *Essays on the Active Powers of the Human Mind.* Cambridge, Mass.: MIT Press.

———. (1799) 1967. "A Statistical Account of the University of Glasgow." In Thomas Reid, *Philosophical Works,* vol. 2, pp. 721–39. Hildesheim: Georg Olms Verlag.

Reisman, D. A. 1976. *Adam Smith's Sociological Economics.* London: Croom Helm.

Rendall, Jane. 1978. *The Origins of the Scottish Enlightenment, 1707–1776.* London: Macmillan.

Riley, P. W. J. 1964. *The English Ministers and Scotland 1707–1727.* London: University of London Athlone Press.

———. 1974. "The Structure of Scottish Politics and the Union of 1707." In T. I. Rae (ed.), *The Union of 1707: Its Impact on Scotland,* pp. 1–29. Glasgow: Blackie & Son.

———. 1978. *The Union of England and Scotland: A Study in Anglo-Scottish Politics of the Eighteenth Century.* Manchester: Manchester University Press.

Robbins, Caroline. 1954. " 'When It Is That Colonies May Turn Independent': An Analysis of the Environment and Politics of Francis Hutcheson (1694–1746)." *William and Mary Quarterly* 3d series 11:214–51.

———. 1959. *The Eighteenth-Century Commonwealthman.* Cambridge, Mass.: Harvard University Press.

Robertson, H. M. (1933) 1973. *Aspects of the Rise of Economic Individualism: A Criticism of Max Weber and His School.* Clifton, N.J.: Augustus M. Kelley.

Robertson, William (1755) 1835. "The Situation of the World at the Time of Christ's Appearance." In *The Works of William Robertson, D.D.*, pp. li–lviii. London: F. Westley & A. H. Davis.

———. (1755–56) 1818. Miscellaneous book reviews. *Edinburgh Review* 1:1–8, 20–24, 51–53, 65–67, 69–70, 79–86, 97–105.

———. (1759) 1818. *The History of Scotland*. Vols. 1–3 in *The Works of William Robertson, D.D.* Edinburgh: Peter Hill.

———. (1769a) 1818. *The History of the Reign of the Emperor Charles V.* Vols. 4–7 in *The Works of William Robertson, D.D.* Edinburgh: Peter Hill.

———. (1769b) 1972. *The Progress of Society in Europe*. Edited by Felix Gilbert. Chicago: University of Chicago Press.

———. (1777) 1818. *The History of America*. Vols. 8–11 in *The Works of William Robertson, D.D.* Edinburgh: Peter Hill.

———. 1788. Sermon. National Library of Scotland. MS 3979.

———. (1791) 1818. *An Historical Disquisition Concerning the Knowledge Which the Ancients Had of India*. Vol. 12 in *The Works of William Robertson, D.D.* Edinburgh: Peter Hill.

Robinson, Jack Fay. 1949. "William Robertson: Scottish Historian (1721–1793)." A.M. diss., University of Chicago.

Ross, Ian Simpson. 1966. "Hutcheson on Hume's Treatise: An Unnoticed Letter." *Journal of the History of Philosophy* 4:69–72.

———. 1972. *Lord Kames and the Scotland of His Day*. Oxford: Clarendon.

Ross, Ian Simpson, and Stephen A. C. Scobie. 1974. "Patriotic Publishing as a Response to the Union." In T. I. Rae (ed.), *The Union of 1707: Its Impact on Scotland*, pp. 94–119. Glasgow: Blackie & Son.

Samuelsson, Kurt. (1957) 1961. *Religion and Economic Action: A Critique of Max Weber*. Translated by E. Geoffrey French. New York: Harper Torchbooks.

Saunders, J. W. 1964. *The Profession of English Letters*. London: Routledge & Kegan Paul.

Saunders, Laurance James. 1950. *Scottish Democracy, 1815–1840: The Social and Intellectual Background*. Edinburgh: Oliver & Boyd.

Schmitz, Robert Morell. 1948. *Hugh Blair*. Morningside Heights, N.Y.: King's Craven Press.

Schneider, Louis. 1967. "Introduction." In Louis Schneider (ed.), *The Scottish Moralists*, pp. xi–lxxvii. Chicago: University of Chicago Press.

———. 1971–72. "Tension in the Thought of John Millar." *Studies in Burke and His Time* 13:2083–2098.

Schücking, Levin L. (1929) 1969. *The Puritan Family: A Social Study from Literary Sources*. Translated by Brian Battersheid. 2d ed. London: Routledge & Kegan Paul.

Schuma, Simon. 1979. "The Unruly Realm: Appetite and Restraint in Seventeenth-Century Holland." *Daedalus* 108:103–23.

Scotland, James. 1969. *The History of Scottish Education*. 2 vols. London: University of London Press.

Scotland, John. (c. 1776) 1789. "The Fear of Divine Goodness." In *The Scotch Preacher: or, A Collection of Sermons, by Some of the Most Eminent Clergymen of the Church of Scotland*, vol. 2, pp. 66–86. Edinburgh: Dickson.

Scott, William Robert. 1900. *Francis Hutcheson*. Cambridge: Cambridge University Press.

————. 1937. *Adam Smith as Student and Professor*. Glasgow: Jackson, Son & Co.

Sefton, Henry R. 1966. "Rev. Robert Wallace: An Early Moderate." *Records of the Scottish Church History Society* 16:1–22.

Segerstedt, Torgny T. 1935. *The Problem of Knowledge in Scottish Philosophy*. Lund: Gleerup.

Shapin, Steven. 1974*a*. "The Audience for Science in Eighteenth-Century Edinburgh." *History of Science* 12:95–121.

————. 1974*b*. "Property, Patronage, and the Politics of Science." *British Journal for the History of Science* 7:1–41.

Sharp, L. W. (1946) 1962. "Charles Mackie, the First Professor of History at Edinburgh University." *Scottish Historical Review* 41:23–45.

Shefter, Martin. 1977. "Party and Patronage: Germany, England, and Italy." *Politics and Society* 7:403–51.

Sher, Richard B. 1979. "Church, University, Enlightenment: The Moderate Literati of Edinburgh, 1720–93." 2 vols. Ph.D. diss., University of Chicago.

Shorter, Edward. 1975. *The Making of the Modern Family*. New York: Basic Books.

Simmel, Georg. (1908) 1971. "Group Expansion and the Development of Individuality." In Georg Simmel, *On Individuality and Social Forms*, pp. 251–93. Edited by Donald N. Levine. Chicago: University of Chicago Press.

Simonds, A. P. 1978. *Karl Mannheim's Sociology of Knowledge*. Oxford: Clarendon.

Simpson, Ian J. 1947. *Education in Aberdeenshire before 1872*. London: University of London Press.

Simpson, John M. 1970. "Who Steered the Gravy Train, 1707–1766?" In N. T. Phillipson and Rosalind Mitchison (eds.), *Scotland in the Age of Improvement*, pp. 47–72. Edinburgh: Edinburgh University Press.

Sinclair, John. 1791–99. *The Statistical Account of Scotland Drawn from the Communications of the Ministers of Different Parishes*. 21 vols. Edinburgh: William Creech.

Skinner, Andrew S. 1965. "Economics and History—The Scottish Enlightenment." *Scottish Journal of Political Economy* 12:1–22.

————. 1967. "Natural History in the Age of Adam Smith." *Political Studies* 15:32–48.

————. 1972. "Adam Smith: Philosophy and Science." *Scottish Journal of Political Economy* 19:307–19.

――――. 1974. "Adam Smith, Science and the Role of the Imagination." In William B. Todd (ed.), *Hume and the Enlightenment,* pp. 164–88. Edinburgh: University of Edinburgh Press.

――――. 1975. "Adam Smith: An Economic Interpretation of History." In Andrew S. Skinner and Thomas Wilson (eds.), *Essays on Adam Smith,* pp. 154–78. Oxford: Clarendon.

――――. 1976. "Adam Smith: The Development of a System." *Scottish Journal of Political Economy* 23:111–32.

Skinner, Quentin. 1966. "The Limits of Historical Explanations." *Philosophy* 41:199–215.

――――. 1969. "Meaning and Understanding in the History of Ideas." *History and Theory* 8:3–53.

――――. 1972. "Motives, Intentions and the Interpretation of Texts." *New Literary History* 3:393–408.

――――. 1974. "Some Problems in the Analyses of Political Thought and Action." *Political Theory* 2:277–303.

――――. 1978. *The Foundations of Modern Political Thought.* 2 vols. Cambridge: Cambridge University Press.

Sloan, Douglas. 1971. *The Scottish Enlightenment and the American College Ideal.* New York: Teachers College Press.

Small, John. 1864. "Biographical Sketch of Adam Ferguson." *Transactions of the Royal Society of Edinburgh* 23:599–665.

Smart, Alastair. 1952. *The Life and Art of Allan Ramsay.* London: Routledge & Kegan Paul.

Smart, Edward. 1932. *History of Perth Academy.* Perth: Milne.

Smart, Robert Noyes. 1974. "Some Observations on the Provinces of the Scottish Universities, 1560–1850." In G. W. S. Barrow (ed.), *The Scottish Tradition,* pp. 91–106. Edinburgh: Scottish Academic Press.

Smelser, Neil J., and Sydney Halpern. 1978. "The Historical Triangulation of Family, Economy, and Education." *American Journal of Sociology* 84 (Supplement):S288–S315.

Smith, Adam. (1755) 1963. "A Letter to the Authors of the Edinburgh Review." In *The Works of Adam Smith,* vol. 5, pp. 567–84. Aalen: Otto Zeller.

――――. (1759; 6th ed., 1790) 1976. *The Theory of Moral Sentiments.* Indianapolis: Liberty.

――――. (1762–63*a*) 1978. *Lectures on Jurisprudence.* Edited by R. L. Meek, D. D. Raphael, and P. G. Stein. Oxford: Clarendon.

――――. (1762–63*b*) 1971. *Lectures on Rhetoric and Belles Lettres.* Edited by John M. Lothian. Carbondale: Southern Illinois University Press.

――――. (c. 1763) 1937. "An Early Draft of the Wealth of Nations." In William Robert Scott, *Adam Smith as Student and Professor,* pp. 315–56. Glasgow: Jackson, Son & Co.

――――. (1763–64) 1896. *Lectures on Justice, Police, Revenue and Arms.* Edited by Edwin Cannan. Oxford: Clarendon.

———. (1776; 5th ed., 1789) 1937. *An Inquiry into the Nature and Causes of the Wealth of Nations.* Edited by Edwin Cannan. New York: Random House.

———. (1795) 1963. *Essays on Philosophical Subjects.* Vol. 5 in *The Works of Adam Smith.* Aalen: Otto Zeller.

———. 1977. *The Correspondence of Adam Smith.* Edited by Ernest Campbell Mossner and Ian Simpson Ross. Oxford: Clarendon.

Smith, Janet Adam. 1970. "Some Eighteenth-Century Ideas of Scotland." In N. T. Phillipson and Rosalind Mitchison (eds.), *Scotland in the Age of Improvement,* pp. 107–24. Edinburgh: Edinburgh University Press.

Smith, Norman Kemp. (1941) 1966. *The Philosophy of David Hume.* New York: St. Martin's Press.

———. 1948. "Introduction." In David Hume, *Dialogues Concerning Natural Religion,* pp. 1–75. Edited by Norman Kemp Smith. New York: Social Science Publishers.

Smith, Preserved. (1934) 1962. *The Enlightenment, 1687–1776.* New York: Collier. ✗

Smith, Robert A. 1972. *Eighteenth-Century English Politics: Patrons and Place-hunters.* New York: Holt, Rinehart & Winston.

Smout, T. C. 1963. *Scottish Trade on the Eve of Union, 1660–1707.* Edinburgh: Oliver & Boyd.

———. (1969a) 1972. *A History of the Scottish People 1560–1830.* Glasgow: Fontana & Collins.

———. 1969b. "The Road to Union." In Geoffrey Holmes (ed.), *Britain after the Glorious Revolution, 1689–1714,* pp. 176–96. London: Macmillan.

———. 1980. "Scotland and England: Is Dependency a Symptom or a Cause of Underdevelopment?" *Review* (Journal of the Fernand Braudel Center for the Study of Economics, Historical Systems, and Civilizations) 3:601–30.

Somerville, Thomas. (c. 1776) 1789. "Heart-Bitterness." In *The Scotch Preacher: or, A Collection of Sermons, by Some of the Most Eminent Clergymen of the Church of Scotland,* vol. 2, pp. 87–103. Edinburgh: Dickson.

———. 1861. *My Own Life and Times, 1741–1814.* Edinburgh: Edmonston & Douglas.

Spalding, John. 1703. *Synaxis Sacra.* Edinburgh: Anderson.

Speck, W. A. 1977. *Stability and Strife: England 1714–1760.* Bungay Suffolk: Edward Arnold.

Stein, Peter. 1970. "Law and Society in Eighteenth-Century Scottish Thought." In N. T. Phillipson and Rosalind Mitchison (eds.), *Scotland in the Age of Improvement,* pp. 148–68. Edinburgh: Edinburgh University Press.

Stephen, Leslie. (1876; 3d ed., 1902) 1949. *History of English Thought in the Eighteenth Century.* 2 vols. New York: Peter Smith.

Stephens, William N. 1963. *The Family in Cross-Cultural Perspective.* New York: Holt, Rinehart & Winston.

Stewart, Alexander. 1818. "The Life of Dr. William Robertson." In William Robertson, *The Works of William Robertson, D.D.*, vol. 1, pp. l–lxxxix. Edinburgh: Peter Hill.

Stewart, Dugald. (1793) 1966. *Biographical Memoir of Adam Smith*. New York: Augustus M. Kelley.

———. (1796) 1966. "Account of the Life and Writings of William Robertson, D.D." In Dugald Stewart, *Biographical Memoir of Adam Smith*, pp. 99–242. New York: Augustus M. Kelley.

———. (1802) 1966. "Account of the Life and Writings of Thomas Reid, D.D., F.R.S.E." In Dugald Stewart, *Biographical Memoir of Adam Smith*, pp. 245–328. New York: Augustus M. Kelley.

———. (1821) 1854. *The Collected Works of Dugald Stewart*, vol. 1. Edinburgh: Thomas Constable.

Stewart, John B. 1963. *The Moral and Political Philosophy of David Hume*. New York: Columbia University Press.

Stocking, George W., Jr. 1975. "Scotland as the Model of Mankind: Lord Kames' Philosophical View of Civilization." In Timothy H. H. Thorensen (ed.), *Toward a Science of Man: Essays in the History of Anthropology*, pp. 65–89. The Hague: Mouton.

Stone, Lawrence. 1969. "Literacy and Education in England 1640–1900." *Past and Present* 42:69–139.

———. 1971. "The Ninnyversity?" *New York Review of Books*, January 28, 21–29.

———. 1974. "The Size and Composition of the Oxford Student Body, 1580–1909." In Lawrence Stone (ed.), *The University in Society*, vol. 1, pp. 3–110. Princeton: Princeton University Press.

———. 1977. *The Family, Sex and Marriage in England, 1500–1800*. New York: Harper & Row.

Strong, John. 1909. *A History of Secondary Education in Scotland*. Oxford: Clarendon.

Sutherland, Lucy. 1973. *The University of Oxford in the Eighteenth Century: A Reconsideration*. Oxford: Oxford University Press.

Swidler, Ann. 1979. *Organizations without Authority: Dilemmas of Social Control in Free Schools*. Cambridge, Mass.: Harvard University Press.

Swingewood, Alan William. 1969. "The Scottish Enlightenment and the Rise of Sociology." Ph.D. diss., University of London.

———. 1970a. "Comte, Marx and Political Economy." *Sociological Review* 18:335–49.

———. 1970b. "Origins of Sociology: The Case of Scottish Enlightenment." *British Journal of Sociology* 21:164–80.

Sypher, Wylie. 1939. "Hutcheson and the 'Classical' Theory of Slavery." *Journal of Negro History* 24:263–80.

Taylor, W. L. 1965. *Francis Hutcheson and David Hume as Predecessors of Adam Smith*. Durham, N.C.: Duke University Press.

Taylor, William M. 1887. *The Scottish Pulpit from the Reformation to the Present Day.* London: Charles Burnet & Co.

Teichgraeber, Richard, III. 1981. "Rethinking *Das Adam Smith Problem.*" *Journal of British Studies* 20:106–23.

Therborn, Göran. 1976. *Science, Class and Society.* London: New Left Books.

Thornton, Robert D. 1968. "The University of Edinburgh and the Scottish Enlightenment." *Texas Studies in Literature and Language* 10:415–22.

Tocqueville, Alexis de. (1856) 1955. *The Old Regime and the French Revolution.* Translated by Stuart Gilbert. New York: Doubleday Anchor.

Trevor-Roper, H. R. 1967. "The Scottish Enlightenment." *Studies on Voltaire and the Eighteenth Century* 58:1635–58.

———. 1969*a.* "Religion, the Reformation and Social Change." In H. R. Trevor-Roper, *The European Witch-Craze of the Sixteenth and Seventeenth Centuries and Other Essays,* pp. 1–45. New York: Harper Torchbooks.

———.1969*b.* "The Religious Origins of the Enlightenment." In H. R. Trevor-Roper, *The European Witch-Craze of the Sixteenth and Seventeenth Centuries and Other Essays,* pp. 193–239. New York: Harper Torchbooks.

Troeltsch, Ernst. (1897) 1925. "Die Aufklärung." In Ernst Troeltsch, *Gesammelte Schriften,* vol. 4, pp. 338–74. Tubingen: J. C. B. Mohr (Paul Siebeck).

———. (1911) 1931. *The Social Teachings of the Christian Churches.* Translated by Olive Wyon. 2 vols. Chicago: University of Chicago Press.

———. (1912) 1958. *Protestantism and Progress.* Translated by W. Montgomery. Boston: Beacon.

Trumbach, Randolf. 1978. *The Rise of the Egalitarian Family.* New York: Academic Press.

Tytler, Sarah, and J. L. Watson. 1871. *The Songstresses of Scotland.* 2 vols. London: Strahan.

Veitch, John. 1877. "Philosophy in the Scottish Universities." *Mind* 2:74–91, 207–34.

Venturi, Franco. 1971. *Utopia and Reform in the Enlightenment.* Cambridge: Cambridge University Press.

Vincent, W. A. L. 1969. *The Grammar Schools: Their Continuing Tradition, 1660–1714.* London: John Murray.

Viner, Jacob. (1927) 1958. "Adam Smith and Laissez Faire." In Jacob Viner, *The Long View and the Short,* pp. 213–45. Glencoe: Free Press.

———. 1965. "Guide to John Rae's Life of Adam Smith." In John Rae, *Life of Adam Smith,* pp. 1–145. New York: Augustus M. Kelley.

———. 1968. "Adam Smith." In David Sills (ed.), *International Encyclopedia of the Social Sciences,* vol. 14, pp. 322–29. London: Macmillan.

Walker, James. 1872. *The Theology and Theologians of Scotland, Chiefly of the Seventeenth and Eighteenth Centuries.* Edinburgh: T. & T. Clark.

Wallerstein, Immanuel. 1974. *The Modern World-System.* New York: Academic Press.

———. 1980*a. The Modern World-System II.* New York: Academic Press.

———. 1980*b*. "One Man's Meat: The Scottish Great Leap Forward." *Review* (Journal of The Fernand Braudel Center for the Study of Economics, Historical Systems, and Civilizations) 3:631–40.

Watson, Goodwin. 1957. "Some Personality Differences in Children Related to Strict or Permissive Parental Discipline." *Journal of Psychology* 44:227–49.

Watt, Ian. 1957. *The Rise of the Novel*. Berkeley: University of California Press.

Weber, Max. (1904–5) 1958. *The Protestant Ethic and the Spirit of Capitalism*. Translated by Talcott Parsons. New York: Scribner's.

———. (1906) 1946. "The Protestant Sects and the Spirit of Capitalism." In H. H. Gerth and C. Wright Mills (eds. and trans.), *From Max Weber: Essays in Sociology*, pp. 302–22. New York: Oxford University Press.

———. (1910) 1978. "Anticritical Last Word on the Spirit of Capitalism." Translated by Wallace M. Davis. *American Journal of Sociology* 83:1105–31.

———. (1915) 1946. "Religious Rejections of the World and Their Directions." In H. H. Gerth and C. Wright Mills (eds. and trans.), *From Max Weber: Essays in Sociology*, pp. 323–59. New York: Oxford University Press.

Wedderburn, Alexander. 1713. *David's Testament Opened up in Forty Sermons upon Samuel 23:5*. Edinburgh: Anderson.

Weingrod, Alex. 1968. "Patrons, Patronage, and Political Parties." *Comparative Studies in Society and History* 10:377–400.

Weinstein, Fred, and Gerald M. Platt. 1969. *The Wish to Be Free*. Berkeley: University of California Press.

West, E. G. 1969. "The Political Economy of Alienation: Karl Marx and Adam Smith." *Oxford Economic Papers* n.s. 21:1–23.

———. 1975. "Adam Smith and Alienation: Wealth Increases, Men Decay?" In Andrew S. Skinner and Thomas Wilson (eds.), *Essays on Adam Smith*, pp. 540–52. Oxford: Clarendon.

The Westminster Confession of Faith; The Larger and Shorter Catechisms. (1647) 1976. Inverness: John G. Eccles.

White, Robert W. 1963. *Ego and Reality in Psychoanalytic Theory*. New York: International Universities Press.

Whitney, Lois. 1934. *Primitivism and the Idea of Progress*. Baltimore: Johns Hopkins Press.

Wightman, W. P. D. 1975. "Adam Smith and the History of Ideas." In Andrew S. Skinner and Thomas Wilson (eds.), *Essays on Adam Smith*, pp. 44–67. Oxford: Clarendon.

Wills, Garry. 1978*a*. "Benevolent Adam Smith." *New York Review of Books*, February 9, 40–43.

———. 1978*b*. *Inventing America: Jefferson's Declaration of Independence*. Garden City, N.Y.: Doubleday.

———. 1981. *Explaining America: The Federalist*. Garden City, N.Y.: Doubleday.

Wilson, Nan. 1968. "The Scottish Bar: The Evolution of the Faculty of Advocates in Its Historical Social Setting." *Louisiana Law Review* 28:235–57.

Winch, Donald. 1978. *Adam Smith's Politics.* Cambridge: Cambridge University Press.

Witherspoon, John. (1797) 1973. "Letters on Education." In Philip J. Greven, Jr. (ed.), *Child-Rearing Concepts, 1628–1861: Historical Sources,* pp. 80–98. Itasca, Ill.: F. E. Peacock.

Withrington, D. J. 1962. "The S. P. C. K. and Highland Schools in Mid-Eighteenth Century." *Scottish Historical Review* 41:89–99.

———. 1965. "Lists of Schoolmasters Teaching Latin, 1690." *Miscellany X* Scottish History Society (4th series) 2:121–42.

———. 1970a. "Education and Society in the Eighteenth Century." In N. T. Phillipson and Rosalind Mitchison (eds.), *Scotland in the Age of Improvement,* pp. 169–99. Edinburgh: Edinburgh University Press.

———. 1970b. "Non-Church Going, c. 1750–c. 1850: A Preliminary Study." *Records of the Scottish Church History Society* 17:99–113.

Wodrow, James. 1789. "The Life of Dr. Leechman, with Some Account of His Lectures." In William Leechman, *Sermons,* vol. 1, pp. 1–102. London: Strahan.

Wolf, Eric R. 1966. "Kinship, Friendship, and Patron-Client Relations in Complex Societies." In Michael Banton (ed.), *The Social Anthropology of Complex Societies,* pp. 1–22. New York: Praeger.

Wood, Marguerite. 1945. "Edinburgh Poll Tax Returns." *Book of Old Edinburgh Club* 25:90–126.

Wright, Erik Olin. 1978. *Class, Crisis and the State.* New York: New Left Books.

Yarrow, Leon J. 1964. "Separation from Parents During Early Childhood." In Martin L. Hoffman and Lois Wladis Hoffman (eds.), *Review of Child Development Research,* vol. 1, pp. 89–136. New York: Russell Sage Foundation.

Young, Douglas. 1967. "Scotland and Edinburgh in the Eighteenth Century." *Studies on Voltaire and the Eighteenth Century* 58:1967–90.

Index

Allan, James, 32
Anonymous (1703), 127–28, 130
Arts. *See* Curriculum, under the pro-
    fessoriate, under regenting
Athole, house of, 217–18
Authority relations. *See* Control
Autonomy. *See* Independence, experi-
    ential basis of

Bailyn, Bernard, 94
Bain, Andrew, 28
Balliol College, 192, 196–98
Baxter, Andrew, 37, 99
Baxter, Richard, 32
Beale, J. M., 28, 146–48
Becker, Carl L., 3 n. 4
Belief
    in Monboddo's thought, 90
    Scottish Calvinist view of, 21–22
    Scottish Enlightenment's view of,
        64–66, 76–78
    in Scottish historiography, 43–44
Bellah, Robert N., 2 n. 2, 4
Bendix, Reinhard, 3 n. 3, 86
Bible
    Hutcheson's view of, 38
    Moderate's view of, 87–88
    in Scottish Calvinism, 21–22, 28,
        141, 151
    Scottish Enlightenment's view of,
        64–66, 69
Bidwell, Charles E., 111
Bierstedt, Robert, 4 n. 5
Black, Joseph, 50 n. 7
Blacklock, Thomas, 88

Blair, Hugh, 89
Borthwick parish school, 160
Bourignon, Antoinette, 32 n. 20
Bower, Alexander, 160 n. 33
Boyd, William, 151
Bradburn, Norman, 133 n. 17
Breer, Paul E., 106–8, 108 n. 24, 113
Brougham, Henry, 138, 188
Bryson, Gladys, 98
Buckle, Henry Thomas, 29
Bullough, Bonnie, 132 n. 14, 134 n. 18
Bullough, Vern L., 122, 132 n. 14, 134
    n. 18, 235–36
Burgh schools. *See* Classical education
Burrell, Sidney A., 13
Bute, Earl of, 219

Cain, Roy Edward, 93
Calvin, John, 13, 22, 29, 66, 87
Calvinism. *See also* Scottish Calvinism
    medieval features of, 3, 18
    modern features of, 2–3, 18
    sociological treatments of, 17–18, 26
        n. 12
    variability of, 14 n. 3
Cameron, James K., 89
Cant, Ronald Gordon, 167, 190
Capitalism, in Scotland, 95–96
Capitalist society, Scottish Enlighten-
    ment's view of, 79–83
Captors, 146, 148, 168, 179–80
Carlyle, Alexander, 131, 138, 159, 184,
    200, 213
Carmichael, Gershom, 37–38, 99
Carstairs, William, 173